F. H. H. (Francis Henry Hill) Guillemard, Alfred Russel Wallace

Malaysia and the Pacific Archipelagoes

F. H. H. (Francis Henry Hill) Guillemard, Alfred Russel Wallace

Malaysia and the Pacific Archipelagoes

ISBN/EAN: 9783743321847

Manufactured in Europe, USA, Canada, Australia, Japa

Cover: Foto ©ninafisch / pixelio.de

Manufactured and distributed by brebook publishing software (www.brebook.com)

F. H. H. (Francis Henry Hill) Guillemard, Alfred Russel Wallace

Malaysia and the Pacific Archipelagoes

STANFORD'S
COMPENDIUM OF GEOGRAPHY AND TRAVEL
(NEW ISSUE)

AUSTRALASIA

VOL II.

MALAYSIA AND THE PACIFIC ARCHIPELAGOES

EDITED AND GREATLY EXTENDED FROM DR. A. R. WALLACE'S
"AUSTRALASIA"

BY

F. H. H. GUILLEMARD, M.A., M.D., CANTAB.
LATE LECTURER IN GEOGRAPHY AT THE UNIVERSITY OF CAMBRIDGE
AUTHOR OF
'THE CRUISE OF THE *MARCHESA*,' 'LIFE OF MAGELLAN,' ETC.

MAPS AND ILLUSTRATIONS

LONDON: EDWARD STANFORD
26 & 27 COCKSPUR STREET, CHARING CROSS, S.W.
1894

PREFACE

THE present volume—an enlargement of that part of Dr. A. R. Wallace's "Australasia" of the former series which deals with the great Malay islands and the numberless archipelagoes of the Pacific Ocean—has been almost entirely re-written, and expanded to nearly twice the number of pages previously allotted to the section. The aim has been to present as comprehensive a view as possible of the regions described, and also to give the latest information obtainable. The history of the islands has been touched upon, fuller details and statistics of their trade afforded, and, lastly, a short sketch of the two capitals, Batavia and Manila, and of the life and manners of their inhabitants, has been added.

As the volumes are intended for separate sale, the Introduction—which is even more needed for this than for the first volume—has, with a few slight alterations, been retained.

Thanks are due to Mr. J. J. Lister of St. John's

College, Cambridge, for the kind loan of various Polynesian photographs; to the Hon. Walter Rothschild for permission to reproduce Mr. Frohawk's sketch of the *Proechidna*; to Professor A. H. Keane and Mr. H. O. Forbes for photographs of Negrito and Papuan types; and to Mr. John Murray and Messrs. Macmillan and Co. for permission to use blocks borrowed from works published by them.

CONTENTS

CHAPTER I

INTRODUCTION

PAGE

Definition and nomenclature—Extent and distribution of lands and islands—Geographical and physical features—Ocean depths—Races of mankind—Zoology and botany—Geological relations and past history—Geographical divisions . . 1

MALAYSIA

CHAPTER II

GENERAL FEATURES

Geographical outline—Physical features; volcanoes—The Malay race and language . . 13

CHAPTER III

THE PHILIPPINE ISLANDS

General features—History—Geology—Climate, typhoons, earthquakes—Fauna and flora—Negritos, Malay tribes—Religion and education—Agriculture, trade, and commerce—Government and revenue—Population, provinces—The capital—Luzon—Mindoro—Panay—Negros—Zebu—Samar—Leyte—Bohol—Masbate—Mindanao—Sulu Islands—Calamianes—Paláwan 27

CHAPTER IV

THE DUTCH EAST INDIES

PAGE

Extent and importance—Dutch policy and its effects on the native populations—System of government of Netherlands India . 97

CHAPTER V

JAVA

General features—History—Volcanoes, geology—Climate and meteorology—Flora and fauna—Inhabitants and language—Religion and education—Antiquities—Trade and agriculture—Government : revenue—Population, provinces, and towns—The capital 101

CHAPTER VI

SUMATRA

General features—History—Geology and orography—Eruption of Krakatau—Plains, valleys, lakes, and rivers—Climate and meteorology—Fauna and flora—Inhabitants and language—The delta and other islands—Bangka—Blitong—Religion and antiquities—Products, trade, and agriculture—Population and political divisions—Chief towns 154

CHAPTER VII

BORNEO

General features—History—Geology and physical features—Climate—Fauna and flora—Native races—Agriculture and products—British North Borneo — Labuan — Brunei — Sarawak — Dutch Borneo 213

CHAPTER VIII

CELEBES

General features—History—Physical features—Climate—Fauna and flora—Native races—The Makassar district—The Menado Residency—Trade and products—Islands 275

CHAPTER IX

THE MOLUCCAS

General description—Geology and natural history—Inhabitants—History and political divisions—Halmahera—Ternate—Tidor and the Lesser Moluccas—Buru—Ceram—Amboina—Banda—Islands east of Ceram—TheKé group . . . 306

CHAPTER X

THE LESSER SUNDA ISLANDS

General description—Bali—Lombok—Sumbawa—Flores—Solor and Allor groups—Wetta and the Serwatti group—Timor Laut—Timor—Savu—Sumba . . . 345

MELANESIA

CHAPTER XI

NEW GUINEA

General description—Physical features—History—Geology—Climate—Flora and fauna—The Papuan race—Mission work in the island—Dutch New Guinea—German New Guinea—British New Guinea—The Papuan Islands . . . 376

CHAPTER XII

OTHER MELANESIAN ISLANDS

The Solomon Islands—Santa Cruz group—The New Hebrides—New Caledonia—The Loyalty Islands . . . 442

CHAPTER XIII

THE FIJI ISLANDS

General features—History—Geology and climate—Fauna and flora—Inhabitants—Religion and education—Agriculture and trade—Government; revenue—Population . . . 467

POLYNESIA

CHAPTER XIV

THE FRIENDLY AND OTHER ISLANDS

Extent and component groups—The Polynesian race—The Tonga or Friendly Islands—Samoa—Niuë or Savage Island—The Union group—Ellice Islands—Hervey Islands—Society Islands—Austral Islands—Paumotu, or Low Archipelago—Gambier group—Pitcairn—The Marquesas—Manahiki or Penrhyn group—Phœnix Islands—America Islands—Easter Island—The Sandwich Islands or Hawaii 487

MIKRONESIA

CHAPTER XV

THE MIKRONESIAN ARCHIPELAGOES

General description—Gilbert or Kingsmill group—Marshall Islands—Caroline Islands—Pelew Islands—Ladrone or Marianne Islands . 542

LIST OF MAPS

1. A Chart of Australasia	To face page		1
2. Chart of Submarine Bank of S.E. Asia		,,	6
3. The Volcanic System of Malaysia		,,	13
4. Philippine Islands	,,	,,	27
5. Settlements in Malaysia		,,	97
6. Java		,,	101
7. Sumatra		,,	155
8. Chart of Effects of Krakatau Eruption		,,	166
9. Borneo		,,	213
10. Celebes		,,	275
11. Moluccas		,,	307
12. Lesser Sunda Islands		,,	345
13. New Guinea		,,	377
14. The Solomon Islands		,,	443
15. Fiji		,,	467
16. The Pacific Islands		,,	487

LIST OF ILLUSTRATIONS

		PAGE
1.	Sultan of Sulu .	*Frontispiece*
2.	A Negrito of Luzon .	48
3.	Manila Hemp (*Musa textilis*) .	57
4.	Hut at Maimbun, Sulu Island	91
5.	Native House, Java .	123
6.	Temple of Boro-bodor, Java .	133
7.	Street in European Quarter, Batavia .	147
8.	Residence of Governor-General, Buitenzorg	150
9.	*Rafflesia Arnoldii* .	178
10.	Palace of a Sumatran Prince .	207
11.	Dyak Village .	236
12.	Sandakan .	251
13.	Brunei .	258
14.	Kuching, Sarawak .	267
15.	Mt. Klabat, from Kema Bay .	279
16.	The Anoa (*Anoa depressicornis*) .	284
17.	The Babirusa (*Sus babirusa*) .	286
18.	House of Raja of Goa, S. Celebes	290
19.	Menado, N. Celebes .	296
20.	Moluccan Cuscus (*C. ornatus*) .	310
21.	Wallace's Bird of Paradise	312

		PAGE
22.	Coco-nut Grove, Ternate	320
23.	Peak of Tidor from Ternate	323
24.	Banda Volcano	334
25.	Fruit of the Nutmeg	337
26.	Royal Palace, Bali	348
27.	Sultan of Bima, Sumbawa	357
28.	Spiny Ant-eater (*Procchidna*)	392
29.	Bower of Amblyornis	394
30.	A Papuan of Dutch New Guinea	399
31.	A Papuan of Dorei Bay	402
32.	Korowaar	405
33.	Native of Heath Island	420
34.	View in Waigiu Island	428
35.	Papuan House, Dorei Bay	439
36.	Natives of New Caledonia	460
37.	New Caledonian Flute-player	463
38.	Suva Harbour, Fiji	469
39.	A Native of Fiji	479
40.	A Native of Tonga Islands	489
41.	Tongan Woman	498
42.	Trilithon at Mani, Tonga Islands	501
43.	Didunculus	505
44.	View in Tahiti	512
45.	Peak of Moörea, Society Islands	517
46.	Ancient Stone Images, Easter Island	531
47.	Head of Hemignathus	536

MALAYSIA AND THE PACIFIC ARCHIPELAGOES

CHAPTER I

INTRODUCTION

1. Definition and Nomenclature.

THE vast region which stretches half-way across the Pacific from the south-eastern extremity of Asia, comprising within its boundaries the richest and largest islands in the world, has from time to time received various appellations: Australasia, the Eastern Archipelago, Oceania, etc. None of these, however, are particularly satisfactory, for none are inclusive. But apart from the fact that some such inclusive name might conveniently serve for a title-page, there is little need to attempt to supply the deficiency. For the innumerable islands which come under our notice in the following pages by no means form a geographical unit, but exhibit many diversified characteristics, and have been divided into various groups, sometimes rather artificially perhaps, but on the whole fairly accurately. Thus, to the west we have the great islands of Sumatra, Borneo, and Java with strongly marked Asiatic affinities; Celebes, occupying a central position and exhibiting a fauna so peculiar as to justify separate consideration; the Lesser Sunda Islands, New Guinea, Melanesia, and Australia; the numerous lesser archipelagoes of the Pacific; and, finally, New Zealand, a country so different from every other in its fauna, that of late many naturalists have considered that it should form a separate zoological region.

Although, as just intimated, there are many reasons why Australia should not be treated apart from New Guinea, the rapid spread of civilisation in the former continent, and its situation to so large an extent within the temperate zone, have more or less differentiated it. Accordingly, since it has been found necessary to divide the "Australasia" of the present series into two volumes, the following pages will deal only with the tropical portion of the Eastern Archipelago, leaving Australia and New Zealand for treatment in a separate volume. The region which we shall now consider may be taken to consist of four divisions, each of which has a distinctive name. These are,—(1) The Malay Archipelago or Malaysia, including the islands from Sumatra to the Philippines and Moluccas, and forming the home of the true Malay race; (2) Melanesia, including the chief islands inhabited by the black, frizzly-haired race from New Guinea to the Fiji Islands; (3) Polynesia, including all the larger islands of the central Pacific from the Sandwich Islands southward; and (4) Micronesia, including the smaller western islands of the North Pacific, inhabited by people of mixed origin.

These will be further subdivided as occasion requires, and will be taken in the order above indicated.

2. Extent and Distribution of Lands and Islands.

That portion of the equator stretching from Singapore across the Pacific to Guayaquil occupies almost exactly 180° of longitude, or half the circumference of the globe, and throughout almost the whole of this vast distance it traverses blue water. This boundless watery domain, which extends northward to Bering Straits, and southward to the Antarctic barrier of ice, is studded with many island groups, which are, nevertheless, very irregularly distributed over its surface. Its northern portion is almost unbroken ocean. Between latitude 30° N. and 30° S., reefs, islets, and groups of coral formation abound, and towards the southern limit of this belt larger islands appear. To the west and south are the great islands of the Malay Archipelago and Australia. In the central Pacific, islands almost wholly cease at the 30th parallel of south latitude. Again, in its eastern part, scarcely a single island is to be found until a few occur near the American coast. It thus appears that all the greater land masses of Australasia form an obvious southern and south-eastern extension of the great Asiatic continent, while beyond, the islands rapidly diminish in size and number till, in the far east and north, we reach a vast expanse of unbroken ocean.

In actual land area this division of the globe is not much larger than Europe, but if we take into account the amount of space it occupies upon the globe, and the position of its extreme points, it at once rises to the first rank, surpassing even the vast extent of the Asiatic continent. From the north-western extremity of Sumatra, in 95° E. long., to the Marquesas in 138° W., is a distance of 127 degrees, or more than one-third of the circumference of the globe, and about 1000 miles longer than the greatest extent of Europe and Asia from Lisbon to Singapore. In a north and south direction it is less extensive; yet, from the Sandwich Islands in 22° N. to Stewart Island, New Zealand, in 47° S., is a meridian distance of 69 degrees, or as much as the width of the great northern continent from the North Cape to Ceylon. From the usual custom of representing the Eastern Archipelago within the limits of a single map, its vast size and extent are generally lost sight of.

3. Geographical and Physical Features.

Within the limits above described are some of the most interesting countries of the world. Beginning at the west, we have the Malay Archipelago, comprising the largest islands on the globe, and unsurpassed for the luxuriance of its vegetation as well as for the variety and beauty of its forms of animal life. Farther to the east lie the countless islands of the Pacific, remarkable for their numbers and their beauty, and interesting from their association with the names of many of our greatest navigators. To the south is Australia, unique in its physical features; and still farther in the Southern Ocean lies New Zealand, almost the antipodes of Great Britain, but possessing a milder climate and a more varied surface.

Being thus almost wholly comprised between the northern tropic and the 40th degree of south latitude, this division of the globe possesses as tropical a character as Africa, while, owing to its being so completely oceanic and extending over so vast an area, it presents diversities of physical features and of organic life not to be found in any of the other divisions of the globe, except, perhaps, Asia. The most striking contrasts of geological structure are exhibited by the coral islands of the Pacific, the active volcanoes of the Malay islands, and the extremely ancient rocks of New Zealand and Tasmania. The most opposite aspects of vegetation are presented by the luxuriant forests of the Moluccas and New Guinea, and the parched ground and thorny thickets of the Eastern Sunda Islands.

Where the land surface is so much broken up into islands, we cannot expect to find any of the more prominent geographical features which characterise large continents, and hence there are nowhere great lakes or rivers of large size. Mountains are numerous, but are for the most part volcanic, and are much higher in the islands than on the continent of Australia. In such remote localities as Sumatra, Borneo, the Sandwich Islands, and New Zealand, there are mountains which do not fall far short of 14,000 feet. Of the snow-covered Charles Louis range in Dutch New Guinea we have as yet no very trustworthy information, but there is little doubt that its peaks attain a very much greater elevation.

4. Ocean Depths

The land and water of the earth's surface is so unequally distributed that it is possible to divide the globe into two equal parts, in one of which—the land hemisphere—land and water shall be almost exactly equal, while in the other—the water hemisphere—there shall be nearly eight times as much water as land. The centre of the former is in St. George's Channel, and of the latter at a spot some 600 miles S.S.E. of New Zealand.

Australasia is therefore situated wholly within the water hemisphere, and many of its islands are surrounded by an ocean which is not only the most extensive, but the deepest in the world.

The Pacific Ocean is deepest north of the equator, where soundings of from 15,000 to 18,000 feet have been obtained over extensive areas, showing the existence of an enormous basin between Japan and San Francisco. Between the Philippines and the Ladrones a depth of nearly 27,000 feet has been obtained, and close to Japan as much as 23,400. But both these have been exceeded at a spot a little to the south of Simusir Island in the Kurile chain, where a depth of 27,930 feet, or about $5\frac{1}{4}$ miles, was found—the greatest as yet recorded. In the South Pacific the depths appear to vary between 10,000 and 17,000 feet; but here, too, the deepest soundings have for the most part been obtained near the larger land masses, as between Sydney and New Zealand (15,600 feet) and a little south-east of New Guinea (14,700), though very deep basins of small extent are found elsewhere. Such, for instance, are shown by the soundings of 19,866 feet near the Phœnix group, and 17,389 feet between the Tonga and Hervey Islands. A comparatively shallow sea extends round the coasts of Australia, which gradually deepens, till at a distance of from 300 to 500 miles on the east, south, and west, the oceanic depth of 15,000 feet is attained. The sea which separates Australia from New Guinea is very shallow, hardly exceeding eight or nine fathoms in depth. The Banda, Celebes, and Sulu Seas are all deep basins, affording maximum depths of 16,202, 15,600, and 15,298 feet respectively, and another such basin occurs in the China Sea a little west of Luzon, where soundings of 14,108 feet have been recorded. In the western portion of the region we are considering, the sea shallows abruptly, so that Borneo, Java, and Sumatra are connected with each other and

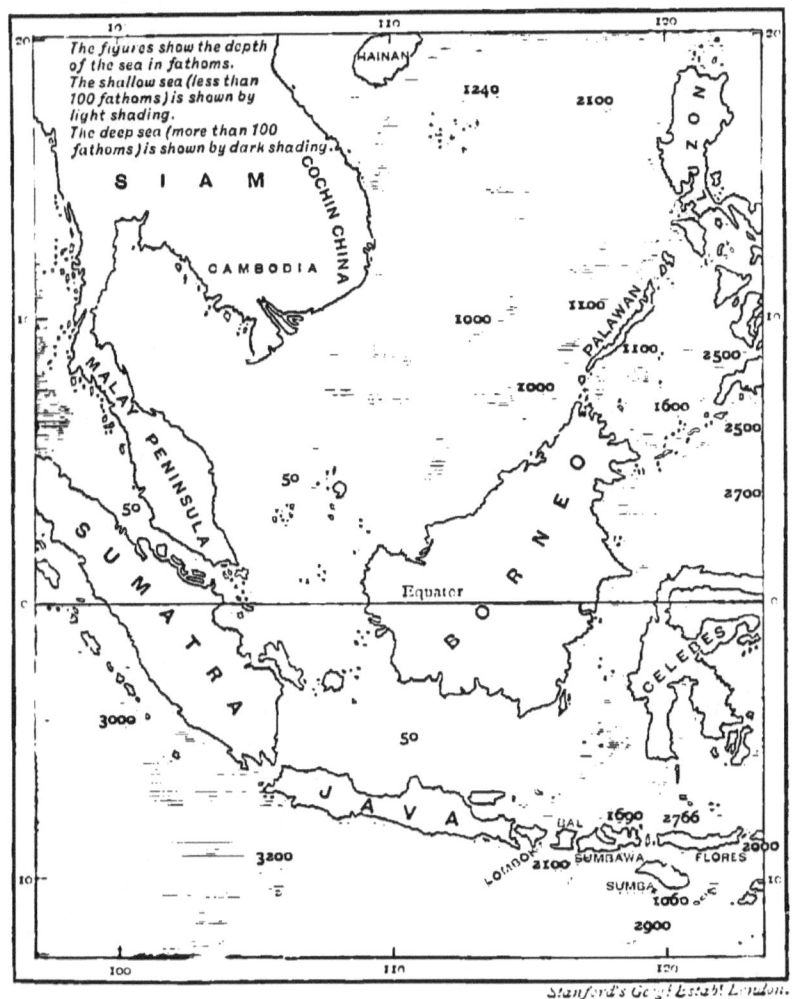

SUBMARINE BANK OF S.E. ASIA.

with the Malay and Siamese peninsulas by a submarine bank rarely submerged more than 200 or 300 feet.

5. Races of Mankind.

In the variety of human races it exhibits, and the interesting problems which these present to the anthropologist, the Eastern Archipelago is hardly surpassed by the great continental divisions of the globe. Concerning the number of distinct races found within its boundaries there are still discrepancies of opinion. For the sake of convenience they may be divided into the two groups of brown and dark, the former including the true Malays, the Indonesians or Pre-Malays, and the allied race of Eastern Polynesians, and the latter the Papuans, the Australians, and the Negritos.

The true Malays (see frontispiece), and the Indonesians who were the earlier settlers of these lands, inhabit all the western part of the Malay Archipelago from Sumatra to the Moluccas. To the eastward of the latter group are the Papuans, whose headquarters are New Guinea, but who range to Timor and Flores on the southwest, and to the Fiji Islands on the east (see illustrations pp. 399, 420). The Australians form a race admitted by most authorities to be distinct. The islands of Eastern Polynesia are for the most part inhabited by a brown people, who have been usually classed with the Malays on account of some similarity of language and colour, and erroneously termed Malayo-Polynesians. They present, however, so many and important differences, both physical and mental, from the true Malays, that the best authorities are agreed in considering them to be altogether distinct. Finally, we have the dark, dwarf, curly-haired Negritos, confined, so far as is known, to the four or five largest islands of the Philippines,[1] and probably allied to the

[1] The Karons of N.W. New Guinea are also considered by some writers to be of Negrito stock.

Semangs of the Malay peninsula and the inhabitants of the Andamans (see illustration p. 48). The distinction that has been drawn between the Papuans proper and a special Melanesian type seems to rest upon insufficient grounds, and is not admitted by those most qualified to judge.

The dark, frizzly-haired Papuan type is not only found in the Melanesian group, but traces of apparently the same dark race may be detected throughout almost the whole of Polynesia and Micronesia. In many of these islands we meet with individuals who in their dark complexions and crisp, frizzly hair closely resemble the Papuans. The light type, on the other hand, is represented by the Malays and by the Polynesians, who in some places, such as Samoa and the Marquesas, are in no respect inferior to the average European, either in complexion, physical beauty, or nobility of expression (see illustration p. 489). Nevertheless, these higher tribes are all disappearing under the fatal influence of our much-vaunted civilisation, and nowhere is this process of extinction developing so rapidly and so inevitably as among the South Sea islanders.

The Eastern Archipelago also affords us an unusual number of examples of immigration and colonisation by the higher races. Malaysia was the scene of the earliest European settlements in Eastern Asia. The Portuguese reached the Spice Islands in 1511, and the Spaniards the same goal ten years later, after discovering the Philippines on their way. Both were soon supplanted in many places by the Dutch, and the English were also not long in obtaining a footing. All these nations have colonies in the Malay islands, while the French have more recently established themselves in New Caledonia and Tahiti, and the Germans in New Guinea and elsewhere. Here, too, we have abundant examples of the overflow of the vast population of China. In almost every city and town in the Archipelago, from Malacca to the Aru Islands, and from Manila to Australia, the Chinese form a by no means unimportant part of the population,—nay, in some places, the bulk of it. In Java the vast ruins of Bora-bodor and other great temples testify to a Brahminical occupation previous to the Mohammedan conquest of the country, and similar remains, though to a much smaller extent, occur in Sumatra and Borneo. And, finally, throughout the whole Archipelago and Polynesia we find evidences of a tolerably recent extension of the Malays at the expense of less civilised tribes.

6. Zoology and Botany.

The eastern half of Australasia forms one of the great zoological regions of the earth—the Australian—characterised by the absence of all the higher and larger forms of mammals, and by the presence of a number of very peculiar types. Its mammalia almost all belong to the marsupials, which are only represented elsewhere by a few opossums in America. Cassowaries, bower-birds, birds-of-paradise, lyre-birds, and other striking genera, are confined to it, as well as numbers of very remarkable parrots, pigeons, and kingfishers, while such widespread and familiar types as vultures, pheasants, and woodpeckers are altogether wanting. The snakes and lizards are numerous and peculiar, and insects and land-shells abound, presenting numberless interesting and beautiful species.

The western half possesses an abundance of the higher mammals, for the most part common to the Asiatic continent — anthropoid apes, monkeys, the great Felidæ, elephants, wild cattle, rhinoceros, and others; all of which in the Australian region are unknown. It belongs, in fact, zoologically speaking, to tropical Asia, and possesses almost all the various forms of life found in Siam and Burmah, although the actual species are to a large extent peculiar.

Plants are equally interesting. The flora of Malaysia proper is a special development of that prevailing from the Himalayas to the Malay Peninsula and South China. Farther east this flora intermingles with that of Australia. The latter, it may be remarked incidentally, is very peculiar and markedly rich in species, while that of New Zealand is poor, though perhaps even more highly differentiated.

7. Geological Relations and Past History.

The western portion of the Australasian Archipelago, as far as Java, Borneo, and perhaps the Philippines, has undoubtedly, at a comparatively recent period, formed a south-eastern extension of the Asiatic continent. This is indicated by the exceedingly shallow sea separating these islands from the mainland, but still more clearly by the essential unity of their animals and plants of which we have just spoken. But, as we go farther east to the Moluccas, New Guinea, and Australia, we have to pass over seas of enormous depth, and there find ourselves among a set of animals for the most part totally unlike those of the Asiatic continent, or of any other part of the globe. Yet these have certain resemblances to the fauna of Europe during the Secondary period of geology, and it is very generally believed that the countries they now inhabit have been almost completely isolated since the time of the Oolitic formation.

New Guinea, the Moluccas, Celebes, and the island chain as far as Lombok—or some pre-existing lands from which these have been formed—were in all probability still attached to the Australian mainland for some time subsequent to its severance from Asia. Cape York, the northern point of Australia, is continued by a chain of high rocky islets all the way to New Guinea, while the depth of Torres Straits between these two countries nowhere exceeds nine fathoms, as has already been stated. The Louisiade Archipelago is nothing more than a submerged portion of the south-eastern extremity of New Guinea. Tasmania must similarly be regarded as the true southern point of Australia, as the intervening Bass's Strait is shallow, and this island was undoubtedly connected with the mainland within comparatively recent geological times. Hence, in Peschel's opinion, Australia was formerly far more extensive than at present. It has clearly been encroached upon along its eastern seaboard, for here stretches the dreaded Great Barrier Reef, whose coral walls sink to considerable depths below the surface, and still shadow forth the former limits of the coast-line in this direction. On this same eastern seaboard, though far removed from the mainland, we find some larger islands which may well have formed part of the Australian continent, though perhaps before the Tertiary epoch. Conspicuous among them is the non-volcanic island of New Caledonia, which is at present slowly subsiding. Australia must, in fact, be altogether regarded as a continent of the Secondary or early Tertiary period, now gradually disappearing, and this phenomenon of subsidence is displayed in many parts of the South Pacific Ocean.

In the following chapter the leading characteristics of Malaysia—the first and most important division of the Australasian Archipelago—will be considered.

MALAYSIA, or THE MALAY ARCHIPELAGO

CHAPTER II

GENERAL FEATURES

1. Geographical Outline.

OF all the great island groups of the globe, the richest in every respect is the Malay Archipelago, lying between Southern Asia and Australia, and made up of fragments of the two continents, although now forming a distinct geographical unit. There is every reason to believe that Asia and Australia were united during the latter part of the Secondary epoch, while the processes of subsidence and upheaval resulting in the present insular formations were not fully developed till a much later period. The Australian continent was probably first broken up, as indicated by the very deep seas which now separate the several islands of the Moluccas from each other; while the Asiatic continent may have remained longer entire, and its comparatively recent subsidence is equally well shown by the very shallow sea—always under fifty fathoms deep—which separates the great islands of Java, Sumatra, and Borneo from each other and from the mainland of Southern Asia. The extensive submarine plateau comes to an abrupt termination at the little island of Bali, east of Java, there being a channel of great depth, though very narrow, between it and the adjacent island of Lombok. The same deep channel is continued northwards through the Straits of Macassar to the Celebes Sea, where it divides, one arm passing between the islands of Mindanao and northern Celebes into the Pacific Ocean, and the other north-westward, between Sibutu and Tawi-tawi islands into the Sulu Sea. Hence one-half only of what is sometimes called the East Indian Archipelago, and included in Asia, is really connected with that continent. The eastern half is essentially Australian, not only as regards the history of its origin, but also in its fauna and flora. Even ethnically this extensive insular system belongs to two clearly distinct peoples—the Malay and the Papuan—so that the current expression "Malay Archipelago," here adopted, is deficient in thorough accuracy. The line dividing the two races lies, however, considerably to the east of that which separates the two zoological regions, the Malays extending to Celebes, Sumbawa, and most of the islands of the Moluccas.

But, while conforming to the hitherto received custom of arbitrarily including under one appellation the whole of the archipelago as far as the Moluccas and Timor, we may still recognise it to be composed of several distinct groups. These groups are—in the north the Philippines, followed to the south by the Moluccas, and by the very remarkable and zoologically distinct island, Celebes. Finally, to the south and to the west are the Lesser and the Greater Sunda Archipelagoes, by the latter of which are understood the three large islands of Sumatra, Java, and Borneo.

All these groups—of which Sumatra, Java, and Borneo belonged in recent geological times to the Asiatic continent

—are separated from each other by straits or passages, each bearing a distinctive name. By far the greater number belong politically to Holland, which here possesses a colonial empire, with its seat of government in Java, rivalling in prosperity the British East Indian possessions. Of all the former extensive dominions of Portugal in these seas nothing now remains to her except a portion of the island of Timor. In the Philippines the Spaniard rules almost exclusively. At the north of Borneo we find two abnormal forms of government— an English raja ruling the extensive territory of Sarawak, while a private company, formed somewhat upon the lines of the old East India Company, administers the neighbouring country now known as British North Borneo. Some islands and portions of islands are still independent, or subject to native sultans.

2. Physical Features—Volcanoes.

The Malay Archipelago is traversed throughout its whole extent by one of the most extensive and continuous volcanic belts upon the globe. Commencing in the north-western part of Sumatra, beyond the equator, it extends through that island and Java, then through the Lesser Sunda Islands to the east end of Timor. Here it turns in a north-easterly curve by Banda, Amboina, and Buru to Gilolo and Ternate. Thence, turning westward to the northern extremity of Celebes, it bends abruptly to the north by the Sangir Islands, and passes through the entire range of the Philippines to the extreme north of Luzon. The number of true volcanic peaks and craters in this belt is very great, and they form a continuous chain, with seldom more than an interval of a hundred miles from one to the other. A very large proportion of them are in a state of activity, and several have devastated the surrounding country within the historic era. Many are perpetually smoking, while others have been frequently in eruption since the occupation of the country by Europeans, and have often been accompanied by disastrous earthquakes. Hardly less remarkable than the extent and continuity of this belt of volcanoes is the complete absence of all volcanic vents in the surrounding districts. The great island of Borneo, and all of Celebes except the extreme northern point, are absolutely free from all signs of recent volcanic action; and the same may be said of almost every island which lies on either side of the band—as the Peninsula of Malacca, Madura, Sumba, Ceram, etc. In all these countries we have ancient crystalline rocks, granite, and extensive Tertiary beds, but no indication of volcanic outbursts. From the acknowledged fact of the very general vicinity of active volcanoes to the ocean, we may perhaps interpret this phenomenon as pointing out to us, in this great volcanic band, the outer limits of very ancient continents, while the lands on either side have once formed inland portions of those continents. This agrees sufficiently well with what we know of the existing distribution of animal life, if we suppose Celebes and the other islands to the eastward, as far as the volcanic belt, to have been separated from Asia at a very early period, when its fauna assimilated much more with that of Australia than it does now; while the islands to the west of Celebes were only separated from the continent at a very much later epoch, after they had participated in all the more recent and higher developments of its flora and fauna. This view will explain some of those great peculiarities of the fauna of Celebes to which we shall have to refer when treating of that island.

In this extensive chain of volcanic mountains many attain great heights, especially in Sumatra and Java. Each of these islands has one mountain about 12,000 feet high, while the former has four and the latter ten which exceed 10,000 feet. In no other part of the chain, except in Bali and Lombok, immediately east of Java, are there any heights which approach these. Lombok Peak is probably nearly 12,500 feet. The highest volcanoes of the Philippines and Northern Celebes are about 7000 or 8000 feet, and those of the Moluccas from 5000 to 6000, if we except Labua in Batjan, which is probably over 7000 feet. Besides Lombok, there is only one mountain in the whole Malay Archipelago that exceeds in height the lofty peaks of Sumatra and Java—the isolated mass of Kina Balu, near the northern extremity of Borneo, which is said to be 13,698 feet high, and which is probably far higher than any other mountain in the island, or than any non-volcanic mountain in the whole archipelago. The summit of Kina Balu is syenitic granite, and it probably represents a portion of the most ancient extension of the Asiatic continent in Tertiary or Secondary times, since it contains plants allied to some now only found in temperate Australia.

From the position of these Malayan islands between 19° north and 10° south of the equator, they all enjoy that equability of climate and abundance of moisture which are so highly favourable to the growth of arboreal vegetation, and which have produced the great forest-belt everywhere girdling the earth in the equatorial zone. Hence the general condition of almost all the islands, where not interfered with by man, is to be covered with luxuriant tropical forests, and this forest-covering is universal except on the very highest summits or precipitous rocky slopes of the mountains. There is only one portion of the region where there appears to be a natural deficiency of forest, due to peculiarities of climate caused by the vicinity of the heated interior of Australia. From the east end of Java throughout the Lesser Sunda Archipelago to Timor Laut, the dense forests which everywhere cover the other islands are the exception rather than the rule, occurring only in valleys and on the moister slopes of the mountains. The country for the most part consists of grassy plains, dotted with palms and thorny bushes, which latter often form dense and impenetrable thickets. During the prevalence of the south-east monsoon, from April to October, scarcely any rain falls in this area, and towards the latter end of this dry season the drought is so great that many small streams dry up, and most of the trees lose their leaves. The heat is then intense; and were it not that the nights are cool and a breeze always blowing, the climate would approach in severity that of Central Australia. As it is, the chief effect of this long-continued dryness of the atmosphere is that it is inimical to that luxuriant forest growth which elsewhere in the equatorial zones clothes the earth with perennial verdure, and affords a constant protection from the rays of the vertical sun. The only other parts of the archipelago where any extent of open country occurs are in Northern Borneo, in Southern Celebes, and some of the Philippine Islands, but in these cases it is probably due to human agency aided by the introduction of cattle which have become wild. The densely peopled plains of Java and the elevated plateaus of Sumatra are highly cultivated, and have been so long the seat of an ancient civilisation that the absence of forest is clearly not to be considered a natural feature.

3. The Malay Race and Language.

Of the two chief peoples of the Eastern Archipelago— the Malays and the Papuans—the Malays are decidedly the more highly developed, the more numerous and important. They have spread their language, their domestic animals, and some of their customs, widely throughout the Pacific and Indian Oceans, in many instances to islands where they have effected no sort of change in the physical or moral characteristics of the indigenous inhabitants. This wide diffusion of Malay influence is an extraordinary phenomenon, for the Malay race itself has by no means such an extensive range, although it has been by some supposed that all the brown tribes with straight or nearly straight hair, generally termed Polynesians, which are widely scattered in the tropical and sub-tropical South Sea Islands, belong to this division of mankind. Since Wilhelm von Humboldt's studies of the old Kawi language of Java, we know that the dominant race in Madagascar and the Comoro group also belongs to the Malay linguistic family. Hence has originated the common statement that this race has spread from the Comoros to Easter Island, and occupies the area between 45° E. long. and 110° W. long., or more than half the circumference of the globe.

But this view as to the extent of the Malayan peoples is held by many modern writers to be quite erroneous, and they accordingly give the Malays a much more restricted habitation. Mr. A. R. Wallace has always maintained that the brown Polynesians are really quite distinct from the Malays, and, except in colour (though in this point he is at variance with most authorities), seem to have more affinity with the dark, woolly-haired races of the Pacific, or are equally distinct from both. This view is supported by two writers who have great knowledge of the races and languages of the Pacific. Mr. W. S. W. Vaux, in a paper on the *Probable Origin of the Maories*, read before the Anthropological Institute in 1876, maintains that the connection of the modern languages of the Eastern Polynesians with the Malay is by no means so intimate as many able philologists have asserted. Still more important and weighty is the evidence of Mr. W. L. Ranken, who, in a paper on the *South Sea Islanders*, read before the same society a few months later, proposes the native term "Mahori" for the Eastern Polynesians, and shows that their language is totally distinct from the Malay, has a different construction, has very few Malay roots, and only a few quite recent Malay words. Though resembling Malays both physically and mentally in some respects, the "Mahoris" differ greatly from them in others. They have a much greater average height, their features are much more of the European type, and their hair is typically wavy. He traces this race to Samoa as their first home in the Pacific, but primarily from some part of the Asiatic continent.

We now come to the view held by perhaps the greatest authority on Australasian ethnology—Professor A. H. Keane—as published in the *Journal of the Anthropological Institute* for February, 1880. In this paper the writer agrees with the opinion that the Eastern Polynesians are distinct from the Malays, but enters more fully into the question of the place of origin of the various races that people the archipelago. His conclusions may be shortly given as follows:—

That the Negritos are the true autochthones of Indo-China and Western Malaysia; the Papuans of Eastern Malaysia and Western Polynesia.

That Indo-China, at some very remote period, became occupied first by a fair Caucasian race, and later by a yellow Mongoloid people. The latter is now represented by the Burmese, Siamese, Laos, Annamese, etc., speaking monosyllabic toned languages, and the former by the Kambojans, Chams, Kûys, and various hill-tribes, speaking polysyllabic untoned languages.

That from these two races have sprung all the peoples—other than Negritos and Papuans—now occupying the entire Eastern Archipelago from Sumatra to the farthest point of Polynesia.

That the earliest wave of immigration was previous to the advent of the Mongol race, and furnished the archipelago with a people of nearly pure Caucasian stock, of whom the Mentawi islanders of western Sumatra and the Eastern Polynesians (Samoans, Tongans, Maoris, Tahitians, etc.) are now the only representatives.

That later waves of immigration, after part fusion of Mongol and Caucasian, brought in a mixed people, but with a preponderance of Caucasian blood—the "Pre-Malays" or "Indonesians" of various writers—who are widely represented in the archipelago (Battaks, Dyaks, etc.)

That at a still later period what is now known as the Malay race developed itself, the Mongol blood predominating. Of this people the Malays of the peninsula, the Javanese, Sundanese, Ache tribes of Sumatra, and Tagals and Bisayans of the Philippines may, among numerous others, be mentioned as examples. It will thus be noticed that the Malay is not ethnically distinct, but a mixture of two races.

These views of Professor Keane have been accepted by many, as they appear to afford a tolerably complete explanation of the difficulties with which the question has been hitherto surrounded. There is in any case no doubt as to the radical distinctness of the Malays and the "brown Polynesians," and the term "Malayo-Polynesian" should therefore be given up as entirely inaccurate and misleading.

The Malays belong then, undoubtedly, to the so-called Mongolian division of mankind, and this is well illustrated by the strong resemblance between some of the higher types of each. The ordinary Malay is, of course, very different from the Chinaman, but in the island of Bali, Mr. A. R. Wallace was unable to distinguish the natives from some Chinese immigrants who had laid aside their national dress. They are of a light brown complexion and rather small, the men being on the average three or four inches below the mean European height. The face is of a somewhat square or rather rhomboid form, not much longer than broad, with high and prominent cheek-bones; the expression often mild and not unpleasing; eyes black, but rarely oblique; mouth wide and large, with rather thick but well-cut lips; broad lower jaw: round and shapely chin; nose small and short and rather broad, not flat like the Negro nor prominent like the European; nostrils very dilated; occiput flat and square, with thick, straight, black hair, but with weak and scanty beard, which is almost invariably plucked out by the roots. The sexes resemble each other not a little, and strangers are sometimes puzzled at first to distinguish between the two (see frontispiece).

The Malay is naturally of an easy-going, indolent character. In his intercourse with others he betrays a certain reserve, diffidence, and even shyness, which has induced many to suppose that there must be some exaggeration in the current accounts of his savage and bloodthirsty nature. He never gives open expression to a sense of astonishment, surprise, or fear, and is probably little affected by such feelings. Slow and deliberate of speech, he leads up in roundabout ways to the subject he may have come expressly to inquire into. In the more civilised parts, where the rules of the Koran are observed with greater strictness, both women and children are timid, and shrink from the unexpected sight of a European. In the society of the male sex they are silent, and in general quiet and submissive. When alone the Malay is gloomy and taciturn, never either singing or talking to himself. But when paddling together in canoes they will occasionally chant a monotonous, wailing song. They seldom offend each other, nor are they prone to wrangling over money matters, scarcely venturing even to claim what is lawfully their own. Coarse horse-play is especially repugnant to them, the Malay being extremely sensitive on all points of etiquette and of encroachments on his personal freedom. The upper classes are exceedingly courteous, comporting themselves with all the quiet dignity of a well-educated European. Yet this outward refinement, strange to say, co-exists in them with the most pitiless cruelty and contempt of human life, traits which belong to the dark side of their character. Herein lies the explanation of the many diametrically opposed judgments which have been given us by various travellers of their mental characteristics.

Some tell us that these dwellers by the sea are ever hospitable and trustworthy, quiet and extremely indolent, but with an insatiable passion for gambling, which all prohibitive measures have failed to suppress. Other accounts describe them as impulsive, without self-control, little to be relied upon, and of fickle disposition. Improvident, lazy, and averse to work, they would gladly assume the *rôle* of superior beings whose lofty aspirations and sense of freedom are degraded by the menial occupations necessary to secure a livelihood. They are, however, distinguished by greater energy and acquisitiveness from the other races of the Indian Archipelago, though Islam has deprived even them of all higher aims in life, splitting up their local communes, and reducing their pursuits mainly to navigation and piracy. Theft and kidnapping are thought lightly of, while insults, real or imaginary, are savagely avenged on the spot. They are, at the same time, unforgetful of wrong, false and wily, so that solemn oaths are uttered with no intention of keeping them, and poisonings are very common. They are passionately fond of opium-smoking, though this is a less common vice than among the Chinese; and of betting over their cock-fights, often staking their very selves and their personal freedom on the issue. On the other hand, they are very frugal; and characteristic of their contentedness is the current expression asking for a present: " Kechil presentie, tuan, poer makan "—" A little present, sir, to eat." Hence the eating-houses take the place of our drinking-houses, and are their chief places of resort. Here they indulge in dry rice, capsicums, little scraps of meat or fish, cooked vegetables, and sweet titbits handed round with a cup of hot water.

The Malays are nominally Moslems, but lack the fanaticism of that religion. The Javanese, especially, consider they have done enough by observing the rite of circumcision, the prescribed ablutions, and the Ramazan fast, at the same time retaining many of the old Hindoo ideas. Some of them are Christians, that is to say, they attend the services of the Dutch Church, abstain from shaving their heads or filing down their teeth, and drink wine and spirits.

The *lingua franca* of the whole East Indian Archipelago is the Low Malay, which contains no rough or harsh gutturals or other consonants difficult of utterance, but is soft and musical, in its liquid sounds somewhat resembling Italian. All Europeans in the Dutch and English possessions speak this language, which is easily and rapidly acquired.

The Malays and Indonesians, to whom the preceding description is generally applicable, and who agree closely with those of the Malayan Peninsula, inhabit all the islands from Sumatra to Sumbawa, Celebes, the Philippines, Buru, and Ternate, with outlying settlements in Gilolo, Ceram, Amboina, Banda, and at several points on the Papuan islands. Only a small portion of these have Malay as their language, that tongue being found chiefly in the central plateau of Sumatra, and around the coast of Borneo. In every other part of the Malayan area other languages are spoken, some of them being merely dialects of Malay, others distinct but allied languages. Many, again, as the Bugis of Macassar, and especially the languages of the people of Ternate and Tidor, are totally unlike Malay.

Again, the Malays may be divided into two great groups—the savage and the semi-civilised peoples. The Dyaks of Borneo are the best example of the former. They have no writing or literature, no regular government or religion, and they wear only the scantiest clothing of the usual savage type. But they are by no means a low class of savages, for they build good houses, cultivate the ground, make pottery and canoes, work in iron, and even construct roads and bridges. In the same stage are some of the inland tribes of Sumatra, Celebes, and Buru. The semi-civilised people comprise all the other Malayan tribes. These possess written languages, and many of them peculiar alphabets; they have some scanty literature, established governments, and some form of religion; they wear a regular costume, they spin and weave cotton or other textile fabrics, and make use of a considerable variety of tools and weapons.

In the foregoing pages we have glanced at the leading features of the Malay Archipelago as a whole. We must now pass on to a more detailed consideration of the various geographical divisions of which it is composed.

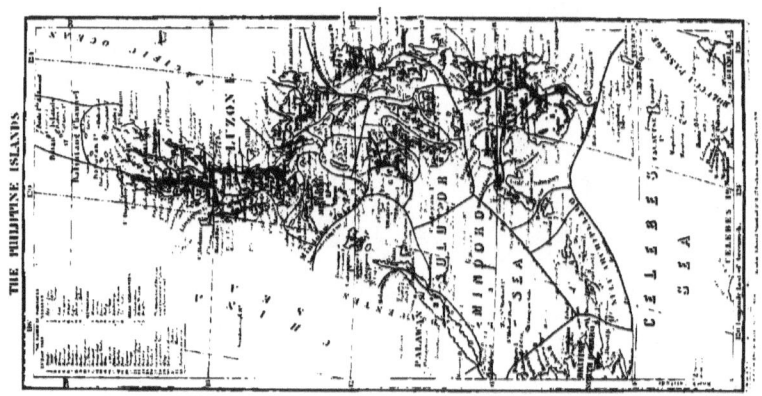

CHAPTER III

THE PHILIPPINE ISLANDS

1. General.

THE Philippines, the most valuable and extensive colonial possessions of Spain, extend almost due north and south from Formosa to Borneo and the Moluccas, embracing an extent of 16° of latitude and 9° of longitude. To the north the nearest land is the island of Formosa, distant about 175 miles. From Manila to Hongkong is $2\frac{1}{2}$ days by steamer. To the west lies Cochin China, to the south Borneo and Celebes, and to the east the open sea. To the south and west the Sulu group and Paláwan project like horns to within a few miles of the coast of Borneo, enclosing the deep basin known as the Sulu or Mindoro Sea. But though a series of stepping-stones are thus formed which would seem to indicate a recent union with that island, a closer examination does not confirm this idea. For the soundings in the Mindoro Strait, to the north of Paláwan, although as yet incomplete, reveal a depth of 600 to 700 fathoms, while between Sibutu and Tawi-tawi Islands, in the Sulu group, a similar channel exists, though of less depth. This, and the shallowness of the sea between Borneo and Paláwan, appear to point to the conclusion that the latter is really Bornean rather than

Philippine—a theory which, as will presently be seen, is more or less borne out by what we know of the zoology of the island. To the west of the Philippine Archipelago is another deep basin separating it from Annam and Cochin China. Along its eastern boundaries, throughout their whole extent, the great ocean depths are soon reached; but to the north a submarine bank connects Luzon with Formosa by way of the Bashi and Babuyan islands, although here also, as in the Mindoro and Sibutu Straits, we find a narrow but rather deep channel intervening close to Formosa.

According to Spanish authors, the Philippines amount to 408 islands, exclusive of mere rocks and uninhabited islets. Two islands are pre-eminently large—Luzon, which is larger than Ireland by a half, and Mindanao, which exceeds it by a fifth. Seven others are of considerable size—Samar, Leyte, Zebu, Negros, Panay, Mindoro, and Paláwan—the largest of these, Paláwan, Samar, and Panay, being each about half as large as Sicily, and the smallest, Zebu, about one-fifth the size of that island. Then come two, Bohol and Masbate, about as large as Majorca; after which are about twenty islands, such as the Calamianes, Marinduque, Basilan, and Catanduanes, all of which are larger than the Isle of Wight. The entire archipelago is said to contain an area of about 200,000 geographical square miles, but this must include the landlocked water-surface between the islands. The actual land area of all the islands, including Paláwan, Balábac, and the Sulu group, is 113,400 square miles, of which Luzon furnishes nearly half, with an area of 47,600 square miles.

Whether considered collectively or individually, the Philippines have their long axis, for the most part, north and south, and—if we disregard the southern groups—

are so closely and compactly situated, with such narrow straits between them, that their appearance is that of a single great island which has been broken up by submersion and volcanic action. There is, indeed, no other archipelago in the world which contains so many islands so compactly massed together.

Lying entirely within the tropics, with an infinitely diversified coast outline, with mountain ranges having a mean elevation of 3000 to 4000 feet, and isolated volcanoes rising to a height of 8000 to 10,000 feet, the Philippines possess all the conditions for the most luxuriant tropical vegetation, and all the elements of the finest tropical scenery. Everywhere the land is abundantly watered, and abounds in rivers and streams, and upland and lowland lakes. In truth, the archipelago is in almost every respect fully worthy to be compared with the most famous tropical regions, such as Brazil, Java, and Ceylon. The light green foliage of the lowlands contrasts vividly with the pine forests of the lofty mountain summits, for here the conifers are wedded to the palm, while the lowland streams are fringed with feathery bamboos. Half concealed by coco-nut palms lie the towns and villages, amid the vivid green of the rice fields and sugar plantations; while the woodlands and gardens are beautiful with the dazzling hues of their blossoms and fruits. From this vegetation the native women seem to have acquired the art of clothing themselves in the brightest colours without offending our more educated taste. For here the wealth of colour in which plants, animals, and man himself are arrayed, harmonises perfectly with the fulness of light poured down by a fierce tropical sun on the bosom of the earth. But, despite this glorious vegetation, no more here than elsewhere does mankind enjoy the cup of peaceful bliss undisturbed. The populous towns and villages are decimated by frightful epidemics—smallpox and Asiatic cholera; while erratic flights of locusts, darkening the heavens like dense clouds, devour the young crops, leaving hunger and famine in their wake. With the change of the monsoons the swollen streams overflow the land; and when the industrious Tagal fancies he has escaped the devastating floods in his log hut or stone house, he is suddenly buried by an earthquake beneath its ruins, stifled in a burning rain of cinders from some new-born volcano, or hurried to a still swifter death in the overwhelming waters of an earthquake-wave.

2. History.

The Philippines will remain for ever famous as the scene of the death of the great Portuguese navigator, Magellan. The Spanish squadron of which he was in command, reduced by desertion and wreck to three ships, sighted the southern point of Samar Island on the 16th March, 1521, but, finding the coast beset with shoals, bore away to the southward, and the admiral landed on the neighbouring island of Malhou the same night. The first place of any note visited by the squadron was Zebu, in the island of that name, and it was in fighting with a hostile tribe who occupied the islet of Mactan in front of the port that, on the 27th April, Magellan lost his life.

To the archipelago thus discovered Magellan gave the name of St. Lazarus, for he had first sighted the group upon the day sacred to that saint. It was not till some time after—in 1542—that Lopez de Villalobos gave them their present appellation of the Islas Filipinas in honour of Philip II., the son of Charles V. Meanwhile they became known to the Portuguese as the Eastern Islands, while the Spaniards called them the Islas del Poniente, for while the latter nation sailed westwards round the world, the Portuguese carried on their explorations in a contrary direction. This curious circumstance involved another. To the first circumnavigators the necessity of altering their day on passing the meridian of 180° was unknown, and so it came about that Hongkong and Manila called the same day Monday and Sunday, and it was not until the 31st December, 1844, that the matter was rectified by the omission of that day from the Manilan calendar. The more civilised people of the archipelago, when first seen by the Spaniards, were very far from being savages. They cultivated corn, wore textile fabrics, and worked iron and gold, had domestic animals for food and labour, and used a phonetic written character.

The Spaniards owe their possession of the Philippines to Miguel Lopez de Legaspi, who with a force of little more than 400 men reached Zebu in 1565. In six years he had subdued the greater part of the archipelago. This facile conquest was effected without much bloodshed, and was not a little due to the efforts of a band of Augustine monks under Andrea de Urdañeta, who had commanded a ship in Loyasa's ill-fated expedition. The gradual settlement and civilisation of the islands, indeed, have been to a very considerable extent the work of ecclesiastics, who dominate the superstitious and *festa*-loving " Indian " without difficulty. In 1571 Manila was taken, the present city founded, and the greater part of Luzon brought under Spanish rule. Legaspi died the same year.

Although at this period the Moors, as they were termed, were well known and numerous in many of the larger ports as traders, the inhabitants of all the northern islands were pagans, and almost ignorant of civilisation of any kind. In Sulu and southern Mindanao the Spaniards found themselves in contact with a very different people. Then, as now, the inhabitants of that part of the archipelago were Mohammedans, fierce and intractable, skilled in navigation, and born pirates. They were, and have been for three centuries, the bitter enemies of the "Castillas," and expedition after expedition was vainly sent to subdue them. In 1731 a fleet of thirty Spanish vessels attacked Jolo, expecting an easy victory, but so well did the Sulus fight that they succeeded in capturing their enemies' colours, and the fleet shortly afterwards sailed away. It was not until 1871 that the Spaniards succeeded in establishing themselves upon the island, but to this day they are in no better position than are the Dutch at Ache.

The Chinese and Japanese, especially the former, have played a considerable part in the history of the islands, but mostly upon pacific lines, as will be seen in a future page. It was otherwise with the Portuguese and the Dutch, who on more than one occasion sought, but ineffectually, to dispossess Spain. Their attempts were not, however, upon such a scale as to need detailed notice here. During the Seven Years' War, in 1762, the English fitted out an expedition from Madras composed of thirteen men-of-war and transports, and a force of 2300 men, and appeared before the walls of Manila. The Spaniards, who had not even heard of the outbreak of the war, were taken by surprise, the city was bombarded, captured, and sacked, and a ransom of four million dollars demanded. Only £200,000 could be furnished, however, and with this sum the commander of the expedition, Sir William Draper, had to be content. This not very creditable conquest did not extend beyond Manila. The city remained in the hands of the English for ten months, and was then restored by the Treaty of Paris.

Much of the archipelago yet remains not only to be subdued by the Spanish, but to be explored. In spite of their three centuries of occupation many of the islands are very little known—some, indeed, such as Palawan and Mindanao, hardly at all. The coasts have been very imperfectly surveyed, and the hydrography leaves much to be desired.

3. Geology.

In few parts of the world are the great subterranean forces of the globe more in evidence than in the Philippine Archipelago. The islands form links in the volcanic chain which runs from Kamschatka southwards to join the even more important range which traverses the Sunda Islands. This chain is for the most part single, but in the Philippines it becomes wider. For, though in central Luzon the Caraballos ridge stands alone, as we progress southward we find it branching to form three main divisions. The eastern passes through Samar, Leyte, and eastern Mindanao to the Talautse Islands and Celebes, and is really the main chain. The other two, curving off to the west by the Calamianes, Palawan, and Banguey in the one case, and Negros, western Mindanao, and Sulu in the other, come to an abrupt end, for Borneo, as already stated, is non-volcanic. The volcanoes will be separately considered in dealing with the islands in which they occur. It is only necessary here to say that Mount Apo, with a height of 10,280 feet, according to Mr. Montano's observations, and Mayon, which has been variously measured, and is probably not far short of 9000 feet, are the two most important volcanoes of the archipelago.

D

The active craters are numerous, the extinct innumerable, and there is scarcely an island which does not give evidence of volcanic action. Although hot springs are less frequently met with than in Japan, they are by no means rare, and fumaroles and solfataras join with the frequent earthquakes to remind the traveller that he can scarcely consider himself upon terra firma. Throughout the archipelago raised sea-beaches and coralline limestones testify to the general upheaval that has taken place in recent years.

But though volcanic action has had so much to do with the creation of the archipelago, it must not be supposed that the islands are all basalts, tuffs, and upheaved coralline rock. The greater part of them is now known to comprise gneiss and schists and other metamorphic rocks, and granites, stratified sandstone, and conglomerates in the north of Luzon and other places. Gold seems to exist over a wide area, though not in any great quantities, and the beds of many rivers show "colour." That the metal has been known for some centuries is evident from Pigafetta's diary of Magellan's voyage, where the natives are described as wearing gold ornaments, and offering to present the Captain-General with a bar of the metal. Mines are worked after a fashion in several places, the richest quartz being in the provinces of Benguet and Camarines Norte. At Misamis and other places in Mindanao a fair amount of the metal is produced. Copper is also abundant, especially in Lepanto, and the ore has been dug and smelted by some of the native tribes for as long as the islands have been known to Europeans, their vessels, ornaments, and weapons being commonly made of the metal. At Camillas, near Mount Data in north Luzon, are copper mines which should pay well, but for the expenses of transport and fuel. Lead occurs in Zebu, and iron ores are very abundant in Luzon and Mindanao. That there are extensive coal-measures in the archipelago there is little doubt, but they have been little exploited, and coal forms one of the largest imports of the group. The Compostela mine only turned out 700 tons in 1881. As yet no deep shafts have been driven, and what has been obtained affords very rapid combustion, and is not well suited for steamers. Zebu and Negros are especially rich in this product. Since the archipelago lies midway between the great coal beds of northern Borneo and Formosa, it is probable that the mineral will in the future be worked to great advantage.

4. Climate, etc.

Situated between 4° and 20° of N. latitude, the Philippines exhibit a purely tropical climate. The mean temperature of Manila, deduced from data extending over ten years, is 81° Fahr.; the extreme minimum 59°, and the extreme maximum 96°. But owing to the great amount of sea which interpenetrates the islands, the sea breezes have free access to the land, and the heat is on the whole not excessive. At Artol, in the province of Benguet, the thermometer occasionally sinks to 38° Fahr. The rainfall is very great, in some places almost incessant. For, owing to their position and elevation, the islands attract the copious rains of each monsoon, and in some localities where the breadth of the land is much reduced, as at the S. Caraballos mountains and the volcano of Majaijay, the rainclouds of both monsoons discharge their contents, and torrential showers fall almost every day. This superabundant rainfall is a leading feature of the group. The rivers overflow their banks and pour deluges of water over the surrounding country, the roads become utterly impassable, and the marshes are turned into lakes in which the unfortunate traveller finds his navigation impeded by the tree-tops. Such is the normal condition of things on the eastern seaboard when the north-east monsoon is blowing with its full strength. At this period the heavy sea running is such as to preclude safe navigation, and the fisherman becomes perforce an agriculturist, while upon the other side of the archipelago there is settled fine weather both on sea and land. The agricultural seasons thus vary with the locality, and when it is seed-time upon one slope of the Sierra the harvest is being gathered upon the other—a peculiarity which has been described by Jagor and some of the older writers. In the Sulu group there are two rainy seasons, occurring at the change of the monsoons, of which that commencing with the onset of the easterly monsoon is by far the heavier. Owing to the conformation of the land and the position of the ranges, the rainfall in the Philippines is subject to great local variation. The Davao Gulf in Mindanao, for example, has its dry season during the N.E. monsoon, when the rain is falling in daily torrents on the east coast of the island. The annual rainfall of Manila is about 99 inches, of the Agusan Valley in Mindanao 156 inches, and of many parts of Luzon considerably more.

Excepting in the southern islands—the Sulu group, Mindanao, and part of Paláwan, which are too near the equator to suffer—the Philippines are subject to the most terrific typhoons, which occur almost invariably at the change of the monsoons, and especially in October, a month dreaded by the navigator of the China Sea. Originating in the Pacific, and progressing along a curved path in a more or less westerly direction, these hurricanes yearly cause incalculable damage in the islands over which they pass on their way to China. Within the last few years the establishment of the telegraph in Luzon has mitigated the loss of life and property resulting from them. Stations at the extremities and east coast of the island warn the Jesuits' Observatory at Manila of the approaching storm, and notice is immediately telegraphed to Hongkong. But in spite of these warnings the destruction wrought is terrible. In 1831, during one of these storms, a vessel of 600 tons burden, which lay in the port of Cavite, was carried on to the ramparts of the fort. In 1856 a terrific typhoon is said to have destroyed 10,000 houses in Manila and the surrounding district. That of 1882, although causing less destruction of life, was almost as violent, the barometer falling to 28·66, and the velocity of the wind rising to 145 miles per hour. Earthquakes are far more frequent, and have wrought even greater havoc than the typhoons. The seismographs of the Manila Observatory reveal an almost constant vibration of the earth. Slight shocks are of the commonest occurrence. Warned by repeated disaster the Manilan now builds his house with a view to guard against accidents. The ground floor alone is stone, the upper story is of wood, and the heavy tiles which once formed the roofs are now abolished by law. In the rooms most frequented it is not unusual to see a sort of "manhole" which acts as a shelter in emergencies, and the tables are made of great solidity for the same purpose. The careful householder screws down the clocks and other ornaments, and holds himself in readiness to dive beneath the table at a moment's notice.

The most disastrous earthquakes of the present century occurred in 1827, 1828, 1863, 1874, and 1880, and of these that of 1863 will be longest remembered from its having caused the collapse of the cathedral of Manila when packed with people, and a fearful loss of life in consequence. On the 18th July, 1880, a sudden shock reduced half the city to ruins, but not more than 150 persons were killed. The shocks were repeated on the 20th, and thenceforward daily and constantly until the 6th August, and to complete the misfortunes of the country, torrents of rain fell almost without intermission from July 21st to the 18th August, and inundated the country. According to the observations of Père Faura, the head of the Manila Observatory, the first shock of this earthquake lasted 70 seconds. The oscillations were excessive, the greatest measured being 22° 11′ to the east and 11° to the west.

Notwithstanding the natural scourges to which the Philippine Islands are thus exposed, they cannot justly be said to be unhealthy. Formerly the natives died in hundreds from smallpox, but this disease has been much mitigated of late since the Spanish Government has established a training post for the instruction of native vaccinators, who are afterwards despatched to every part of the islands. Asiatic cholera, however, claims numberless victims. The most important diseases are dysentery, ulcers,—probably of parasitic origin,—and malarial fevers, but the latter are not of a severe type. Contrary to what is usual in tropical climates, frequent instances of extreme longevity have been recorded among the native inhabitants.

5. Fauna and Flora.

The flora of the Philippines is not even yet thoroughly known, the difficulties till recently thrown by the Government in the way of scientific investigation, together with the heavy cost of travelling, having deterred naturalists from visiting the country. Lately, however, Don Sebastian Vidal, Conservator of Forests in the Philippines, has added considerably to our knowledge by the publication of his *Sinopsis de Familias y Generos de Plantas Leñosas de Filipinas*, and Mr. R. A. Rolfe of Kew has rendered equal service to science by his able paper upon the flora of the archipelago,[1] in which its derivation and the elucidation of the past history of the group receive detailed consideration. So far as is at present known, 723 genera of 2108 species of Dicotyledons, and 273 genera of 1340 species of Monocotyledons exist. The proportion of the latter to the Dicotyledons is thus more than one-half, which—since in tropical insular floras it seldom exceeds one-fourth—must be considered very unusual. In the ferns, of 467 species no less than 52 are peculiar, which is alone sufficient to stamp the islands with a marked individuality. But one of the most peculiar features is the large number of endemic species and the exceeding paucity of endemic genera. The former reach the large total of 769, but while Borneo has 28 endemic genera and Java 30, there are only 6 in the Philippines.

The general features of the flora are certainly Malayan; but at the same time a large number of typical Malayan genera have not yet been found in the archipelago, in spite of their occurring in Borneo. Yet more striking is the presence of a considerable Australian and Austro-Malayan element. Space will not permit detailed reference; but the characteristic genera *Stackhousia, Osbornia, Leptospermum, Psoralea* are found, and numerous like examples could be given. A considerable connection with Celebes would prob-

[1] *Jour. Linn. Soc. Bot.*, vol. xxi. No. 135.

ably be revealed if we were possessed of a better knowledge of the flora of that island. Three species are only known from Celebes and the Philippines, and besides these a number of plants collected at Gorontalo in the former island by Mr. Riedel are considered by Mr. Rolfe to be either identical with, or closely allied to Philippine species. The connecting link is doubtless to be found in the south, in Mindanao and the Sulu islands, as indeed Mr. Burbidge's researches in the latter group have proved. Bearing in mind the existence of the submarine bank between Luzon and Formosa, and the shallowness of the sea intervening between the latter island and China, a northern element might certainly be expected to be found existing to a greater or less extent in the group. This surmise is borne out by facts, and although not extensive, the connection is very well marked. There are three endemic species of *Carex*, a typical northern genus, as indeed is *Pinus*, of which we find two species—*P. insularis* and *P. Merkusii*. Other forms exist which, if not specifically identical with, are nevertheless closely allied to Chinese species. The genus *Pinus* only occurs in Luzon, and is confined to the western side, *P. insularis* not growing south of 15° N., although *P. Merkusii* occurs in the province of Zambales in a restricted area, and is met with again in the island of Sumatra. The richness of the forests is shown by the fact that the timber of more than 200 different trees has been experimented on in the arsenal of Manila, resulting in the selection of six as specially adapted to shipbuilding. Two of these are species of *Vitex* (*Verbenaceæ*), one is a *Vateria* (*Dipterocarpeæ*), another is a *Sterculia*. Of these Molave wood (*Vitex geniculata*) is practically indestructible, resisting alike the teredo and white ant, as well as the destructive effects of climate. Dyewoods are abundant, and the sapan-wood, produced by *Cæsalpinia sappan*, obtains the highest price in European markets. Teak is found in Mindanao and also in the Sulu group, although it is said not to occur elsewhere in the Malay Archipelago except in Java and Sumbawa. Gums, resins, and textile materials are also abundantly produced. *Musa textilis* is largely grown for its fibre, which when prepared is known by the name of abaca or Manila hemp. This, with sugar, forms the chief export. The St. Ignatius's bean (*Ignatia*), yielding the deadly poison strychnine, is commonly sold in the market at Manila. Most of the fruits of the other Malayan countries abound, excepting the mangosteen and durian. For these a strictly equatorial climate appears to be indispensable, and they only thrive in the extreme south of the archipelago.

If we pass to the fauna of the group we find that it bears out to a great extent what may be surmised from a study of the flora. Although generally agreeing with the fauna of the larger Malay islands, that of the Philippines exhibits some remarkable deficiencies. These are most prominent in the mammalia, which are very few in number as compared with those of Borneo or Java. Thus, the numerous apes and monkeys of those islands are represented in the Philippines only by the common *Macacus cynomolgus* and the curious little Tarsier, one of the lemurs. Of carnivora there are three species only, two civets and a wild cat,—all the larger felines, the weasels, bears, and wild dogs, being entirely wanting. Of the Ungulates there is a wild pig, a mouse-deer, which is confined to the Bornean islands, Balabac and Palawan, three kinds of deer, and a very curious representative of the *Bovidæ*—*Probubalus mindorensis*, whose nearest ally is the antelopean buffalo of Celebes (*Anoa depressicornis*). This interesting animal, which has only recently been obtained by Professor Steere's expedition, is confined to the island of Mindoro. There are no tapirs, rhinoceroses, or elephants. Even the small rodents are very scarce, there being only five squirrels, one flying squirrel, a porcupine, and two or three of the rat tribe. The flying mammals, on the other hand, are numerous, there being nearly thirty species of bats, many of which are peculiar. Some half-dozen insectivora only are known—the "flying lemur" (*Galeopithecus*), two or three shrews, and the curious squirrel-like *Tupaia*. The Edentata are represented by a Manis, which only occurs in Paláwan.

Altogether, although a few more may yet remain to be discovered, there are only twenty-three terrestrial mammals known to inhabit the Philippines, and of these several are confined to the island of Paláwan, which, as has already been stated, cannot be said, geographically speaking, to form a portion of the Philippine Archipelago. Java has nearly 100 mammals, of which more than half are terrestrial, and it is therefore remarkable that the Philippines with a larger area should have so few.

The birds show many peculiarities and deficiencies when compared with those of the great islands of western Malaysia. To the revised list published by Captain Wardlaw Ramsay in the appendix to the Marquis of Tweeddale's "Ornithological Works," Professor Steere has added 53 new species, bringing the total number of land birds to 303. And although many of these are subspecies, or species only slightly differentiated by more or less long-continued separation in different islands, the number is large as compared with the 270 odd species known from the much better explored island of Java.

In spite of this richness there are many very important genera found in all the other Malay islands which are wanting in the archipelago. This isolation is further marked by the fact that more than two-thirds of the Philippine species are peculiar to the group, and that they include such birds as cockatoos and mound-builders (*Megapodius*), which are essentially typical of the Moluccas and the other eastern islands. Similarly the preponderance of parrots and pigeons points out a strong eastern connection, and although woodpeckers—a group characteristic of the western regions—are rather numerous, no pheasants exist, except upon Palawan, an island which, as has already been shown, is so conclusively Bornean, that it should not be taken into consideration in discussing the geological history of the Philippine Archipelago. The only game birds found in the islands are the common jungle fowl (*Gallus bankiva*) and one or two small quail.

Of the other vertebrates little is known. There are crocodiles, lizards, and snakes in abundance, and among the latter are pythons, which destroy young cattle, and are said in some cases to exceed 40 feet in length. Insects are abundant and of great beauty. As in the case of the birds, mammals, and plants, they differ in many respects from those of the other Malay islands, and show in numerous instances an affinity with those of the eastern islands.

Instructive as is the distribution of all the foregoing classes of the animal kingdom in the archipelago, the land mollusca yield to none in interest, both in themselves and in their relation to those of the neighbouring islands. Pre-eminent among them is the group known as *Cochlostyla*, a genus of large and handsome snails with affinities both with *Helix* and *Bulimus*. This group, of which more than 200 species have been described, appears to be quite peculiar to the Philippines,—the few extra-Philippine forms which have been referred to it being better grouped elsewhere. The Sandwich Islands alone in the Pacific form another instance of a group of islands possessing so large and so well-marked a genus of peculiar land-shells.

A study of the various subgenera of *Cochlostyla* reveals several facts of importance. Firstly, with regard to the island of Mindoro, it appears that not only are two of them (*Orthostylus* and *Hypselostyla*), which are abundant in Luzon and the central islands, entirely absent, but two well-marked subgenera (*Chrysalis* and *Prochilus*) occur which are found nowhere else in the archipelago. The small island of Luban, to the north-west of Mindoro, also has a peculiar subgenus. Siquihor, an island of equally small size lying between Mindanao and the central group, is likewise conspicuous as possessing the only species of *Clausilia* known from the Philippines. Three subgenera (*Chlorœa*, *Corasia*, and *Calocochlea*) are universally distributed, occurring on all the islands, and it seems probable that these were developed at a time when the Philippines were all united together, or, at all events, were much less of an archipelago than they now are. It is evident, from their isolation being so specially marked, that Mindoro and Luban became separate at a very early period.

With regard to the land mollusca in general, and their relation to the neighbouring lands and islands, Mr. A. H. Cooke remarks that two distinct faunæ, the Indo-Malayan and the Polynesian, find their meeting-place in the group. Palàwan and the Sulu Islands form two arms or ridges which tend to connect the Philippines with Borneo. On these ridges the mollusca are of a mixed type — partly Philippine, partly Indo-Malayan; but there can be little doubt that they have formed, at a period more or less remote, the passage by which the Indo-Malayan mollusca have entered the archipelago to mingle with the indigenous genera. Thus we find the great *Nanina* and *Cyclophori* of the Sunda Islands largely represented, as well as *Amphidromus*, *Kaliella*, and others, all of which are represented in Java, Sumatra, and Borneo, as well as in India or Indo-China, but scarcely at all, or in greatly diminished numbers, in the islands farther east.

The Polynesian and eastern connection is exemplified by the occurrence of *Tornatellina*, *Endodonta*, numerous species of *Helicina* and *Leptopoma*, and a considerable number of *Pupina* and *Diplommatina*. About fifteen species of land shells are common to the Philippines and Amboina, and some writers have considered it probable that a land connection existed at one time with the countries to the east and south, but in this opinion Mr. Cooke does not share.

From the foregoing it will be seen that the zoology of the group is of unusual interest, presenting problems in geographical distribution which have as yet not been satisfactorily explained. Taking all the facts yet known, we find a wonderful amount of peculiarity throughout, great luxuriance of development in some of the lower groups, and many deficiencies in the higher, especially in the mammalia. This luxuriance and peculiarity, combined with poverty in the forms of life, implies great antiquity and long-continued isolation from adjacent countries. The presence of a tolerable variety of mammalia, closely allied to those of other Malayan countries, shows that the time from which the isolation dates is not very remote geologically; but it is less easy to account for the absence of so many important groups of mammalia. Two explanations are open to us. Either the former union with Borneo, and, perhaps, with Formosa, was limited in extent and of short duration, so that only a few mammalian types ever entered the country; or, the union having been more complete and of sufficient duration, the islands became well stocked with mammals, but a great amount of subsidence has since so reduced the land area and altered the physical conditions, that numbers of them, especially those of the largest size, have become extinct. This latter hypothesis is supported by the fact, that almost everywhere are found large tracts of elevated coral reefs containing shells similar to those now living in the adjacent seas—proving that at a comparatively recent period the islands have been partially submerged, and therefore less extensive than they are now. Mr. Rolfe, too, considers the present flora to have been differentiated when the islands were much more immersed than is now the case. We know that all volcanic countries are subject to elevations and subsidences, and it is highly probable that so pre-eminently volcanic a district as the Philippines has been repeatedly subject to partial elevations and depressions; at one time effecting a union with adjacent lands, and thus favouring the introduction of new animals, at another submerging extensive areas, and thus leading to the extermination of many forms of life. Changes of this kind, if continued through the latter portion of the Tertiary period, would inevitably produce such a limited yet peculiar fauna as is now found to characterise these islands. Minute geological investigation, combined with a more complete knowledge of the existing fauna and flora, will alone enable us to determine how far these suppositions are correct. There is not much doubt, however, that we have in Mindoro the sole remnant of a pre-existing land which was at one time unconnected with the great Malay islands, and probably prolonged to the east and south.

6. Inhabitants.

The Philippines are inhabited, so far as the indigenous population is concerned, by two distinct races of men—the Negrito and the Malayan. Ethnologists are for the most part agreed in looking upon the former as the remnant of the aboriginal inhabitants of the group, who have been gradually supplanted and driven to the mountains by the more civilised and capable Malays. That this invasion took place at a very remote period there is every reason to believe.

The Negritos are a diminutive, dark race, with crisp and woolly hair and a facial appearance of a Negroid type. They are found in Luzon, Mindoro, Negros, Panay, and Mindanao; probably in Paláwan according to Marche, and possibly in Zebu. The pure race is now rare. Their total numbers are put by Blumentritt at 20,000, an estimate only 5000 short of that given by Crawfurd forty years ago. Although wild, and living in districts for the most part remote from civilisation, they have mixed very largely with the pagan Malay tribes, and traces of Negrito blood are very frequently to be seen. In the pure Negrito the height is said to average 4 ft. 10 in., but Semper's estimate is two or three inches less. The skull is brachycephalic, the chest small, the legs without calves, and the feet turned inwards. Their prognathous and deeply-lined faces give them an ape-like appearance. The nose is broad and flat, and the nostrils dilated, and the slender build and small size of the body cause the head to appear disproportionately large. They are somewhat timid and gentle by nature, and great affec-

A NEGRITO OF LUZON.

tion exists between parents and children. The chief or only weapons used by them are the bow and arrow, the former being constructed of the midrib of a *Caryota* frond. The arrows are always poisoned. Their intelligence is of a very low type, and according to Montano they are unable to count above five. Excepting where they have become partly civilised, they are more or less nomadic of habit. Such religion as they have would appear to consist chiefly of a sort of ancestor-worship. They are monogamists without exception. The chief or headman is chosen from among the oldest and most respected of the tribe. Circumcision is universally practised. Little appears to be known of their language, except that spoken by them in some parts of Luzon. Oscar Peschel and some other ethnologists class the Negrito with the Papuan, an opinion little likely to be shared by those who are well acquainted with the latter race. The slender build, flat nose, diminutive stature, and gentle retiring manners render such a classification impossible. Mr. J. Barnard Davis, from the examination of three fine crania, considers the Negrito to be distinct from any other race. Taking all their physical characters into consideration, they seem more nearly to resemble the Andaman islanders and the Semangs of the Malay Peninsula than any other existing peoples.

To the Spaniard of the present day the people of Malayan stock who inhabit the Philippines are known as *Indios*, *Infièles*, and *Moros*—an ecclesiastical rather than scientific classification. The *Indios* are all those who have come under Spanish influence, and are professed Christians; the *Infièles* are the wilder pagans of the interior who have always rebelled against Spanish rule, and the *Moros* are the Sulus and other Mohammedan tribes occupying south-west Mindanao, the Sulu group, and part of Paláwan. The people included in this nomenclature have certain characteristics in common which are collectively typical of the Malay race, namely,

E

a moderate stature, an olive-coloured complexion, broad nose, full lips, a head broader than in Europeans, and hair straight, nearly black, and somewhat coarse. They are divided into numerous distinct tribes speaking different languages, of which there are twenty in the island of Luzon alone. Many are doubtless still unknown, particularly in the unexplored recesses of Mindanao and Paláwan. The two chief tribes are the Tagal and Bisayan, the former occupying the greater part of Luzon and the whole of the islands Marinduque and Mindoro, and numbering about 1,500,000 souls. They appear to be increasing somewhat rapidly, more by the assimilation of neighbouring tribes than anything else, and are the most civilised of all the *Indios*. The Bisayans occupy all the islands lying between Luzon and Mindanao, as well as a considerable portion of the north of the latter island, and number over 2,000,000. Their language is akin to Tagalog, but is spoken with an infinity of dialects. Formerly they had a peculiar alphabet, or rather syllabary, but this seems to be now unused. The Tagalog writing-system is still to be found, based like the other, according to Mr. Keane, upon the archaic Devanâgiri of the Asoka inscriptions, though now departing greatly from that type in form. The Tagbuanas of Paláwan appear to be allied to the Bisayans, and still make use of a very similar writing system, writing from the bottom of the page to the top in columns, and beginning on the right hand.

These two peoples will probably in time include and assimilate their less powerful neighbours, but there are still other tribes of considerable importance, numerically or otherwise, in the archipelago, the chief of which are the Bicols and Ilocanos. The former inhabit the Camarines or southern peninsula of Luzon, the Catanduanes

Islands, part of Masbate, and the islands lying between it and Luzon, and are related to the Tagals, especially by their language. They number about 350,000. The Ilocanos are more numerous, and occupy, with various tribes with which they have more or less intermingled, the northern part of Luzon. Besides these there are an infinity of other sub-Malayan peoples—Pangasinans, Pampangos, Tinguianes, Busaos, etc., to which particular reference is unnecessary. The Spanish apply the name Ygarrotes very loosely to a number of different tribes, but, strictly speaking, it should be given only to the natives of the mountains in the Benguet, Lepanto, and other neighbouring districts at the north of Luzon. They appear to differ not a little from the other Malayan inhabitants of the island, and according to some authors are a mixed race, partly of Japanese or Chinese origin. M. Marche, who visited them in 1880, describes them as being a short, hairy race with low forehead and thick lips, large thick feet, but small hands, the hair straight, black, and fine, and worn long by the men. A remarkable feature is the great elaboration of their tattooing, the designs being extremely florid and ornamental, with flowers, serpents, etc., and still more curious is their wood-carving. They dig and work gold, silver, and copper, and make very ornamental pipes, for which they themselves grow the tobacco. They breed both cattle and horses, and are great dog-fanciers. With all these characteristics, which serve to differentiate them markedly from their neighbours, they are nevertheless a wild and savage race, committing frequent raids, and at bitter enmity with the Spaniards, whose bullets have frequently thinned their ranks.

The *Moros*, as the Spanish commonly term the Mohammedan inhabitants of the southern islands, are probably as mixed a people as any in the Philippines. Centuries of piracy have recruited their harems with the women of numberless tribes of Malaysia—with Europeans even, for before the days of steamers few vessels were a match for the crowded praus of the Sulu pirates. In the south of Mindanao the Illanuns had their headquarters, while the Sulus make Sulu Island and Tawi-tawi the base of their operations. The sultans of Sulu claimed authority over the north-east end of Borneo, together with the island of Cagayan Sulu, as well as over their own group, but the former district was ceded some few years ago to the British North Borneo Company, and the rule of the sultans over their turbulent subjects does not ever appear to have been very strong. Such obedience as the Sulu nature is capable of rendering is paid to the small rajas, panglimas and datus, many of whom are not on the best of terms with their sovereign. These rajas are in many cases of Bornean extraction, and the sultan has a species of court with numerous retainers after the fashion of the Sultan of Brunei. The Sulu language is closely allied to the Bisayan, although quite distinct from it, and containing a large number of Javanese and Bugis words, but from the frequent intercourse with the Bornean Malays almost every Sulu is bilingual. The language is written in the Arabic character, and the manners and customs are Malay, but their adherence to the precepts of the Koran is anything but strict, as is shown by their indulgence in alcohol, and by the fact that their women are unveiled.

The Chinese form a very important part of the population of the Philippines, amassing considerable wealth as merchants and shopkeepers. It is probable that they established themselves in the country from the very earliest times, and would long ago have overrun the archipelago but for the repressive measures adopted by the Spaniards. The history of Manila records several wholesale massacres of the "Sangleyes," the last of which took place in 1819, when they were accused of poisoning the wells. Their numbers were limited to 6000, but frequently rose to 30,000 or 40,000, only to be reduced by slaughter and exile. In 1603 some 23,000 were killed. Heavy taxes and strict regulations drove them to revolt in 1639, when over 30,000 of them fell victims. In 1762 they helped the English at the taking of Manila, and on our evacuation of the city some months later, an edict was published by the Spanish Governor that all the Chinese on the islands should be hanged, and this order was said to have been very generally carried out. Notwithstanding these checks to their increase they have thriven and prospered, and at the present time the pure race probably number about 55,000. Of those of mixed blood it is impossible to arrive at an estimate. The number of Chinese women who leave their country is infinitesimally small, and the Celestial has from time immemorial chosen his wife from the native women. To such an extent has this mixture of race been carried on that the Chinese element has left an indelible stamp upon the inhabitants of the Philippines, and its influence throughout the archipelago is very considerable.

The number of Spaniards, who with the exception of the priests are chiefly resident in Manila, is stated to be 14,000. But here the same difficulty of estimation obtains as in the case of the Chinese, for, like the latter, they have mixed freely with half-castes and natives from the time of their first arrival. The Philippines, indeed, show as great confusion of races as any country in Australasia. Even the American element is present, for, as Reclus points out, it must not be forgotten that the Acapulco galleons brought over a powerful colony of Peruvians and Mexicans, and history furnishes us with several instances of the establishment of Japanese in the north of Luzon and in Manila, where they were encouraged to counteract the influence of the Chinese.

The Negritos, as already stated, must be regarded as having in past ages formed the chief or sole population of the Philippines, but it seems probable that another race or races must at some epoch have lived there in great numbers. M. Marche and other naturalists have found numbers of cave burial-places in Marinduque, Catanduanes, and other islands. These caves yielded remains of coffins with handles of carved wood, and urns containing crania, all of which had been deformed by art, pottery, both rough and glazed, some of the jars decorated with dragons in alto-relievo, and fragments of porcelain. Gold ornaments were also discovered, and small rings of that metal, of a form similar to those used in Japan as money in ancient times. These burial-places are supposed to be of great antiquity, and certainly point to the conclusion that the people by whom they were used were largely subject to both Chinese and Japanese influence.

7. Religion and Education.

The Philippine Archipelago presents the anomalous instance of a country which has been conquered as much by ecclesiastical as by military power. Legaspi landed with his body of Augustines, who were followed by the Dominicans and Franciscans, and later—but not until the main work had been accomplished—by the Jesuits. The administration, whether civil or "politico-military," is aided in no small degree by the clergy, who have a great influence over the *festa*-loving and superstitious natives. The Archbishop of Manila directs a large territory, the Ladrones, Carolines, and Pelew Islands being comprised in his province. He has as suffragans the Bishops of Nueva Cáçeres (Camarines-Sur), Nueva Segovia (Ilocos-Sur), Zebu, and Jaro (Iloilo). The public exercise of any religion other than the Catholic is forbidden. The Spanish secular clergy, about 400 in number, reside chiefly in Manila. The parishes are administered by the Spanish ecclesiastics of various orders, or by native clergy who receive their education in the large seminaries attached to each diocese. The Augustines number 500, the Dominicans and Franciscans each 200. The missionary work in the island of Mindanao is almost entirely carried on by the Jesuits. The Spanish regular clergy thus number about 1200. The Church is chiefly supported by a capitation tax and fees.

The Christianised Indians have in a manner grafted their new religion upon their former cult. Deeply superstitious and with boundless faith, the religious orders found them ready converts. The brilliant processions and rich robes and images of the Church appealed most strongly to them. Now the smallest village has its fêtes and its band of musicians to accompany the processions, and plays of a religious or semi-religious nature are very commonly given. The priest is the practical king of the village, and does not regard with a too favourable eye the spread of knowledge, except it be through himself. For, despite the censure, newspapers and posts have begun their work, and there is no doubt that the railway scheme, if completed, will bring a great change in the condition of the native. Not that education is by any means neglected. It is probable, indeed, that a larger percentage of the Christian natives can read and write than the peasantry of Spain, but the education does not go far. In every village where there is a church there is a school where the children are taught to read and write Spanish. In 1886 there were 1608 such schools, affording instruction to 177,113 pupils. Tagal and Bisayan alike have relinquished their peculiar alphabet, and the native officers are chosen, if possible, from those only who can speak the language of their European masters. There are eight or ten Spanish newspapers published in the islands, and a single paper in Tagalog, but all are subjected to ecclesiastical censure.

8. Agriculture, Trade, and Commerce.

As in most parts of the Malay Archipelago, the system of agriculture is that of small holdings. Only one-fifteenth of the entire land area of the archipelago is cultivated. Rice is, of course, the staple crop, but the cultivation is not as careful as in Java and elsewhere. Maize, which is gathered in two months from the time of sowing, has been much grown of late, especially in Luzon, Zebu, and Mindanao, and partly takes its place, but large quantities of rice are annually imported. Abaca or Manila hemp is the chief export. It is the fibre of *Musa textilis* or *Musa abaca*, a species of banana which produces a small and uneatable fruit, and requires peculiar conditions of soil and climate for its growth. It is cultivated in Samar, Leyte, Zebu, and Bohol, but the best comes from the Camarines provinces and Albay in southern Luzon, Legaspi being the port of shipment to Manila. North of Manila this plant will not thrive. The export of the fibre appears to be increasing, although the drought of 1889 largely affected the supply. Thus, while in 1880 it was

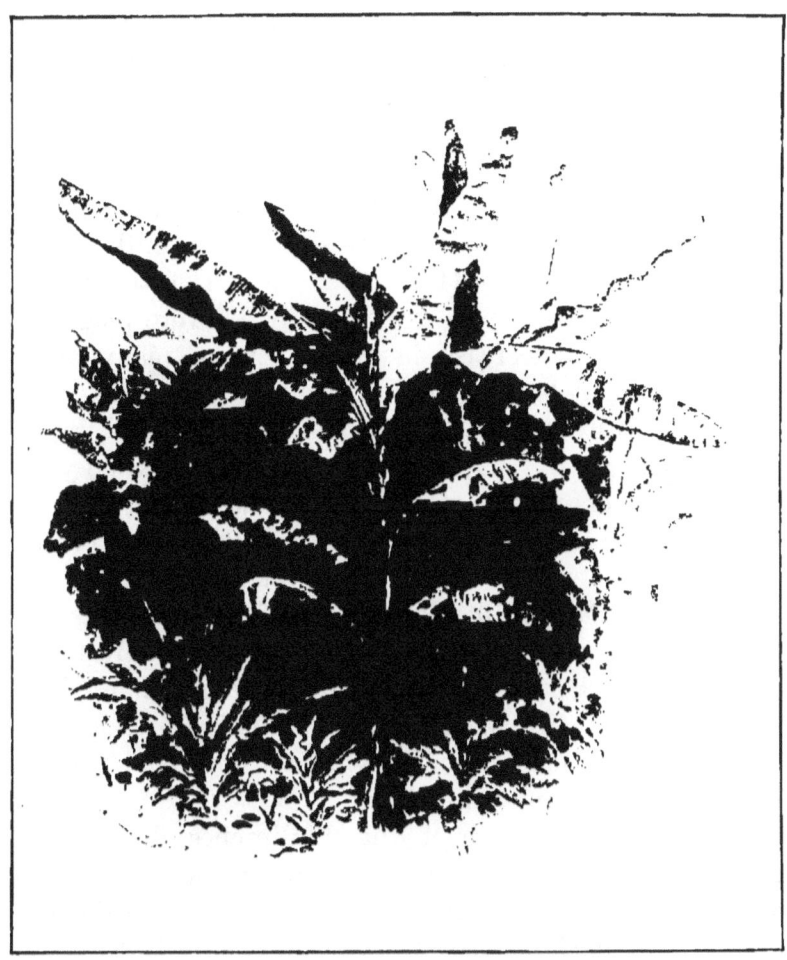

MANILA HEMP (*Musa textilis*).

returned at a value of £1,040,000, the total value of that exported in 1890 was £2,150,000, and even this large figure was less than the estimated value of shipment for the year 1889 by over £1,000,000 sterling. The variation in price of this article is enormous. Sugar is the export next on the list in point of importance, Panay being the principal island upon which it is grown, although it is also cultivated largely in Luzon and Zebu. Of late, owing to the fall in price and the manipulation of the American market, this produce has been much discouraged, and from a value of £2,600,000 in 1880 the total shipments of 1890 were only estimated at £1,330,000, which was not far short of a million less than the value of the 1889 crop. Much of this shortcoming may, however, be explained by a severe plague of locusts, but the decrease in the export of many other products cannot be thus accounted for. Thus indigo fell from 354,500 lbs. to 37,400 lbs. in 1890, and sapan wood from 5000 tons to 2800 tons in the same year. Coffee, another export of importance, has suffered from the ravages of an insect which attacks the heart of the tree and kills it, and the 1890 shipments were only to the value of £420,000—less by £80,000 than those of the preceding year. Other articles of export are hides, mother-of-pearl, gum-mastic, and the perfume ylang-ylang from the plant *Uvaria aromatica*. This is worth £9 per lb. in the Paris market, and has been a good deal planted lately in Luzon and Sulu Island.

The tobacco culture of the Philippines demands a separate word. The policy of Spain in the islands has always been that of monopolies. Little by little she has had to relinquish them. The last to fall, in July, 1882, was that of tobacco. First instituted by Governor Basco in 1780, it has always been productive of difficulties. The enforced culture of the plant in the chief tobacco districts entailed great hardship on the natives, who were unable to work their rice crops at the same time;

while, on the other hand, it was found impossible to keep down illicit fields in the wilder districts and the sale of the leaf to private buyers. The abandonment of the *régie* is a step in advance, and will tend to improve the export in quantity, though possibly not in quality. The best tobacco comes from the province of Cagayan in the extreme north of Luzon, but since 1884 plantations have been established in Sulu Island for the growth of "wrappers" (as the outer leaves of cigars are technically termed) for the best Havana cigars, and with some success. In 1890 some 8000 tons of leaf tobacco and 110,000,000 cigars were exported from Manila, showing a slight falling off from the previous year.

Manufactures are chiefly of two kinds—cigars and textiles. The great cigar factories of Manila employ several thousands of hands. The textile fabrics are chiefly made for home use, an immense quantity of abaca, cotton, and silk stuffs being produced. The fibre of the pine-apple, known in the islands as *piña*, is wrought into fabrics of excessive fineness,—to such a fineness even that some of the looms are protected with curtains to prevent the breaking of the thread by a current of air. These *piña* dresses often fetch enormous sums, a single one having been sold for over £300. The Philippines practically clothe themselves, for there is very little importation of stuffs for the people. Mat-making is also a great specialty, as well as hats and cigar cases, made from palm leaves and split rattans. The chief other native manufactures are gold filagree work and coarse pottery.

The buffalo is the chief beast of labour, and is bred in vast numbers. It is specially suited for a country in which the roads and tracks are for a great part of the year half under water, and utterly impassable for horses. In some of the islands both buffaloes and horses have become completely wild: in many parts they are half-wild, being only caught and used as occasion demands. Oxen are bred numerously, but sheep are rarely seen.

The principal ports in the Philippines are Manila and its secondary harbour of Cavite; Iloilo in Panay; Zebu; Aparri in the extreme north of Luzon, the port of the tobacco district; Ilocos, also in North Luzon; and Capiz in Panay. About two-thirds of the shipping trade is British. In 1890 the number of British vessels which entered the port of Manila was 153. The import trade will, however, doubtless be checked by the establishment of a new Customs tariff, which has raised the duties considerably. This was promulgated in April, 1891, and is apparently protective in its aim, for by its provisions all Spanish manufactures arriving in Spanish vessels are admitted free of duty. The total value of imports and exports, according to the last published official report (1888) is as follows: Imports, £4,000,000; Exports, £5,000,000. After the British the German trade comes next in importance.

A project for the establishment of a general network of railways throughout the most populous parts of Luzon and elsewhere has been under consideration for some years, but up to the present time the only line constructed is the Manila-Dagupan, which is about 120 miles in length. This was opened for traffic in November, 1892. The telegraph is confined to Luzon, and the service has been established in 59 towns and villages. It extends to both extremities of the island, and has been found of the greatest benefit in giving warning of the approach of typhoons. The postal service is largely carried on by the interinsular steamers, for in the less civilised districts the want of bridges and the execrable condition of the roads greatly impede inland communication.

9. Government and Revenue.

The supreme authority in the colony is vested in the hands of a *Gobernador Capitán General*, under the direction of the Crown and Cortés. Under his orders a General of Division commands the army and a Rear-Admiral the sea forces. The islands are divided for political purposes into four governments—Luzon, the Bisayas, Mindanao, and the Islas Adjacentes. The first is administered by the Governor-General, the others by general officers under his command. A Council of Administration, composed of the chief Spanish officials, assists the Governor-General in the exercise of his functions at Manila.

These four districts are subdivided into provinces, fifty-three in total number, which are variously administered by "Civil Governors," "Politico-Military Governors," "Politico-Military Commandants," and "Military Commandants," whose powers are sufficiently indicated by their titles. Roughly speaking, the rule of the Luzon district is civil, that of the others military, but to this there are many exceptions. Each province is again divided into *pueblos*, which word should be rendered rather as small canton than as village. Each *pueblo* is ruled by its *Gobernadorcillo*, elected biennially, who is very often a native; and every little village or hamlet has its *Teniente*, responsible in turn to his gobernadorcillo. The latter acts as a magistrate, trying small cases and remitting the more important to the Alcalde, who is often at the same time the Governor of the province. The office of gobernadorcillo is unpaid, but much coveted for its position and the wealth it brings. The *Real Audiencia* at Manila constitutes a final Court of Appeal.

The gobernadorcillo, in addition to acting as mayor and magistrate and headman of the district to whom (or to his teniente) the European traveller applies for men and animals to continue his journey, was formerly also the tax collector, or rather the collector of "tribute," for by this name was known the impost levied upon every person not of European parentage. Each married couple paid a *tributa*, amounting to about 4s. 4d.; unmarried adults paid half that sum. In addition there was a forty days' corvée for road mending, which could be compounded for by an annual payment of 12s. In 1884 all this was abolished, and a passport (*Cedula personal*) system adopted. The passports are of nine classes from 25 dollars downwards; those holding lower than a $3\frac{1}{2}$ dollar rating being obliged to submit to 15 days' corvée, or to pay an equivalent of half a dollar per diem. These passports are compulsory for every person above the age of 18 years of whatever nationality.

The army is composed of seven regiments of infantry; a squadron of cavalry; a *Guardia Civil* of native troops numbering four regiments; a battery of peninsula artillery; a corps of engineers, with four native companies attached; and a corps of carbineers. The total strength, on a peace footing, is 11,000 men, 12 guns, and 120 horses. Recruiting is by conscription, and the length of service eight years, but a native can purchase freedom from conscription by the payment of about £10. The navy comprises 26 vessels, mostly of small tonnage, although a corvette of the first class and three smaller unarmoured ships are stationed in the archipelago. Of the rest 13 are gunboats. One vessel is employed in survey work. The total number of officers and men on active service, including marines, is about 3000. At Cavite, the naval station of Manila, there is an arsenal and a slip.

The revenue is derived from various sources, the most important being the passport tax above mentioned. Customs dues (considerably raised in 1891), State lotteries, post and telegraphs, excise on palm-wine, and licenses for cock-fighting — the ruling passion of the islanders — are the chief items. The Budget shows generally a deficit. In 1886 the expenditure was £2,326,000, the revenue £2,300,000. The estimates for 1891 are given as £2,145,763 and £2,119,467 respectively.

10. Population and Provinces.

The population of the Philippines has been very variously estimated. It is chiefly arrived at by the number of those who paid the capitation tax. The last statistics of these given by Dr. Meyer show that 1,232,544 paid tribute in 1870, and the total population was estimated at six times this number, or in round numbers about $7\frac{1}{2}$ millions. The persons living between the ages of 16 and 60 (the age of taxation) are usually about half the total population, so that the Christian natives and Chinese would together only amount to $2\frac{1}{2}$ millions. The official census — if it can thus be termed — of 1877 gave 5,559,020 as the population of the Philippines, and 75,000 as that of the Sulu group. The latest estimate of the Archbishop of Manila places the total number of the inhabitants of the archipelago at 7,500,000, and calculates that of the Sulu group at 200,000 more. This latter is without doubt much too high an estimate. From the subjoined table given by Réclus, which claims to be calculated from the latest available data, the total numbers appear as 6,142,452.

Governments.	Provinces.	Capitals.	Population.
Luzon.	1. Manila	Manila	324,367
	2. Cavite	Cavite	69,794
	3. Laguna	Sta. Cruz	141,900
	4. Morong	Morong	48,663
	5. Bulacan	Bulacan	264,375
	6. Pampanga	Bacolor	207,205
	7. Bataan	Balanga	49,273
	8. Zambales	Iba	80,230
	9. Tarlac	Tarlac	57,713
	10. Pangasinan	Lingayen	252,892
	11. La Union	San Fernando	115,911
	12. Benguet	La Trinidad	9,311
	13. Ilocos Sur	Vigan	114,675
	14. Ilocos Norte	Laoang	148,204
	15. Abra	Bangued	37,791
	16. Cagayan	Tuguegarao	70,881
	17. Batanes	San Domingo	500
	18. Isabela	Tumauini	39,391
	19. Bontoc	Bontoc	7,757
	20. Lepanto	Lepanto	18,009
	21. Principe	Baler	3,268
	22. Nueva Vizcaya	Bayombong	26,857
	23. Nueva Ecija	San Isidro	92,970
	24. Infanta	Binangonan	8,483
	25. Batangas	Batangas	308,110
	26. Tayabas	Tayabas	103,310
	27. Camarines Norte	Daet	29,009
	28. Camarines Sur	Nueva Cáceres	88,712
	29. Albay	Albay	245,972
	30. Island of Mindoro	Calapan	37,648
	31. Island of Burias	San Pascual	
	32. Island of Masbate	Masbate	44,000
	33. Romblon Islands	Romblon	
Bisayas.	1. Island of Zebu	Zebu	518,032
	2. Island of Leyte	Tacloban	278,452
	3. Island of Samar	Catbalogan	183,000
	4. Iloilo	Iloilo	500,000
	5. Concepcion	Concepcion	27,000
	6. Antique	San José	106,000
	7. Capiz	Capiz	197,000
	8. Island of Negros	Bacolod	226,000
	9. Island of Bohol	Tagbilaran	277,387
Mindanao.	1. Misamis	Misamis	
	2. Surigao	Surigao	
	3. Davao	Davao or Vergara	
	4. Bislig	Bislig	650,000
	5. Cottabato	Cottabato	
	6. Zamboanga	Zamboanga	
	7. Island of Basilan	Isabela	600
	8. Jolo (Sulu)	Jolo	100,000
Islas Adjacentes.	1. Calamianes	Tai-tai	19,500
	2. Puerto Princesa	Princesa	12,000
	3. Balábac	Balábac	800

11. The Capital—Life and Manners.

The traveller visiting Manila for the first time will be struck by the scene of busy life which the port affords. The anchorage is full of shipping, and the quays thronged with people. Although the larger vessels anchor off the town, the quays afford sufficient depth of water to permit the greater number to warp alongside and discharge or load direct. The Pasig river, which bisects the city, admits vessels of three or four hundred tons, but a new harbour is in course of construction in front of the citadel, which will materially advantage shipping. The Spanish men-of-war lie in the harbour of Cavite, about 10 miles to the south, where is the arsenal and slip.

The Pasig is a small stream, some 150 yards in breadth, which drains the great lake known as the Laguna de Bay. It is less than 10 miles in length, but is lined with villages throughout its course, and but for a bar at its origin would admit vessels of considerable size into the lake. In its course through the city it is spanned by three bridges, which connect the old and fortified "Manila *intramuros*" with its populous suburbs. The city itself, situated at the head of a magnificent bay, on a navigable river leading to a lake whose waters teem with fish and whose shores are specially favourable for agriculture, possesses advantages of site which were at once recognised by Legaspi on his arrival in 1571, and he commenced its founding without delay. It is therefore the oldest European town in the East after Goa. Before this, Zebu had served as capital for the first Spanish settlers. When the English seized Manila in 1762 the Spanish temporarily removed the seat of government to Bacolor in the province of Pampanga, to the north of Manila Bay.

The old town, triangular in shape, is surrounded with walls of solid masonry, now cracked and shattered by innumerable earthquakes. To the north and south-west it is protected by the river and the sea respectively. The land-face has strong bastions and a double fosse, but the fortifications would be of little use against modern artillery, and only serve to render unhealthy the town which they enclose. Within, the streets are gloomy and narrow, and show frequent evidences of the earthquakes. Here are the chief official buildings, the cathedral, the convents, and the barracks, and outside the walls on the river-face are the wharves and a monument to Magellan. Commercial Manila lies across the river, upon its right bank, in the quarters of Tondo and Binondo, where the Chinese stalls and stores gradually give place to busy thoroughfares lined with European shops. Canals which become partly dry at low water intersect the streets, and leave much to be desired from a sanitary point of view. But otherwise this part of the city is well kept, and the main street—the Escolta—where are situated the chief cafés and shops, is well paved and lighted. The officials and merchants reside chiefly in the suburbs of San Miguel and San Sebastian, while Quiapo and Ermita are the most important native quarters. Three or four miles to the north is Malabon, with a gigantic cigar factory, which employs sometimes as many as 10,000 hands.

Manila owns nothing of importance in the way of buildings. The cathedral built in 1654 was destroyed in the frightful earthquake of the 3rd June, 1863,[1] but

[1] The following account of this catastrophe is given by the German traveller Jagor:—

"On the 3rd of June 1863, at thirty-one minutes past seven in the even-

was afterwards rebuilt and consecrated in 1879. There is a small museum and a public library, which are not too crowded. The Manilan prefers the promenade in the Paseo de la Luneta, whither he drives at top speed in his *calesa* when business is over for the day. Here the whole world of the city, from the *cigarera* to the wife of the Governor, meets to chat and listen to the band, of which Manilans are justly proud. Music of some sort—good, bad, or indifferent—the *Filipino* must have. Other amusements are scanty enough. There is a European theatre, and two or three others where the performances are in Tagalog, but the evenings are chiefly devoted to *tertulias*, or "At Homes," of which, as is not infrequently the case in other countries, it may be said that they are more numerous than amusing.

The population of the old town in 1879 was 17,950, and that of the immediate suburbs 116,670, making a total of 134,620, but it appears that there has been some decrease of late years, since the official returns of 1891 give the number of inhabitants of the town and suburbs as 107,171. There is apparently no agreement, however, as to what should be described as Manila. The outlying

---

ing, after a day of tremendous heat, while all Manila was busy in its preparations for the festival of Corpus Christi, the ground suddenly rocked to and fro with great violence. The firmest buildings reeled visibly, walls crumbled, and beams snapped in two. The dreadful shock lasted half a minute; but this little interval was enough to change the whole town into a mass of ruins, and to bury alive hundreds of its inhabitants. The cathedral, the government house, the barracks, and all the public buildings of Manila, were entirely destroyed, and the few private houses which remained standing were seriously damaged. Subsequent examination showed that 46 public and 570 private buildings were thrown down, 28 public and 528 private buildings were nearly destroyed, while all left standing were more or less injured. Four hundred persons were killed, and two thousand injured, and the loss of property was estimated at eight millions of dollars."

villages are sometimes included, and the population misleadingly estimated at a quarter of a million or more.

The Christianized natives of the Philippines are for the most part a simple race,—docile, easy-going, credulous, rather excitable, and very superstitious. The Spaniards say that they are as easily led by Europeans who take pains to understand them as the horse or the buffalo. They are, in fact, led, guided, and virtually governed by the Catholic priesthood, who may be truly said to have originally conquered them, and to have maintained them ever since in subjection. This has made them less dignified and polished than some of the true Malays, but they yet have many estimable qualities. They are a good-natured, cheerful, contented, and hospitable people; and though, when first visited by the Portuguese and Spaniards, they were inferior in civilisation to the Malays and Javanese, they may now be considered as equal if not superior to them. Of all Asiatic people they are perhaps those who have made the most advance under European rule. Mr. W. G. Palgrave calls them "as industrious, steady, and persevering a race as any under a tropical sun."

Most of these people wear a national costume somewhat resembling that of the Malays; the women a "camisa" and "saya," and the men a shirt hanging outside the trousers like a blouse. On festa days and other holidays they are often very expensively clad in *piña* of fine texture freely embroidered. Their amusements, with one exception, are of a harmless and simple order. Plays, secular or semi-religious, the latter preponderating, dances, festas, and processions with as much music as can conveniently be introduced, for a brass band is a *sine quâ non* in every Tagal village: these are the chief. The exception is cock-fighting—" une véritable passion que les Indiens des Philippines poussent jusqu'au paroxysme," as M. Montano justly remarks. Every village that can afford to pay the tax has its pit for the *galleras*, each peasant rears his fighting-cock, which he carries with him almost wherever he goes, whether to market, fishing in his canoe, or working in his field. It is the possession by which he sets most store, and it is commonly said in the islands that in the event of fire the native flies to rescue his bird rather than his wife or child. The spurs used are made of razors ground to excessive thinness, and the issue of the combat is thus greatly an affair of chance. Despite this fact, the Tagal does not hesitate to stake all his available cash upon his bird, and it has been well remarked that the *galleras* work more ruin than the earthquakes and typhoons put together.

Travel in the Philippines is not only expensive, from the high price of labour, but also an affair of no little difficulty owing to the condition of the country. For six months in the year, and in some places for considerably more, much of the low country is under water, and so great is the deposit of mud left behind that it is impossible to progress either on foot or on horseback, and the buffalo is the beast of burden for the traveller and his baggage. The torrential rains tear up the roads and render them next to impassable, and swollen streams and rivers bar the track with annoying frequency. Since bridges are almost unknown except in the civilised districts, recourse must be had to cane rafts, which often render the passage of these rivers a matter of considerable danger. There are no inns of any kind, but hospitality is freely dispensed by the priest, or in his absence the traveller rests at the house of the gobernadorcillo, or establishes himself in the little court-house which serves equally the purposes of a town-hall and a dâk-bungalow.

12. The Islands.

LUZON.

Luzon is the largest island of the Philippines, is as fertile as almost any island in Australasia, and is nearly as populous as Java and Madura. It lies between north latitudes 12° 35′ and 18° 43′, and has a length of about 420 miles in a straight line, but owing to its irregular shape, its actual length is not less than 550 miles. In breadth it varies from about 140 miles in its northern part to less than five at the isthmus of Tayabas. Its total area is about twice as great as that of Ireland. Throughout its whole length it is traversed by mountain ranges, all of which are of moderate, but none of very great height. In the northern peninsula there are two parallel ranges. The highest mountain in Luzon is the Mayon volcano in the province of Albay, which has been lately measured and found to be 8970 feet. This height is exceeded by the mountains of Mindanao, and possibly by others, but accurate information upon the subject is wanting. The mountains are generally loftier towards the eastern coast of the island, where they form a bold and inaccessible shore exposed to heavy seas and bad weather during the prevalence of the N.E. monsoon. The soil here is poor and the population scanty, and the interinsular steamers do not ply north of the Catanduanes Islands.

The island affords very different conditions of climate, agriculture, and race: the rainfall everywhere abundant, but very variable; in the north the great tobacco district of Cagayan, and the Ilocanos, with numerous Negritos in the less known mountain fastnesses; in the central provinces around Manila a careful but mixed agriculture and the Tagals; to the south the vast hemp-producing regions, Albay and Camarines, with the Bicols as the chief inhabitants. Near Manila there are the particular industries connected with large cities, as the " petite culture"; and land fetches a high price. One of the great sights of Luzon is Pateros, or Duck-town, as it may be rendered, where many hundreds of thousands of ducks are annually reared for the Manila market. These establishments occupy the banks of the Pasig river for nearly two miles. The birds are hatched by incubators, and are fed upon shell-fish taken in Manila Bay. Ascending the Pasig, the great sheet of water known as the Laguna de Bay is reached, which has an average length and breadth of about twenty-five miles. It has been suggested, and with some probability, that it was formerly an arm of the sea which was cut off and formed into a lake by the eruption of one of the neighbouring volcanoes, as the lake of Taal a little further to the south undoubtedly has been. Sharks and other sea fish are reported to be found in its waters. At the present time its surface is said to be 58 feet above the level of the sea, and its depth to average about 100 feet. Fifteen rivers flow into it, but the Pasig is the only exit. Its shores are extremely fertile and the scenery is beautiful, and owing to the number of towns and villages surrounding it, its waters are covered with native boats.

Occupying the region to the north of Manila Bay are the two provinces of Bulacan and Pampanga, which are perhaps the most flourishing parts of the island. Magnificent haciendas and sugar plantations evince the fertility of the soil, but the earthquake of 1880 wrought tremendous damage, and its effects are still to be seen. Daily steamers connect the capital of the first-named province with Manila. Farther north, in the province of North

Ilocos, is Lavag, which claims to be the largest town in the archipelago after Manila, but it is without a port and is the centre of a purely agricultural district. Off the extreme northern point of Luzon lie the Bashi and Babuyanes groups, which are claimed by Spain. They have few inhabitants, and are not subjected to the passport or poll-tax. On the coast opposite the Babuyanes is Aparri, the port of the province of Cagayan, whence large quantities of tobacco are shipped to the capital to be made into cheroots. The district is a fertile valley—the Llano de Dijun—lying between the two great ranges of the Sierra Madre and the western Cordillera, and drained by the Rio Grande de Cagayan or Tajo, the largest river in Luzon, which is navigable by small vessels for a considerable distance, and has a course of about 200 miles. The inhospitable east coast affords no important towns in its northern part, and scarcely a single harbour until Port Lampon, opposite Manila, is reached.

Southern Luzon, but for its abaca, would be of less agricultural importance than the central parts of the island, but its geographical position is superior, and the San Bernardino Channel, which bounds it to the south and west, permits of navigation in most weathers. Legaspi, the port of shipment of the hemp, is used only in the summer. When the north-east monsoon is blowing the vessels lie at Sorsogon, and the produce is sent across the narrow isthmus to that port. The Albay district is conspicuous for the excellence of its roads—a rare characteristic of any part of Luzon—and planting has been progressing with great energy and success of late years, the Government selling the unreclaimed forest land at from one shilling to half a crown the acre. But the district is famed not only for its abaca, but for its volcanoes, and the peasant works under the shadow of the smoking cone of Mayon with a full knowledge of the disaster which may at any moment befall him.

The volcanoes of Luzon demand special consideration. Although, as has been already stated, the whole archipelago is more or less of volcanic origin, the acme of the manifestation of these subterranean forces appears to be reached in the southern part of the great island of which we are treating. Bulusan, situated within a few miles only of its terminal cape, is still partly active, but though two or three eruptions have taken place within the last half century, they have not occasioned any great destruction. This cannot be said of Mt. Mayon, whose stupendous cone of nearly 9000 feet dominates the town of Albay. The first eruption known to the Spaniards was in 1616, and another occurred in 1766, which was attended with great loss of life and property, but both of these were eclipsed by that of 1st February 1814— one of the most appalling of the many volcanic catastrophes which have visited the islands of Australasia. The rain of ashes was such as to bury whole villages and their coco-nut groves to a depth of 120 feet or more, and more than 12,000 people lost their lives. In Manila, 208 miles distant, the ashes lay nearly two feet deep in the streets. Since then eruptions have been very frequent, but not so violent. The mountain has been ascended both by Jagor and von Drasche, and has been found to be without a crater—the steam and gas escaping from a mass of scoriæ. The shape of the volcano is a nearly perfect cone, an evidence that its formation has been due to constant and prolonged action. In the Bay of Sorsogon—celebrated as the harbour in which the Acapulco galleons were built and fitted out—the land has recently sunk five or six feet. At Tibi, on the coast to the N.E., are fumaroles and hot springs somewhat resembling those of the New Zealand "Pink Terrace," and phenomena of like nature exist in the surrounding country.

To the north numerous volcanoes occur in the Camarines, forming a sort of group. The chief of them are Isarog, Kolasi, Labot, and Bernacci. At the present time they are extinct, but there is no doubt that at no very distant epoch their eruptions added the Camarines and Albay provinces to Luzon, and that Albay was also formerly a distinct island from the Camarines. Immediately south of the Laguna de Bay is another similar group—Majaijay or Banahao (7326 feet), S. Cristobal (7654 feet), Maquiling (3780 feet), and Taal being the principal peaks. All except Taal are inactive, but Maquiling has solfataras and hot springs at its base, and the latter, being of considerable therapeutic repute, are the site of a hospital which, though only commenced a few years ago, was never finished, and has now fallen into ruin. Taal is one of the most singular volcanoes on the surface of the globe. It consists of a volcanic cone emerging from a lake, which appears to occupy the enormous crater of an ancient volcano. This lake (Lake Taal or Bombon), which is 17 miles long and 11 wide, is so surrounded with steep hills as to have the appearance of a huge cauldron of water. It is about 600 feet in depth, and from its centre rises the island cone, which, though 3 miles in its longest diameter, is only 767 feet high, and is thus remarkable as being probably the lowest active volcano in existence. The crater is an irregular oval, and is about three-quarters of a mile across in its widest part. At the bottom are two or three lakes, the water of one of which is of a brilliant apple-green in colour. Another, bright yellow, smokes and boils over perpetually. The principal eruptions of Taal occurred in the years 1709,

1716, 1740, 1754, 1867, and 1880—the most severe being that of 1754, when for eight days the crater threw out ashes and lava, darkening the sky to such an extent that artificial lights had to be used at mid-day in Manila, while the shocks of the explosions were sensible at a distance of 300 leagues. The red-hot lava falling into the lake raised the temperature of the neighbouring water to boiling point, and the fish, perishing in countless thousands, gave rise to an epidemic which is said to have cost the lives of 40,000 of the natives. The last eruption, that of July 1880, commenced before the great earthquake, and stones of enormous size were projected to some distance into the lake. The lake of Taal is bounded on its south-west side by a low isthmus, formed entirely of volcanic ashes, which separates it from the sea, and it is evident that at some past period the walls forming the ancient crater yielded at this spot, and that the sea irrupted. At a later date a succeeding volcanic eruption cut off this arm of the sea and turned it into a lake. It is said to be still partially salt, and to contain various marine fish. Previous to the 1716 eruption the island itself used to be cultivated, but the great showers of ashes which fell in 1754 destroyed everything, and in 1880 nothing was growing upon it but the coarse lalang grass. Since then this too has disappeared, and the island is now only a heap of cinders.

Between Manila and the extreme north of Luzon there are few volcanoes, and none of them are active, but near Cape Engaño, the north-east extremity of the island, Cagud (3920 feet) appears as the first of another isolated group. It is in a semi-active state, but has had no eruption in the present century. Of the Babuyanes Islands two are active, Camiguan and Babuyan Claro. In 1856 a volcano suddenly rose from the sea-shore of the island of

Dedica, and gradually grew till it attained its present height of about 800 feet.

The lakes of Luzon are very numerous, especially in the province of Pampanga. The Laguna de Canaren, on the highest part of this plain, has two rivers flowing from it in opposite directions—one northward to the Gulf of Lingayan, the other south to Manila Bay. The Laguna de Cagayan in north Luzon is another great sheet of water. The term *Pinag* is applied to the temporary lakes which are so abundant in the rainy season from the overflow of the rivers. Of these one of the most important is the Pinag de Candava, about 30 miles north of Manila. During the rains it is 15 miles or more in length, but in the dry season it becomes a verdant plain of grass with a few permanent pools of water.

According to the latest estimate, the population of the island of Luzon is 2,964,933. It is divided among twenty-nine provinces, and there are many populous *pueblos* of from 10,000 to 20,000 inhabitants. That a steady increase has taken place in some parts of the island is evident from the following statistics of the Tayabas Province:—

Year	Population
1754	21,000
1831	59,000
1850	81,000
1882	104,000

Manila, Sual (Lingayan), and Legaspi (Albay) are free ports, but few British vessels enter the two latter.

MINDORO.

Mindoro, though one of the great islands, and the nearest to Manila, is one of the least known and least inhabited. It lies immediately to the south of the Batangas district of Luzon, from which it is separated by a narrow strait about seven or eight miles in breadth. It has a length of about 90 miles, and is from 40 to 50 miles wide. Its area is about 4050 square miles. With the neighbouring islands of Marinduque and Lubang it forms one of the thirty-three provinces of the Luzon administration, its population amounting to 37,648. It is under a civil governor, who resides at Calapan on the north coast. There is no other village of large size in the island, and no civilisation except upon the coast.

Mindoro was discovered by Legaspi, who sent his nephew, Juan de Salcedo, to take possession, a task which he accomplished with thirty Spaniards and some native allies. The island was always the haunt of Illanun and Sulu pirates, but the Spanish gunboats have now effectually suppressed them. Still, little attempt at cultivation and civilisation has been made of late. The Jesuits did much, but since their evacuation there has been almost no advance. Many formerly populous *pueblos* in the interior are now deserted and ruined. The inhabitants of the coast are Tagals, but the people of the interior—the Manguianos—are in a state of almost complete savagery, though of harmless disposition. They are of sub-Malayan stock, speaking a peculiar language, and living in a very miserable manner on the products of a rude agriculture.

Mindoro has lofty mountain ranges, which culminate in the north in Mount Halcon (8865 feet), and are covered everywhere with dense forest. Near the coast there is much marsh land, and the island bears the reputation of being extremely unhealthy. There are no active volcanoes in Mindoro, and its geological structure is almost unknown. In the north-west a valley crosses the island from Abra de Ylo to Mamburao, along which there is a road which can be traversed in the dry season, but is so flooded during the rains as to be impassable. In the north-east is a lake about five miles across, which lies in a depression behind the coast-range between the towns of Nanjan and Pola. The floods of the wet season leave an annual deposit of mud in this valley, which raises its level so rapidly that the church of the old town of Nanjan, situated near the lake, became buried in the course of fifteen years to the top of the arch of the door, and the town had to be removed to near the sea.

The curious *Anoa depressicornis*, an antelope-like buffalo which is peculiar to the island of Celebes, has been reported to exist in Mindoro, but Dr. Steere's recent visit has shown that the wild bovine animal of the island is quite a distinct and new species, although apparently closely allied. The occurrence of this animal in Mindoro alone of all the islands is very remarkable. The land shells also show a striking peculiarity, and the avifauna, if not so distinctive, nevertheless comprises many peculiar species. Taking these facts into consideration, and that of the existence of very deep water completely surrounding the island, it is probable that we have to do with a remnant of a very much older continent, which was at one time possibly connected with Celebes and land to the south and east in the direction of Australia.

Panay.

This island is situated to the south-east of Mindoro, and including Guimarás, has an area of 4831 square miles. It is in shape an irregular triangle, and the island of Guimarás to the south-east appears to have once formed a part of it. A chain of mountains runs from the centre to each point, thus dividing the island into three natural districts, which form the provinces of Antique, Capiz, and Iloilo. The little province of Concepcion occupies the north-east corner, and is the smallest in the archipelago with the exception of Batanes—the group of islands at the extreme north.

Panay is exceedingly fertile, being well irrigated by numerous mountain streams, and is very populous, the last returns giving 830,000 as the number of its inhabitants. It is, in fact, after Zebu, the most densely peopled and highly cultivated island of the group. The natives, with the exception of a few Negritos in the mountains, are exclusively Bisayans. The land near the coast is low, easily irrigated, and specially adapted for sugar growing. The mountains scarcely exceed 3000 feet. There are no active volcanoes, but fumaroles and other evidences of dormant volcanic forces exist in the province of Iloilo. Gold, copper, iron, and quicksilver have been found, and coal in Antique, but none of these are worked. Next to Manila, Iloilo is the most important town in the Philippines. It is a free port with an excellent harbour, and is frequented largely by British vessels. A municipal corporation was established in 1891, from which great benefits are expected to be derived with regard to public lighting, police, repair of roads, and other improvements which up to the present have been much neglected. The decrease in the price of sugar has, however, proved a great blow to the island, as it is upon this crop that its welfare chiefly depends. The export for the year 1890 amounted to 96,000 tons, and was less than that of the previous year by 14,000 tons. Tobacco is also largely grown—to the amount of 2,314,100 lbs. in 1890, and large quantities of sapan wood, piña fabrics, cacao, coffee, and rice are produced. The latter cereal is, however, not grown in sufficient quantities for the consumption of the island, and some twenty or twenty-five thousand tons are annually imported. While in 1887 a total of 174 vessels entered the port, rather less than half that number were registered in 1890, and with increased taxes and dues the prosperity of the island seems seriously threatened.

Negros.

Negros lies to the south-east of Panay, from which it is separated by a strait about 15 miles in width. It is 130 miles long, and on the average about 30 miles wide. Its area is 4650 square miles. Its coast is comparatively little broken by bays or inlets, and it has no good harbours. A central chain of mountains runs through its entire length. For the most part these are of no great height, but the Malaspina or Canloon volcano, situated towards the northern end, forms an exception. Its height is estimated at 8192 feet, and it is in a state of intermittent activity. Owing to the narrowness of the island there are no navigable rivers. The inhabitants are chiefly Bisayans, and number with the Negritos, from whose abundance the island received its name, about 226,000.

The island is fertile, and produces sugar, rice, tobacco, and the textiles abaca and piña, and in common with Zebu and Samar, a large amount of cacao. Its coal mines appear to be no longer worked. The capital is Bacolod on the west coast, opposite to Iloilo, where the "politico-military" governor resides, and there are numerous large villages around the coast, though few in the interior. Hinigaran, the former capital, contains over 12,000 inhabitants.

Zebu.

Zebu or Cebu is a long and narrow island, lying immediately to the east of Negros, from which it is separated by a strait from 5 to 15 miles wide, and over 100 miles in length. Zebu is 130 miles long, and not more than 20 broad in its widest part, and contains 2275 square miles, or rather less than half the area of Negros. Several chains of mountains of no great height traverse it from north to south, but little is known of its geology except that it produces gold, silver, and lead, and has no active volcanoes. Coal occurs abundantly, and is of fairly good quality, but the complete neglect of all mineral wealth by the Spaniards is exhibited here as elsewhere. The inhabitants are almost exclusively Bisayans, but there are said to be a few Negritos. The population has greatly increased of late years owing to the great development of the sugar and abaca cultivation, and now numbers 518,000, but locusts and low prices have recently dealt as heavy a blow to Zebu as to Panay. In all these islands sugar-growing will probably give place to hemp or some more paying crop. In 1890 only 3000 tons were exported as against 11,000 tons in 1889, and while in the latter year thirty-four vessels—almost all of which were British—entered the port, the number in 1890 only amounted to 14.

The capital, Zebu, dignified by the title of city, is the oldest settlement in the Philippines, and was the seat of government until the founding of Manila. It was the first place of any importance visited by Magellan on his discovery of the group, and it was upon the little island of Mactan which forms the harbour of Zebu that he met with his death on the 27th April, 1521. Fifty years later Legaspi planned and built the city. It is picturesquely situated, and has a fine cathedral and several churches, but the population is not large. The island forms a province by itself, under the administration of a military governor.

Samar.

Samar lies within ten miles of the extreme southern point of Luzon, and is one of the larger islands of the archipelago, being about equal in size to Panay, and having an estimated area of 4680 square miles. From Luzon it is separated by the San Bernardino Channel, and from Leyte by the narrow winding sea-passage of S. Juanico, which has more the appearance of a river than a strait. The island is 150 miles in length, and is very mountainous. Its eastern shores are exposed to the full force of the north-east monsoon, and are very imperfectly known, but the western side has some tolerable harbours, and it is here that the capital, Catbalogan, is situated. The rivers are numerous, and owing to the irregular disposition of the mountains, penetrate far into the country. Coal is found, but no attempt has been made to investigate the minerals of the island. The interior is covered with dense forest, and only inhabited by a few scattered Negritos. There is hardly any trade, but there are large groves of coco-nut palms, and cacao is also grown. The population is estimated at 190,000, and is almost exclusively Bisayan. The thirty-six *pueblos* are administered by a politico-military governor.

Leyte.

Across the narrow Juanico Strait to the south-west

lies Leyte, an irregularly shaped island, whose southern arms approach within a few miles of Mindanao. It is about 110 miles long, has an area of 3075 square miles, and, like almost all the islands of the group, is mountainous, although the chain which traverses it from north to south is of no great elevation. Mount Sacripante, one of the highest peaks, is under 4000 feet. The formation is volcanic; there are hot siliceous springs, and many extinct craters which produce sulphur in abundance. Gold mines are worked, but in a desultory fashion. The east coast is said to be rising, while the west is being destroyed by the sea, which at Orinog has advanced fifty yards in six years. The rivers are all small and not navigable. There are two lakes, Jarnaran in the north-west, and Bito near the centre of the island, but both are of insignificant size. The former is an old crater and has acid water. The inhabitants of Leyte are Bisayans, who are said by Jagor to be more idle and dirty than the Tagals, although friendly and tractable, crime being almost unknown. The whole of the interior is forest, the settlements being on or near the coast. The capital town is Tacloban, at the southern entrance to the San Juanico Strait. It has direct communication with Manila, and is a free port, but there is no large trade as yet. A recent calculation gives the population of the island as 278,452.

Bohol.

Bohol lies between Zebu and Leyte, and at no distant period probably formed a part of the latter island, to which it is joined by a submarine bank of coral reefs and rocks covered by very shallow water. It has an area of 1250 square miles, and is of remarkably compact shape, its length being about 60 miles and its breadth 30. It is hilly and volcanic, with abundant streams and a fertile soil, the chief product of which is tobacco, although almost all the crops usually cultivated in the archipelago are grown. It is united with the small island of Siquihor to form the province of Bohol, whose population, according to the latest census, numbers no less than 277,387 souls. The capital town is Tagbiloran, and there are four *pueblos* of over 10,000 inhabitants. The density of the population is, in fact, nearly as great as that of Zebu and Panay. The people are all Bisayans. Siquihor is notable for possessing an active or semi-active volcano.

MASBATE.

Off the southern end of Luzon, and forming with Ticao Island a province of that government, is Masbate, partly peopled by Bicols and partly by Bisayans. It is rather smaller than Bohol, having an area of about 1200 square miles. A crescent-shaped mountain chain of considerable elevation occupies the middle of the island, probably composed of ancient crystalline rocks, as the river sands produce a considerable quantity of gold, and copper is also found. It possesses several good harbours, but in spite of this and its potential mineral wealth it is sparsely inhabited and cultivated, and has little or no trade.

MINDANAO.

Mindanao, or Magindano as it was formerly called, is the most southern of the Philippines. In size it is scarcely inferior to Luzon, having a total area of 37,680 square miles. In shape it is very irregular, its outline being broken on every side by deep bays and gulfs. Its rough measurements from north to south and from east to west are about 300 miles, and it may therefore be considered to be about equal in size to England, the shape of which, if the orientation be changed, it very much resembles. It is generally mountainous, with extensive plains and valleys and numerous lakes. Three separate volcanic ranges traverse it from south to north. That from the western extremity, proceeding from the Sulu range, curves and passes north by Siquihor Island to the Bisayas. The middle chain is a continuation north of the volcanoes of Celebes and the Sangir islands, and is connected by the active crater of Camiguin Island with the ranges in the islands to the north. The third chain closely borders the east coast, and reappears in Leyte. The middle range exhibits the greatest altitudes, which culminate in Mount Apo, near the Gulf of Davao. This mountain, which is the highest in the whole archipelago, was ascended in 1880 by M. Montano, who assigns to it an altitude of 10,280 feet. It is in a state of semi-activity, its sides rent by a huge crevasse which emits dense sulphurous fumes. The summit is nearly bare, but dotted here and there with stunted junipers, and is succeeded below by a zone of melastomas and rhododendrons. At the base of the mountain is a forest of huge tree ferns. Another active volcano is known to exist near the centre of the island, and there are boiling springs in the Surigao district. Of the recent elevation which has taken place Mindanao affords an excellent example in the valley of the Agusan river at the northeast, where huge coral masses are to be seen blocking the river bed at an altitude of some hundreds of feet above the sea-level.

Mindanao, with high mountains, extensive plains, and exposed to a superabundant rainfall, is watered by many rivers, some of which are navigable. Of these the two chief are the Mindanao, or Rio Grande, on the western side, and the Agusan river, which debouches into Butuan Bay in the Surigao district. The lakes are scarcely less numerous, but many are *pinays*, and disappear in the dry season. So little is the interior known that the position of Lake Mindanao, a large sheet of water reported to exist near the centre of the island, has never been determined. M. Montano, whose bold journey from the Davao Gulf to Butuan Bay in 1880 added considerably to our knowledge of the country, crossed the Linao Lake in lat. 8° 12′ N., and found it to be of small size, and Mainit is only a crater lake. In the Cottabato or Cota Batu district Lakes Liguasan and Buluan feed the Rio Grande, and are said to unite in the rainy season. The whole island, being within ten degrees of the equator, avoids the terrible typhoons which so frequently devastate the islands to the north, but is by no means stormless. From November to April a heavy sea and strong currents render the navigation of the east coast very dangerous, the more so as it is almost without harbours. The climate is more equable than that of Luzon, and the rainfall still heavier.

The inhabitants of Mindanao are of three, if not more, distinct peoples. A line drawn from Iligan Bay on the north coast to Davao roughly divides the island into halves, the west of which is inhabited by the *Moros* or Mohammedan Malays, who have gradually extended eastward from Borneo, while the eastern half is occupied by savage tribes of sub-Malayan stock, who appear to be allied to the Bisayans. A Negrito race is found in the mountains to the north-east. There are also the Mandayas, a people of doubtful origin, whose height and fairness of skin have led some writers to suggest that they are partly European! Of all the *Moros*, the Illanuns bear the worst reputation. For centuries their pirate praus have been the terror of the Eastern seas, and the Spanish settlement at Zamboanga was established with the special object of suppressing them. At the present time it may be said that piracy is within measurable distance of extinction. The tribes of supposed Bisayan stock chiefly occupy north-eastern Mindanao, and are specially numerous in the Agusan valley. They are complete savages, constantly engaged in inter-tribal war, and are partly cannibals. Captives are made slaves, and there is a title of honour for those who have succeeded in slaughtering as many as sixty of their enemies—a distinction which M. Montano found to be far from uncommon. Of these tribes the best known are the Mandayas of the Sahug River and the Manobos of the Agusan. The former people number some 30,000, of whom about 8000 have been converted to Christianity. In some parts of the Davao Gulf these people are more civilised, knowing how to weave and to forge krisses, and breeding good horses. All the work in civilising the natives has been done by the Jesuits.

Mindanao is both rich and fertile. It is probable that gold exists in tolerable quantities, and coal also. Sulphur is exported, and quicksilver has been discovered. There is considerable cultivation, especially in the north of the island; and in addition to the ordinary vegetable products of the archipelago, cacao and coffee are grown, and of the latter, which is said to be of better quality than that of Puerto Rico, a considerable quantity appears to be exported. The island is densely forested, and grows a great deal of valuable timber, including ebony and teak. The latter tree is found nowhere else in these islands, excepting in Sulu. The mangosteen and durian also abound, fruits which will not flourish farther to the north.

The island is divided into six provinces, the largest and most populous of which is Misamis, extending along the north coast between E. long. 123° and 125°, the chief town, also called Misamis, being situated in a deep inlet of Iligan Bay, forming a secure harbour. East of this, occupying the whole northern peninsula, is Surigao, at the extremity of which is the chief town of the same name. On the east coast is Bislig, a small province, and of less importance even than Davao, a little explored territory around the gulf of that name. Cota Batu, wrongly written Cottabatto by the Spaniards, embraces not only the larger part of the southern land-mass of the island, but also the country around Illana Bay. Its capital, formerly termed Mindanao, is situated a short distance up the Rio Grande. Another Spanish settlement, Pollok, ten miles farther north, was at one time connected with it by an excellent road, but, like other undertakings in the Philippines, it has been neglected, and is now impassable. There are few settlers here, and the population is chiefly composed of the garrison and the officers of the gunboats, of which one or two are always kept on the station to watch the movements of suspicious craft on the neighbouring coast, which does not bear the best of reputations. Of all the Spanish settlements, however, Zamboanga is the best known. Lying at the entrance of the Sulu Sea, and guarding the Strait of Basilan, it is frequently made a port of call. It was established in 1635, and is of some size and commercial importance, boasting of being the healthiest town in the archipelago. Its inhabitants are chiefly half castes, descended from Tagal women and Spaniards, and speak pure but old-fashioned Spanish. The total population of Mindanao is estimated to be about 650,000.

The Sulu Islands.

From Zamboanga south-westward to Borneo the Sulu Islands form, as it were, a series of stepping-stones. They number over 200, but are for the most part of very small size, the only exceptions being Basilan, Sulu, and Tawi-tawi. They are remarkable for their beauty, and, until lately, for affording shelter to the praus of the most bloodthirsty pirates of the Eastern seas. Politically, they fall under the jurisdiction of the administrator of the Mindanao district, and form two provinces, Basilan and Jolo (as the Spaniards term Sulu) each of which is looked after by a military governor. Until lately the "Castillans" had enough to do to hold their own within the walls of their settlements, and did not venture to exercise any real authority over the fanatical and turbulent Sulus, except by means of occasional punitive expeditions. Nor had the Sultan of Sulu much more power over his lawless subjects. Each rendered obedience to his own panglima or small raja, who was often at war with his neighbour a mile or two distant, and hardly on better terms with his nominal sovereign. When Dr. Guillemard visited Sulu in 1883 and 1884, four or more of these small potentates were more or less at war with each other. Lately, however, with the establishment of fresh posts in the archipelago, the check to piracy, and the civilising influence of trade, the "Castillans" have been gradually gaining the upper hand. They have settlements at Basilan, Jolo, Siassi, and Lapac, Tataan in Tawi-tawi Island, and Bongao off its western extremity, and two or three gunboats are always stationed in the group. The establishment of the British North Borneo Company has also done much towards purging these seas of piracy.

Basilan has been longest in the possession of the Spaniards, the sparseness of its population rendering its reduction easier than Sulu Island. It is thirty miles long by twenty broad, and is the largest island in the group. The capital is Isabela, on the north coast, a good harbour, which was considerably improved by the French during their occupation in 1845. A few plantations exist, and the natives have a good deal of intercourse with the Spaniards, but it is still hardly safe to travel alone in the interior. There is an arsenal here, where good foundry work is done by native workmen.

Sulu Island has been for more than three centuries the scene of oft-recurring struggles between the Spanish and the natives. In 1628, 1637, 1731, and 1871 the former despatched large expeditions against it, but it was not until 1876 that they fairly established themselves on the island. Jolo was then completely destroyed, and the town rebuilt and surrounded with fortifications. The Sultan now lives at Maimbun, on the south side. The other settlements of the group are mere outposts guarded by a handful of soldiers. The network of reefs and mangrove islands round Tawi-tawi gave shelter to swarms of pirates, but these are gradually being driven out by the Spanish gunboats. This island, or at all events the southern part of it, is inhabited chiefly by the Bajaus or sea-gipsies, a people quite distinct from the Sulus, and of a much lower type.

Sulu, which is about thirty miles in length, is volcanic, well cultivated, and very fertile. There are no active volcanoes, and the last eruption occurred in 1641, but the ground is in many places covered with scoriæ and pumice, upon which nothing but the coarse lalang grass flourishes. The teak tree grows well, as in Mindanao, and the durian and mangosteen are found. Deer and wild pigs are numerous, and pig-sticking is one of the favourite native amusements. The elephant is said to have been wild at the beginning of the present cen-

HUT AT MAIMBUN, SULU ISLAND.

tury, but there is no doubt that this statement is entirely erroneous, although the sultans possessed these animals, and some may have escaped into the forest. The fauna and flora are distinctly Philippine, and widely different from Borneo. The inhabitants, as has been already stated, are Mohammedan Malays, speaking a peculiar language allied to Bisayan and written in the Arabic character. They are considerably advanced in civilisation, making beautiful *parangs*, as the Sulu krisses are termed, and breeding horses with a special eye to racing them. Since 1885 the German Borneo Company has established tobacco plantations upon the island, the labourers being Chinese coolies from Singapore. The ylang-ylang plant is also cultivated. Liberian and Arabian coffee has been proved to do well, but there are as yet no white planters. Many valuable articles of commerce are produced, such as tortoise-shell, tripang, edible birds' nests, pearls, and pearl-shells. The islands are also a great mart for slaves, the piratical expeditions having for centuries brought captives from every part of the archipelago, so that here are to be found pure Malays from Sumatra, Papuans from New Guinea, and even natives from Siam in the north, and of Java and Timor in the south. These slaves are bartered with traders, and thus find their way to remote islands, and must have helped to produce those mixtures of various races which often render it difficult for the anthropologist to determine the affinities of many of the so-called Malay peoples. Although the check upon piracy has also had considerable effect upon this trade, there is no doubt that it is still largely carried on, and the Spaniards are powerless to stop it. The chief market and port of export is Maimbun. Official returns give the population of the Sulu Archipelago at 100,000, which is probably too high an estimate.

Between Tawi-tawi and Sibutu intervenes the deep channel known as the Sibutu Passage, which zoologically and geographically separates the Philippine Islands from Borneo.

THE CALAMIANES AND CUYOS ISLANDS.

These islands form, with part of Paláwan, the province of Calamianes, which has a population of about 20,000. The principal islands of the first-named group are Busuanga and Culion, which are inhabited by a race of dark Bisayans. There is a certain amount of trade in birds' nests and tripang, as well as wax and tortoise-shell, and a steamer puts the group in monthly communication with Manila. In many of the islands are found the burial caves to which allusion has been already made, and a colony of Chinese seem to have been established in Culion in ancient days. The Cuyos are for the most part of very small size, but the Spaniards have had settlements on them for a long period. The island of Cuyo, which is entirely under cultivation, is now the capital of the Calamianes province—the former capital, Tai-tai, in north Paláwan, having had to be abandoned on account of its unhealthiness. The town is provided with a large square fort, whose walls are 30 feet high by 12 feet in thickness, with towers at each of the four corners; but in 1884 there was only a single cannon serviceable. The military force is of the *Guardia civil*. Cattle form almost the only article of commerce.

PALÁWAN.

The long and narrow island of Paláwan, known to the French and Spanish as Paragua, projects like a horn from the northern extremity of Borneo, running north-east towards Mindoro. It has a length of about 250, and an average breadth of 20 miles, although at Ulugan Bay it is only 3 miles across. Its area is probably about 5000 square miles, and it is thus the third in size of the Philippine Islands. Its northern extremity is much broken, and studded with small islands, so as to form several good harbours, while its whole north-western coast is bordered by an extensive submarine bank, with numerous reefs and islets. Considering its breadth the island is very high throughout its whole extent, many of the peaks reaching 5000 feet, and one 6843 feet. Towards the north the coast is formed by vertical limestone cliffs. Although the island is not known to have any volcanoes, it is possible that they may exist, as there are two active craters on the island of Dumaran at its northern end.

Politically Paláwan is one of the Philippine Archipelago, but it cannot be considered so geographically. The soundings show that, together with the Calamianes and Cuyos islands, it is connected with Borneo by a bank which is hardly submerged 50 fathoms. North of the Calamianes, in the Mindoro Strait, the great depths of 700 to 800 fathoms are reached. Not one of the few mammals peculiar to the Philippines is known to inhabit Paláwan, while, on the other hand, the genera *Hystrix*, *Manis*, and *Mydaus*, abundantly found in Borneo, occur there, but in no other island of the Philippines. The avifauna shows similar evidence of a preponderating western element, and of this element being the original,[1] and we must therefore conclude that the island forms an integral portion of the Bornean group rather than of the Philippines.

The greater part of Paláwan is unexplored, owing in part to the untrustworthy character of the natives.

[1] See Mr. A. H. Everett in *Proc. Zoolog. Soc.* 1889, p. 220.

Along the eastern coast, especially in its southern portion, many Sulus have established themselves, most of them being refugees from the pirate haunts of Sulu and Mindanao. Inland are Dusun and Murut Dyaks, and to the north a people of uncertain race, probably a mixture of Dyaks and Bisayans—the Tagbuanas—interesting as being an almost savage people who possess a peculiar alphabet, somewhat similar to that once used by the Bisayans, but distinct (see Marche, *Luzon et Palaoan*, p. 327). Negritos are said to exist.

The only place upon the island which can really be said to be occupied by the Spaniards is Puerto Princesa, better known to the English as Port-Royalist, an excellent harbour on the east coast. Here is a convict settlement, looked after by two companies of a native regiment, a small arsenal, and a slip, and two gunboats are stationed at the port, which boasts of one of the few lighthouses existent in the Philippines. Tai-tai, at the north of the island, has been almost deserted by the Spaniards on account of its unhealthiness.

There are few or no roads in Paláwan except that crossing to Ulugan Bay, and very little is done in the way of trade or agriculture. Such trade as there is consists chiefly of forest and sea produce, and is in the hands of a few Chinamen on the east coast. But even these do not obtain their goods direct from the natives, but through the Sulus, who act as middlemen, and not infrequently make a more rapid profit by murdering the Chinese and sacking their stores. Dumaran Island, to the north, was once covered with pine plantations, but a few years ago these were completely destroyed by a plague of rats.

On Balabac Island, to the south of Paláwan, the Spanish have established an agricultural convict colony, but the experiment has not been attended with success. The Spanish and British North Borneo Company's steamers touch here, and the post is of some importance as commanding the Balabac Strait, but it has hitherto proved very unhealthy. Balabac forms the capital of the province of that name, which includes the neighbouring islands, together with Cagayan Sulu. Banguey, however, falls within the territory of the North Borneo Company.

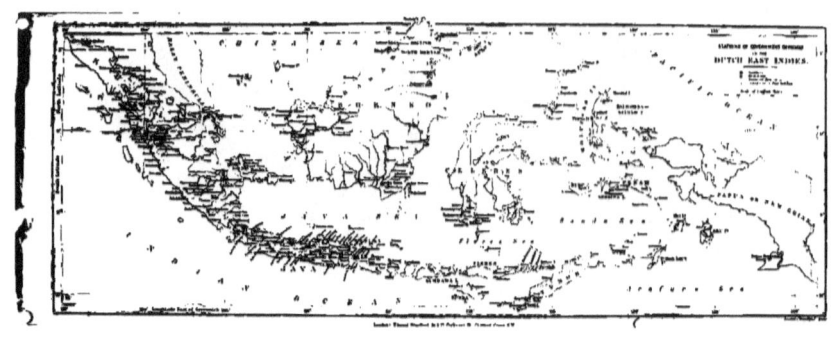

CHAPTER IV

THE DUTCH EAST INDIES

1. Extent and Importance.

ALMOST all the groups south of the Philippines—extending from Pulo Nias on the west of Sumatra to the Aru Islands near New Guinea, a distance of nearly 2500 geographical miles—are comprised in the Dutch Colonies, forming altogether a state nearly twelve times the size of England, with a population of over 30,000,000, abounding in gold, tin, diamonds, pearls, coal, and salt, and producing pepper, cinnamon, tea, coffee, rice, tobacco, sugar, camphor, and spices. The actual land area is estimated at 562,540 square miles. Thus, these Dutch possessions rank next in importance to the British Empire in Asia, and their trade with the home country amounts to at least one-half of that carried on between the East Indies and England. The total value of the exports in 1890 amounted to £14,657,975, while the floating capital of this trade can scarcely be estimated at less than £25,000,000. Of all these great possessions the most important by far is the island of Java. It is intersected in every direction with railways and telegraphs, has been for centuries the seat of civilisation, and is as well known as most European countries.

2. Dutch Policy, and its effects on the Native Populations.

The army, and the policy pursued towards the natives, are the two mainstays of the Dutch power in these remote regions. The army, purely of colonial origin, and amounting to about 30,000 men, of whom more than 14,000 are Europeans, is administered by the Indian Council of six members. About two-fifths of all the forces are stationed in Java, the heart of Netherlands India. They consist both of Dutch and Malays, drilled and officered by Europeans, who are very often mercenaries. The fleet numbers twenty-five vessels, and these combined forces have gradually overcome all resistance as far as they could reach; so that the Dutch authority is firmly established, especially in Java, where one or two nominally independent sultans are mere tools in the hands of the authorities in Batavia.

The Dutch Government has a monopoly of salt, opium, and coffee, so that native planters are obliged to dispose of their coffee to the State on fixed terms. By this system a large revenue is obtained. Slaves are no longer employed on the plantations, slavery having been abolished some few years ago. But the natives are bound to a sort of statute labour, besides their obligation to serve their own sultans in the same way. Many of the hardships inherent to this "heerendienst" have been mitigated, but it still remains substantially true that the Dutch colonies are farmed for the benefit of the mother country. The natives feel the yoke, but endure it patiently—partly through obsequiousness to their sultans, who are so many Dutch puppets, partly through their own natural temperament. The Malays have, no doubt, some good qualities, but at the bottom of their character lies a material and sensuous element; for them the *panem et circenses* argument has irresistible attractions; they are satisfied with their rice, fish, and betel, which they easily earn as careful agriculturists and skilful mariners. If to these blessings be added an occasional exhibition of dancing girls, a concert, a visit to the play-house, or a cock-fight, they are more than rewarded, and think no longer of revolting. The natives even thrive under the system, as shown by the enormous increase of the population. That of Madura, for instance, rose from 393,426 in 1856 to 676,818 in 1871, thus almost doubling itself in fifteen years. It will also be readily allowed that the condition of affairs in the districts under Dutch rule is far superior to that of the native states, where the old barbarous systems of slavery, piracy, and spoliation still flourish unrestrained.

3. System of Government of Netherlands India.

At the head of the Dutch East Indies is a Governor-General with the authority of a viceroy. He is supreme commander of the land and sea forces, with the right of declaring peace and war, and concluding treaties with the native princes and peoples, within the limits of his instructions from the Home Government. He is aided by a council of five of the higher officials, who are nominated by himself. The colonies are divided into two main divisions, the first comprising Java with Madura, the second the so-called external possessions (Buitenbezittingen), that is, all the other possessions and tributary states. They are further subdivided into "Residencies" and "Governments." In Java there are twenty-one of these provinces, each of which is administered by a "Resident."

These, again, are split into "regencies," with a "regent" at their head. This regent is always a native chosen from the nobles, especially of former dynastic families, whose influence over their subjects, cemented as it is by religious associations, still remains undiminished. Under the regent are the district and "dessa" chiefs, charged with the collection of the taxes, who are chosen by the inhabitants, and who represent the interests of the "dessa" or commune, a social organisation somewhat resembling the Russian "mir." With the regent, called by the Javanese "pangerang," "adhipatti," or "tummonggong," according to his rank, is associated a European "Assistant Resident," who is instructed to treat his compeer as a younger brother, and while keeping him well in hand to put him forward as ostensibly the real agent. Under the Assistant Residents are other European functionaries— "Controleurs" and others, who, besides their political duties, have the administration of justice or the superintendence of the culture-system mainly in their hands.

In the "Buitenbezittingen," omitting those of Sumatra and Borneo, there are the following residencies only:— Bali, Timor, Amboina, Ternate, and Menado. Of these Ternate is much the largest, as it embraces the large island of Gilolo, and the whole of Dutch New Guinea. The extent of Holland's possessions in the East Indies is so vast that she has done little to exploit them, but there are not very many even of the smaller groups of islands without some resident representative of the Government, whether "Controleur," "Posthouder," or a native in whom some authority is vested.

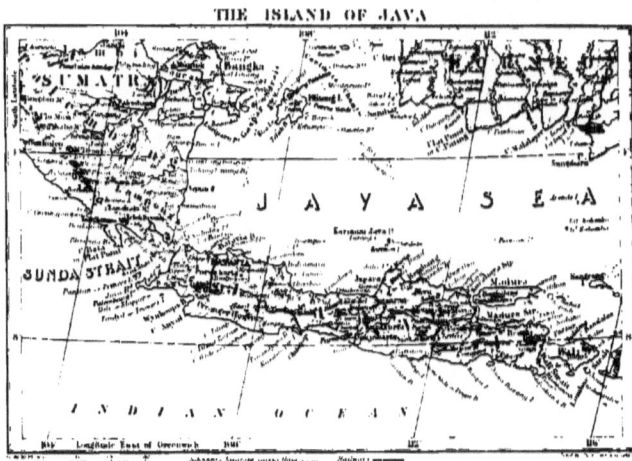
THE ISLAND OF JAVA

CHAPTER V

JAVA

1. General.

CHIEF of the Dutch possessions is the fine island of Java, situated on the southern margin of the great Asiatic submarine plateau. Not only has it been a great source of wealth to the mother country, but it is remarkable for other reasons. It is one of the few islands of the Eastern Archipelago which possesses a history. Its antiquities are in point of size not far inferior to the Pyramids, and in workmanship far above them. It exhibits throughout its whole extent a series of volcanoes of great height, of which more than twenty are active,— such a series, in short, as cannot be surpassed by any other region of the globe. And, finally, its population has increased in a most astounding manner of late years, so much so, that the density per square mile considerably exceeds that of England, and most probably even that of Belgium.

Java is separated from Sumatra on the west by the Straits of Sunda, at the narrowest part only fourteen miles wide, and from Bali on the east by a strait not two miles across. Borneo lies immediately north of it, at a distance of about 200 miles, while due south of it the Indian and Southern oceans extend uninterruptedly to the Antarctic continent. In form it is long and comparatively narrow, lying in a nearly east and west direction. Its extreme length is 575 geographical miles, while its breadth varies from 28 to 105 miles. Its area has been computed at 49,176 square miles, or about one-third part larger than Ireland. Its north coast is somewhat low and comparatively sheltered, and here are several small islands, the chief being the Karimon Java group, and Bawean; and one large island, Madura, which at its western extremity is only separated from the main island by a strait a mile wide. The southern coast is bold and precipitous, and has only a few islands situated close to the shore, the most important being Barong towards the eastern extremity, and Kambangan a little west of the centre. The coast-line presents many bays on the north, but none of them penetrate deeply, so that there is only one good harbour, that of Surabaya, formed between the main island and Madura. The southern coast is still less indented, and is exposed to a heavy and dangerous surf, which rolls in upon the shore at all seasons. It is therefore little frequented, and it has hardly any safe harbour but that of Chilatjap, situated between the island of Kambangan and the mainland.

The western part of Java, as far as Cheribon, is from 75 to 95 miles broad, and, except the plains on the northern coast, is very mountainous, the mountains being crowded together with narrow intervening valleys, but not reaching such great elevations as elsewhere, the highest being a little over 10,000 feet. This, however, is the most luxuriant part of the island, owing to the moister climate, so that the forests reach the summits of some of the highest mountains. Here is the country of the Sundanese, who speak a language distinct from the Javanese proper. Eastward as far as Samarang the island is hardly more than 50 miles wide, mountainous in the centre, but with plains both on the north and south coasts. Here the mountains exceed 10,000 feet. Then comes a portion which is about 100 miles wide, as far as Surabaya, at which spot an extensive valley nearly crosses the island. Beyond this the eastern end is only 50 miles wide, yet it contains the great mountain of Semeru, over 12,000 feet in height, and the highest in all Java. Dr. Junghuhn estimated the mean height of the island at about 1600 feet.

The island of Madura forms one of the "Residencies" of Java, and is always grouped with it in Dutch statistics, a position which physical geography tells us it has every right to occupy, for it has undoubtedly been separated from the main island at no very distant geological date.

2. History.

Although from a very early period Java has been the seat of a more or less advanced civilisation, the records concerning it are remarkably scanty. It is probable that the Hindus established themselves upon the island about the sixth century of our era, but even this indefinite date is at best conjectural, and the date of the construction of their great temples, whose ruins still remain to astonish the traveller by their size and magnificence, is likewise in many instances doubtful or unknown. It is, however, a tolerably well established fact that the death-blow to Hindu influence was inflicted in 1478, when Majapahit, near Surabaya, the capital of the chief Hindu state, was destroyed by the Arab traders who had established themselves upon the coast. Still, nothing much more was known of the island for a long period, and though Marco

Polo, who passed through the archipelago in about 1290, makes mention of it by name, he did not visit it, and Ludovic Varthema, the Italian traveller, was probably the first European to land upon its shores, in 1505.

The taking of Malacca by Albuquerque in 1511 brought the Portuguese in close proximity to Java, and Antonio d'Abreu's fleet, despatched to the Spice Islands a month or two later, coasted its shores and passed through the narrow straits dividing it from Madura. But in spite of its known richness the Moluccas were considered to offer greater advantages, and d'Abreu did not attempt to open negotiations with the people, although he touched at Agaçim, the present Gressi. The Portuguese, indeed, never established themselves upon the island, and had only a few trading posts upon its coasts. So little was it known, that fifty-two years after the taking of Malacca it was described by Barros as consisting of two islands. The Dutch landed for the first time in 1595 under Houtman, and in 1610 built a fort at Batavia, which, nine years later, the English helped the natives to take, but on its being relieved by the Dutch fleet the assailants retired. It was not until 1677 that any territorial acquisition was made, the principality of Jacatra being then ceded. From that time up to 1830 the Dutch have been engaged in five great wars, lasting from five to fifteen years each, but all ending in important acquisitions of territory. The last was the final effort of the natives, and Java is now securely in the hands of Holland.

The British temporarily occupied Java for the five years from 1811 to 1816, a period which will always be remembered for the energetic, though not altogether successful, administration of Sir Stamford Raffles.

3. Geology and Physical Features.

The southern coast-line of Java forms part of the lip of the vast basin of the Indian Ocean, and within a short distance of the shore the great ocean depths are reached. To the north and west a shallow sea dotted with many small islets separates it from Sumatra, Banka, and Blitong, while eastward a prolongation of Madura may be traced to Kangeang and the Paternosters, and Bali is separated by a strait barely a mile and a half wide, and having a depth of only nine fathoms.

It was formerly believed that Java was almost exclusively volcanic, but it is now known that this is far from being the case, the volcanoes resting upon sedimentary rocks of which the greater part appear to be of the Tertiary period, although it has been lately shown that certain fossiliferous strata must be ascribed to the Quaternary period. Granite occurs at the western end of Java, but the plutonic rocks are not common, as in the neighbouring island of Sumatra. With these geological conditions it is not to be wondered at that few minerals are to be found. Coal, indeed, is plentiful, but it is poor, occurs in thin strata, and hardly repays working. Sulphur is abundant, and a further exploitation of the mineral oils should give good results.

The great mountains of Java are all volcanic cones. Two of them, Karang and Muria, are isolated from the others, which are situated for the most part near the central line of the island. In the west these volcanoes are grouped together in a mass, and spring from high ground. In the east they are more discrete, and the ground upon which they rest is lower and more open. There are not less than fifty volcanic peaks in the island, about half of which are more or less active. The highest is Semeru, with an altitude of 12,044 feet; ten exceed 10,000 feet, five more exceed 9000 feet, and ten are between 7000 and 9000 feet. The following are the names of the most important, with their heights. Those that are more or less active have the names given in italics :—

DETACHED.		CENTRAL AND EASTERN GROUP.	
Karang	5834	*S'lamat*	11,240
Muria	5234	Sundara	10,249
		Prau	8,389
WESTERN GROUP.		*Sumbing*	10,941
		Merapi	9,404
Salak	7266	Merbabu	10,223
Gede	9718	*Lawu*	10,676
Patuwa	7828	Wilis	8,369
Tangkuban Prau	6808	Pennggungan	5,413
Malabar	7683	Arjuna	10,935
Tunggul	7224	Butak (Kawi)	9,381
Papandayang	8611	Tengar	8,937
Guntur	7362	Semeru	12,044
Chikurai	9242	Lamongan	5,370
Galunggung	7313	Argopura	10,138
Cherimai	10,073	Raun	10,925
		Ijen (Merapi)	9,187

Of the western group, Salak, which from its proximity to Buitenzorg is one of the best known of the volcanoes of Java, is now inactive, but was in 1699 the scene of a great catastrophe. Enormous masses of mud were ejected from the crater, and impeding the course of the rivers, caused the formation of lakes, which burst and devastated the country below them. Papandayang, or "the forge," so called from the deafening noise produced by its crater, exhibits a series of sulphurous mud pools, which boil and eject stones and mud. In 1772 occurred its last eruption, which was one of the most destructive in the history of the island, and was specially remarkable for its suddenness and short duration. A great part of the mountain is said to have been engulfed, and 40 villages and 4000 people were destroyed. The eruptions of Guntur—"the mountain of thunder"—are innumerable. It is bare from base to summit, and although history does not show it to have been so destructive to human life as many other volcanoes of the island, it has nevertheless ruined the coffee-plantations around it on many occasions.

Terrible in their effects as have been many of the eruptions of the volcanoes of Java, few have been so disastrous as that of Mount Galunggung, a peak some few miles north-east of Papandayang. At noon on the 8th October, 1822, not a cloud was to be seen in the sky, and no preliminary earthquake or noises within the mountain gave warning of what was about to occur. Suddenly a frightful thundering was heard, and from the top of this apparently extinct volcano a dark dense mass was seen rising higher and higher into the air, and spreading itself out over the clear sky with such appalling rapidity that in a few moments the whole landscape was shrouded in the darkness of night. Through the thick darkness flashes of lightning gleamed incessantly in every direction, and many natives were instantly struck down to the earth by stones falling from the sky. Then a deluge of hot water and flowing mud shot up from the crater like a waterspout, and poured down the mountain-sides, sweeping away trees and beasts and human beings in its seething mass. At the same moment stones and ashes and sand were projected to an enormous height into the air, and, as they fell, destroyed nearly everything within a radius of twenty miles, while quantities of the ejecta fell even beyond the River Tandoi, which is forty miles off. A few villages that were situated on high hills on the lower declivities of the mountain escaped the surrounding destruction by being raised above the streams of hot water and flowing mud, while most of the stones and ashes and sand that were thrown out passed completely over them, and destroyed villages that were farther removed from the centre of this great eruption.

The thundering was first heard at half-past one o'clock. At four o'clock the extreme violence of the eruption was past; at five, the sky began to grow clear once more, and the same sun that at noon had shed its light over a rich and peaceful landscape, at evening was shining over the same spot now changed into a scene of utter desolation.

But this was not all. A second eruption followed on October 12th, even more violent than the first. Hot water and mud were again vomited forth, and great blocks of basalt were thrown to a distance of seven miles from the volcano. There was at the same time a violent earthquake; the summit of the mountain was broken down, and one side, which had been covered with forest, became an enormous semi-circular gulf. The rivers bore down to the sea the dead bodies of men and the carcases of deer, rhinoceroses, tigers, and other animals. The base of the mountain could not be approached for a month, and it was found that the surrounding country had been covered with a layer of greenish-blue mud, which in places was 50 feet in depth. The official accounts state that 114 villages were destroyed and 4000 persons killed.

Passing to the central and eastern groups of volcanoes, we find them to be uniformly of greater height than those of the western portion of the island. No less than nine attain an altitude of over 10,000 feet. Of these S'lamat is remarkable as much for the regularity of its shape as for the thick cloud of smoke which it continually pours forth from its summit. Of the great crater of Prau one-half of the lip alone remains, the southern portion having been blown away in some giant convulsion of Nature. On a small plateau, half within it, is the unduly celebrated Guwa Upas, or "Poison Valley," a small depression whence carbonic acid gas escapes, in no way more remarkable than the Grotto del Cane. Far more interesting are the numerous Hindu temples around, of which more than twenty remain tolerably entire, though many others have fallen into ruin. They are all Brahminical, and show no admixture of Buddhism as do those of Boro-bodor. Inscriptions have been found, but none bearing dates, although it is probable that the buildings were erected about the 12th century. Although Merbabu is inactive and cultivated nearly to its summit, its sister cone Merapi emits a constant jet of smoke, but an eruption seldom occurs. Lawu, and Wilis, "the green mountain," are quiescent, only showing signs of their former activity by the hot springs and solfataras of their slopes. The first-named is chiefly noteworthy for the extraordinary phallic Hindu temples whose ruins occupy its slopes. Arjuna shows many remains of a similar cult, and with Kawi appears to be now nearly extinct. Not so Kelut, which, though of insignificant height, is much dreaded from the nature of its eruptions. In that of 1848 its terrific detonations were heard over the greater part of the Malay Archipelago.

Semeru and Tenger are perhaps the most remarkable of all the Javanese volcanoes, the former as being the highest peak in the island, the latter as possessing the largest crater. There is little doubt that Tenger was at one time higher than its neighbour, and that some Titanic convulsion blew away the upper part of the mountain, leaving the base only to serve as the walls of a crater which is at the present time about six miles in its largest and four and a half in its smallest diameter. The floor is perfectly level, in one part sandy and barren, but elsewhere covered with prairie and other grasses, and from its centre rises a little group of small peaks. The chief of these (600 feet in height), known to the natives as Bromo (Brahma), is in a state of constant activity, and having been in past times a sacred mountain to those professing the Hindu religion, is still held in awe by the Javanese. Tenger is connected by a high ridge with Semeru, whose summit lies about eight miles south of it. The latter ejected in 1885 a stream of lava of considerable volume.

Although the earthquakes occurring in Java are neither so frequent nor so terribly destructive as those of the Philippine Islands, they are nevertheless far from uncommon. The most celebrated is that of 5th January 1699, on the occasion of the eruption of Salak already referred to, when 208 considerable shocks were felt, and many houses in Batavia destroyed. Again, in 1867, a violent earthquake occurred in central Java, which caused great havoc and killed numbers of people. In the capital of Jokjokarta alone a thousand are said to have perished.

In a country so eminently volcanic as Java, the occurrence of the rarer phenomena owing their existence to the agency of volcanic forces might be expected, and accordingly we find not only an abundance of hot springs, solfataras, and the like, but various manifestations of the great subterranean fires which are not so frequently seen. The wondrous tales of the deadly "Poison Valley"—the celebrated Guwa Upas—have long ago been proved to be mythical, as has been already stated, but they may perhaps have been confused with hearsay accounts of Pajagalon, a valley near the lake of Talaga Bodas, where the ground emits carbonic acid gas in sufficient quantities to kill animals traversing it. Here may be found the bodies of civet-cats, squirrels, birds, etc., and, at the time when Junghuhn wrote, of tigers and rhinoceroses. The fabulous stories of the deadly "Upas tree," which was said to destroy all creatures which slept beneath its shade, or any birds which flew over it, have originated in the word "upas" (poison) being applied to these places, and also to a tree—*Antiaris toxicaria*—which, though poisonous, has none of the deadly properties above mentioned. An analogous phenomenon is a lake in the crater of Taschem, in eastern Java, which is so strongly impregnated with sulphuric acid that no fish can live in it, or in the river which flows from it, and where the river empties itself into the sea it destroys or drives away all fish for a considerable distance. Jets or fountains of inflammable gas in one locality, at least, point to the existence of considerable quantities of petroleum. Brine springs are very numerous, especially in the province of Japara, where they are dispersed through a district several miles in circumference, forcing themselves upwards through apertures in the rocks with some violence and ebullition. The salt obtained by evaporation from these springs is of very fair quality. In this same district of Grobogan are some curious mud volcanoes which have been described by Dr. Horsfield as follows :—

"About the centre of this limestone district is found an extraordinary volcanic phenomenon. On approaching it from a distance, it is first discovered by large volumes of smoke rising and disappearing at intervals of a few seconds, resembling the vapours arising from a violent surf, while a dull noise is heard like that of distant thunder. Having advanced so near that the vision is no longer impeded by the smoke, a large hemispherical mass is observed, consisting of black earth mixed with water, about sixteen feet in diameter, rising to the height of 20 or 30 feet in a perfectly regular manner, and, as it were, pushed up by a force beneath, which suddenly explodes with a dull noise, and scatters about a volume of black mud in every direction. After an interval of two or three, or sometimes four or five seconds, the hemispherical body of mud or earth rises and explodes again. In the same manner this volcanic ebullition goes on without interruption, throwing up a globular body of mud, and dispersing it with violence through the neighbouring plain. The spot where this occurs is nearly circular and perfectly level. It is covered with the earthy particles impregnated with salt which are thrown up from below. Its circumference is about half a mile. A strong, pungent, sulphurous smell, somewhat resembling that of petroleum, is perceived on standing near the explosion, and the mud recently thrown up possesses a degree of heat greater than that of the surrounding atmosphere. During the rainy season these explosions are more violent, the mud is thrown up much higher, and the noise is heard to a greater distance."

On the southern coast, not far from the meridian of Surakarta, is the curious phenomenon known as Gunong-gunong Sewu—the Thousand Mountains—a plateau covered by innumerable and closely approximated white limestone hills which are from 100 to 200 feet in height. A perfect labyrinth of narrow winding valleys and innumerable small lakes are thus formed, the milky waters of the latter being in many cases drained by subterranean channels into the sea, where they may be seen staining the water in patches at some distance from the shore. This district is spoken of by Junghuhn as one of the most beautiful in Java.

Besides the true volcanoes there are many hill ranges and lesser mountains in Java; and skirting the southern shore there is a great range of low mountains about 3000 feet in height, formed of basalt, trap, and sometimes of limestone. This latter appears to be of Miocene age, as it contains shells and corals allied to those of the European Miocene, as well as others similar to those which now live in Eastern seas, three out of twenty-two being living species.

The rivers of Java, especially on the north side, are almost innumerable, but from the form of the island they are of comparatively small size, and a few only are navigable for boats. Their rapid flow and perennial supply of water are excellently adapted for irrigation, to the practice of which much of the fertility of the country is due. The largest and most useful river of the island is that usually called the Solo River, from its passing the native capital of that name. It has its source in one of the low ranges of hills towards the southern side of the island, and after a tortuous course of 310 miles empties itself into the sea by two mouths opposite the western end of Madura. Except for three months, from August to October, it is navigable by large boats, and at all times by small ones. It would even be accessible to ocean vessels but for the bar at its mouth. The next largest river is the Brantas, or river of Surabaya. This also rises near the southern coast, on the west side of the Semeru mountain, and after receiving many affluents, enters the sea by two mouths, one of which passes the town of Surabaya and contributes to form its harbour. In the west of Java the Chi Tarum (Chi, or Tji as it is usually written, being the Sundanese word for river) and the Chi Manuk are the most important rivers, but they

I

are of little value except for irrigation. Much detritus is brought down by them in the rainy season, and from this and other causes their bars are silting up and the neighbouring land is encroaching upon the sea to the extent of over 21 feet annually. In like manner the Surabaya Strait has been filling up for years, and although much was gained in 1854 by the diversion of one branch of the Solo into a new channel, it is doubtful how long the improved condition of affairs will last, and steps are already being taken to prevent the closing of the harbour which again threatens.

The valleys of Java, like its streams, are innumerable, but there are few inland plains of any extent. The physical conditions of the country are not favourable to their existence, and the same may be said concerning lakes, of which there are none worthy of particular mention. The most important plain, perhaps, is that of Surakarta. Of the valleys, in point of beauty, the palm must be yielded to Kadu, dominated as it is by the magnificent volcanoes Merbabu and Merapi on the one side, and Sumbing and Sundara on the other.

4. Climate and Meteorology.

The climate of Java is on the whole hot and uniform, as might be expected from its geographical position, but its elevated plains and plateaux, from 1000 to 5000 feet above the sea, afford a variety of climates, some of which are as near perfection as any that can be found. The wet season is from October to March, when the north-west monsoon blows, and the so-called dry season from April to the end of September, during the prevalence of the south-east winds; but, as in all countries near the equator, rain and sunshine are more or less distributed throughout the year. At the change of the monsoons the weather is often unsettled and tempestuous, with violent thunderstorms, which in the mountains are often destructive of life. Batavia experiences annually an average of over one hundred thunderstorms. That the permanent winds from the eastward prevail over the monsoons at the higher altitudes is made evident by the westerly direction taken by the smoke of the volcanoes, and the constancy of this current is shown by the erosion of the western side of the lips of the craters, as may be well seen in the case of Merapi. Land and sea breezes are experienced within fifteen miles of the northern and southern coasts, while in some parts of the east end, which exhibits a considerably greater aridity than the west, the south-east monsoon blows violently across the entire island.

Although Java has not such a great rainfall as Sumatra, owing in a measure to its being protected by that island, it is nevertheless considerable, although naturally varying very much with the locality. At Batavia the mean annual rainfall is 75 inches, but at Buitenzorg, the hill-station of that city, it averages 185 inches, or more than four times that recorded from the eastern end of the island. December, January, and February are the most rainy months, averaging in Batavia about 18 inches in each month, while in July and August the amount recorded is little over 2 inches. The island, lying out of the track of typhoons, shows a very steady barometer, and during observations extending over some years ·36 inch was recorded as its extreme range of variation. The variations of temperature are likewise very small upon the coast. The result of twelve years' observations at the Government

Observatory at Batavia show an extreme range of only 30° Fahr. during that period. The monthly mean temperatures do not differ more than 2°, that of January being 77°·48, and that of May 79°·59. The usual daily range is from about 74° to 84°, and during the whole year the temperature seldom falls much below 70° or rises above 90°. At elevations of from 3000 to 5000 feet above the sea the thermometer is usually about 20° lower than the figures above given, producing a climate very agreeable to European constitutions, and suitable to the corn, fruits, flowers, and vegetables of the temperate zone, which have long been acclimatised. Java may be said on the whole to be very fairly healthy. The malarial fevers are milder and less common than in the other great islands of the archipelago, and diseases of the lungs are rare. But on the other hand zymotic disorders are prevalent, beri-beri and smallpox are very fatal, and the towns are ravaged from time to time with severe epidemics of cholera. In 1889 no less than 16,000 persons fell victims to this scourge of the East.

5. Flora and Fauna.

The botany of Java is exceedingly rich and diversified, and the peculiar Malayan flora is here developed in its highest luxuriance and beauty; over 9000 phanerogamous plants being known to exist in the island. The villages, and even the towns are in great part concealed from view by the luxuriant abundance and perpetual verdure of the vegetation. Patches of sandy shore or of bare lava-coloured peaks are the exception, and quite one-fifth of the island is still covered with forest, despite the denseness of the population. The vegetation varies with the soil, whether composed of the debris of volcanic matter, of calcareous rocks, or of sandstone; but it varies far more according to the elevation of the land, which gives rise to at least six different botanical zones, which are thus described by Dr. Bleeker:—"On the low coast-lands we find superb palms, bananas, aroids, Amaranthaceæ, papilionaceous plants, and poisonous Euphorbiaceæ. Scarcely do we ascend 1000 feet above the sea when our eyes are struck by the quantity of ferns which already preponderate over other plants, and here, too, we find magnificent groves of slender bamboos. The farther we ascend the greater is the change in the aspect of the vegetation. Palms and leguminous plants become rare, and bamboos less abundant. In place of these we find forests of *Ficus*, with their tall trunks, spreading branches, and thick foliage, overshadowing more lowly trees and a variety of humble plants, and exhibiting a majesty which even surpasses in splendour the palms of the coast. Here, too, the ferns increase in number, and beautiful tree-ferns abound, often covering the sides of the valleys with their aerial crowns of fronds. Orchideous plants now present themselves in considerable numbers, clothing the old trees with a parasitic vegetation. Higher still the figs are mingled with gigantic Liquidambars, with white trunks. To the Orchideæ are added the curious Nepenthes, or pitcher-plants, while the numerous ferns are accompanied by Loranthaceæ and elegant Melastomas. Above these comes the region of oaks and laurels, and here the Melastomas and orchideous plants become still more abundant, while the vegetation receives a new ornament in the elegant Freycinetias, which are found as pseudo-parasites. rubiaceous plants being at the same time abundant, growing by themselves, and flourishing in the shade. There is but one region above that of oaks and laurels, where

Rubiaceæ, conifers, heaths, and other plants familiar to countries beyond the tropics, present to us the flora of higher latitudes. Cryptogamous plants, especially, are infinitely multiplied; fungi are abundant, and mosses cover the ground and invest the trunks and branches of trees. The ferns are now smaller in size, but are of an infinite variety of forms, and constitute an important portion of the vegetation." The lowest zone is by far the most extensive, and is chiefly given up to cultivation, especially to rice. On the second zone are grown tea, coffee, cinchona, and the Sagueir palm (*Arenga*), while at still higher altitudes cabbages and potatoes are to be seen in the gardens.

Another interesting feature of the higher mountains of Java is the appearance upon them of plants closely allied to those of northern Europe. On Pangerango, one of the peaks of the Gede volcano, we meet with eatable raspberries at 6000 feet, cypresses at 7000, while at 8000 feet we come upon such familiar types as the honeysuckle, St. John's wort, and guelder-rose; and when we reach 9000 feet, we meet with the imperial cowslip, allied to species inhabiting Japan and the Himalayas, but of a peculiar species (*Primula imperialis*). The following genera, characteristic of north temperate regions, were found upon the summit by Mr. Motley:—Two species of violet, three of ranunculus, eight or ten of rubus, and species of primrose, St. John's wort, swertia, lily of the valley, cranberry, rhododendron, gnaphalium, polygonum, foxglove, honeysuckle, plantain, wormwood, oak, and yew.

Java affords many timber trees of considerable value, but as yet, with the exception of the Teak (*Tectonia grandis*), they have not received the attention they commercially deserve. Forests of this tree are to be found throughout the island, but they exist chiefly between Samarang and Surabaya in the lower ground. Injudicious felling had at one time reduced them considerably, but under careful management matters are now more satisfactory, and it is stated that at the present time the forests of this tree occupy an area of about 2500 square miles. Afforestation with the Blue Gum, *Cassia florida*, and other trees, has been of late largely carried out by the Government. In fruits the island is remarkably rich, and the markets of Batavia exhibit innumerable different kinds, most of which are strange to European eyes. It is here that the durian, mangosteen, rambutan, and other typically Malayan fruits are tasted in perfection.

While the zoological features of Sumatra, Borneo, and the Malay peninsula are more or less identical, those of Java exhibit certain marked differences. The island is very rich in mammalia, possessing about 90 distinct kinds. The majority of these are identical with those of Sumatra and Borneo; but many of the forms inhabiting those two islands are wanting, and there are a few peculiar to Java, or common to it and the Siamese peninsula, but wanting in the other islands. Thus, Java has no tapir, or elephant, or Malay-bear, or orang-utan, while the Javan rhinoceros and hare are identical with species found again in the Indo-Chinese countries. Among birds we meet with similar but still more remarkable facts. No less than 240 species of land-birds are known to inhabit the island, and at least forty are peculiar to it. There are, however, no less than sixteen genera found in Malacca, Sumatra, and Borneo, which are absent from Java, among which are such conspicuous birds as the Indian magpies (*Dendrocitta*), the green gaper (*Calyptomena*), the large bee-eater (*Nyctiornis*), the Argus and fire-back pheasants, and the crested partridges (*Rollulus*). On the other hand, there are twelve Javan birds whose nearest allies (sometimes the identical species) occur in the Indo-Chinese countries or the Himalayas, while they are quite unknown in Sumatra and Borneo, the most popular example of which is the pea-fowl of Java, found also in Siam and Burmah, but not in the intervening islands.[1]

In reptiles, fresh-water fishes, and insects, Java is very rich, the forms agreeing generally with those prevalent in the other Malay islands, and in the Indo-Malay countries. The insects are especially fine, and among the beetles and butterflies are some of magnificent dimensions and gorgeous colours; but, as in the birds, many of them are quite peculiar to the island and unlike those of Sumatra and Borneo.

Among the more remarkable large animals of Java are the rhinoceros, the tiger, the leopard, the wild dog, the wild ox, and two species of wild swine. Deer are abundant and of several species, but there are no antelopes or goats. Squirrels are very plentiful, and there are several species of monkeys. A singular animal, somewhat intermediate in appearance between a polecat and a badger, is the Mydaus, remarkable for its distribution on the higher mountains only. Dr. Horsfield states that it is confined exclusively to those mountains which have an elevation of more than 7000 feet above the sea, and that on these it occurs with the regularity of some plants, extending from one end of the island to the other on the numerous disconnected mountain summits. It emits an offensive stench like the skunk of America. Besides the peacock,

---

[1] For the details of these peculiarities and their probable causes, see *The Geographical Distribution of Animals*, by A. R. Wallace, vol. i. p. 349.

two species of jungle-fowl inhabit Java—one a very beautiful species (*Gallus furcatus*), peculiar to the island and those eastward of it as far as Sumbawa; the other the common jungle-fowl of India and the Malay countries (*Gallus bankiva*), and the original stock of all our domestic poultry. There are also several species of partridge and quail, and some very beautiful pigeons, pre-eminent among which is the mountain fruit-dove (*Ptilopus roseicollis*), whose entire head and neck are of an intense rosy-pink, contrasting exquisitely with its otherwise green plumage.

6. Inhabitants and Language.

Setting aside Europeans and other immigrant races, the inhabitants of Java belong to three nations, speaking allied but distinct languages—the Sundanese, Javanese, and Madurese. The Sundanese inhabit the country west of the meridian of Cheribon, and from the mountainous character of the district have remained the purest race. There are fewer Sanscrit words in their language than Javanese, owing to the greater absence of Hindu influence, and although nominally of the Mohammedan religion, have retained and incorporated with it not a little of their former superstitions and customs. The second nation, the Javanese, are by far the most numerous, comprising nearly three-quarters of the entire population, and extending over the entire centre and east of the island, excepting the northern portion of the eastern peninsula. They are the most civilised and advanced of the native inhabitants, their civilisation having been early brought about by the wave of Hindu immigration which spread with rapidity over a country well cultivated and easy of access. The Madurese inhabit Madura and a great part of the eastern peninsula of Java lying directly to the south of it, and are increasing rapidly round Surabaya. They exceed the Sundanese in number.

All these people are of Malay race, and are physically not easily distinguishable from the Malays of the other great islands and the Malacca peninsula, except for the fact of their being somewhat taller. Like all Malays they are of slight build, and Von Scherzer has recently called attention to the extreme fineness of the bones in female skeletons. As regards character, Crawfurd, who had long and intimate experience of them in the earlier part of this century, pronounced them to be peaceable, docile, sober and industrious, and the most truthful and straightforward Asiatic people he ever met with—an opinion that will probably be shared by most of the modern travellers who have known them. They have, without doubt, improved under a settled government, which has given them peace and security; for an old writer, Barbosa, describes them, in the beginning of the sixteenth century, as being "very malicious, great deceivers, seldom speaking the truth, and prepared to do all manner of wickedness;" and this was no doubt true, as the same terms will apply to many of the Malay people at the present day under the rule of despotic native princes, who govern by favouritism and intrigue, spend their lives in amusements and debauchery, and hold the property, the families, and even the lives of all their subjects at their disposal.

Java was a populous and wealthy island long before it was known to Europeans, for the Portuguese found there a comparatively civilised people, carrying on a great trade with surrounding countries, which they supplied with rice and native manufactures. The Javanese are good agriculturists, and are especially skilful in irrigation.

Extensive valleys and mountain sides are terraced and levelled in steps, and water is carried from the mountain streams so that every plot can be flooded or dried at pleasure. These terraced lands are of very great antiquity, but they are continually being extended, and they enable the ground to produce a constant succession of crops all the year round, and year after year, without manure, because the fertilising matter held in solution and sus-

NATIVE HOUSE, JAVA.

pension by all streams is retained upon the land instead of being carried away to the sea and wasted. This mode of terracing the land and compelling the streams to fertilise it effectually, is probably the most perfect system of agriculture conceivable, and could it only be applied in our own country, it would enable us at once to solve the problem of the economical utilisation of sewage; for we should then have, in all parts of the country, water ready to carry and dilute, and land ready levelled to receive the rich manures that are now thrown into the sea, having first contaminated our streams and done as much mischief as possible.

The Javanese are careful and skilful workmen, whether in wood or iron. They build admirable boats and canoes, which cannot be surpassed for speed and elegance. Their *krisses* or daggers are also excellent, the steel blades being finely figured, and the handles and sheaths worked in the finest woods or in ivory, and ornamented with gold or jewels. They weave native cloths of fine quality, often intermixed with gold thread, and of beautifully blended colours; while they dye cottons in elaborate and tasteful patterns with a few simple tints obtained from earths and vegetables, whose permanence and artistic merit put our more gaudy and evanescent colours to shame.

Like all Malays, and most uncivilised peoples, the Javanese are great gamblers, and are also very fond of cock-fighting. The upper classes, however, are fond of hunting, and are admirable horsemen. They hunt deer on horseback, killing them with a short sword; and tigers are often surrounded and killed with spears. They have a peculiar kind of theatrical performance, in which the shadows of flat wooden figures are thrown upon a transparent screen, behind which the performer speaks the several parts, altering his voice to suit the different characters. In the *wajang*, or puppet plays, the figures are dressed in leather and occupy the front of the stage. The pieces are almost always historical dramas, taken from the ancient and legendary history of the island. The Javanese excel in music, every chief or wealthy man having a *gamelang*, or band of musicians, generally ten or twelve in number. The instruments consist of gongs of various sizes for the deeper tones, and strips of metal or bamboo for the higher notes, arranged in frames so that a set of each can be conveniently struck by the performer. A *Biola*, or one-stringed violin, leads the band, which is in constant requisition at all festivals. Some of the musical pieces performed are long and elaborate, but all are played by ear, the performers generally practising from childhood. On grand occasions, as at the wedding of a raja's daughter, the *gamalang* will keep on playing at short intervals day and night for several days in succession.

Besides these three peoples—the Sundanese, Javanese, and Madurese—there are probably at least a million and a half, if not more, of other nationalities. Not the least numerous are the true Malays, the immigrants, that is to say, from the Peninsula and elsewhere. They are chiefly to be found in the great towns, whither trade and commerce attract them. So, too, with the Chinese, who act as opium merchants, *compradores*, money-lenders, and middlemen generally, and, as elsewhere in the archipelago, become men of property. According to a recent writer their possessions in the island are valued at over £11,000,000 sterling. Suspicious of their prosperity, the Dutch Government, in the early part of the century, forbade absolutely all immigration of Chinese, but this decree was rescinded in 1837. Even now some difficulties are made to their settling, and capitation fees, passports, and liberal taxation place some check upon their increase. They number at the present time about 250,000 individuals, but a large proportion of these are *Penakan*, or half-breeds, the children of Chinese fathers by native women. Of much the same trades and employments as the Chinese are the Arabs. In part new arrivals, in part the descendants of the "Moros," whom the Portuguese on their advent found established at all the ports of the East, they act as merchants of European goods, as pedlars, and so forth, while others, as *talebs* or scribes, figure as learned men, and are held in great respect by the simple-minded Javanese. There are probably under 15,000 of this race, who are thus numerically far inferior to the Europeans. But as among the Chinese are reckoned the half-bred race who, little by little, are becoming insensibly mingled with the Javanese, so the term European embraces all those who can claim European blood for two generations. Throughout the archipelago there is none of the feeling towards the Eurasian which is so marked a feature in India, and people of mixed blood are to be seen at almost every social gathering in the large towns—a result to which the long term of service without furlough endured by the Dutch officials has helped to contribute. Yet, despite this classification, the Europeans in Java are far from being numerous. Had the island been an English colony it would long ago have been the home of large numbers of planters, engineers, and professional men and artisans. The Dutch Government, however, have, until lately, discouraged the settler in every possible way, making the island, as it were, their private property. Even now, although these difficulties have been removed, and European immigrants are permitted, it cannot be said that much in the way of help or encouragement has been afforded them, and the settler is rarely permanent.

Of all the languages spoken in Java, Javanese is the most important and most widely employed. Its alphabet is peculiar, it is based on the Dewanâgari, and is found in inscriptions and manuscripts of the 12th century, although in its present form it is not more than 400 years old. Professor Keane considers the language to be the most cultivated of all the Malayan tongues, and intermediate in structure between the simple Malay and the more developed Tagalog of the Philippines. Omitting the *kawi*, or ancient language, there are two distinct forms of it: the *krama* or court speech, and the *ngoko* or vulgar dialect. Something of the same kind obtains in Malay, where we have the *bahasa dalam* and the *bahasa dagang*. or "Raja Malay," and "bazaar Malay," as they are often termed. But the two dialects of Javanese are more distinct. The *krama* appears to be a factitious language made by changing all familiar words either by altering their terminations, or by adopting words from other languages, and is undoubtedly a modification of Javanese by the Hindu conquerors. It is used by every one in addressing a person of higher rank than the speaker, while the person thus addressed replies in the *ngoko*, which includes *tutoiement* among its peculiarities. From this custom it is evident that the lower the rank of the individual, the more frequently he is called upon to use the *krama*, and the curious result ensues that the poorer class speak the court language far better than do those of high rank. In writing, this court language is always used, though addresses and proclamations are in the vulgar tongue. Still another language, a species of mixture between these two, appears to be in use—the *madyo*—which is employed among intimates, as is also the *ngoko*.

The *kawi*, first brought prominently into notice by the labours of Wilhelm von Humboldt, was the ancient or religious language, and bears the same relation to the *ngoko* that Sanscrit does to the modern languages of Hindustan. In Bali and Lombok it is still the language of the priesthood, but in Java it is entirely a dead tongue, only found in ancient inscriptions and manuscripts. Kawi literature is abundant, and is wholly metrical, consisting of romances and histories founded on Hindu legends and ancient Javanese story, the authors and dates of which are entirely unknown.

Sundanese is ruder and less cultivated, although still possessed, like Javanese, of the two forms of court and vulgar language. It is spoken purest in the west extremity of the island, and is believed to have been introduced by some of the Malay tribes of Sumatra, in parts of which it is also spoken. Madurese, though allied to Javanese, is still sufficiently distinct to take rank as a language.

7. Religion and Education.

Little now remains, save the wonderful temples of Brambanam and Boro-bodor, to mark the wave of Buddhism and Brahmanism that overspread the island in the Middle Ages. Almost all the Javanese are Mohammedans by religion. But, just as the Hindu influence penetrated but little into the fastnesses of the western highlands, so the creed of the Prophet is considerably modified among the Sundanese of the present day. Every Javanese, indeed, of whatever nation, is more or less of a pagan, whose beliefs and superstitions place him scarcely on a higher level than the Papuan. Attributing to the action of good or malevolent spirits every incident of their lives, and adopting the saints of every calendar, they have succeeded in evolving a religion of their own, so different from that enjoined by Mohammed, that it has even been dignified by the separate title of Javanism. "The whole life of the Javanese, indeed, is enveloped in a mesh of mystery; not the stars only, and the heavens, rain influence, but from every object a spiritual emanation, invisible for the most part, but potent and exhaustless, flows forth to him for blessing or for curse. Even Mohammedanism with its One God has done little more than increase the number of supersensual beings to whom he prays. To Joseph he presents offerings that he may obtain beautiful children, to Solomon for honour and rank, to Moses for bravery, to Jesus for learning. The ritual of his religion—and his whole round of life is part of his religion—is intricate almost beyond conception, and at the same time rigid and precise. Everything must be done by rule and rubric; the unwritten law handed down from father to son admits of no curtailment or modification. Each individual class of offering must be prepared in its own peculiar way; the rice, for example—which is one of the chief sacrificial substances—must now be white, now red, now hard, now soft."[1]

The state of education in Java is far from being creditable to so cultured a people as the owners of the land. While in the Philippines we find a church in almost every village, and nearly 2000 schools which afford instruction to about 200,000 children, the Dutch have until lately studiously set their faces against both the education and the Christianising of the natives. Java at the present day has under 11,000 Christian natives. Everything which tended to lessen the distance between the two races was discouraged. The island was to be farmed by the Government, and was looked upon as private property. Nothing which could in any way become a source of difficulties and complications was to be permitted, however right or desirable it might be. The island was *terra clausa*, and the missionary was considered to have hardly more claim to enter it than the settler. Even as late as the second or third decade of this century the New Testament was considered a revolutionary work, and Herr Brückner, who translated it, had his edition destroyed by Government. All this, of course, is past, but so also is the opportunity for the moral and

[1] Mr. H. A. Webster in *Encyc. Brit.*

intellectual improvement of the native. The prestige of race might very well have carried in its train both Christianity and education, as it did with the Spaniards in the Philippines, but it is now disappearing, to leave behind it a semi-pagan Islamism and the knowledge gained by attendance at Mohammedan schools. The "culture-system" of the Dutch in Java has often been severely attacked, but there is much to be said in favour of it, and a far more serious charge to which Holland has to answer is her neglect of the education and religion of her Javanese subjects in past years.

8. Antiquities.

The original source of the Hindu religion in Java is not known. All that is known with any certainty is the date of its overthrow. In 1478, as has been already stated, the principality of Majapahit was conquered by the Mohammedans, and its great city destroyed. But between the time of the Hindu immigration and this date, whether we place the former in the sixth century or earlier, a period of many centuries must have elapsed, and from time to time, at dates which are for the most part conjectural, a vast number of magnificent palaces, temples, and cities, together with sculptures and other works of art, were erected, whose ruins now astonish the traveller as he comes upon them in the midst of the forest or on the mountain side. Volumes have been written upon these ruins from the time they were first brought to the notice of the antiquarian world at the beginning of this century to the publication of Dr. Leemans' great work on Boro-bodor, in 1884, and it would be impossible to notice here a tenth part of those already known and described. The ruins of the ancient city of Majapahit cover miles of ground, and consist of paved roads, walls, tombs, baths, and gateways, while sculptures of Hindu gods and goddesses in hard trachytic rock are often found in the forest, or remain *in situ* in the temples. Some of these buildings were of brick, and in their ruins show a degree of perfection of workmanship perhaps not equalled in any other part of the world. The bricks are exceedingly fine-grained and hard, with very flat surfaces and sharp angles. They are laid together with the greatest accuracy without any perceptible mortar or cement, yet often joining so closely that a penknife cannot be inserted between them. The surfaces seem, in fact, to adhere together in some incomprehensible manner. These brick buildings were richly ornamented with mouldings, projecting courses, recessed panels, and bold cornices, so as to produce a very fine architectural effect. The great temples and religious buildings, however, some of which remain in a sufficiently perfect state to give an idea of their size and beauty, were much more remarkable, and a short sketch of some of them will not be out of place.

One of the most extensive collections of sacred buildings is at Brambanam, near the centre of Java, between the native capitals of Jokjokarta and Surakarta. One set, called Loro-jongran, which has lately been fully excavated, consisted of twenty separate buildings, six large and fourteen small, the larger supposed to have been 90 feet high. They were all constructed of solid stone, everywhere decorated with carvings and bas-reliefs, and adorned with numbers of statues, many of which still remain entire. At Chandi Sewu—the "Thousand Temples"—in the same neighbourhood, are many colossal figures. Captain Baker, who surveyed these ruins, said that he had never seen "such stupendous and finished specimens of human labour, and of the science and taste of ages long since forgot, crowded together in so small a compass as in this spot." They form a quadrangle of 540 by 510 feet, exactly facing the cardinal points, and consist of an outer row of 84 small temples, a second row of 76, a third of 64, a fourth of 44, and the fifth forming an inner parallelogram of 28—in all 296 small temples, disposed in five regular parallelograms. In the centre is a large cruciform temple surrounded by lofty flights of steps, richly ornamented with sculpture, and containing many apartments. The tropical vegetation has ruined most of the smaller temples, but some remain tolerably perfect, from which the effect of the whole may be gathered. About half a mile off is another temple, called Chandi Kali Bening, 72 feet square and about 60 feet in height, in very fine preservation, and covered with sculptures of Hindu mythology surpassing any that exist in India. Other ruins of palaces, halls, and temples, with abundance of sculptured deities, are found in the same neighbourhood.

The great temple of Boro-bodor is situated in the Kedu residency, near the Praga River, and not far from Jokjokarta. It is one of the largest and most striking ruins in the world, and may be roughly described as an enormous block of building 530 feet square and about 120 feet high, occupying the summit of a hill, and consisting of six terraces raised one above the other, and culminating in a dagoba-like cupola, which is surrounded by 72 smaller temples of a similar shape, arranged in a triple row. The terraced walls are surmounted by 400 sedent figures of Buddha in covered niches, and the walls of the terraces on both

TEMPLE OF BORO-BODOE, JAVA.

sides are covered with bas-reliefs, elaborately executed in hard stone, and illustrative of Hindu mythology in the strangest mixture of Buddhism and Brahmanism. These sculptures have been estimated to occupy an extent of wall of nearly three miles in length, and the amount of labour and skill expended upon this stupendous temple must have been as great as, if not greater than, that required to build the Great Pyramid. Unlike the dagobas of Ceylon, the apical cupola—which is 50 feet in diameter—is a hollow chamber, which shows no trace of a shrine. The enigmatical verse, which, as in the case of the Hindus, serves as Javanese chronology, places the date of the construction of the building at A.D. 1344, which may possibly be correct, for the perfect preservation of the greater part of the structure is against its being of any great antiquity.

Although few or no remains of temples are to be found in the mountainous Sunda lands, where, indeed, the Hindu influence never established itself, the mountains of Central and Eastern Java were special objects of veneration by those who followed the cult of Siva, and innumerable *chandis* or temples are found upon their slopes and summits. The plateau of Dieng, overlooking the vast extinct crater of Gunong Prau, has the most remarkable group of this nature. Vast flights of steps lead up to it from opposite sides of the mountain, each flight consisting of more than 1000 steps. Traces of nearly 400 temples have been found here and in the neighbourhood, all of which appear to have been decorated with rich and delicate sculptures, and others of smaller size are met with at or near the actual summit of the mountain. Upon the great volcano Lawu, to the south-west of Samarang, are temples of a later date and different character. They rise in terraces one above the other, are roughly built, and ornamented with sculptures of a grotesque and obscene nature and rude execution. There are no Hindu images, but representations of animals and monsters only, and the temples were no doubt dedicated to the worship of the Linga or Hindu Priapus in its grossest form. The whole country from Gunong Prau to Jokjokarta, a distance of 60 miles, abounds with ruins, so that fine sculptured images may be seen built into the walls of enclosures, or lying neglected in ditches. When all these wonderful buildings were in their full perfection Java must have presented a very different appearance from that of the present day, when wooden houses or low white-washed huts are alone to be seen through the greater part of the interior. The Mohammedans destroyed most of these temples as signs of paganism, and they are now looked upon by the natives as the work of superior beings or of demons, and the arts of architecture and sculpture are totally lost.

9. Agriculture and Trade.

The Malay of Java is perhaps more essentially an agriculturist than any others of his race in the archipelago. Rice being the staple food, enormous quantities of it are needed and produced for the twenty-three million persons inhabiting the island, and the harvest may be put at an average of $4\frac{1}{2}$ millions of tons. Very little is exported, and indeed in some years importation is even necessary. The common *Oryza sativa* is grown chiefly upon the irrigated lower grounds or *sawatis*, but other varieties of the cereal are used for the non-irrigated or *tagal* lands. Its cultivation with the natives is almost a religion, and is hedged about with countless superstitions which often interfere with good farming. On the whole, however, it may be said that the better part of the land is highly cultivated. In Madura, maize partly supplies the place of rice, owing to the flatter nature of the country. A system of communal proprietorship obtains in most parts, the land being annually redivided, but much is held by individual owners. All new land won from the forest by clearing becomes the property of the person clearing it.

Although there were in 1890 over five million acres of rice-land in cultivation in the lowlands, it is not to this, but to the higher botanical zones that the Government looks for its profit. Coffee has been said to be the pivot upon which everything in Java turns, though how much longer it will remain so is another question. It was first introduced in 1696, and early in the last century was being exported in fair quantity. Upon the introduction of the "culture-system" in 1830 a considerable increase took place, and before the devastation caused by the appearance of the *Hemileia vastatrix* in 1879, some 60,000 tons were annually sent to Holland. In 1887 the return was only 17,750 tons, and although that of the following year was somewhat better, the decrease has been steady. In 1890, the lowest crop of the half century, 15,578 tons, was obtained, and that of 1891 was estimated at not more than 11,000 tons. This is the Government export; that of private growers is rather greater in amount. At the last computation there were 114 million coffee trees in cultivation as against 250 millions in former years. The Government, while admitting that the future prospects of the island in this respect are far from favourable, and that there is no product which in the immediate future can be looked for to take the place of coffee, are averse to a modification of the existing culture-system, "which may result in a sacrifice of certain interests in order to secure other uncertain advantages." The favourable points of the case are that during the last two or three years a considerable area has been newly planted on cleared lands in eastern Java, and the cultivation of the disease-resisting Liberian tree has been largely instituted in the low-lying grounds. In spite of the events of recent years, the island is only surpassed by Brazil in the value of its annual crop. The Pasuruan and Preanger districts together furnish more than half of the entire quantity grown upon the island.

Sugar, like coffee, was formerly a Government monopoly, but is no longer so, and the greater proportion of it is grown by large companies. It is the most valuable of all the island exports, for Java again holds the second place in the production of this article, and only yields to Cuba. The growth of sugar is an old industry which has much increased of late years, for while at the beginning of the present century the annual crop was only 6000 tons, that of 1890 amounted to 400,000 tons, of which 362,344—valued at over £4,000,000—were exported. The production has been very steady since 1884, and the improved returns of 1890 are ascribed to a new system of cultivation. Surabaya is the centre of the principal sugar-growing districts.

Although the three crops above mentioned—rice, coffee, and sugar—may be said to be the staples of Java, the island yields many other valuable products in great abundance. The cinchona bark obtained in 1890 was not far short of 7 million lbs., and the estimated crop for 1891 nearly 8 million, or about four-sevenths of the world's consumption. Of greater value still is the tobacco, the worth of the 1890 crop being estimated at about £2,000,000. Other noteworthy products, placed in the order of their value, are indigo, tea, hides, pepper, gum-dammar, copra, and coco-nuts, while large quantities of teak find their way from the Government forests to European shipbuilding yards. The import trade is a thriving one. Cotton goods to the value of two million pounds annually pass the custom-house, and the mineral oil lamps which light nearly every peasant's hut consume over 20 million gallons per annum. Concessions were granted in 1890, both in Java and Sumatra, for the working of petroleum, and the prospects are said to be very encouraging.

The villages, embowered in fruit trees and coco-nut palms, appear like gardens. Vast quantities of bananas are grown, of many different varieties, among them a bright red plantain from 12 to 16 inches in length. Cassava and yams are also much cultivated. The island is said to be insufficiently stocked with cattle, especially in the Sunda districts. The census of January 1889 showed a slight increase. There were then 2,630,400 buffaloes, 2,208,100 bullocks, and 536,900 horses. The latter animals, although useful and strong for their size, are not equal to the smaller race from Sumbawa and Sandalwood Island, or even to the ponies of Sumatra. The total value of the exports from Java in 1890 amounted to £10,494,353.

10. Government and Revenue.

The system of administration in Java has already been described (p. 99). It remains only to be said that the aim of the Government is to rule the natives by natives—if not actually, at all events nominally. The native "Regent" is treated with a considerable amount of respect and ceremonial, but he is, nevertheless, a mere puppet in the hands of the Dutch. Drawing a large salary in virtue of his post, and having merely nominal duties, he is wise enough in most cases to carry out the wishes of his European masters. If not, he is dismissed, and dismissal means virtual ruin. Other native officials are the *waidonos* and *mantris*, with whom the Dutch "Controleur" is chiefly brought in contact. A large portion of the time of the latter officer is employed in business connected with the "culture-system."

No account of Java would be complete without some description of this "culture-system," and its connection with the *corvée*, which has been so fiercely attacked since the publication of *Max Havelaar*. Introduced by General van den Bosch in 1830, it has survived in a modified form to the present day. It was based upon the plan, which has already been alluded to, of excluding Europeans and making the island a Government farm. It aimed at bringing the most scientific farming to bear upon the most remunerative products, and at utilising such time and labour of the peasant as was not needed for the cultivation of his necessary bread-stuffs. The natives of the *dessas* where the land appeared suitable were called upon to plant the various trees or seeds provided for them by the Government. Their number or acreage was decided by the same authority, as were also the site, the season, and the method of cultivation. A fixed rate of wages was paid to the labourers engaged in clearing the ground and forming the plantations, and the produce was bought by Government at a fixed price. This money, after the deduction of a certain percentage for the chiefs, was divided among the labourers, the sum in good years being considerable. In this manner were established the greater part of the numerous plantations of coffee, sugar, tobacco, tea, pepper, and other products which cover the island. Of these, coffee alone is now thus grown, and even here the "system" has been considerably modified, no person being required to plant more than fifty trees annually, and the labourers being no longer called out *en masse* as was formerly the case. The Government cultivation of sugar was given up in 1890. In 1882 it was decided to commute part of the labour by the introduction of a capitation tax of one florin, and it was found that the sum thus obtained was larger than was required for carrying out the works previously performed by *corvée*. For road repair, however, and various other minor duties, this system is still in force, and will probably remain so for some time.

From a European point of view, the "culture-system" and its attendant *corvée* is no doubt indefensible. But it should be remembered that what is suitable among civilised nations is by no means always advisable in the case of a people who are socially and educationally immature. From time immemorial the natives of Java have been accustomed to render labour service to their chiefs and princes, and it is doubtful whether the substitution of money-taxes will be in any way more acceptable to them. The experiment of passing at one stride from the feudalism of the Middle Ages to the civilisation of the nineteenth century would not have been a wise one. The method of paternal government adopted by the Dutch has taught the people habits of steady industry and the art of scientific farming, and whether it be abolished now or retained for some years to come, it will still have served good purpose in bridging over this gulf, which with us has been filled up and effaced by many centuries of time. Taxation and the free admission of the white man will be a doubtful benefit to the labourer, since it will open the way to greater commercial activity, which will lead to the gradual alienation of the land to capitalists, give an unnatural stimulus to the population, and inevitably introduce the evils of feverish competition, pauperism, and crime, from which the country has hitherto been comparatively free. European rulers, imbued with ideas of freedom of labour and of commerce, will not understand that a child-like people can only be raised to independence and national manhood by means of a paternal government. It may safely be predicted that if the Dutch Government freely throw open Java to the world, the result will be that many capitalists will make fortunes, but the native inhabitants will not be benefited. But the system must be judged by its results. The island may have been " bled to the extent of nearly 50 millions of pounds for the benefit of the mother-country," as has been alleged, but this bleeding has been done without any oppression of the natives, who are well fed, decently clothed, and as happy and contented as any people are likely to be under the rule of an alien race. One of the best tests of the general well-being of a community is that of the growth of the population; for where this is steadily increasing, where there is no pauperism, where serious crime is rare, and where famine and rebellion on any important scale are almost unknown, the Government cannot be otherwise than suitable to the people governed. This is the case with Java. In 1850 the population was about $9\frac{1}{2}$ millions, in 1890 it had increased to 23 millions, and notwithstanding that a large portion of its surface is covered with virgin forest and lofty mountains, it supports a population of greater density than Great Britain. With such facts as these before us, it must be conceded that however theoretically wrong the "culture-system" may be, it has at least been productive of considerable benefit to the Javanese.

The revenue and expenditure of Java occupies about two-thirds of the Netherlands India Budget, and upon the abundance or deficiency of its crops the variations in that document largely depend. Apart from customs and other dues the revenue is chiefly derived from coffee, the opium and salt monopolies, and the rent of land. The Budget for the eight years inclusive, from 1884 to 1891, shows extraordinary irregularity. Thus in 1887 the revenue exceeded the expenditure by £2,091,652, while in 1891 there was a deficiency of £1,702,194. The mean surplus for these eight years was about £75,000. No surplus, however, can safely be counted upon, and there is no doubt that the prosperity of Java, which was formerly so great as to admit of a large and certain annual contribution being made towards the revenue of the mother-country, has been for many years diminishing.

11. Population. Towns.

In January, 1890, the census gave the united population of Java and Madura as 22,819,074, of which 233,717 were Chinese, and 13,365 "Arabs." The Europeans numbered 42,364. Central and some parts of Eastern Java and the island of Madura show the densest population, the Sunda lands being only sparsely inhabited. The mean density of the population of the nine provinces of Central Java is 657 to the square mile, while that of Belgium, the most thickly populated of European countries, is only 530. In the province of Bagelen the density reaches the astonishing figure of 964 to the square mile. It is said that in the year 1780 the population was not much more than 2,000,000. At the end of 1892, it was certainly not much less than 24,000,000, and that there is room for still further increase is evident from the fact that not more than one-third of the entire island is under cultivation.

The following are the names of the provinces and their capitals :—

Division.	Provinces.	Capital.	Area in sq. Miles.
Western Java	Bantam	Serang	3190
	Batavia	Batavia	2631
	Krawang	Purwakarta	1785
	Cheribon	Cheribon	2608
	Preanger Regencies	Bandong	8170
	Tagal	Tagal	1466
	Banyumas	Banyumas	2147
	Pekalongan	Pekalongan	691
	Bagelen	Purworejo	1324
Central Java	Samarang	Samarang	2002
	Kedu	Magelang	791
	Jokjokarta	Jokjokarta	1192
	Japara	Pati	1205
	Surakarta	Surakarta	2404
	Rembang	Rembang	2910
	Madiun	Madiun	2506
	Surabaya	Surabaya	2091
	Kediri	Kediri	2610
Eastern Java	Pasuruan	Pasuruan	2066
	Probolingo	Probolingo	1126
	Besuki (with Banyuwangi)	Besuki	3723
	Madura	Pamekasan	2033

Total area of Java, 48,638 square miles; of Madura, 2033—total, 50,671 square miles. There are three towns with over 100,000 inhabitants—Surabaya, Surakarta, and Batavia.

After Batavia, which, with its hill station, Buitenzorg, demands a separate notice, SURABAYA (pop. 129,000) is the chief town. In population and commercial importance it surpasses the capital, its port being the best in the island. It is, in fact, with the exception of Chilatjap on the south coast, the only natural harbour that Java possesses, the others being merely open roadsteads. The Government dockyards and arsenals are situated here, and large sums have been spent on the fortification of the place. The river is navigable by boats far into the interior, and is the means of bringing down an enormous quantity of rice, sugar, and other products, the surrounding province being exceedingly fertile and thickly populated. A little to the north is Gressi, now almost deserted, but at one time a place of considerable importance, and of interest as being the chief town frequented by the Portuguese after their conquest of Malacca.

SAMARANG suffers, like most of the ports of Java, from being without protection, and is a very dangerous anchorage in the north-west monsoon. It is, nevertheless, one of the chief commercial cities of the island, and had a population of over 70,000 in 1886. It appears to be decreasing, for by the census of 1878 there were nearly 80,000 inhabitants, but there is no great falling off in the exports. Its situation is ill adapted both for health and commerce, a mile or more of low-lying marshy ground intervening between it and the sea, which is only to be reached by a raised causeway. As at Surabaya and other towns the river has been canalised, and piers protect its mouth. In many ways, however, Samarang rivals the last-mentioned port. The buildings are finer, and the town has been arranged after the home model.

CHILATJAP possesses the best harbour upon the south coast. It is an open port both for export and import trade, and its favourable position has caused a wonderful increase in its consequence. It is in connection by the

Eastern Railway system with Samarang and Surabaya, and a line is in course of construction to Garut and Chichalengka, which will join it with Batavia. It is guarded by the forts on Kambangan island and by batteries on the mainland, and has a considerable garrison. CHERIBON, a town almost opposite to it on the north side of the island, is of secondary rank only, and is chiefly celebrated for its horses.

The above are the only towns in Java with many European residents. SURAKARTA, or Solo, the chief junction of the Eastern Railway system, although almost entirely native, possesses a larger number of inhabitants than any of them, the population at the last census being over 130,000. It is here that the Susuhunan, or Emperor of Java, still exercises a nominal sway over a province of more than a million of his subjects, but under the supervision of a Dutch Resident, with a force of 500 soldiers and a fort. The Emperor lives in considerable state, and is surrounded by an amount of luxury and magnificence hardly surpassed by any of the native princes of India. JOKJOKARTA, the capital of the province of that name, is not far from Surakarta, and, like it, is a native city ruled by a sultan. It is finely situated beneath the great cone of Merapi, and from the proximity of Brambanam and other ruins is very frequently visited by tourists. It has about 90,000 inhabitants.

12. The Capital; Life and Manners.

Towards the end of the sixteenth century the Dutch formed their first settlement in Bantam, driving out the Portuguese, and making the city one of the most important in the East, at a time when Batavia was not even in existence. It was only in 1619 that this latter city was established on the ruins of the Javanese town of Jacatra by the Dutch general Koen, but it was not long in supplanting its rival, and the capital is now of considerable extent, although its population, which, by the census of 1886, was 100,485, is inferior to that of Surabaya. Various misfortunes have hampered its growth. In 1699 the terrific eruption of Mount Salak swept away its houses and gardens, choked its streams with mud, and rendered it so unhealthy from malaria that it is said that over a million people perished between 1730 and 1752. Until lately the shoaling of its roadstead has still further interfered with its prosperity. At the time of its foundation Batavia consisted of a citadel built at the mouth of the little river Liwong, and a small town to the south of it, situated in the bend of the stream and protected by a fosse and a wall of fortifications upon its eastern side. The streets were intersected by canals after the Dutch fashion, and these combined with the walls to aggravate the natural unhealthiness of the site,—a fact that was recognised early in the present century by Marshal Daendels, at that time Governor. Under his administration the mass of suburbs, of which Weltevreden is the nucleus, was first commenced about two miles to the south of the city, and in a few years the latter was deserted by Europeans for the new town.

There is little either of interest or beauty in the first view of Batavia usually obtained by the traveller. His vessel anchors a mile and a half or more from the shore, the flatness of which is its most noticeable feature. The river, as in many of the Java ports, has been canalised, and here the canal extends not only to its mouth, but is built out seaward for nearly three-quarters of a mile. Up this the traveller rows for some distance, past many

STREET IN EUROPEAN QUARTER, BATAVIA.

unsavoury native suburbs, to the city, whence the train, or a showy open cab drawn by a pair of horses, conveys him to the European quarter. By road he passes Molenvliet, a connecting link of houses and huts, surrounded by gardens, and bordered by a canal which joins the city to Noordwijk, Rijswijk, and Weltevreden—the three European villages or districts grouped around the Koningsplein. This Koningsplein, which, in spite of latitude, reminds the Englishman not a little of Woolwich Common, is similarly used by the troops here quartered, and its vast open space is no doubt of great service in ventilating the district, and freeing it from malaria. The walks and roads in these suburbs, although not equal to those of the towns of the Spice Islands, are nevertheless charming in their beauty and in the wealth of their tropical foliage, and the houses, with their neat appearance and characteristic white-pillared entrances, are equally attractive. The broad roads are bordered with trees meeting overhead to form arched avenues, and as most of the houses are low and are surrounded by gardens full of fruit trees, palms, and flowering shrubs, the general effect is very pleasing. While Batavia proper is given up to warehouses, shops, and offices, and peopled by Malays, Chinese, and Arabs, the European suburbs just named have within their limits all the chief hotels, clubs, museums, theatres, and other places of amusement. In Rijswijk is the Governor-General's residence and the Government offices; the museum and other public edifices are in the Koningsplein, and the barracks and civil and military hospital in Weltevreden. The Dutch in Java have done much to further science, and their various learned societies established here have published numerous valuable papers upon the fauna and flora as well as upon the ethnology of the islands, of which their museums and the magnificent botanic gardens at Buitenzorg are excellently illustrative. Meester Cornelis, with 71,000 inhabitants, is a suburb still further to the south, but is hardly sufficiently connected with the capital to be included with it. It is memorable as the site of the engagement with Daendels in 1811, which brought Java under English rule. Two other towns, Tangerang and Bekasi, inhabited chiefly by Chinese, lie respectively to the west and east of the old town, and much of the intervening ground is occupied by the huts and holdings of small cultivators, so that the city of Batavia, taken as a whole, occupies a very much wider area than might from its population be expected. Nevertheless, as has been said, it is neither the largest nor the most thriving city in the island, and the explanation of this doubtless lies partly in the difficulties that the roadstead offers to shipping. So rapidly does the land gain on the sea that the shore-line is over a mile seaward of its position on the founding of the city. After many proposals, it was at length settled to make an artificial harbour at Tanjong Priok, a point some six miles east of Batavia, and the work was successfully concluded in 1887. Two enormous piers, each over a mile in length, project from the shore into a depth of four fathoms, sheltering between them a sheet of water half a mile in width, which is capable of receiving the largest ships at low water. Two large dry docks are also in course of construction, and the new harbour is connected by road, railway, canal, and telegraph with Batavia. The only drawback to this splendid harbour is its great unhealthiness.

Although in no way a suburb of Batavia, from which it is distant some 45 miles, BUITENZORG may be mentioned here as the hill-station of that city, and the usual place of residence of the governors-general. The railway

RESIDENCE OF GOVERNOR-GENERAL, BUITENZORG.

renders it easy of access, and the European residents visit it in large numbers to escape the heat and malaria of the capital. Its height above the sea (870 feet) scarcely entitles it to be called a sanatorium, and for this purpose Sindang Laja, a station on the northern slopes of Gede at an elevation of 3500 feet, is used, but the climate is delightful as a change from Batavia, the mornings and evenings being deliciously cool. Here are the celebrated botanic gardens, in which nearly every vegetable product of the East is cultivated; to the number, it is said, of over 9000 species. The country around is wonderfully picturesque, and the view southward looking towards the striking peak of Salak is celebrated as one of the most beautiful in the world.

Life in Batavia may be taken, *mutatis mutandis*, as a good example of life in any other settlement in the Dutch East Indies. In the lower town the Malays and Chinese lead a semi-aquatic existence around the canals, in whose unsavoury waters the germs of cholera may be said to be endemic. The same trades, the same street scenes are here as the traveller finds at Singapore, but there is an even greater mixture of nationalities. Roggewein, writing in the early part of the seventeenth century, speaks of this heterogeneous mixture of different races, and it is probable that they have increased rather than diminished since his day. Batavia is the great emporium of this vast archipelago of Australasia, and from almost every island come the praus of the traders laden with every sort of product, from the dye-woods of Sumatra to the paradise birds of New Guinea. The only industry specially characteristic of Batavia is the weaving of bamboo hats, mats, and boxes, which employs many thousands of people during a portion of the year. Vast numbers of these hats are made for the Paris market, and the value of the export is very considerable.

But if native life is much the same in Netherlands India as it is in our own Eastern possessions, the manners and customs of the Europeans show little similarity with those of the English in India. "*Cœlum non animum mutant*," is less true of the Dutch than of ourselves, and there is more of England in India and the Straits than of Holland in Java. The inordinate length of service without furlough which the officials of the Netherlands India have to endure partly explains this, and it is partly due to many, both of this and the merchant class, making the island their permanent home. At Buitenzorg and in Weltevreden they are within reach of a wide social circle, and in command of every comfort of modern civilisation. The skies are kinder, and the exigencies of fashion less strict than at home. In most parts of the East Indian Archipelago the Dutch ladies adopt the native dress in the morning—a silk *sarong* or petticoat, a loose lace-edged linen jacket (the *kibaya*), and a pair of gold-embroidered slippers, and in this costume walk about or take their customary morning drive. In the morning and late afternoon the merchant or official devotes himself to business, the midday hours being given up to the siesta. The midday meal or *rijsttafel* corresponds to the French *déjeûner*, and consists largely of curry dishes, for which Java and the Moluccas are celebrated. Business over, the Dutchman seeks the "Harmonie," or club, drinks his *pijtje*, and plays a game of billiards or cards. Games demanding much exertion and sports do not find much favour in his eyes, albeit he has a taste for horse flesh, breeds most wonderful little ponies, and is always riding or driving. Afternoon calls are generally paid during the hour before late dinner, and if of a ceremonial nature, custom ordains that the gentleman must wear a black tail-coat, and at least carry a hat, even if he do not wear it. Under ordinary circumstances no head-covering is ever worn during the daily evening walk or drive. Balls are frequent, and the hospitality offered to the stranger in Java is on the most liberal scale. The ceremonial and state surrounding the person of the Governor-General is as great as that attending our own Viceregal court in India, and some of the sultans have retinues and surroundings not less magnificent than those of our own native princes.

Travel in Java has of late years been considerably simplified by the construction of an elaborate railway system, which serves chiefly the central and eastern parts of the island, placing Samarang, Surabaya, Surakarta, Jokjokarta, Chilatjap, and all the other large towns in communication with each other. Batavia is the starting-point of another system in the western portion of the island, which is very soon to connect with this at Chilatjap. At the beginning of 1890 there were 762 miles of railway open to traffic, of which about half belongs to the State. There are also nearly 150 miles of steam tramway. The magnificent road system, which forms a network over the whole of Java, connecting all the principal towns, is very largely due to the initiative of Marshal Daendels, who at the beginning of this century constructed the great trunk road from end to end of the island, 800 miles in length. The law which compels every peasant to give a certain number of days' work upon the roads, results in their being kept in excellent condition, and the posting system which serves them is equally good, although extremely expensive. The post-houses are at short intervals along the main road, and the traveller may either get coolies or horses to carry him, day and night, at the rate of ten miles an hour.

CHAPTER VI

SUMATRA

1. General.

SUMATRA, the westernmost of all the Dutch Indian possessions, is one of the largest islands in the world, and in the archipelago is surpassed in size only by New Guinea and Borneo. Its extreme length is about 1060 miles, its greatest breadth 260, and its area, so far as an insufficient survey can admit of its being calculated, about 170,000 square miles. It lies with its long axis in a N.W. and S.E. direction, and is traversed from north to south by an almost unbroken chain of mountains, many of which are volcanoes. This chain lies close to the western shore, and hence the island may be roughly described as presenting a high, steep wall, and straight, almost harbourless coast-line, to the Indian Ocean, guarded by an outlying chain of large islands; while the eastern portion, which goes to form the Strait of Malacca, is low, flat, and alluvial, intersected with large rivers forming great deltas, and consequently provided with numerous harbours. At the south, Sumatra is separated from Java by the great ocean highway known as the Straits of Sunda, and memorable of late years as the site of the appalling eruption of Krakatau. A considerable portion

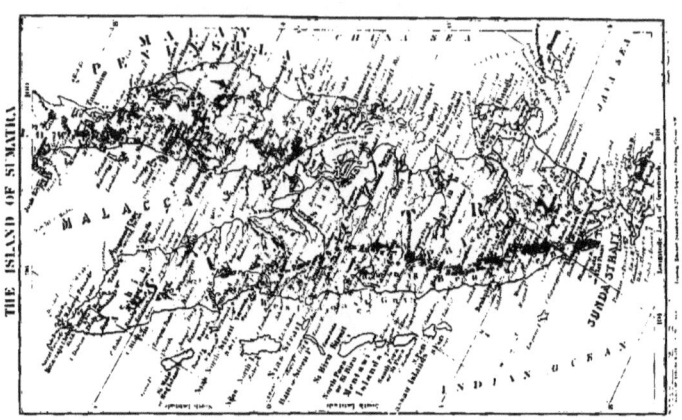

of the centre of the island remains yet unexplored, and in the north the Dutch have for more than twenty years been vainly endeavouring to subdue Ache (Atjeh or Acheen), of the interior of which little or nothing is known. While Java is throughout its whole extent brought under the influence of civilisation, and covered with a network of roads and railways, Sumatra still remains to all intents and purposes a wild and savage land; the only parts at all well known and settled by the Dutch being the district lying between Palembang and Benkulen, the country around Padang and Deli, and the Lampongs. In this respect European civilisation has but followed in the footsteps of Hindu influence. We have seen Java to be everywhere strewn with the ruins of innumerable temples of the Indian cults, except perhaps in the Sunda lands, but here in Sumatra such remains are not nearly so common, and are of no architectural importance. The marked inferiority and lack of progress in Sumatra is not very easily explained; it is certainly not to be entirely accounted for by any peculiar advantages of Javanese soil.

2. History.

The first account which we have of Sumatra is that of Marco Polo, who states that he was delayed five months in one of its ports by the S.W. monsoon during his passage through the archipelago in 1291. He calls it Java Minor, and claims to have visited six out of the eight kingdoms into which it was said to be at that time divided, but much of the story is obviously fictional. Ludovic Varthema is the next European we know certainly to have visited it, but not until more than 200 years later, landing at Pedir, in Ache, in 1505. He identifies the island with Taprobana, but calls it Sumatra, using the orthography of the present day. He speaks of the pepper, aloes, silks, and other products of the island, and states that it was divided into four kingdoms, that gold, silver, and tin coin was current, and that the practice of suttee or concremation was in vogue. Diego Lopes de Sequeira, with Magellan as one of his officers, landed at the same port in September 1509, and concluded a treaty with the raja. Thenceforward, and especially after the fall of Malacca in 1511, the island was frequently visited, and in Schöner's globe of 1523 we find it represented with very tolerable accuracy. In the *Carta Universal* of Diego Ribero, published in Seville in 1529, it is extraordinarily well plotted, both as regards outline and position; while, on the other hand, it is curious to note that the northern coast of Java is alone depicted, so that it is probable that the former island had been circumnavigated before southern Java had been visited by Europeans. For many centuries before the arrival of the Portuguese in the archipelago, the commerce of the ports had been in the hands of the Arabs, and in Ache this appears to have been especially the case, resulting to a certain extent in the fusion of the immigrants with the native population—a fact which may partially account for the marked difference in type of the Achenese of the present day from the other island tribes. From the earliest times the Hindus carried on trade with Sumatra, and there is sufficient evidence in the remains of Hindu temples to show that they had at one time established their religion among the natives. But it was earlier ousted by Islamism than was the case in Java, and Marco Polo found the people of the eastern coasts Mohammedans at the time of his visit in 1291.

At some period to which it is impossible to assign a date, the southern part was largely colonised from Java, and the two kingdoms of Menangkabo and Palembang established, or at all events largely peopled. That this was long anterior to the advent of the Europeans is evident from the fact that Malacca was a colony founded by settlers from Palembang, and that the former city had been in existence for more than 200 years before its fall in 1511. The Portuguese never succeeded in establishing themselves in Sumatra any more than in Java, although they had many unimportant trading settlements, and were involved in many small wars with the natives. The Dutch first came in 1598, and in 1685 the English, driven by them out of Bantam in Java, built a fort and factory at Benkulen. This was not, however, their first acquaintance with the island, for Sir James Lancaster, with a fleet of four vessels, had already borne a letter from Queen Elizabeth to the King of Ache in 1602, and had concluded a friendly treaty with him. The British tenure of Benkulen lasted until 1824, when the settlement was handed over to the Dutch in exchange for Malacca, after an expensive and useless occupation of 140 years. The history of the Dutch in Sumatra is that of slow but steady progress in the acquisition of territory, although the Ache war, which has lasted over twenty years, shows at present no sign of termination.

3. Geology, Orography, etc.

The physical structure of Sumatra is a combination of that of Java with that of the Malay peninsula. The great mountain masses appear to be composed largely of Palæozoic rocks; slates, and clay schists, etc., and much granite, from amid which rise the peaks of volcanoes, both active and extinct. Carboniferous limestones and marls occur freely, but rocks of the Secondary Period are conspicuously absent. It is otherwise with the Tertiary formation, which is strongly developed. The coal-measures, which are recent, appear to be very extensive.

The central mountainous ridge, the general name for which is Barisan or the "Chain," consists in the broadest parts of the island of more than one crest, the intervening plateaux, lakes, or valleys, and secondary connecting ranges. The nearness of this chain of mountains to the west coast causes the larger part of the drainage to find its way to the Straits of Malacca and the Java Sea, and hence the detritus from the mountains has been for ages forming the great alluvial belt which extends along the whole of the eastern side, and silting up the straits. The island, in point of fact, is slowly but surely altering its position, and gaining steadily to the eastward, so that the time is, geologically speaking, not far distant when it will have reunited itself to the mainland from which it has so long been separated.

The two islands at the north end of Sumatra, Pulo Bras and Pulo Wai, familiar to all who navigate the Straits of Malacca, are in reality the commencement of the chain just mentioned. The first peak upon the mainland itself lies at no great distance from Ache, and is known to the natives as Selawa-jantan or Yamura (5663 feet), and to the Dutch as Goudberg. From here a secondary range runs eastward to Diamond Cape, but the mountains are of no great height, and not comparable in grandeur to Mounts Abong-abong and Lusé to the south. These volcanoes, being in the territory of the hostile Achenese, have never yet been ascended, but their heights have been estimated at over 11,100 and 12,100 feet respectively, and if these be correct there is no doubt that Lusé is the highest peak in Sumatra. A little farther to the south the main range forks, and at this point is the most important of the mountain lakes of Sumatra, many of which, it may be remarked, are formed in extinct craters. This sheet of water, known as Lake Toba, is of considerable size, being 45 miles in length and 15 in breadth, and is occupied in the centre by a large insuloid mass of land which is joined to the shore by the narrowest possible connection. This lake thus resembles very closely Lake Taal in the Philippines, for the central island, if we may so term it, although not now active, is, like that of Taal, a volcano, and the narrow connecting causeway has been formed by ashes ejected from its crater. The shores of Lake Toba are thickly populated by Battaks, among whom the Dutch are represented by a "Controleur." Almost on the equator is Mount Ophir (9610 feet), the isolated position and fine outline of which render it a well-known object to seamen. It is a volcano, but is now extinct. Merapi, the next peak of any importance, is very far from being so, and its eruptions have been more numerous than those of any other Sumatran volcano—at all events during the present century, a fact which partly explains its Malay name, the Fire Destroyer. Although by no means the loftiest mountain in the chain, the Malays have adapted a form of the story of the ark to it, and regard it as their Ararat.

During the Central Sumatran Expedition of 1877, Mr. Veth ascended the Talang and Korinchi or Indrapura volcanoes. The former, which is 8343 feet in height, dominates the city of Padang, and although now inactive, affords the natives an inexhaustible store of sulphur. Korinchi, which was found to measure about 3600 metres, in other words, not far short of 12,000 feet, is a far finer peak, with an enormous crater, some hundreds of yards in depth, which appears to emit steam almost without intermission. Other volcanoes, of scarcely less importance, occupy the more southern portion of the chain, the chief of which are Kaba and Dempo. The former, although of comparatively low altitude (5413 feet), has been quite recently the scene of a succession of eruptions which, though not destructive to human life, have covered the surrounding districts with sand, and destroyed its vegetation and animals. Dempo, visited and described by Mr. H. O. Forbes, attains a height of 10,562 feet. It is in a state of constant activity, and every three or four years discharges a "sulphur rain" which injures or destroys all the crops in the adjacent country. The Merapi, or present active crater, is about half a mile in diameter, with a lake of liquid mud at the bottom, some 70 yards across, which is from time to time converted into a gigantic geyser. Mr. Forbes thus describes the phenomenon:—

"We had sat thus for ten or twelve minutes when I noted that the centre of the white basin had become intensely black and scored with dark streaks. This area gradually increased. . . . The lake was becoming engulfed. A few minutes later a dull, sullen roar was heard, and I had just time to conjecture within myself whence it had proceeded, when the whole lake heaved and rose in the air for some hundreds of feet, not as if violently ejected, but with calm, majestic upheaval, and then fell back on itself with an awesome roar, which reverberated round and round the vast caldron, and echoed from rocky wall to rocky wall like the surge of an angry sea; and the immense volume of steam, let loose from its prison-house, dissipated itself into the air. The wave circles died away on the margin of the lake, which resumed its burnished face, and again reflected the blue sky, and silence reigned again until the geyser had gathered force for another expiration. .... Thus all day long the lake was swallowed up and vomited forth once in every fifteen or twenty minutes."

The most important mountain in the Lampong district is Tangkamus, better known to the Dutch as Keizers Spits, which dominates the head of Samangka Bay, and is estimated to be 7422 feet in height. The peaks at the extreme end of the island are of no great height. All the mountains we have mentioned are volcanoes, whether extinct or active, as are probably almost all in Sumatra. Their number has been estimated at sixty-six, but so much of the interior remains unexplored that these figures can only be approximate.

Of all the volcanic eruptions known to have occurred, either in ancient or modern times, that of the island of Krakatau, in the Sunda Straits, which will be fresh in the mind of every reader, was at once the most stupendous, the most wide-spread in its effects, and the most destructive of human life. As far as regards the actual amount of matter ejected, and the area and duration of the darkness caused by the volcanic dust, other eruptions have exceeded it, as for example that of Tambora, in Sumbawa, in 1815, and of the Skaptar Jökull, in Iceland, in 1783. But in the suddenness and violence of the explosions, and in the disastrous effect of the resulting "seismic wave," it is without an equal. By this great eruption the volcano was completely eviscerated. A mass of matter, of not less than $1\frac{1}{5}$ cubic mile in size, was blown into the air in the course of a few hours, and nearly 40,000 people perished.

Of the former history of the volcano, geology tells us something. The island of Krakatau and its satellites, previous to the eruption, formed in reality only the lip or edge of a crater, the wreck of some former volcanic cone, which was probably not less than 10,000 or 12,000 feet high and 25 miles in circumference at its base. That this great mountain must have been gradually built up in comparatively modern times is evident from the fact that beneath the mass of which its ruins are composed there are deposits of post-Tertiary age, which in turn rest on the widely distributed Tertiary rocks so well developed in Java and Sumatra. Subsequent to the ancient eruption which destroyed this mountain, secondary craters must at some time have formed within and around the eviscerated cone, and the volcano was in this condition when the great eruption of 1883 ensued. The only outburst previously recorded in history occurred in 1680, when all the forests clothing the islands are said to have been destroyed.

On the morning of May 20th, 1883, the dormant volcano again woke suddenly to life. The explosions were sufficiently violent to be heard at Batavia, 100 miles distant, where dust fell on the following day, and the officers of a German man-of-war in the vicinity estimated the height of the column of matter vomited forth as over 36,000 feet. Considerable as the disturbance must have been, it does not appear to have been attended with any very injurious results, and although the eruption lasted without intermission until the appalling finale on August 26th and 27th, it steadily decreased in violence until the end of June. Pleasure-parties were even arranged in Batavia to visit the island, and photographs were taken of the scene. Towards the beginning of July an exacerbation of the phenomena took place, other craters having opened in the centre of the island. On the 11th August the island was approached upon its north-east side by Captain Ferzenaar, of the topographical staff of Bantam, who discovered that no less than three large and eleven secondary craters were in action. The whole island was covered with a thick white dust, and the forests and vegetation utterly destroyed.

On Sunday the 26th August the volcano entered upon its paroxysmal and culminating stage of eruption. From the commanders of two or three vessels which were then passing through the strait, and in some remarkable manner escaped destruction by the frightful wave that submerged the villages on its shores, we have full accounts of the phenomena presented at this period. The various craters appear to have united, and the mountain was vomiting forth enormous columns of smoke which, according to one observer, presented the appearance of "an immense wall with bursts of forked lightning like large serpents rushing through the air." Chains of fire appeared to ascend between the volcano and the sky, while on the south-west side huge white-hot fragments of lava rolled down the sides of the peak. On the ships the yard-arms and mast-heads were studded with "*corpisanti*," and the entire deck and rigging were covered with brilliant phosphorescence, due to showers of warm mud which fell at times at the rate of six inches of depth in ten minutes. Occasionally a peculiar pinky flame appeared to come from the clouds and touch the mast-heads and yard-arms; and the sounding-lead was hot when brought to the surface. A strong wind was blowing at the time, hot and choking, with a pungent sulphurous smell. The explosions, which began on the afternoon of Sunday, continuing at intervals of ten minutes, increased in violence, until at night there was an almost continuous roar. The sounds thus caused were indescribable, as may indeed be easily conceived, seeing that we have only the discharge of heavy cannon or thunder to serve as means of comparison. By one observer they were stated to resemble discharges of artillery at every second of time, combined with a crackling noise which was probably due to the collision of the fragments of the ejecta. But at Buitenzorg, 100 miles distant, a similar comparison was used, and the noise compared to the firing of a park of artillery close at hand,—so violent, indeed, were the explosions that the windows were blown in and sleep was rendered almost impossible.

Such were the phenomena witnessed by the onlookers who escaped with their lives from the horrors of the night of August 26th. Precisely what occurred at the focus of eruption will always remain a matter of doubt, but it is probable that from long-continued eruptive action the lip of the crater became gradually removed, and the sea gained admission to the white-hot mass of lava in the interior. The extraordinary violence of the explosions may have been due to the immense amount of steam thus generated, or the inrush of a vast body of water may have had a merely mechanical action, blocking the vent like the clods of earth thrown in to cause the eruption of a geyser. It is not unlikely that the succession of smaller seismic waves which left the island at various times during the night of the 26th, owed their origin to these causes, but the great wave, which will be presently referred to, and which was productive of the most wide-spread results. is considered by most authorities to have been aided, if not entirely caused, by some upheaval of the sea-bottom. It is worthy of remark, however, that at no time and in no place was any earthquake recorded during the eruption.

Throughout the 27th August the eruption continued, though with decreasing severity, but the exact nature of the phenomena then occurring is unknown, as the Straits of Sunda and much of the surrounding country were enveloped in complete darkness during the whole day. The vast quantity of dust and watery vapour which had been ejected hung like a pall over the scene, assuming the "pine-tree" shape noticed in the eruptions of Vesuvius. But while in the latter the cloud has been recorded as only attaining the height of four miles, the enormous body of ejecta thrown out by Krakatau was estimated by various observers as being from seventeen to twenty-three miles high. Then, slowly, the mass began to descend. For the most part it seems to have been composed of fine dust and watery particles, which deposited as a smooth mud, but in other cases pieces of pumice fell, some of which were as large as a pumpkin. A great part of this volcanic dust was no doubt caused by the collision of the individual pieces of the ejecta as they were shot out from the mouth of the crater, for the pumice was of a peculiarly brittle character, and crumbled easily between the fingers. The darkness in the straits only lasted during the 27th. On the morning of the 28th the explosions of the volcano, which had gradually been growing weaker and less frequent, finally ceased, and the great eruption of 1883 was at an end.

The foregoing is a brief account of the events which occurred in the immediate neighbourhood of Krakatau at the time of the disaster. But, terrible as they were, the enormous loss of life which followed on them was not immediately suspected, while the wide-spread character of the resulting phenomena was not known until months later. It may be said without exaggeration that the effects of the eruption manifested themselves in one way or another over the greater part of the surface of the globe.

The changes at the focus of eruption are best realised by a comparison of the survey of the straits after the disaster with the former Admiralty charts. Shortly they consist of the blowing away of the whole of the northern part of the island of Krakatau, a mass of land $3\frac{1}{2}$ miles in length by 2 in width. Where there was formerly dry land there are now soundings of 90 fathoms, while in one place bottom was not reached at 164 fathoms. Of the two neighbouring islands one, Lang Island, remained much as before; the other, Verlaten Island, was increased to more than thrice its original area. The bed of the sea for some five or six miles to the north appears to have been raised many fathoms, and in depths of 60 feet or more two islands were formed by the scoriæ. These, however, were not able to resist the action of the sea and have since disappeared.

That this elevation of the sea-bottom was connected with the production of the great seismic wave already mentioned, which overwhelmed all the villages of the littoral, is most probable. However produced, it will long be remembered as one of the most astonishing natural phenomena on record. It does not seem to have been felt by any person on board the vessels at that moment in the neighbourhood of Krakatau, and although the sky and land phenomena were of such an appalling character as doubtless to divert attention in great measure, still it is evident that, had the wave approached the height it was recorded to measure on striking the shores of the strait, it would probably have overwhelmed the ships, and certainly could not have escaped observation. It may

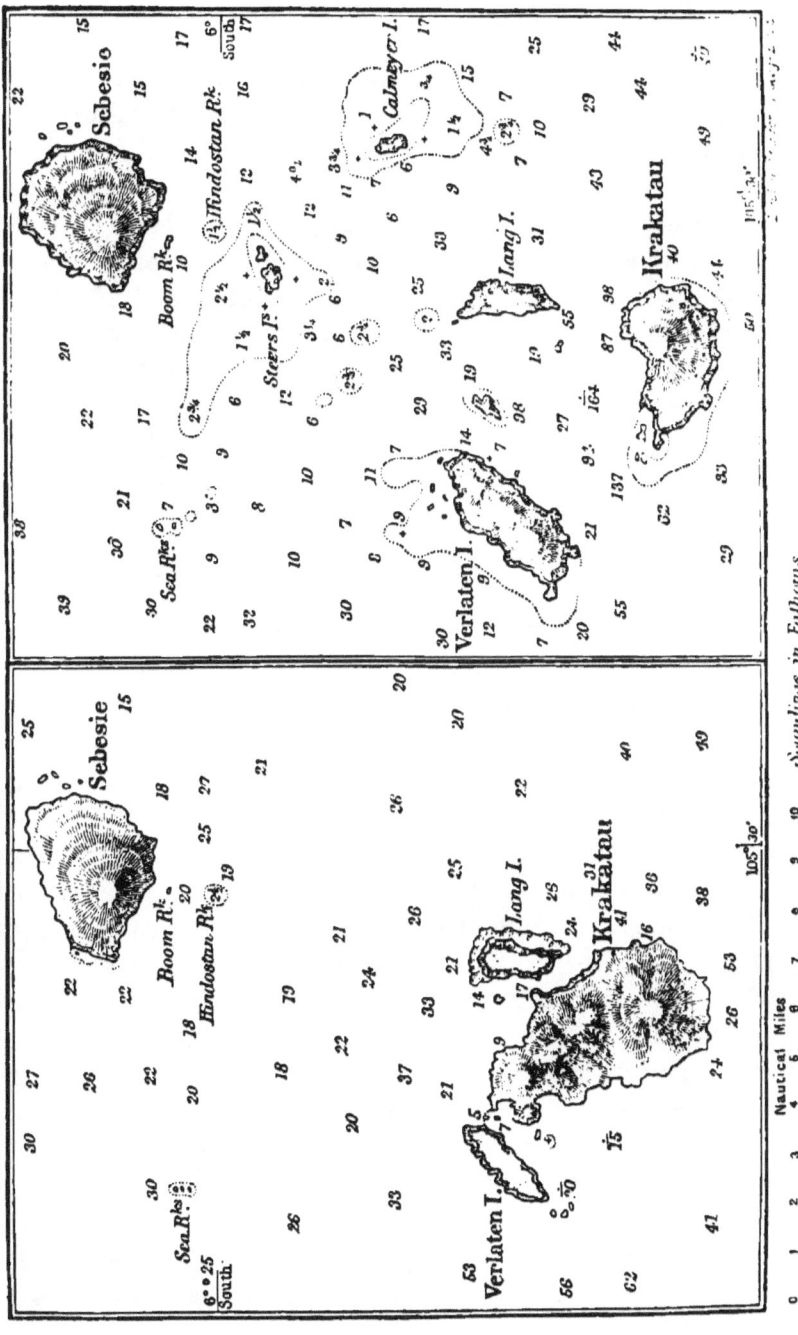

therefore be assumed that the wave did not originate merely from the island, but from a wider submarine upheaval. The hydrographic surveys subsequently undertaken show that over an area of 72 square miles the depths were greatly reduced by the eruption. Over a large portion of this there are now soundings of 12 feet only where formerly there was an uniform depth of 120 feet. Although, as has been stated, various seismic waves were recorded on the neighbouring shores, most of them were not of extraordinary height. The great loss of life and property was chiefly occasioned by the single gigantic wave which occurred at 10 o'clock on the morning of the 27th August. The destruction caused by it was immense. It may be said, roughly speaking, that all the coast villages and towns of the Straits of Sunda were overwhelmed. The actual height of the crest of the wave above sea-level has been variously estimated, and no doubt varied greatly according to the locality. Mr. Verbeek, in his plan, shows the hills of Merak to have been washed by the water to the height of 115 feet, and at Telok Betong, on the Sumatran coast, the water reached within 6 feet of the Residency, which stands on a hill 78 feet above the sea. A still better illustration of its height and volume is afforded in the case of the Dutch man-of-war "Berouw," anchored off this place, which was carried more than one mile and three-quarters inland, and left more than 30 feet above the level of the sea. The distance to which this wave was propagated is very remarkable. It was felt not only in South Africa, distant some 5000 miles from the scene of the eruption, but also at Cape Horn (7500 miles), and, possibly, in the English Channel (11,000 miles). In Ceylon even the smaller waves were distinctly recorded. To the north the numberless islands of the archipelago soon destroyed it, but to the south-east the tide gauges of West Australia showed marked evidences of its having reached those shores.

Still more extraordinary were the air waves produced by the violent explosions. Here, again, we find, as in the case of the sea waves, that there was one pre-eminent in strength and volume. It appears very nearly to have coincided with the gigantic seismic wave just discussed, and the character of the disturbance would seem almost incredible, were it not for the fact that it is attested by the barograms of every great meteorological station on the world's surface. Shortly, it was this: that the circular wave or oscillation having Krakatau as its centre propagated itself over the entire surface of the globe until it reached the antipodes of the volcano; that it was thence reflected back or reproduced, travelling backwards to its point of origin, from which it again returned; and that in this manner the occurrence of the wave was observed no fewer than seven times—four passages having been those of the wave travelling from Krakatau, and three those of the wave travelling from its antipodes. From this the time of its genesis could easily be calculated with tolerable exactitude. It is given by Lieutenant-General Strachey as 2 hours 56 minutes Greenwich mean time, which in local time would correspond with 9.58 o'clock on the morning of the 27th August.

The distance at which the sounds of the eruption were audible is much in excess of anything previously recorded; indeed, one of the reports is of special interest, as being the only instance known of sounds being heard at anything like so great a distance from their place of origin. The island of Rodriguez in the Indian Ocean is about 2968 miles from Krakatau in a direct line, yet the noise of the explosions was heard during the night of the 26th-

27th "like the distant roars of heavy guns." In the opposite direction Dr. Guillemard records that the sounds were audible on both days at Dorei Bay, on the north coast of New Guinea, 2014 miles distant. Roughly speaking, the eruption was heard over one-thirteenth of the entire surface of the globe. It is very remarkable that in the more immediate neighbourhood of the volcano the sounds were inaudible after the culminating explosion at 10 a.m. on the 27th, and this curious phenomenon can only be accounted for by the supposition that the enormous mass of ejecta formed a sort of wall or curtain so thick as effectually to exclude all sound. With regard to the extraordinary sunset glows and coloured suns so widely noticed during the autumn of 1883 and at subsequent periods, Messrs. Archibald and Rollo Russell's exhaustive treatise proves beyond all possibility of doubt that they were caused by the impalpable dust and vapour particles ejected from the crater of Krakatau during this memorable eruption. The pumice, which lay so thick in the Straits of Sunda that a bank of it was reported on one occasion to have almost stopped a vessel passing a few weeks later, drifted completely across the Indian Ocean from about 0° to 20° S., and reached Natal about the end of September 1884.[1] Three years after the eruption the island was visited by Dr. Treub of the Buitenzorg Botanic Garden, who found the cinders and pumice entirely covered with fresh-water algæ of various species. He also collected eleven species of ferns and twenty other plants.

The plains, table-lands, and valleys of the mountain region of Sumatra are often of great extent, and differ

[1] For further information the reader is referred to "The Eruption of Krakatoa"—the Report of the Krakatau Committee of the Royal Society, and M. Verbeek's "Krakatau."

very much in character, some being forest-clad, others bare; some extremely fertile, others sterile. Of the latter class is the plain of Pertibi, situated in the country of the Battaks, in lat. 1° 20′ N., on the eastern side of the mountains. Mr. Willer, a Dutch writer, thus describes it :—" Descending from Gunong-Tuah we see unrolled before us a plain without horizon, and without variety except such as may be caused by the presence or absence of the rank and worthless lalang grass (*Andropogon caricosum*). On this plain not a single living creature appears to move ; trees are rare, and have the appearance of being stunted and dwarfed. At the distance of miles we may descry, as an oasis in the desert, an insignificant thicket, or a small strip of brushwood along the banks of a marsh or brook. A fell, scorching wind blows for months together, and from the numerous conflagrations spreads a dull haze, through which the sunlight scarcely forces itself — wavering and heavy. In a word, all nature appears to have gone to an eternal sleep. Such is the appearance of Padang-luwas (spacious plain), whose naked and flat surface offers no other diversity than the ravines and morasses with which it is intersected. The upper soil is of the most meagre and unfruitful kind, and is seldom more than six inches in depth. Beneath, we come to layers of white clay, limestone, and sandstone. The climate is extremely variable. Frequently, in the afternoon, we have a temperature of from 92° to 97° Fahr., and in the night of from 63° to 66°. The heat is accompanied by great dryness. A violent storm, for the greatest part of the year, day after day bellows from the west over Padang-luwas. Like the *mistral*, this wind has a strong desiccating power, cracking the ground, and in a few minutes removing all traces of mud and rain."

The neighbouring district of Mandeling, on the western

side of the watershed, offers a totally different aspect, and is thus described by the same writer:— "The appearance of Mandeling is as varied and luxuriant as that of Pertibi is monotonous and arid. To the south are high and naked mountains, over which the lalang grass again spreads its monotonous mantle. Here hamlets and cultivated tracts appear, stuck on frightful steeps, where unfruitfulness and poverty have established their hungry seat. The northern Ankola valley also presents some dry and desert places like those of Padang-luwas. But for the rest, the district consists of one chain of beautiful valleys hemming the banks of the Batang-gadis (Virgin River), which runs between the central mountains of Sumatra. These valleys, like the river itself, become wider and wider as we proceed to the north and west. The high chains of mountains are covered to their summits with stately forests, which afford abundance of good timber and other valuable products. On the lower mountains, too, are woods here and there, and these are commonly adorned with the wine-yielding Areng palm (*Saguerus sacchariferus*). Here we see well-watered rice-fields, which, in small valleys like amphitheatres, climb up a considerable portion of the acclivities, and, in the distance, extend to an invisible boundary. Nowhere does the landscape weary. The eye rests constantly on ornamental groups of bamboos and various trees, or on the small clumps of fruit-trees in which the villages lie concealed, their position being especially marked by the abundance of coco and areca palms. Towards evening we observe near the villages numerous herds of buffaloes, oxen, and goats; while men, well fed and well clothed, and, what is more, a superabundance of children, prove that in this favoured region the greatest prosperity has reigned for some years."

To the great alluvial plain which occupies the entire eastern portion of Sumatra allusion has already been made. It is about 700 miles in length, and from 50 to 200 in breadth, and in area is equal to England. It is intersected with large and navigable rivers, by means of which trade is carried on almost to the opposite shores of the island. Much of it is flooded in the rainy season, and, with the rare exception of a few cultivated patches on the river banks, it is covered with a stupendous forest, coeval probably with the formation of the land itself. The greater part of this vast territory is of ample fertility, and suited to the growth of most of the products of tropical countries, but much of it is in the hands of rude tribes who are quite unable effectually to cultivate it.

Like Luzon, the great island of the Philippines, Sumatra abounds in lakes. But while in the former these are for the most part either inlets of the sea shut off by upheaval or by volcanic ejecta, or the temporary sheets of water occurring during the rainy season and known as Pinags, those of Sumatra are chiefly mountain lakes, many of which occupy the craters of extinct volcanoes. The largest of them is the Toba Lake in the Battak country (see p. 159), and although no others approach its area of nearly 500 square miles, there are several of considerable size. Lakes Singkara and Maninju, near Padang, are each about 12 or 13 miles in length by 3 or 4 in breadth. The latter is fed by thermal springs which are much used for their curative powers by the natives. The Danau or Ranau Lake (Danau signifying lake in the Malay and other allied languages) is of similar nature. It was visited in 1881 by Mr. H. O. Forbes, who describes it as appearing to occupy the site of an old crater at the foot of the Siminung volcano. It is about 12 miles in length, and is of very great depth. At various points round the margin hot springs of 127° Fahr. bubble up, and warm the western end some 10° higher than the temperature of the air. It is abundantly stocked with fish and bivalve mollusca, but when they approach too near the warmer shore the temperature instantly proves fatal to them.[1] This lake is widely celebrated throughout the Western Archipelago for the tobacco grown upon its shores. The finest quality is made only from the topmost leaves, and commands a very high price. Two or three other mountain lakes occur in the Battak country, but little is known of them, and there are probably others in Ache. Of lowland lakes and swamps there are many in the neighbourhood of the great rivers.

From the orography of the island it is evident that there can be no rivers of any length on the western side of the main range of mountains. Upon the other side, however, we find the alluvial plain intersected by streams of great size and depth, by which the whole interior of the country is rendered accessible to commerce. Owing to the great rainfall and the steepness of the Barisan chain the erosion which takes place is excessive, and the rivers bear down enormous quantities of débris which deposits around their mouths, blocking the channels and adding to the numerous islands and sandbanks by which they are beset. The change thus effected in the physical condition of the island is enormous. The rapid gaining of the east coast upon the Straits of Malacca has already been mentioned. It is said that at the time of the founding of Palembang the town was situated at the mouth of the river, from which it is now distant some 40 miles as the crow flies. Yet for the most part the rivers are not only of great size, but of considerable depth,

---

[1] *A Naturalist's Wanderings in the Eastern Archipelago*, H. O. Forbes.

and admit of steamer service far into the interior. The
Jambi River, better known as the Batang-Hari, is the
largest, and, disregarding the windings of the upper part
of its course, exceeds 500 miles in length. It is practicable for the transport of merchandise for quite 480
miles, and the Dutch Government vessel *Barito*, a paddle-wheel steamer with a draught of over five feet, navigated
it for a distance of 370 miles without difficulty. It
drains a vast area, and is connected with some of the
most beautiful and fertile districts of the Padang highlands by its affluents, many of which are of large size.
It is thus not only valuable as affording an easy means
of access to the Ombilin coal-fields, but eminently important for commerce both with the eastern parts of the
"West Coast Government" and with the inland districts
of Jambi and Korinchi, and before long its farthest
navigable point will doubtless be connected with the
network of Government roads on the western side of the
island. The Musi or Palembang River is scarcely inferior
to the Batang-Hari, being about 400 miles in length, of
which distance the *Barito* was able to navigate rather
more than half. The upper part, however, together with
its numerous tributaries, is navigable right up to the
mountain range by praus and *rakits*, or large bamboo
rafts, upon which a vast amount of produce is carried to
Palembang. From the fact of this district having been
for some time settled, the trade is very considerable, and
gutta, rattan, and other forest products, together with
large numbers of buffaloes, are shipped from the large
up-country towns of Muara-Rupit, Tebbing-Tinggi, Muara
Inim, and Muara Dua, the river thus tapping the trade
of the districts along the mountain range for a distance
in width of more than 150 miles. Other great rivers
are the Siak, navigable for large vessels for 80 miles, the

Kampar, Rakan, and Indragiri, all of which form vast deltas with labyrinthine intersecting channels at their mouths. Upon the western side of the island the only river of importance is the Singkel, which debouches opposite Banyak Island, and is navigable for a considerable distance by small vessels.

4. Climate and Meterology.

Sumatra differs considerably in its climate and rainfall from Java. In the latter country—at all events in its eastern portion—a strong S.E. monsoon blows from March to November, which produces a marked degree of aridity, causing trees to shed their leaves and filling the air with powdery dust. This dry season, produced by the winds sweeping over the parched and heated deserts of the Australian continent, becomes less and less marked as we increase our distance from the latter country, until at the Straits of Sunda it becomes almost non-existent. The position of Sumatra, bisected as it is by the equator, causes the winds and seasons of Ache to differ from those of the Lampongs at the southern extremity. For at the north the monsoons blow from the north-east and south-west; in the centre is a wide belt of variable winds with alternating calms and squalls; and in the south the monsoons blow from the south-east and north-west. A series of observations at Palembang show that from November to March the prevalent winds are westerly and north-westerly, this being the regular rainy season. April is the month of the change of the monsoons, when thunderstorms are most frequent. From May till September easterly and south-easterly winds prevail, and the "kentering," or change of the monsoon, comes in September or October. During the shifting months of the S.E.

monsoon sailing vessels are often five or six weeks in making the passage from Singapore to Bangka Strait, and squalls are common.

The heavy squalls affecting the eastern lowlands of Sumatra and the Straits of Malacca are as marked a feature of this region as the "Bora" is of the Adriatic. They are known to sailors as "Sumatras," and are generally accompanied by heavy rain and thunder. They occur most frequently during the S.W. monsoon, and are supposed to be due to the obstruction offered to the course of the wind by the Barisan chain. Not having strength at all times to overcome this barrier the current becomes pent-up and checked, and the condensed air thus formed at high altitudes rushes down to displace the heated and rarefied atmosphere of the east coast lowlands, and driven by the pent-up force of the monsoon, spreads far and wide over the straits.

As in most equatorial climates rain occurs very generally at all seasons of the year, and the fall is excessively heavy, especially in the mountain districts. At Padang on the west coast the average is about 187 inches, and at Palembang it is said to be still heavier. This great humidity, combined with a continued high temperature, makes the island unhealthy, and the low-lying alluvial plains of the east coast, half under water for some months in the year, generate paludal fevers of a severe type. Cholera, too, is more or less endemic, and the almost equally deadly "beri-beri" annually claims hundreds of victims.

5. Fauna and Flora.

Sumatra may be regarded as exhibiting, with Borneo and the Malay Peninsula, the truly typical Malayan fauna and flora. From Java it differs not a little in both. One of the most characteristic features of the Sumatran flora is the superabundance of the *lalang* and *glaga*—rank and worthless grasses which cover a vast extent of ground in the plateau region, and flourish at comparatively low altitudes, while in Java they are not met with much below 3000 feet. This pest is one of

RAFFLESIA ARNOLDII.

the most troublesome with which the agriculturist has to deal, as cleared and fallow land becomes rapidly covered and the soil exhausted. Among characteristic plants are the enormous *Rafflesias* (*R. Arnoldii*, *R. Hasseltii*), the largest flowers in the world, and the giant arum, *Amorphophallus titanum*, sometimes seventeen feet or more in height, and with tubers seven feet in circumference. The Melastomas, Ternstrœmiaceæ, Cyrtandraceæ, and Eriocaulaceæ are better represented here than in Java, and in the highlands of the north *Pinus Merkusii* occurs—the only other locality for it in the archipelago being the island of Luzon in the Philippines. The island is specially rich in its forest trees, which Mr. Forbes mentions as being larger than any he had ever seen; and that the species are very numerous is evident from the fact that the Central Sumatran Expedition collected specimens of some 400 kinds of timber.

It has often been remarked that, from a variety of circumstances, the flowers of tropical regions are less conspicuous, or at least form less showy masses of colour, than those of the temperate zones, but exceptions to this rule are not infrequent in Sumatra, as may be realised from Mr. Forbes's descriptions of the descent of the upper reaches of the Palembang River:—"Very many trees were in flower and fruit—tall Melettias hung with immense pods, and wild nutmeg trees with their pretty, drop-like fruits. The oaks were one mass of white inflorescence, and formed a characteristic feature of the vegetation of the banks; while bushy Sterculiaceous trees made a greater show of colour in the rich pink of their young foliage and the bright scarlet of their fruits than in their inconspicuous flowers. Between these more outstanding trees dark-foliaged figs and slender bamboos gracefully bending over the bank filled up the ranks shoulder to shoulder. Tall Sialang trees, with lightning-conductor-like stairs up their white stems, by which the wild bees' nests are reached, and Pangiums, bearing six to seven hundred brown velvety fruits, each several pounds in weight, so that one marvels that the branches are able to sustain the load, marked the vicinity of villages. . . . Every lifeless stem, to the very tips of its withered arms, was festooned with dark foliaged climbers, yellow and purple *Papilionaceæ* and *Convolvulaceæ*, like the grotesque shrubbery cut out of boxwood, but with all the natural grace which is conspicuously wanting in Dutch gardens. No tree, however, was more abundant or brighter than the *Layerstræmia*, whose fine red tops could be seen a long way off." Lower down "the Jambus (*Jambosa* sp.) seemed to be among the most common trees, and their long white-stamened flowers falling on the water glided down the stream like so many stars. The whole surface of the water was covered, absolutely in a close sheet, with petals, fruits, and leaves of innumerable species. . . . To recall the magnificent flora of the upper reaches of the river almost makes me retract the statement that the tropics present few flowers, for so blossom-spangled a road it would be difficult to match anywhere."

From many of these trees and plants economic products of great value are obtained. Sumatra exports large quantities of gutta-percha, rattan, dammar, and other gums and resins. Dammar is chiefly collected from various species of the *Dipterocarpeæ*, some of which are trees of enormous size, which will yield nearly a hundred pounds weight of the resin. The "eye-dammar," which is the best description, and is that sent to Europe, is the exudation from *Hopea dryobalanoides*, but the common "stone-dammar," used chiefly for paying the seams of vessels, is obtained from *Vatica eximia*, also of the order *Dipterocarpeæ*. Benzoin, the gum of *Styrax benzoin*, is also collected in considerable quantities, together with catechu and other medicinal products. Recent travellers have remarked upon the reckless destruction of the forest by the natives, but bearing in mind the vast area of land known to be entirely covered by virgin forest, it is unlikely that any real injury will result for many years to come.

Turning to the fauna we find that it, too, offers great similarities to the Malay Peninsula and Borneo, and differs much from that of Java. The orang-utan exists in the north-eastern part of the island, but probably very locally. The Siamang (*Siamanga syndactyla*), a very powerful animal, not much inferior in size to the orang, is common. It is not found in any other of the islands, the Malay Peninsula being the only other locality in which it occurs. On the whole Sumatra is rich in monkeys, and has probably as many species as Borneo. All the great mammalian forms of the continent are found here, such as the elephant, rhinoceros, tapir, and tiger, but of these species only the latter exists in Java. The elephant, considered by some authors as a peculiar species, has been driven out of some of the cultivated districts, but it is still very common in the Lampongs and in the thick jungles of the eastern lowlands. The rhinoceros (*R. sumatranus*) is rarer. It is a species peculiar to the island, smaller than that found in Java, and carrying two horns. It is found not only in the marshy jungles of the coast, but also, like its Javanese congener, at considerable altitudes, and Mr. Forbes noticed its spoor at a height of nearly 6000 feet on the Tengkamus mountain. Tigers are very plentiful, especially in the east coast, in which district alone twenty-two deaths were registered by the Dutch officials as having been caused by them in 1889—figures which probably do not represent a tithe of the loss of life really occasioned. The clouded tiger (*F. macroscelis*) also exists, as does the Malay sun-bear and the wild dog, but the fine Banteng, *Bos sondaicus*, is not found. The "kambing-utan," or "wild sheep," is an antelope (*Antilocarpa sumatrana*) which frequents the mountain ranges, and of which not much is known. In addition to the above there are a Manis (*M. javanicus*), and a peculiar hare (*Lepus netscheri*), the common Malayan deer, and the muntjac. Between sixty and seventy mammals have been described, and the total number is possibly in excess of that of Borneo, for the numbers are about equal, while Sumatra is certainly less explored.

The avifauna of Sumatra is practically the same as that of Borneo and the Malay Peninsula. Among the most striking birds are the great Argus pheasant and the yet more showy *Euplocomus;* crimson-breasted Trogons ; bush-shrikes of a glossy cobalt-blue (*Irena*) ; vivid green gapers (*Calyptomena*), and the curiously marked rain-birds (*Cymborhynchus*); the lovely rose-crested bee-eater (*Nyctiornis amicta*), and the pheasant-cuckoos (*Carpococcyx*), besides numerous woodpeckers, barbets, spider-hunters, and brilliantly-coloured *Pittas*. The peacock does not exist, but is found in Java. There are but few peculiar species on the island, and the genus *Psilopogon*, which was supposed to be confined to it, has lately been discovered in the mountains of Perak. It is interesting to note that, as in the case of the flora, there is an occurrence of certain Himalayan forms in the high mountain regions, such as *Niltava, Sibia*, etc., most, if not all, of which are probably to be found in the elevated chain of the interior of the Peninsula. About 330 different species of birds are now known from Sumatra.

6. Inhabitants and Languages.

The natives of Sumatra, from Ache Heads to the Straits of Sunda, are all of the great Malayan stock, although the different tribes vary much in language, customs, and social condition. No dark and woolly-haired race, such as exists in the Philippines, has ever yet been found in the island, although it has by some been considered possible that the Kubus are partly of Negrito origin. Many different nations, speaking distinct languages, inhabit the main island, while at least three others are found in the adjacent small islands. Most of these are comparatively civilised, building good houses, practising elaborate agriculture, weaving cloth, and having written languages, while others are almost pure savages, their civilisation on a par with that of the Dyaks of Borneo.

At the extreme north lies the Sultanate of Ache, a country, roughly speaking, about the size of Ireland, which has remained unconquered and uninfluenced by the Dutch. For centuries one of the most important sites of commerce, its people—at all events those in the neighbourhood of the capital—yielded early to such civilisation as was introduced by the Arabs, and intermarried with them. For more than 700 years the Achenese have been Mohammedans, and although the Arab influence is less marked now than formerly, it is still evident in the dress of the well-to-do and the character in which their language is written. Other elements have been introduced to form the nation. The traders from the Malabar and Coromandel coasts, Ceylon, Pegu, and Tenasserim have mixed with them, and as they were formerly renowned as pirates, whose raids extended over a considerable portion of the Archipelago, it is probable that their harcems were stocked by the women of many different nations. The language, as might be expected, is far from pure. It is written in the Arabic character, although it probably had at one time a native alphabet, as have the Battak, Rejang, and other tongues at the present day. The outcome of this mixture of races is not without marked characteristics, as is evidenced by the vigour of the resistance which the Dutch have experienced. Physically the Achenese resemble the Malays, but are darker and slightly taller, and with none of the good looks of that people. They have long borne a bad name, both for treachery and cruelty, but since it is impossible to penetrate their country, and since all our accounts of them are derived from the accounts of their natural enemies the Dutch, it is possible that these characteristics may be exaggerated. They possess, at all events, the simpler virtues of courage and industry, and, considering the backward condition of their civilisation, are rather clever handicraftsmen, weaving cotton and other stuffs, and a peculiarly delicate silken fabric, and producing gold and silver filagree work of a very remarkable kind. They are, moreover, good shipwrights, and their vessels, which at one time used to sweep the seas far beyond Java, are now, whenever they can escape the Dutch gunboats, engaged in trade with the Malacca coast and Singapore.

In former days, when Queen Elizabeth and James I. sent their duly accredited ambassadors to the court, Ache was a great kingdom, and embraced half the island of Sumatra. Captain Thomas Best, in his mission of 1613, speaks of the king as "a proper, gallant man of warre, strong by sea and land, his country populous, and his elephants many, whereof we saw one hundred sixty, or one hundred eighty at a time." He possessed "gallies and frigates carrying in them very good brasse ordnance," and made treaties with great nations. Little or no trace of this former greatness now remains, and the country, although nominally under a sultan, whose office is hereditary, is largely republican in its form of government. As among the Battaks and other peoples of this part of the world, the system is communal. The country is divided into *saguis*, corresponding to the *margas* of the Lampongers and Battaks, to which we shall have presently to refer. There are three of these clans, called the "XXII," "XXV," and "XXVI *Mukims*," from the number of districts each comprises—the *mukim* being a partly religious, partly political division. Formerly each of the three *saguis* was administered by a Chief Panglima of the Sultan, but the Dutch claim to have abolished the title. One died in battle, another is an adherent of the Dutch, and the third is one of their most redoubtable enemies, whose headquarters are at or near Pedir, and who is said to command about 100,000 men, of whom 20,000 are armed with breech-loading rifles of modern pattern. Each *mukim* is ruled by headmen, and in its turn is subdivided into *binasas* or townships, each of which enjoys self-government, the law being administered by a council of elders.

The Achenese are Mohammedans, but, like others of this sect in the archipelago, are by no means strict, and have never distinguished themselves by their persecution of other religionists. This tolerant spirit is illustrated by the saying current among their neighbours, that "an Achenese will curse a Christian, and then invite him to bread and salt." Their chief amusements appear to be fighting, gambling, and opium-smoking. The soil is for the most part not very fertile, but pepper, camphor, and other commodities are produced for the foreign market, and of late, in consequence of the war, a considerable quantity of rice for home consumption. The civets also yield a valuable product, and their breeding is said to form a special branch of industry.

The main characteristic of the Achenese is his love of fighting. Every man is a soldier, and every village thus has its little army, which is bound to present itself equipped for service at the outbreak of war. This it is, combined with thick jungle and want of roads, which has caused, and is still causing, the Ache war. The constant acts of piracy in the Straits of Malacca led to the English Treaty of 1871, which gave Holland a free hand. Hostilities were commenced in 1872, but the Dutch suffered a reverse. It was not till a year later, and after a siege of forty-seven days, that the Sultan's fortress, situated about two miles inland from Olélé, was captured. After a struggle of twenty years, an expenditure of over £20,000,000, and the loss of many thousands of lives, the Dutch find themselves in a hardly better position than at the beginning of the war. The greater part of the interior is still independent, and will probably remain so for many years to come. A new experiment has lately been tried,—the blockading of the various ports. By this means an opium and tobacco famine has been created, from which favourable results are anticipated. But the chief weapon upon which the Dutch rely to place Ache eventually in their hands is the want of cohesion among the numerous petty states of which a great part of the country is composed. Of these may be mentioned the Gaious and Allas, and the Karos, who inhabit the country between the Battaks and the Allas, of all of whom little or nothing is known.

South of Ache comes the country of the Battaks, a territory of great extent, for people of this race extend south nearly as far as Mount Ophir, up to the head waters of the Siak river. They are essentially an inland, hill people, and are most thickly grouped around the Toba Lake, which they themselves consider as the cradle of their race. Those on the Ache border were visited by a Dutch Government expedition in 1891, and were found inhabiting an immense plain country, for the most part covered with lalang grass and intersected with deep ravines. Rice was almost the only crop cultivated, and cattle were rarely seen. The more southern tribes have been long in contact with the Dutch, and are gradually becoming civilised. They nevertheless present, even to this present day, the extraordinary anomaly of a people who possess a written language of their own, yet are at the same time cannibals.

The Battak is of Malayan stock, and has by some travellers been considered to resemble the Bornean Dyak. He is taller and darker than the true Malay and is more bearded, but the hair is straight, not frizzled, as in the Kubus, and if there be any Negrito blood in the race, no trace of it is now evident. Some consider that they are partly of Hindu origin, and it is probable that they must have come under the influence of that race to a considerable extent at the time of its immigration. In their customs, however, there are few if any points of resemblance. The more civilised, and especially those around Lake Toba, are good agriculturists and stock farmers, and understand working in iron. They weave and dye cotton, make jewellery and krisses, which are often of beautiful workmanship, and bake pottery; but their skill is especially exhibited in the construction of their houses, many of which are two-storied and with carved timbers, though in this form of decoration they do not approach the work of the natives in some parts of the Palembang district. The form of government obtaining is not unlike that of the Achenese, as already described, the people being divided into clans, communes, and families—a system, it may be remarked, which is found through the greater part of Sumatra, and, with various modifications, in Java also. The *kota* of the Battaks and of the Menangkabo people corresponds with the *mukim* of the Achenese, and there are thus districts known as the "XIII kotas," and the "IX kotas," just as there are the "XXII" and "XXV" mukims."

The cannibalism of the Battaks has doubtless existed for centuries, and we find Barros mentioning it in his *Decades*. It appears to have been practised rather from enmity, or as a punishment, than from any desire for human flesh as an article of food. Their victims are, or were, either criminals, prisoners of war, or occasionally slaves, and the established punishment for certain crimes, such as adultery with the wife of a Raja, midnight robbery, or being taken prisoner in war, was to be cut to pieces and eaten alive. The Dutch have found no difficulty in abolishing these practices wherever they have sway, and when this is done the people are found to be no whit worse than their neighbours, among whom such customs did not exist. The civilised Battaks declare that cannibalism has entirely died out, but there is little doubt that it is still existent in the more out-of-the-way and unexplored districts. The race is still pagan, and is noteworthy as being the only example in the archipelago of a lettered people who have not embraced Mohammedanism, whose converts surround them on all sides. Their faith is apparently chiefly confined to a belief in evil spirits; but they recognise three deities, a Creator, a Preserver, and a Destroyer, and carry small images, of the nature of amulets, about with them, like the Papuans of New Guinea. It is probable that they will in time become converted to Islamism, but Christian missionaries have not met with much success. The race is partly becoming absorbed in the Achenese and Malay tribes of the coast, and the constant wars of tribe against tribe have done much to lessen their numbers. The art of reading and writing is pretty generally understood. The alphabet, according to Professor Keane, is based on the Dewanagiri, but others hold it to be probably original. It is written from left to right on palm leaves, and the character differs entirely from the Rejang, Korinchi, and other of the peculiar Sumatran languages, being curved and not rectilinear in its form.

In the hill-country, near Mount Ophir, are two tribes —the Orang Lubu and Ulu—of whom next to nothing is known, except that they are pure savages and few in number. East of them, inhabiting the lowlands opposite Malacca and Singapore, are the Siak people, a pure Malay race, as are the Jambi tribes lower down on the same coast. But of all the true Malays inhabiting Sumatra, the most important and highly civilised are those occupying the mountain district of Menangkabo, above Padang. They comprise several tribes, and are divided into *sukus* and *kotas* on the same principle as the Achenese and Lampongers. By many people this district is regarded as the original cradle of the Malay race. In spite of foreign influence this language has here remained singularly pure—purer, indeed, than in many places in the Peninsula—and few words of foreign origin have been introduced. According to the theory of others, these people are the remnant of the original conquerors of the island, and the word Menangkarbau—"buffalo's victory"—is held to commemorate symbolically the victory of the champion of Sumatra over its rival, the tiger, the representant of Java. Of all parts of the island this district is the most highly cultivated and prosperous. Sir Stamford Raffles, describing it, says:— "As far as the eye could reach was one continued scene of cultivation, interspersed with innumerable towns and villages shaded by palms and fruit trees. I may safely say that the view equalled anything I ever saw in Java. The scenery is more majestic and grand, the population equally dense, the cultivation equally rich." The marriage system is matriarchal, as indeed is occasionally, but not habitually, the case among the Battaks. The husband cannot choose his wife from his own *kota*, and when married does not always reside with her. The children belong to the mother, and must remain in her village. Yet these customs, curiously enough, co-exist with the religion of Mohammed, in the practice of which these people are said to be more strict than is usual among Malays. At the early part of this century a new religion sprang up in Menangkabo—a noteworthy fact, as being the only instance of the kind ever known in the archipelago. The sect were known as the "Padris," from the missionary zeal inspiring them; or the "Orang puti" or "white men," from the converts being dressed entirely in white. They prohibited the use of opium, and punished with death all those found indulging in it; and tobacco and betel were also forbidden. Every man shaved his head and wore a skull-cap, and none was permitted to converse with his neighbour's wife. The women were obliged to cover their faces with a white cloth, having only two small holes for their eyes, and no coloured garments of any description were allowed. The reformers in time became conquerors, subduing a large portion of the interior; and it was through them, indirectly, that the Dutch acquired possession of the Menangkabo country. The neighbouring tribes appealed to be protected from them, and the Netherlands troops entered upon the campaign in 1837. It was not till 1840, however, that they were entirely subdued, and the sect subsequently became extinct. It could only have come into existence among the lax and easy-going

Malays by virtue of its very austerity, as Commonwealth followed upon Caroline manners, to be again succeeded by them; and it was equally predestined to extinction; but it served its turn in bringing Dutch influence and civilisation to bear upon a country that had been until then but little known. Menangkabo has met with more success in colonisation than in preaching the creed of the "Padris." About the fourteenth or fifteenth century a fleet of twelve ships is said to have left the neighbourhood of Padang, and sailing northward, established settlements at various places along the coast, both in the Battak and Ache lands. Each ship founded a town, and hence this part is still sometimes called the Twelve Colonies, though to the British sailor it is perhaps better known as the Pepper Coast. The descendants of these settlers still retain the title of Datu, and have preserved both the race and language pure. To such an extent does this custom prevail, that any Malay marrying an Ache woman, or giving his daughter to one of that race, would be obliged to quit the country.

Still proceeding southwards, after passing the Korinchis, who are grouped on the eastern slopes of the Indrapura peak, and are a tolerably civilised sub-Malayan race, with a written language, the Rejang country is reached. These people are interesting as being the tribe with whom the English were brought in contact during the occupation of Benkulen. They, too, are of sub-Malayan stock, and are probably a mixture of Malays with immigrant Javanese. South and east the Passuma and Lampong people border on them, and on the east the mixed riverine Palembang tribes. They are a numerous and civilised people, possessing a written language like the Korinchis and other nations already mentioned, but inscribed in a peculiar character of rectilinear form, based on the Dewanagiri. The communal system, so widely spread in Sumatra, obtains among them, and the tribal divisions are known as *sukus*, as in the Menangkabo lands, although the headmen and chiefs have the Javanese appellations of Pangerang and Adhipatti. Javanese influence, indeed, has no doubt left its impress upon these as upon other of the southern peoples of the island, and has given them a good deal of their civilisation. Mr. Marsden's description of the character of the Sumatran native is in reality drawn from the Rejang people, and as it is more or less accurate even at the present day, it may be reproduced here. "The Sumatran of the interior," he says, "though partaking in some degree of the Malayan vices, possesses many exclusive virtues, but they are more of the negative than the positive kind. He is mild, peaceable, and forbearing, unless his anger be roused by violent provocation, when he is implacable in his resentments. He is temperate and sober, being equally abstemious in meat and drink. The diet of the natives is mostly vegetable. Water is their only beverage, and although they kill a fowl or a goat for a stranger, they are rarely guilty of that extravagance for themselves; not even at their festivals, where there is plenty of meat, do they eat much of anything but rice. Their hospitality is extreme, and bounded by their ability alone. Their manners are simple; they are generally, except among the chiefs, devoid of the Malay cunning and chicane, yet endued with quickness of apprehension, and on many occasions discovering a considerable degree of penetration and sagacity. They are modest, particularly guarded in their expressions, courteous in their behaviour, grave in their deportment, being seldom or never excited to laughter, and patient to a great degree. On the other hand, they are litigious, indolent, addicted to gaming, dishonest in their dealings with strangers, which they esteem no moral defect, suspicious, regardless of truth, mean in their transactions, and servile. Although cleanly in their persons, they are dirty in their apparel, which they never wash. They are careless and improvident of the future, because their wants are few; for though poor they are not needy, Nature supplying with extraordinary facility whatever she has made necessary for their existence."

Of the tribes of the eastern lowlands, the Siak and Jambi have already been mentioned as true Malays. The people inhabiting the Palembang valley are of like origin, but they have been much mixed with Javanese settlers from the earliest historical period, if, indeed, these latter were not the first inhabitants of the locality. They speak a mixed language in which Javanese words occur largely, and their manners and customs resemble those of that people. The court language is Javanese, and is written in the peculiar character of Java. At the head waters of the Musi and Batang-Hari rivers, on the confines of the Jambi country, live the nomadic and totally wild Kubus, who probably correspond in the south with the Ulus and Lubus of the northern part of the island. From the accounts of Mr. H. O. Forbes and other travellers, more is known of them than of the latter tribes. They inhabit the thickest forest country, making only temporary shelter-huts, and, like the Veddas of Ceylon, avoid all communication with those not of their own race. They cultivate no crops whatever, living on fruits, roots, and such animals as they are able to kill, and are without manufactures, even of the simplest kind. They collect beeswax, dammar, and other forest produce, and barter it with the Malay races, also by a method similar to that of the Veddas, laying the objects of barter on the ground, disappearing until the Malay has in like manner deposited what is considered the equivalent, and then returning to carry it away. They appear extraordinarily timid, and have no sense of shame. Monogamy is the rule, but a few have two or more wives. Intermarriage with Malays is extremely rare. Yet, with all this, it would seem that they are in reality a Malay people, which have merely developed their characteristics by isolation. Their language, according to Forbes, is "a corrupted Malay with a peculiar accentuation," but they are said to have a language of their own, unintelligible to their neighbours. The skulls brought to Europe bear out the evidence afforded by their language, although a slight tendency to frizzling in the hair seems to indicate that the race may at some remote period have intermingled with Negritos.

South of the Palembang district, and occupying the terminal point of Sumatra, are the Lampongers, dwelling in a country fairly well known to Europeans, and leading a settled and agricultural life. They claim to be descended from the Menangkabo Malays, but that there has been a considerable admixture of Javanese blood there can be no doubt. The spoken language contains a very large number of corrupt Malay and Sundanese words, but the character employed is not Arabic or Javanese, but peculiar, as in the case of other of the Sumatran languages of which mention has been made. The communal system also exists, and here, as elsewhere on the island, the Dutch, in dividing the country for administrative purposes, have retained as far as possible the boundaries of the old native districts, here called *margas*. The country is not peculiarly favourable to agriculture, and the native does not seek to improve it by irrigation, so that the *sawah* or wet rice-fields are rare, and the crops are taken for the most part from the cleared forest land. But a ready source of wealth lies at hand in the shape of pepper, and could the natives but abstain from gambling and cock-fighting, they might amass considerable fortunes. The unmarried women are often nearly covered with necklets, bracelets, and ear-rings of solid silver, their dowry being thus displayed on feast days and great occasions at the *balai*. This building is a characteristic institution among the Lampongers, though halls or meeting-places of a somewhat similar nature are to be found not only in Sumatra, but as far east as New Guinea. It occupies the most central position in the village, and bears evidences of having much labour bestowed upon it. Mr. Forbes thus describes its uses :—" The Balai is in reality the town-hall of the Lamponger. It is the common property of every man, woman, and child in the village. In Mohammedan lands a man's house is sacred; for a man rarely enters the dwelling of his neighbour, and never without the head of the house; but the Balai is the assembly-room, the meeting-place for all. Its doors stand ever open. All business is transacted under its roof, all *bicharas* (discussions) are held there. At whatever hour one enters, its most characteristic occupants—lazy, sleeping villagers—are to be seen dotted over its floor. During the day the *orang-jaga*, or watchman, who occupies an open guard-room during the night, makes the Balai his watch-tower. All travellers passing through the village are free to its shade and shelter. The *orang-bedagang* or itinerant pedlar finds at once a free lodging, a market-place for his goods, and an eager crowd to listen to the news he brings. Here all civic feasts and festive gatherings are held. Here they enjoy the pleasures of the dance for unbroken days and nights. . . . Under its roof their love is consummated in the wedding and attendant ceremonies. Here before a crowded audience they are invested with their equivalent knighthoods and peerages; and here, in many villages, they are at last laid out, and pass from it to the grave. Around the Balai, therefore, centres as it were the whole life of a Lampong village."

In brief, then, we may describe the inhabitants of Sumatra as consisting of various nations of either pure Malayan or sub-Malayan stock, those in the north being the most hybrid. The majority follow Islamism with more or less laxity, but the centre of the island is occupied by tribes of pure pagans, such as the Battaks, Ulus, Lubus, Kubus, and others. Of these, the Battaks are conspicuous as affording the only known instance of lettered cannibalism. These pagans, chiefly on account of the inaccessibility of their country, have come very little under Dutch influence. The Ache people have resisted it to the death for the past twenty years, but it has spread steadily though slowly in the north-east, near Dili; in the Palembang, Lampong, and Benkulen Residencies; and, more especially around Padang and the upland districts behind it. In the south there are abundant evidences of a large Javanese immigration having occurred at some past epoch, while scattered ruins and sculptures in various parts of the island testify to the probability of the existence of some Hindu influence at a remoter period, which influence, however, can never have in any way approached that which held sway in Java. Throughout a large portion of the island we find a communal system obtaining, upon which the Dutch attempt to graft their own administration. Lastly, the languages, which are all either pure Malay or sub-Malayan, are remarkable in certain instances (Battak, Korinchi, Rejang, Lampong) as being written in a peculiar character.

7. The Islands of Sumatra.

The islands of Sumatra, omitting those of no great importance, may be divided into four groups. These are (1) the barrier islands off the west coast, from Simalu or Hog Island to Engaño: (2) the delta islands at the mouths of the great rivers of the east coast; (3) the mass of small islands south of Singapore, known to the Dutch as the Rhio-Lingga Archipelago: and (4) the two large and important islands, Bangka and Blitong (Billiton).

(1) The islands of the west coast in their order, beginning from the north, are Simalu, the Banyak Islands, Nias, the Batu, Mentawi, and Nassau groups, and Engaño. All possess certain features in common. They are situated at a tolerably uniform distance of from 70 to 80 miles from the coast; are not simply of volcanic origin, but exhibit the older rocks of the main island, granites, sandstones, etc.: and possess, roughly speaking, its fauna, although the larger animals, such as the tiger, elephant, and rhinoceros are, as might be expected, wanting. Of Simalu, otherwise known as Pulo Babi, or Hog Island, not much is known. The inhabitants are partly Achenese and partly descendants of Menangkabo settlers, and profess the Mohammedan religion, but they are almost savages, and the Dutch have not attempted to establish a settlement either here or on the Banyak group, which may be described in similar terms. Nias is of far greater importance. Here, at Gunong Sitoli, a colony of Malays and Chinese, is established a Controleur, but very little has been undertaken in the way of exploration, and we are indebted for our knowledge of the people to the accounts of Signor Modigliani, who spent a year upon the island in 1885. It

is about 80 miles in length, and has an area of over 1700 square miles, and as its population has been estimated at about a quarter of a million, it is evidently thickly inhabited. The people of the south differ essentially from those of the north. They are taller and more robust, their hair is more curly, and their cheek-bones more prominent, and they exhibit a fierceness and irritability quite foreign to the milder inhabitant of the north. Each village appears to be at war with its neighbours, and the people are confirmed head-hunters. The houses are very skilfully constructed, and are raised on stout piles 12 or 15 feet from the ground, partly, it is said, on account of the earthquakes, which are both frequent and violent, but partly as a means of defence. They are oval in shape, and are often decorated with human heads, examples of the prowess of the owner against some neighbouring tribe. The Nias people, in spite of their barbarism, are good handicraftsmen, weaving cotton stuffs, forging weapons, and working in copper and gold. Their agriculture is also good, the art of irrigation is understood, they make excellent roads, and have domestic animals, using oxen for ploughing. Rude attempts at carving are common, and statues of their deities adorn the villages, for the people are not Mohammedans, but pure pagans like the Battaks, of whom they are supposed by some to be an offshoot. Formerly a great trade in slaves was carried on, the Nias women being celebrated for their beauty, and even now the coast Malays of the mainland try to obtain them as wives. The island produces large quantities of coco-nut oil, but in this respect is surpassed by the Nacco group of islets off its western coast, which Signor Modigliani describes as presenting the appearance of vast gardens of coco-palms, intermingled with plantations of rice and sweet potatoes.

The small group known as the Batu or Rock Islands come next in the chain. There are three chief islands Pingi, Masa, and Bala, each of which is about 30 miles long. Their inhabitants seem to be a similar race to the Nias people, with whom they keep up a friendly intercourse. There are many Malays and Chinese settled on the coast, the latter, as in Nias, having the whole trade in their hands. Upon the little islet Pulo Telo the Dutch have a resident Controleur.

The Mentawi Islands are two only in number—Sibiru and Sipora—of which the former is much the larger, being not much inferior to Nias in size. The Nassau Islands—North and South Pagi or Poggy Islands—may conveniently be grouped with them as being inhabited by the same race—a people whom Von Rosenberg declares to be totally distinct in physique and speech from any other tribe of the adjacent islands and mainland, and strikingly like the Eastern Polynesians. Their language is soft, full of vowels, and of a very primitive character, possibly possessing affinities with some of the Polynesian dialects. They love to decorate themselves with flowers, tattoo themselves on the breast, and file their front teeth; all of which customs are characteristic rather of the Pacific Islands than Malaysia. They are very peaceable in disposition, firearms are unknown, and their only weapons are the bow and arrow. They live chiefly by fishing, and rice seems to be little if at all cultivated, their chief food being the products of the sago and coco palms. Professor Keane regards these people as possibly autochthones—"the only remnant of the western Mahoris that has escaped contact and fusion with the intruding sub-Mongolian and other Asiatic races." Both the Nassau Islands are high and densely wooded, the largest about 30 miles in length by 10 in breadth. Sibiru is said to have an active volcano.

Engaño, the last of this great chain of islands, is not more than fifteen miles in length, and is surrounded by coral reefs. Its hills nowhere exceed 400 feet, and it is covered with timber, like all the islands in this chain. The inhabitants, under 1000 in number, are half savage, were unacquainted with the use of iron until a short time ago, and speak a language which is described as being wholly unintelligible to Malays. The coco-nut is largely grown, together with bananas, sugar-cane, and pine-apple.

(2) The delta islands of the eastern coast, although of large size, are not important. Two, Mendang and Rupat, separated by a narrow strait, lie off the mouth of the Rakan river. Farther south, the Siak and Kampar Besar rivers disembogue by a network of canals to form a group of four large islands, each more than 30 miles in length —Bankalis, Padang, Rantau, and Panjor. Two others, Sabon and Mandol, are a little farther to the south. All these islands are alike in being low, flat, and densely jungled. They have a very sparse population, and produce little besides sago.

(3) The Rhio-Lingga Archipelago exhibits a vast collection of reefs, shoals, and islands clustered around the terminal point of the Malay Peninsula. The northern group has two chief islands, Batam and Bintang, while in the southern division there are also two which considerably exceed the rest in size—Lingga and Singkep. Geologically, all these islands are continuations southwards of the Malay Peninsula, showing the granites and sandstones of that region, and in every way differing from the low alluvial formations of the eastern coast of Sumatra. The islands are more or less undulating and hilly, and Lingga Peak rises to a height of 3920 feet.

Not long after the occupation of Singapore by the British, the Dutch established a post on Rhio Island, on the south-east side of Bintang. Originally designed to counteract the trade of Singapore, it has merely added to it, but has itself also become prosperous. The archipelago is the chief seat of the gambir trade, and some millions of pounds of this commodity are annually exported. Black pepper is also much grown, and considerable quantities of the forest products—gutta, dammar, wax, timber, etc.—find their way from here to the Singapore markets. All this trade has caused a large influx of Chinese and coast Malays, especially of the former, and the port of Rhio is visited by the Dutch lines of steamers. Innumerable ships pass through the Rhio Strait, for it is now the recognised highway in both monsoons for vessels proceeding eastwards, or bound through the Strait of Sunda.

The only post of the Dutch in the southern group is upon Lingga, where an Assistant Resident is established. The town is very prettily situated beneath a striking peak, upon a river nearly a mile from the sea, and contains 7000 or 8000 inhabitants, the Chinese having substantial houses of stone. The produce is chiefly rattans, gambir, and pepper. Gold is obtained in small quantities, but tin has not yet been discovered, although it occurs in the neighbouring island of Singkep. The Rhio-Lingga Archipelago, together with the valley of the Indragiri river on the opposite shore of Sumatra, and the Anamba and Natuna Islands north-west of Borneo, forms the political district known as "Rhio and its Dependencies."

(4) Bangka (Banca or Banka) is situated opposite the eastern coast of Palembang, from which it is separated by a long strait of a tolerably uniform width of 15

or 20 miles—well known to navigators as the Bangka Strait and as the chief highway for all shipping passing between the great islands of Borneo and Sumatra. Bangka is 138 miles in length, and has an area of nearly 5000 square miles. It is comparatively sterile, is full of small valleys and swamps, and is everywhere covered with thick forest. Its surface is rugged and irregular, and a series of high hills not disposed in ranges runs through its whole length, parallel with and of similar character to those of the Malay Peninsula. The greatest heights attained are those of Mount Maras, 2760 feet, and the Parmasang Mountains, 1608 feet, but it is remarkable that, notwithstanding their low elevation, the summits of these hills are generally covered with clouds, which has caused their height to be much over-estimated by some writers.

Like the islands of the Rhio-Lingga Archipelago, and like its near neighbour Blitong, Bangka is Peninsular in its affinities, not Sumatran. The formation is principally granitic, and in situations of less elevation there occurs the red ironstone clay (laterite) which forms so marked a feature of the landscape in Singapore and Ceylon. In the lowest lands is an alluvial formation, intermixed with sandstones and breccias, in which is found the tin for which the island is famous. Zoology bears out the evidences afforded by geology. Although so near Sumatra, all the large Carnivora are absent, except the Malay bear, and neither the elephant, rhinoceros, nor tapir exist. More remarkable is the occurrence of numerous peculiar species of birds and a squirrel, which differ from those of Sumatra and Borneo sometimes more than the species of those islands differ from each other. There is therefore every reason to suppose that Bangka was once a southern extension of the Malay Peninsula, from which it has been isolated by subsidence of the intervening land. The animals now inhabiting it may thus be the unmodified descendants of ancient Malayan species which in the larger islands have undergone progressive changes.

The history of Bangka practically dates from the discovery of its tin, which occurred in 1709. From the Sultan of Palembang, to whom the island belonged, the Dutch acquired the monopoly of the metal. In 1811, when the English gained possession of the Sumatran settlements, the Sultan, in the hope of gaining favour with them, massacred all the Dutch in his dominions, an act of treachery which was fitly punished by his dethronement by the British. From 1812 to 1816 the island remained a British possession, at which latter date it was again resigned to the Dutch, who, after a few native wars, have since remained in undisturbed possession of it.

The original inhabitants of Bangka are few in number. They consist of hill tribes, said to resemble the Battaks, cultivating a little rice, but existing largely on the products of the forest; and the Orang Laut, or fishermen, who live chiefly in their praus. The bulk of the population is immigrant, and is almost entirely formed by Malays from the north and by Chinese. The census of 1st January, 1887, gives the entire population as nearly 75,000, of which 21,000 are Chinese, over 53,000 Malays, and only 165 Europeans. The Chinese are chiefly engaged in digging, washing, and smelting the alluvial tin ore, which is widely spread and worked in many parts of the island, although chiefly in the north-west, around Merawang, of which district the well-protected but narrow harbour of Klabat forms the port. Gold and iron are also worked, and lead, silver, copper, and arsenic have been found. The chief town of Bangka is Muntok, which is fortified and garrisoned, and is the seat of the Resident. It has a population of about 4000, and is a port of call for all the mail steamers between Batavia and Singapore. The Dutch are represented by Controleurs at eight different towns and villages in various parts of the island.

East of Bangka, and separated from it by the dangerous, reef-beset Gaspar Strait, lies Blitong (Billiton), a considerable island of an irregular, sub-quadrangular form, and about 40 miles across. It has an area of about 1800 miles, and the highest point attains an elevation of 3117 feet. Geologically it resembles Bangka and exhibits the same alluvial deposits of tin, and like that island it is covered with dense forest. The iron ore has been worked by the natives for a very long period, but the value of the tin deposits was only recognised about the year 1850. At the present time nearly as much is obtained from this island as from Bangka, but it is the extreme southern limit of the stanniferous formation. This begins in Tenasserim, and occupying more than 20° of latitude, is thus the most extensive in the world.

The chief town of Blitong is Tanjong Pandang, on the Chiruchup river. There is but little trade except in forest produce and tin. The population of the island in 1887 was 35,000, of whom over 9000 were Chinese. The total output of tin for Bangka and Blitong in tons for the five years 1886-1890 was as follows:—6175, 7906, 11,712, 10,383, 8876, and the average may therefore be placed at about 9000 tons. The industry is a Government monopoly, and is leased to a company. Of late the island has been politically separated from Bangka, and is now an Assistant Residency.

8. Religion. Antiquities.

It is impossible now to fix the date of the introduction

of Hinduism into Sumatra, or to discover how far and to what extent it became adopted. The temple-remains, though found more or less all over the island, are very scattered, and nowhere do they approach in importance those of Java. At Kuta-bangan, in the Dili district, there is a stone temple about 60 feet square, having the figures of men and animals sculptured upon its walls, and various inscribed stones have been found in the neighbourhood. That the cult of Siva existed in the Jambi valley is evident from the statues of the bull Nandi, the vehicle of Mahadewa, and the elephant-headed god Ganesa discovered there. The images are carved out of granite, and were therefore probably made in the highlands of the interior. At Muara Takus, on the Kampar river, are other Hindu ruins of importance, and the Menangkabo district has perhaps afforded more examples than any other part of the island. The Hindu influence doubtless came as much from the south as from the north, with the stream of Javanese immigration which has more than once been alluded to. Of how long it lasted we have not much more knowledge than we have of its establishment. About the thirteenth century Islamism began to gain a footing, and is now the accepted religion of almost all the civilised and semi-civilised tribes. Over a vast area, however, pure paganism exists, and Christianity, both here and among the Mohammedans, has met with little or no success.

9. Products, Trade, and Agriculture.

While Java may be regarded as the garden of the Netherlands India, where, under the "culture system," almost every tropical product has the benefit of the most careful farming, Sumatra still labours under the disadvantages of non-development, and a very large portion of her exports are forest products. The rice—although in certain districts almost as carefully cultivated as in Java—is for the most part grown by the *ladang*, or dry system, instead of by the carefully terraced and irrigated *sawahs*, or wet-field culture, which is the rule in the sister island. The same may be said of the less important food stuffs, though the Menangkabo valleys form a marked exception, and show most careful farming. Almost all the fruits, cereals, and farinaceous roots belonging to Java and Malacca are found in the island, and some other commodities, such as benzoin, are only obtained here and in Borneo. The vast extent of lowland in the eastern part of the island, together with the large delta islands lying off the mouths of the rivers in this part, produce sago in great abundance. But the product for which Sumatra is chiefly renowned is black pepper. For nearly two centuries the Dutch endeavoured to retain the monopoly of its culture, and the efforts of the British in Benkulen were directed to the same end. The western portion of the island was the chief seat of the trade, and this part was, and is still, known to mariners as the "Pepper Coast." The spice at the present time is most grown at the north and at the south extremities of the island—in the Ache and Lampong districts— and in a good year the export reaches the amount of nearly 18,000 tons, which is said to be two-thirds of the world's consumption. About eight years are needed for a pepper garden to reach maturity, but once in full bearing, the annual yield in value of each shrub should be about 10s. The only other products of great importance are coffee and tobacco. The returns have of late decreased considerably, but a few years since coffee was exported to the value of nearly half a million sterling annually. It is grown principally in the upland districts around Padang, and finds a market chiefly in the United States. The great agricultural feature of East Sumatra is the tobacco industry of the Dili district, which is of recent establishment, but has proved an unqualified success. The

PALACE OF A SUMATRAN PRINCE.

Sumatra crop has now actually exceeded that of Java in quantity, while the quality is much superior. The object is largely, though not solely, the growth of what are technically termed "wrappers"— leaves of great excellence both in quality and appearance, which are used as the outer or folding leaves of Havana cigars of the finest quality. These are sent to Europe, and thence re-exported to Cuba, while the smoking-tobacco remains for home consumption in Holland. The industry is in the hands of a few large companies, and is not permitted to Chinese capitalists, although Chinese labour is very largely employed on the fields, the Battaks and Malays being less valuable as labourers. The export during the last decade has been very considerable. That of 1886 exceeded 11,000 tons, and its estimated value was nearly £3,000,000, the crop averaging two shillings per lb. The sugar-cane is not cultivated. A great trade is carried on, on the east coast especially, in beeswax, camphor, gutta, dammar, benzoin, and other resins, rattans, gambir, cotton, and various sea-products such as *béche-de-mer*.

The mineral wealth of Sumatra still remains for the most part undeveloped, although it is probable that, before long, the rich coal-fields of Ombilin, which are situated towards the head waters of the Batang Hari, will be opened. They were discovered in 1869, and have been estimated by M. de Grève to contain 370,000,000 cubic metres. The mineral is of the Tertiary period, as it is probable that most of the Sumatran measures will prove to be. Mr. Forbes found coal in the Palembang district, and it exists near Malabu and other places in Ache. South of Padang, at Moko-moko, it is worked. Gold is even more widely distributed. The fields around Padang, which have been known for centuries, are now exhausted, but the Menangkabo placer diggings, which are equally ancient, are still in operation. The metal is found at Malabu in Ache, and at many places on the eastern slopes of the Barisan range, but the amount obtained is trivial, though, were a thorough exploration undertaken, it would probably lead to good results. Tin exists on the eastern side in the Siak district, and there are copper mines in the Padang "bovenland," near the Merapi volcano, but the output of both metals is insignificant. Iron has been dug and smelted for ages by the Menangkabo Malays. Concessions were granted in 1891 for working some petroleum wells lately discovered, sulphur is abundantly obtained from the craters of various volcanoes, and it is probable that antimony is also existent.

The industries of the island are not numerous. Krisses are largely made, especially in Menangkabo, and the workmanship is often excellent, as is the embossed gold-work of their sheaths. The silk *sarongs* worked with gold thread are as fine as those made in Brunei, and as costly, but they are chiefly made by immigrant workmen. Palembang is celebrated for its manufacture of furniture, but this also is foreign labour, the greater part of it being constructed by Chinese.

10. Population and Political Divisions.

The population of Sumatra has been given at $3\frac{1}{2}$ millions, but it is probable that this is an under-estimation. So much of the country, however, is unknown, that guesswork rather than calculation comes into play. Ache, the highlands of Padang, and the Palembang divisions are all stated to have over 500,000 inhabitants, and the two first named are the most thickly populated portions of the island. The Dutch have divided the island and its satellites into nine administrative divisions, viz. (1) The Government of Ache and its Dependencies; (2) the Government of the West Coast; (3) the Residency of Benkulen; (4) the Residency of the Lampongs; (5) the Residency of Palembang; (6) the Residency of the East Coast; (7) the Residency of Rhio and its Dependencies; (8) the Residency of Bangka and (9) the Assistant-Residency of Blitong.

The system of administration varies with the condition of the inhabitants. Thus the Ache "Government" is such only in name except at certain of the coast towns, and over a great portion of the centre of the island the Dutch have no rule or authority whatsoever. In other districts a species of suzerainty exists, the chiefs paying tribute or acknowledging the Government, but ruling their subjects without intervention. In others again the Dutch have engrafted their administration firmly upon the old communal native system, and rule much as they do in Java. The most settled districts are Dili, Benkulen, and the country between this town and Palembang, and the highlands of Padang.

11. Chief Towns.

The four chief towns of Sumatra are Padang, Ache (Kota Raja), Benkulen, and Palembang. Padang is in some ways the most important; it has about 16,000 inhabitants, and is a place of considerable trade, there being many European merchants, with Arabs, Chinese, Javanese, Battaks, and Nias islanders settled within its limits. The town presents the aspect of a beautiful park, and is situated on the right bank of the Padang river, whose mouth is dominated by the picturesque Apenberg. The port is inferior and exposed to westerly weather. The country to the north is flat, with extensive rice fields, and good roads shaded by avenues of trees lead inland. Westward, at a distance of a few miles, the hills begin, on ascending which the rich Padang plateau or "bovenland" is reached, where the climate is well suited for coffee cultivation. Here, at an elevation of about 3000 feet, are Fort de Kock, the seat of the Resident, and the garrison; and a few miles to the south, in the neighbourhood of the Singkara Lake, Fort van der Capellen.

Ache, known to the Dutch and natives as Kota Raja, lies some three miles from the port Olele, with which it is connected by railway. The latter town is built on piles on the shores of a creek, and, like many of the Sumatran sea-ports, is not very healthy. Kota Raja is prettily placed and well built. The population numbers about 12,000 without the Europeans. The garrison is very large, five or six thousand troops being stationed here and at one or two villages on the coast. Owing to the enormous loss of life from beri-beri, the Dutch have given up many of the earlier forts and rebuilt others more in accordance with modern ideas on hygiene. It is indicative of the unsettled condition of the country that the windows of the railway carriage are made of steel plates, as the trains are frequently fired upon. Trenches surround all the fortified positions, artillery is mounted on elevated bastions, and powerful lights illumine the foreground at night. Like precautions have to be taken by the neighbouring friendly Achenese, sentinels keeping guard day and night from high watch-towers. The railway above mentioned, although the first constructed in Sumatra, is not the only line, another of 30 miles or more in length connecting Medan and other villages in the Dili districts with the sea-port.

Benkulen, on the southern part of the west coast, and in about 4° south latitude, is chiefly interesting as having been a British possession for nearly a century and a half. Driven out by Dutch influence from Bantam, the English established themselves here in 1685, and for a period of a hundred years—up to the time of the foundation of Penang in 1785—held it as their sole possession in the Malay Archipelago. In 1824 they obtained Malacca from the Dutch and yielded them Benkulen in return.

The town has now lost whatever greatness it possessed. Although it is said to have 12,000 inhabitants, the trade is of no importance, the surrounding territory infertile, and the situation unhealthy. The coffee cultivation has been more or less abandoned, and earthquakes have partially destroyed some of the buildings and given an air of desolation to the town.

Palembang differs greatly from Benkulen, being the seat of a vast and increasing trade. The town lies about 45 miles up the Sungsang or Palembang river, and is one of the largest and most curious in the whole archipelago. It is accessible at all times to vessels of the heaviest burden, the width of the stream at the town being about three-quarters of a mile, and its depth five or six fathoms close to the shore. The town lines both banks of the stream for a distance of 6 miles, and large numbers of the population inhabit the praus and rakits anchored in the river, much as the floating population of Canton and other Chinese cities, so that all marketing and general business is carried on by water. A Resident and other officials reside here, and with various merchants number altogether about 100 Europeans. The entire population is estimated at from forty to fifty thousand, and, in spite of the surrounding marshes, the climate is considered so healthy that convalescent soldiers are sent here from Bangka. A small garrison is stationed here, and there is a kraton, or fort, of substantial construction, capable of containing 1500 men, with walls 8 feet thick and 50 feet high, and mounting eight guns on each of the bastions at the four corners. The export trade has already been alluded to. Owing to its numerous affluents, the river taps a vast area, and it is said that a hundred or more praus laden with produce often arrive from up country in the course of a single day.

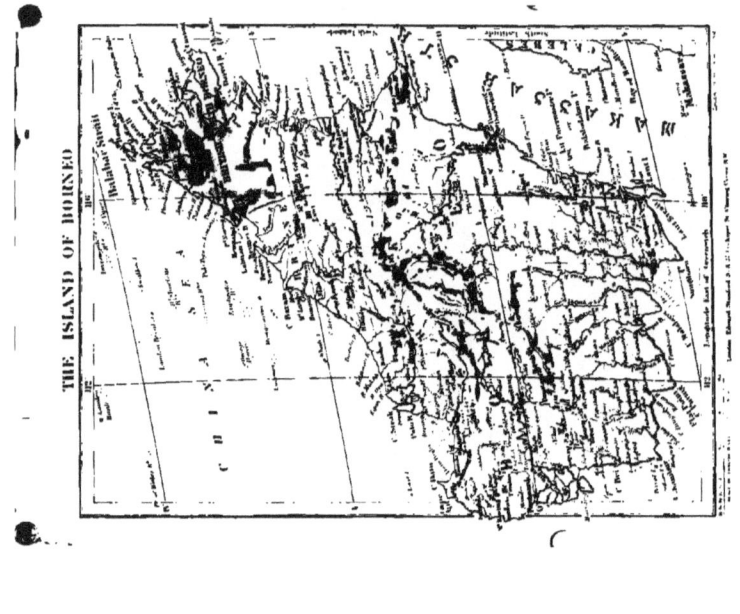

CHAPTER VII

BORNEO

1. General.

IF we consider Australia to be more properly a continent, Borneo is undoubtedly the second island in the world in point of magnitude, for New Guinea alone surpasses it. Its extreme length is about 850 miles, and its greatest breadth 600. Its compact mass is somewhat pear-shaped, lying in a north-east and south-west direction. It has a coast line of about 3000 miles, without measuring the smaller bays and inlets, and its area is about 285,000 square miles, being nearly three and a half times as large as Great Britain.

Extending from 7° 3′ N. to 4° 10′ S. latitude, and being nearly bisected by the Equator, Borneo occupies a central position amid the greater Malay islands, being, roughly speaking, equally distant from the Philippines on the north-east, from Celebes on the east, from Java on the south, and from Sumatra and the Malay Peninsula on the west. It is thus removed from the violence of typhoons, and enjoys on all its coasts a tolerably calm sea. There are comparatively few islands around its shores, the most important being the Natunas off the western promontory, and Pulo Laut on the south-east; but at the north-east, from the country now called British North Borneo, two separate chains of islands run to form connecting-links with the main group of the Philippines, the most eastern being known as the Sulu Archipelago.

The coast of Borneo is very little indented with bays, and nowhere by deep inlets. The few bays it possesses are towards the north-eastern extremity, where the coast is somewhat higher and more abrupt. As a rule the island is bordered throughout by a considerable width of swamp and lowland, except at a few points where there are high promontories or a small extent of hilly country. Various ranges of mountains, which may be roughly described as radiating from a common centre, divide the island into sections, the intervening land being low, flat, and marshy, and it has been pointed out that a subsidence of 500 feet would allow the sea to fill the great valleys of the Kapuas, Barito, and Koti rivers almost to the centre of the island, greatly reducing it in size, and causing it to assume a star-shaped outline much resembling that of the neighbouring island of Celebes.

Politically, Borneo is divided into four separate territories—British North Borneo or Saba occupying the northern portion, and Sarawak the greater part of the north-western. Between them lies the small independent state of the Sultan of Brunei. The rest of the island belongs to the Dutch, and is considerably larger than the aggregate of the other three territories. The island is, on the whole, very sparsely inhabited. It is impossible to obtain any exact data as to its population, but it is estimated as under 2,000,000.

2. History.

So far as is known, the Italian traveller Varthema

was the first European to visit Borneo, probably at the end of 1505, but he appears to have made no stay there. Malacca fell to the Portuguese in 1511, and it seems improbable that for ten years after that date the island should have remained unvisited, especially when it is remembered that the far-distant islands of Banda and Ternate were reached before the year had ended. We have, however, no trustworthy account of any such visit, and the next mention of " Bornei " occurs in Pigafetta's diary. After the death of Magellan in the Philippines, the two remaining ships of his squadron sailed south-westward, and reached the city of Brunei in July, 1521. Pigafetta's description of the town would almost serve for the present day. The Malays had been long established there, and were in a high state of civilisation. They had forts mounting heavy guns, and used horses and trained elephants. In the king's house were silver candlesticks, and gold spoons of European shape were used at his table. Although Pigafetta makes no mention of Chinese being settled in the city, it is very probable that they had even then established themselves. Considerable Chinese trade must at all events have existed, as is proved by the description of the silks, brocades, and porcelain vases in the king's possession, while the currency was entirely of that country, bronze or brass coins pierced for stringing, and stamped with Chinese characters.

Except for a possible visit by Lorenzo Gomez in 1518, the first acquaintance of the Portuguese with the island was in 1526, when Jorge de Meneses touched at Brunei on his way to the Moluccas. A few years later they established trading posts at various ports, but no attempt at conquest was made then or at any subsequent period. Oliver van Noort brought the Dutch to the island in 1598, and commerce was soon initiated by them, as it was a few years later by the English, so that in the middle of the seventeenth century three European nations were busily engaged in trying to supplant each other at the various ports. For more than half a century, however—from 1670 to 1733—the Dutch left the field, and were followed by the Portuguese, and in 1707 the English, who had a settlement at Banjarmasin, then a place of considerable trade, were driven out by the natives. In 1733 the Dutch returned, and fifty-two years later a civil war placed them in possession of the large territory belonging to the Sultan of Banjarmasin. The country nevertheless remained undeveloped, and it was only subsequent to the restoration to the Dutch in 1816 of their Malayan dominion that anything was done in the way of settlement. Since that time considerable additions have been made to their possessions, and the entire island, with the exception of the Brunei, Sarawak, and British North Borneo Company's territories, now belongs to Holland. The history of the English occupation of these latter countries will be separately considered on a later page.

The medieval history of the island is chiefly conjectural, and we have even less knowledge of it than of that of Java and Sumatra. Numerous ruins of Hindu temples in various parts of the island, as for example at Pontianak on the west, Sangkulirang on the east, and 400 miles in the interior on the Koti river, prove that the Borneans must in bygone ages have come under a western influence if not an actual dominion, but it is probable that the immigration took place largely from Java. Borneo, however, could at no time have been a political unit. Later, Malays from the Peninsula or from Sumatra invaded the island, and, settling on the coasts, drove the aborigines inland; but although they brought with them a tolerably advanced civilisation, as we can see from Pigafetta's description, their influence did not penetrate far into the interior.

3. Geology and Physical Features.

Borneo in pre-Tertiary days exhibited a very different configuration from that of the present time. It consisted almost certainly of a mass of islands, now represented by the central range, Kinabalu, the Sarawak and western districts, the Tana Laut Mountains, etc., which in geological structure resembled the islands of Bangka and Blitong. In his work on the geology and mineralogy of Borneo, Dr. Theodor Posewitz remarks that in this ancient archipelago crystalline schists played only a subordinate part. "The rocks belonged mainly to the 'Old Slate Formation' of Devonian age, and in the northern portion of the islands to the Carboniferous. The stratigraphical position of these strata was disturbed by the eruption of igneous rocks, granites, and diorites. The eruption took place partly after the formation of the Devonian, partly in pre-Devonian times. . . . Then began a deposition of sedimentary matter in the seas surrounding the islands. The Eocene strata containing the thick coal-beds were formed, and then disturbed by the eruption of andesite. Further, younger Tertiary beds containing brown coal were deposited. The separate islands were now united, the Tertiary beds being deposited not only between them, but also as a belt on all sides. The configuration of Borneo was thus brought nearer to its present shape, first acquiring a form similar to that possessed at the present day by the neighbouring island of Celebes. Wide arms of the sea ran far into the interior. In the beginning of the Diluvial period these gulfs began slowly to give place to dry land; a strip of flat land was formed along the foot of the mountains, and gold, diamonds, and platinum, swept down by running water, were here deposited. The seas became shallower and retreated, and the present period commenced."

From the above sketch, the general configuration of Borneo of the present time can be gathered. We find a skeleton mountain formation in which the mountains, although arranged in chains, are not continuously elevated, but more or less separate and insular in nature; a hill-land of Tertiary age surrounding it, and in turn bordered by a dry plain land, which merges imperceptibly into vast swamps and morasses, through which large and tortuous rivers find their way to a shallow sea. This rough outline does not, of course, hold equally good for all localities. Thus in British North Borneo the land is more elevated, and the older rocks in close approximation to the sea, and the formation in Brunei and in the western promontory of the island is likewise irregular. It is in the southern and eastern portions that the characters mentioned are most apparent. Here we have four main basins, drained principally by the Kapuas, Barito, Koti, and Kayan rivers, and separated from each other by mountain chains.

The Tertiary beds of which the hill and lower lands are composed have been separated into Eocene, Oligocene, and Miocene. Dr. Posewitz states that "all four stages of the Eocene are developed in Borneo. The first or breccia stage, consisting of conglomerates and sandstones, is up to the present only known in West Borneo. The second, or sandstone stage, is of great thickness and wide development; it yields the Indian coal, and consists of quartz, sandstones, shales, and coal seams. The third, or marl stage, consists of marls and shales, with isolated nummulites, many orbitoids, lamellibranchs, and crustaceans. The fourth, or limestone stage, which forms coral reefs, contains numerous fossils, among which are nummulites and many orbitoids. These strata are broken through and disturbed by basalts, augite- and hornblende-andesites, which are associated with breccias, conglomerates, and tuffs of eruptive origin. The age of these rocks is probably Miocene, for the limestone stage is also pierced by them. As to the composition of the younger Tertiary formations little is known. They appear, however, to consist also of sandstone, marl, and limestone beds, and the limestones are said to occur as coral reefs."

The abundance and wide distribution of coal in the island is remarkable. In this respect Borneo is by far the richest of all the islands of the Malay Archipelago. Schwaner says:—" The occurrence of coal is more widespread than one might be led to think by a first examination. In the whole of the hill-formation it constitutes a most important and almost never-failing factor. All fissures and openings that have been made use of for the investigation of the underground geology have led to the discovery of coal seams, and even the banks of the great rivers disclose them in many places." As far as is known, there is no coal of greater age than the Tertiary period. Most of it belongs to the Eocene, but the brown coals of the Miocene also occur plentifully.

Mr. Motley, in his Report on the Geology of Labuan and neighbourhood, gives the following interesting description of its peculiarities:—" The coal, dense and perfectly carbonised as it is, yet exhibits most unequivocally its vegetable origin; and not only that, but even the kind of vegetation of which it has been composed is evident from the most cursory inspection of the heaps of coal brought out of the levels. It is clearly the product, not of a bed of peat produced by the decay of small vegetation, but of a mass of huge timber. At least one half of the mass displays the grain and structure of wood, and frequently it separates naturally into the concentric layers of dicotyledonous wood. All the specimens I have examined have exactly the structure of the dipteraceous trees now forming the bulk of the timber growing above them. The trees must have been of vast dimensions. I traced one trunk upwards of 60 feet, and for the whole of that distance it was not less than 8 feet wide. They are all prostrate and slightly compressed, and lie crossing each other in all directions. What makes the resemblance of this coal to the wood of the Dipteraceæ still more striking is the existence in it of thickly scattered masses of semi-transparent resin dispersed through its substance. The clay below the coal contains a few carbonaceous particles, but no trace of Stigmaria or any other forms of fossil roots. In the shale above the coal are found occasionally erect trunks of small size, apparently, from the coats of their bark, dicotyledonous, but their whole substance converted into soft pulverulent coal; and, more rarely, palm trunks, also erect but solidified, and excessively hard. Impressions of leaves are in vast abundance, though rarely perfect. I have procured specimens of nine species of dicotyledons, of which two so closely resemble an existing species of Barringtonia and a dipteraceous plant which yields an oily resin named 'druing,' that it is difficult to believe them not identical. Besides these are two or three species of ferns, a large flag-shaped leaf like a Crinum, something closely resembling a large thick-stemmed confervoid alga, and four or five species of palms, one flabelliform and four pinnate, one of the latter very closely resembling an existing species. These vegetable remains are chiefly, but not entirely, in the lower part of the stratum. Sparingly among them, but more abundantly in the upper half of the thickness of the bed, are found a good many casts of bivalve shells, much like some species of Unio." In some adjacent beds of shale are found marine shells consisting of species of *Cardium*, *Tridacna*, *Arca*, *Ostrea*, *Tellina*, *Murex*, *Turbo*, *Cerithium*, and *Pecten*, all genera now living in the adjacent seas.

It is remarkable that such an evidently recent formation should be so much upheaved, the coal-measures of Labuan and Brunei dipping from an angle of 24 to nearly or quite vertical, the dip being N.N.W., or about at right angles to the direction of the great chain of mountains which rises nearly parallel to the coast. Mr. Motley's account of this coal formation would lead us to conclude that dense tropical forests growing on an extensive plain or river delta had been suddenly overthrown by flood or earthquake, or by sudden depression of the land, and had been covered with a deposit of clays or sands. He well remarks on the quantities of trees and shrubs which in the tropics grow on the sea-shore, or even in the salt water, and thus accounts for the presence of marine shells in the shales, and even in the coal itself.

Until recently, Borneo was supposed to differ from all the other great islands of the archipelago in not possessing a single volcano, either active or extinct, but this supposition has lately been shown to be not quite correct. It is highly improbable that Kinabalu is volcanic, as Mr. Little, who ascended one of its peaks in 1887, declared, but a small volcano, which is probably of late Miocene or Pliocene age, was discovered by the mining-engineer Van Schelle in the Menteradu district, situated to the west of the Bawang Mountains, and about 40 miles from the most western point of Borneo. Other ancient volcanoes have been described lately (1889) as existing in the same district. They appear to occur in the region of the Old Slate formation of the Devonian age. Hot springs, though not common, exist in many places and are widely distributed, being found in South and West Borneo and in Sarawak.

The exploration of the island having been of necessity chiefly carried out by the rivers, our knowledge of the mountains is exceedingly limited. Land travel is both difficult and dangerous. Few travellers have crossed any of the great ranges, and details of their height are thus almost entirely wanting. Even concerning Kinabalu, whose vast mass appears as one of the most conspicuous features of the country to those navigating on the northern coast, the differences of opinion are very great, and of the central mountain group nothing is known. Kinabalu, or the "Chinese widow," which is situated towards the extreme north of the island, is, however, almost certainly its loftiest mountain, and possibly is not excelled by any other in the archipelago. The results of a triangulation by Sir Edward Belcher made its altitude to be 13,698 feet. It is an isolated mountain mass, consisting of several peaks forming a vast wall, which is higher at the western part. The northern face appears as a gigantic precipice, but, owing to the size of the mountain and the difficulties connected with its ascent, its exact conformation is unknown. Low was the first to attain the summit, but it has since been ascended, entirely or in part, by Spenser St. John, Bove, Hatton, Little, and Whitehead. The view from the higher peaks is said to be magnificent, and numerous ranges estimated at 7000 or 8000 feet in height are visible to the south.

In a general south-west direction from Kinabalu an

interrupted range extends at a tolerably uniform distance of 80 or 90 miles from the coast, bending sharply at right angles towards its termination at Cape Datu, and forming the natural inland delimitation of the Sarawak and Brunei territories. In the greater part of its extent it is unknown, but Mounts Malu and Marud at the head of the Brunei river are estimated at 8000 feet, and Mount Baling at over 7000. Between the Batang Lupar and the Seriang Lake the range appears to be discontinuous, as it also is towards the western boundary of Sarawak, where the hills—for the elevation becomes much diminished—have frequently the character of abrupt isolated blocks. The highest elevation in this part is Mount Pu, in the neighbourhood of Tanjong Datu, which is believed to be about 6000 feet in height. Still farther west, in the Menteradu (Montrado) district, Mounts Bawang, Pandan, and others form a separate group of insignificant height.

From near the middle of the chain just considered, three principal ranges are believed to originate, and not far from the centre of the nucleus thus formed lies Mount Tebang, which is as yet unvisited by Europeans. Native accounts on the whole concur in describing this mountain as of great height, and giving origin to the four great rivers of Borneo, and it is further stated to have its summit white. It is, nevertheless, improbable that a snow mountain should exist without having been viewed by some of the many travellers who have explored the rivers, and it may be concluded that the story in this respect is without foundation. The three main ranges have a general direction of E., S.S.E., and S.S.W., and mark out the basins of the Kayan, Mahakkam (Koti), Barito, and Kapuas. They are composed, for much of their extent, of isolated hills or mountains, so that it is often possible to pass from one river-basin to another without any great ascent, and this arrangement of the mountains may be regarded as a characteristic feature of the orography of the island.

Borneo is remarkable both for its plains and rivers. The southern and eastern portions of the island are, in the main, areas of flatness and little elevation, as may be gathered from a glance at the map, which shows the rivers to be of almost phenomenal tortuousness. In some places quite flat, in others gently undulating, these plains occupy the spot where, in pre-Tertiary days, the sea flowed. Towards the coast, and in the vicinity of rivers, this flat land often exists as vast and impassable morasses, which in the wet season become much enlarged, so that enormous areas become submerged. Schwaner estimated that 160 square geographical miles are daily flooded by tidal action in the basin of the Barito, and 580—or more than one-third of the entire basin—in the rainy season. Like phenomena may be witnessed upon many, if not most, other of these rivers, and Dr. Posewitz, in his work on the geology of the island, gives the following graphic description of the appearance of the district surrounding the Negara, an affluent of the Barito. "During my first journey everything, as far as the eye could see, was covered with water: it appeared to extend to the mountain-chain skirting the eastern horizon, the foot of which is surrounded by steep Tertiary coral reefs. In the midst of the flooded district one could see Negara, an important seat of industry, extending along the end of the great sheet of water, as if it were situated on an inland sea. In the swampy parts there were thick patches of rushes, which formed welcome resting-places for dense swarms of mosquitoes, and the oarsman in threading his way is obliged to keep a sharp look-out in order not to lose himself, for should this happen, he would be compelled to lie by until the following morning. In the dry season the district bore quite another aspect. The immense sheet of water had disappeared, its place being taken by a black soil, traversed by numerous canals and filled with clear darkbrown water. During the dry season, between Barabai and Amuntai, I could clearly distinguish the districts subject to periodic floods. The vegetation consists entirely of thickly tangled bushes, while the boundary was marked by the gigantic trees of the virgin forest."

Few countries are so plentifully furnished with rivers as Borneo, and, although in most cases the existence of bars prevents the entrance of large vessels, small craft can navigate them for a very large portion of their course. The rivers of the north-west are necessarily the smallest, from the proximity of the mountain range to the seaboard. Taking them in their order from the north, the first of any importance is the Limbang, better known as the Brunei river. From the absence of nipa palm and mangrove, and the bareness of its banks, it differs greatly from the majority of the rivers of tropical Malaysia, and the plentiful outcrop of coal visible in ascending the stream renders it still more peculiar. It is supposed to admit vessels of 20 feet draught, but the entrance is very intricate and dangerous. The Rejang, a large stream which rises near the central mountain mass, and debouches by two mouths, is of more importance, and much forest produce descends its stream. It is the largest river in Sarawak, and will admit vessels of 1000 tons. The fort, where a Resident of the Sarawak service is stationed, lies 25 miles from the entrance, and ships can anchor off it in 7 fathoms. A small Government steamer ascends the river for 200 miles. The Batang

Lupar also admits large vessels, but has a very much shorter course, and the Sarawak river is only of importance as the stream on which Kuching is built. It is not till we come to the more southern part of the island that the characteristic Bornean rivers are met with, and of these one of the largest is the Kapuas, which reaches the sea at Pontianak. It has its sources in the central mountains, probably near Mount Tebang, which is also reputed to give origin to the Barito, the Mahakkam, and the Kayan or Bulungan. Thence it pursues a tortuous course in a south-west direction, forming an enormous delta at its mouth. As it is beset by a bar carrying only 10 to 12 feet of water at high tide, it is unnavigable by large vessels, but small Government steamers ascend it for 200 miles. Until lately, large lakes were formed in the middle part of its course during the rainy season, a common feature in Bornean rivers, but now these have become to a great extent silted up, and the detritus brought down by the floods has caused the land to gain rapidly on the sea at the river's mouth.

Between the Kapuas and the Barito occur various considerable rivers, the Lamandu, Pembuan, Mentaya, Katingan, Kahayan, and others, but they are of little importance commercially. It is otherwise with the great Barito, upon which Banjarmasin is situated. It is 3 miles wide at the mouth, is supposed to exceed 570 miles in length, and is thus the longest river in the Malay Archipelago. In its upper course it is very rapid, and is said to abound in waterfalls, and lower it expands in the wet season into lakes and morasses, which occupy, as has already been stated, an area of some hundreds of square miles, in which respect it is almost equalled by the Mahakkam or Koti river. A bar prevents the entrance of large vessels, but the stream is navigable for smaller craft for some fifty miles, and trading praus ascend it for an immense distance.

The Mahakkam, like all the great rivers of Borneo, rises in the unexplored regions of Mount Tebang, and follows a south-east course for over 400 miles, to pour its waters into the Strait of Makassar. It receives numerous tributaries, and exhibits in a marked degree the phenomenon of lake expansion. The permanent lakes in its course are filling up gradually, but they are still of considerable depth, for Mr. Carl Bock, who lately travelled in this region, speaks of getting soundings of 80 feet or more. The Mahakkam has the large town of Samarinda at its mouth, and forms, like the Kapuas, a very considerable delta. Farther north, the rivers in Dutch territory are little known. The most important waterway in British North Borneo is the Kinabatangan, which debouches between Darvel and Sandakan Bays, and is navigable by boats for about 200 miles.

Certain marked characteristics, then, are exhibited by the majority of Bornean rivers, but more especially by those of the southern and eastern portions of the island, and these peculiarities are determined to a great extent by the flatness and slight elevation of the surrounding land. Most are surrounded in the lower part of their course with a greater or less extent of impassable morass. In most cases deltas are formed, sometimes of very large size, and here, aided by the mangroves, the land gains very rapidly on the sea. The slight fall in the river beds causes daily tidal inundation, and periodic flooding of vast areas occurs in the rainy season. For like reasons the rivers are extremely serpentine in their course, and in flood time the intervening land is often cut across at the narrow part of the bend. The old bed becomes partially blocked, and the phenomenon is thus exhibited of a series of lakes lying on either side of the river. Occasionally, rivers change their beds entirely, or a complete network of anastomoses is formed with other streams, in which it is an easy matter for the traveller to lose his way. Finally, the mouths of almost all are beset with bars, which prevent the ingress of large ships.

Borneo is, apparently, without permanent lakes of any great size. For many years a large sheet of water was represented in the maps as lying to the south of Kinabalu, but recent travellers have shown that it is only low land submerged in the rainy season, similar to that existing on most rivers, as already described. In the upper basin of the Kapuas are two lakes of minor importance, the Seriang and the Luar. Mr. Crocker found the former a fine sheet of water with four Dutch gunboats anchored in it, but it was said to have completely dried in 1877. It also appears to be subject to tremendous inundations. The diary of the same traveller records that a Malay, his informant, on the occasion of one of these floods, found a boy eating sugar-cane, and on asking where he got it, as he saw nothing but water, the boy told him he had dived down to their garden, which was at that time several feet under water.

4. Climate.

Bisected as it is by the equator, Borneo is exposed to the action of the four monsoons: in the northern portion theoretically to the N.E. and S.W., and in the southern to the S.E. and N.W., but those winds become considerably altered with the locality. At Banjarmasin the westerly monsoon blows as a south-west or west-south-west wind, and is steady from December to March, when it blows more northerly. The south-east monsoon is prevalent from April to October, and brings the greatest amount of rain, though thunderstorms — of which there are on the average about fifty in the year— occur most frequently in December or at the change of the monsoon. There is, strictly speaking, no dry season on the island, although droughts—some of which have been severe—sometimes occur.

In British North Borneo the wet season is from October to February, and April and May are the driest months. Rain occurs, however, at all seasons, and even during the severe drought which affected Borneo, Sumatra, and the Peninsula in 1885, the longest rainless period registered in Sandakan was twenty-two days. The mean annual rainfall of that town is 124 inches, and the showers are sometimes extremely heavy. Thus in June, 1884, over 2 inches fell in forty minutes, and in January, 1886, 9 inches were registered in twenty-four hours. Mr. Whitehead, who spent eight months on Mount Kinabalu, records that the weather was extremely wet. Sometimes rain fell for three days without ceasing, and the general average was six hours per diem, generally from 1 P.M. to nightfall. The maximum temperature on this coast is considerably higher than that of Java, varying from 81° in February to 93° Fahr. in April. In point of healthiness, Borneo must, on the whole, be considered more trying to European constitutions than any country hitherto described, although it is probably superior to New Guinea and to some parts of Sumatra. The large area of low and marshy land, subject to alternate flood and drought, the heavy rainfall, and, in the new settlements, the disturbing of the soil, combine to generate malarial fevers, which, though not nearly so fatal as those of Western Africa, are often of a severe type. Beri-beri, the scourge of the native races in the Malay Archipelago and Eastern Asia, is a common disorder among the plantation coolies, and cholera, which appears, at all events in Northern Borneo, to be a disease of recent introduction, has upon more than one occasion caused great mortality in the coast towns. In August, 1882, the village of Kimanis numbered just under 300 souls, of whom 177 were attacked and 144 died. About the year 1870, smallpox ravaged Northern Borneo and carried off vast numbers of the natives; so many, indeed, that it is said that more than one-half of the population perished. Lately, vaccination has been largely carried on, and the recurrence of any such epidemic rendered impossible. With regard to the prevalence of malaria, it may be said that the position of the European settlements, though at present unavoidable, is to a great extent responsible for it. They are situated for the most part either upon the sea-coast, often in close proximity to mangrove swamps, or upon rivers in the low country, and in this respect, therefore, it is not possible to make comparisons with a country such as Java, where the land has been for centuries cleared and settled.

5. Flora and Fauna.

The vegetation of Borneo is exceedingly luxuriant, the whole island being, with few exceptions, one vast forest. It is especially rich in palms and forest trees, many of which have not yet been botanically described. The vegetation is, of course, thoroughly Malayan, but the lofty mountain of Kinabalu contains a curious mixture of Indian, Malayan, and Australian plants. Here are numerous rhododendrons, forming trees 20 feet high, as in the Himalayas; here the characteristic Malayan pitcher-plants (*Nepenthes*) reach their maximum of size, variety, and beauty; and here are found such typical Australian genera as *Leptospermum*, *Leucopogon*, *Coprosma*, *Dacrydium*, and several others, among which is the Antarctic genus *Drimys*. In the lowlands, too, there are rhododendrons growing parasitically on trees or on exposed rocks; ferns and orchids are in endless variety; and the strange *Vanda Lowii* hangs down its elegant flowers, like crimson stars, strung upon slender cords sometimes 10 feet in length.

The zoology of Borneo has its closest affinities with that of Sumatra, thus differing considerably from Java. It is rather remarkable that the tiger, which is common in both the latter islands, should be unknown. There are, however, two smaller felines, *F. macroscelis*, the Clouded Tiger, and *F. marmoratus*. The elephant is tolerably common in British North Borneo, but its range appears to be very limited—a curious fact when the suitability of the rest of the island is taken into consideration. Some naturalists have sought to explain the fact by suggesting that they are the descendants of the trained animals formerly in possession of the Sultans of Brunei, an explanation which is possible, but not probable. For the Sumatran rhinoceros shows the same tendency to confine itself to this north-eastern promontory, and here no similar explanation can hold good. Both animals are found quite close to Sandakan. The elephants have destroyed plantations in the vicinity of the town, and rhinoceros have been known to enter its suburbs. The tapir is also reported to exist. Wild cattle (*Bos banteng*) are very numerous in parts, and here again we find that British North Borneo is the favourite locality. The island is very rich in monkeys, and has many peculiar species. The most remarkable, perhaps, are the Proboscis monkey (*Presbytes nasutus*), whose long and fleshy nose gives it a very man-like aspect, and the orang-utan, or "mias," of which there are two species, the largest being superior in size to all the anthropoid apes excepting the gorilla. The mias is abundant in the swampy forests of the south, and hardly less so in the Company's territory, and the smaller species is very readily domesticated.

The birds of Borneo show few marked differences from those of Sumatra and the Malay Peninsula. The island has no family confined to it alone, and only a very few genera, and even these become steadily reduced as our knowledge of the latter countries increases. The most notable peculiar genera are *Chlamydochara* among the Campophagidæ, and the striking *Lobiophasis* among the pheasants. Hornbills are very varied, and the island may be regarded as the headquarters of the beautiful family of the *Pittas*, or ground-thrushes, and the long-billed *Arachnotheras*, or spider-hunters. Mr. Whitehead's late zoological explorations of Kinabalu, during which he spent eight months upon the mountain at various altitudes, have added greatly to our knowledge of the Bornean fauna, have revealed many new and several most striking species, and have shown a marked connection with the ornis of the Himalayan sub-regions. The Sumatran and Peninsular affinities have been confirmed, but no special connection with Javanese mountain species appears. A slight Celebesian element, however, is revealed by a *Dicæum* closely allied to a species found only in that island, and is strengthened by Mr. Whitehead's discovery of a small rat (*Mus musschenbroeki*), previously only known from Celebes.

Reptiles abound, as in all the Malayan islands, but there are in Borneo many peculiar species, including two kinds of crocodiles not found elsewhere. These are much feared by the natives, and not without reason, for in the southern division of Borneo forty-one persons are officially recorded as having been killed by them during 1889, and this probably does not represent anything like the true total. Insects are excessively abundant, and many are of the largest size and of extreme beauty, but they show no great divergence from those of the Malay Peninsula.

6. Native Races.

Occupying a central position in the archipelago, Borneo exhibits considerable diversification among its inhabitants. Briefly, the island is populated as follows:—In the centre—or more accurately, in almost every part with the exception of a belt extending round the coast—are an aboriginal race of Indonesians, collectively known as Dyaks. No Negritos are known to exist. All round the seaboard, except in the northern portion of the east coast, and settled for the most part at the mouths of the rivers, are a thriving population of Mohammedan Malays. On the eastern and part of the southern coast the Bugis of Celebes—from time immemorial a race of traders—have settled themselves. The north-eastern part of the island is peopled by a large proportion of Sulus, that region having, until the advent of the British North Borneo Company, formed part of the territory of the Sultan of Sulu. The Chinese are extremely numerous in Borneo, carrying on a flourishing trade in the sea-ports, and occupying large areas in Western Borneo, to the exclusion of the Dyaks and Malays. Finally, the Bajaus, a race of Malays who have been well described as the "Sea-gipsies" of the archipelago, are well known in most of the creeks and rivers of the island.

Dyak is the generic name applied to the wild tribes which were found living on the island when the Malays first settled upon its shores. Whether they are the aboriginal inhabitants, or whether they were preceded by a Negrito race, it is impossible to say. It is quite possible that the latter may be the case, and that they are the descendants of a former immigrant pre-Malayan horde who overwhelmed a yet earlier race. They are divided into innumerable tribes, speaking distinct languages, forming distinct political units, and, in the wilder parts of the country, engaged in constant inter-tribal warfare. Physically, these people differ little from the Malays except in being somewhat lighter, taller, and more active, and they are generally of a more cheerful and child-like disposition. In point of civilisation they vary considerably. Some are described as exceedingly low in the social scale, living, like the Lubus and other Sumatran tribes, as forest vagrants, building no houses, but only temporary shelters. Others, like some of the Milanaus, are almost as civilised as the Malays. But in this respect Borneo is far behind Sumatra, for while in the latter island several of the tribes have separately and independently invented writing, with rather complex alphabets, no instance of this kind is known in Borneo. The majority of the Dyaks are heathen, but in many places contact with the Malays has converted them to Islamism. Tattooing is very generally practised, and it is a favourite custom to wear a quantity of brass ear-rings, so that the lobe of the ear becomes enormously dilated, and hangs almost on the shoulder. The Milanaus cause the malformation of their children's heads by boards, in the manner of some South American tribes. Others immure their young girls for two or three years or more at the age of puberty, and there are many curious customs, especially among the Kayans, for the knowledge of which we are indebted to Mr. Dalton, who resided for a long period with the head-hunting Dyaks in 1828.

As a rule the Dyak pagan tribes wear rude clothing of bark or cotton cloth, and the women deck themselves with abundance of beads, brass wire, and plaited girdles. The men generally wear only the *chawat*— a long band of bark or strip of cotton cloth passed between the legs and round the loins, with sometimes a jacket. The women wear a short petticoat, and in some tribes have a belt of bark or bamboo bound together with brass wire or rattans, and sometimes also a jacket. The women, as with most savage tribes, do much hard labour, whereas among the Malays and other Mohammedans they are almost wholly confined to housework, occasionally assisting in the fields at harvest-time. The practice of taking heads as trophies was common among almost all the Dyak tribes, but has been to a great extent abolished where European influence is predominant. A young Dyak could not marry, nor a parent or widower leave off mourning, till a head was obtained. These heads were dried and carefully preserved in their houses. It was a custom, and as a custom was observed, but it did not imply any extraordinary barbarism or moral delinquency. On the contrary, it is the general opinion of all who know them well that the Dyaks are among the most pleasing of savages, that they are kind, truthful, and have many excellent qualities. The Dyak houses are generally very large, many families residing together, and there is in every village a *balai*, or council-house, where the young unmarried men sleep, where councils are held, and where travellers are lodged. The houses are always raised on posts, often to a great height where subject to attacks from other tribes; or they are built perched up on almost inaccessible mountains, only to be reached by ladders up the face of lofty precipices.

DYAK VILLAGE.

The Dyaks cultivate rice and many kinds of vegetables, and have large plantations of fruit, which often cover whole mountain sides, and furnish them with an important part of their food. They also grow tobacco and sugar-cane for luxuries. Their weapons are spears, the *sumpitan* or blow-pipe, snares, and pitfalls, and with these they capture all kinds of wild animals for food. They collect beeswax, edible birds' nests, and other products of the forest, and exchange them for tools, clothing, or ornaments, and especially for brass wire, gongs, and brass guns, which constitute the wealth of every Dyak chief. Earthenware vases and other vessels are also greatly prized, and some of the chief's houses are quite full of them. The Dyaks of the interior of Sarawak are celebrated for the construction of ingenious bamboo suspension bridges over the rivers, to enable them to cross to their plantations or to other villages during floods. Mr. St. John tells us that the rivers sometimes rise forty feet during a flood, and that even a single heavy shower will render the fords impassable. The bridges are generally placed where large trees overhang the river. These are connected by strong bamboos lashed together, and supported at several points by cords of rattan. A light but shaky hand-rail is fixed a few feet above, but the whole is so slender and elastic, and the foothold on the smooth bamboo so insecure, that it requires some nerve in a European to cross such a bridge.

It is worthy of note that the Dyaks of the northern and north-western part of the island show in many instances a striking resemblance to the Chinese. That the latter have been an important factor in the production of the race there can be no doubt. They have for centuries settled on the coast, and have taken their wives from the native women. The Dyak of pure blood is only to be found in the interior. A recent writer, indeed, declares that in some parts of British North Borneo the Dyaks are more than half Chinese.

Of the date of the arrival of the true Malays in Borneo nothing certain is known. From the condition of the court of Brunei as described by Pigafetta, it is evident that they must at that time have been long established. Some centuries must have been needed to build up so solid a dominion. It is not necessary, however, to conclude that the Malay power was established by the single invasion of a conquering host, and it was more probably the outcome of the long-continued immigration and settlement of a trading people. The tradition current among these people is that they are the descendants of Malays from the great kingdom of Menangkabo in Sumatra, who left their country about 600 years ago. Whatever may have been the case, they are now found as settlers on the seaboard of the greater part of the island, gradually—though slowly—extending their influence over the tribes brought in contact with them, and converting them to Mohammedanism. Their headquarters are, as in bygone days, at Brunei. The Sultan of Brunei was in Pigafetta's time a great monarch, ruling actually a very large portion, and theoretically the whole of Borneo, and it is from his capital (the Burnai, Porne, Bornei, etc., of the old writers) that the whole island has obtained its name. It is on the western and north-western coasts that the Malay is most numerous and has made most progress. In the south he has mixed with and almost absorbed the Javanese, of which people there must at one time have been a considerable immigration, as is shown not only from the evidence of language, but possibly also from the numerous temple ruins; for by some writers the Javanese are credited with the introduction into Borneo of the Buddhist and Brahman cults.

The Sulus are found almost exclusively in British North Borneo, over part of which country their sultan ruled until the Company purchased his rights. They have preserved their own language, akin, as we have seen, to another widely spoken Philippine tongue, Bisayan, but Malay is used by most as the *lingua franca* of that region. Of mixed blood, largely Arab and Malay, the Sulus of Borneo resemble those of the neighbouring archipelago in being independent, rather fanatical, and not very trustworthy; but they are good seamen and successful fishermen, and in addition carry on a certain amount of trade in forest produce.

The Chinese are perhaps the most important people in Borneo. They have been traders and settlers on the coast from beyond historic times, and, as has just been stated, have for an equally long period mixed with the natives; so that some Dyaks—the Dusuns especially— might almost be classed with them. They are not only traders who amass wealth merely to return with it to their own empire, but miners, agriculturists, and producers, without whom it would be difficult to develop the country. The Philippines, Singapore, and Borneo receive, perhaps, a larger number of these immigrants than any other countries. In Borneo they are scattered over the whole seaboard, carrying on a good deal of the river trade, and supplanting in many ways the less energetic Malay. But they are chiefly to be found in West Borneo, especially in the mining districts, as in Sambas and Montrado (Menteradu) in Dutch territory. Numbers are settled around Bau and Bidi, in Sarawak, and in the capital, Kuching. In North Borneo an irruption of some thousands occurred on the opening up of the country, and great numbers are employed on the tobacco plantations lately established. In Labuan, and in Pengaron in South Borneo, the coal mines were worked by Chinese, and they still act as sago-washers in the former island. Bound together by societies with stringent laws, their system of co-operation enables them to prosper where others would fail. In West Borneo they thus became so powerful as to defy the Dutch Government, who had great difficulty in subduing them. In Sarawak, also, they rose in revolt in 1857, obtained temporary possession of the capital, and nearly succeeded in killing Rajah Brooke, who only saved his life by swimming the river. His Malay subjects, however, inflicted a severe but well-deserved punishment upon the insurgents, and it is not likely that any similar incident will again happen.

The Bajaus, who in Blitong and some parts of Borneo are known by the name of Sikas, are a wandering race of Malays, who pass their lives in boats from the cradle to the grave. In some places they have changed their mode of life, have built houses, and cultivated the ground; but this is seldom the case, and the majority act as cattle-stealers, petty pilferers, and kidnappers, and are not averse from more serious crimes if the occasion should offer. They have given a good deal of trouble to the North Borneo Company's Government, some of whose officers they have murdered, while boats' crews have more than once been cut off by them. These occurrences are nevertheless rare, and are becoming still rarer as European influence extends. The days of piracy are practically over, thanks to the establishment of the Spanish in Sulu and the British in North Borneo, but hardly more than a decade ago these seas were scoured by the Illanuns and Balagnini, the most dangerous and blood-thirsty pirates of the Malay Archipelago. The former are a race who had their original home in the island of Mindanao in the Philippines. They have of late been compelled to lead a less lawless life, and some have formed settlements in Borneo. The Balagnini, or Balangnini, inhabited an island of that name in the Sulu group, which is memorable as the scene of the most signal punishment ever inflicted on Malay pirates by a European power. "In 1848," says Mr. Crawfurd, "it was attacked and captured by a Spanish force of 650 infantry and artillery, with a squadron of three war-steamers and sixteen smaller armed vessels, under the Governor-General of the Philippines, and the resistance made will show the formidable character of these pirates. The Spaniards had 1 officer and 20 men killed, and 10 officers and 150 men wounded. They stormed four redoubts, captured 124 cannon, mostly of small calibre, and burnt 150 praus. Four hundred and fifty of the enemy were killed, refusing to take quarter, and 200 captives rescued from slavery. The forts and houses of the inhabitants were levelled to the ground, and in order to make the place uninhabitable the coco-palms were cut down to the number of between 7000 and 8000." In 1879 the Balagnini murdered or kidnapped sixty-five people in North Borneo, and have since then committed other minor acts of piracy, but it is believed that these outrages are now, practically speaking, things of the past.

7. Agriculture and Products.

Agriculture, as we understand it, is hardly known except in those parts of the country where the people have been taught by Europeans. Horses and oxen are almost unknown among the Dyaks, but buffaloes are very numerous, and are specially suited for work in so marshy a country. A good account of the native system of cultivation is given by a writer in the *Handbook of British North Borneo*. "A piece of ground is selected—usually one that has undergone the same treatment a few years previously—the felling and clearing is conducted in the usual manner, after which Indian corn and paddy (rice) are planted simultaneously. Ploughs and hoes are quite unknown, and not a clod is turned over. The mode of operation is for a man and woman to walk one behind the other, the man in front, dibbling a hole with a sharpened stick, into which the other drops one or two seeds, and then scratches a little earth over the hole with her toes. In this manner a large field is very soon planted with crops without any lengthened operation. In seven or eight weeks the corn is ready to pull, the paddy in the intermediate lines between the corn being rather poor-looking in consequence of being overshadowed by its long stalks. As soon as the corn is cleared off, however, the paddy springs up rapidly, and in two months more it too is ready for cutting. During the time the paddy is coming to maturity the fields require weeding three times. In some cases, while the paddy is half grown, tapioca cuttings are planted. In all cases no sooner is the paddy cut than something else is coming on, either tapioca, kaladi, or what not, and before such crops as the last named are ripe, banana suckers and sugar-cane are planted. The ground being cleared of the tapioca, sweet potatoes are put in round the bananas, no further weeding is undertaken, and the sweet potatoes are left to fight it out with the grass. As soon as the potatoes begin to ripen, the yield is continuous, but when the weeds finally get the mastery, the people desert that place and make a new start somewhere else. . . . These operations occupy a term of two years or so, during which time crops of one sort or another are following each other in quick succession and without intermission. Paddy they store up, but nothing else, and from year's end to year's end, whatever else they require for the day's consumption, they send into the fields and fetch." So prolific is nature that the inhabitants of six crowded huts on the Kinabatangan have been known to draw their entire subsistence, day after day, from a little plot under two acres in extent.

It is only in the neighbourhood of the European settlement that the native embarks in agriculture for trading purposes, and even then only under the direction of a civilised master, excepting in the case of the Chinese. Copra, coco-nuts, areca-nuts, rice, pepper, and tobacco are the only field products which appear in the export lists of Dutch Borneo. Gambir and pepper and a tolerable quantity of rice are cultivated in the Sarawak territory; but coffee, sugar, and tapioca have not proved very remunerative. The Milanaus, however, grow large quantities of sago for export, and the trade is steadily increasing; but this article may be regarded as a forest product rather than as the result of agriculture. British North Borneo has developed rapidly of late, not a little owing to the success of the tobacco plantations, of which there are now many in operation. The land has proved to be as suitable for the growth of the special quality used for " wrappers " of cigars as Dili in Sumatra, and the high price of three shillings per lb. has been obtained for the leaf in the London market. This, however, is almost the only agricultural product as yet worthy of mention, although it is very probable that both pepper and Manila hemp will eventually bring a large revenue into the country.

The natural products of Borneo are innumerable, but the country being so little known, and the natives in many parts so untrustworthy, very little has as yet been done to develop them. Timber of many kinds, of which *bilian*—a species of ironwood resisting the attack of white ants—is perhaps the most valuable; rattans; the nipa and nibong palms—which furnish the material for the construction of almost every Bornean house; gum dammar and gutta-percha—the latter a product of great value: all these are largely exported. Considerable quantities of beeswax are brought down to the coast by the natives, especially in North Borneo; but, excepting rattan, by far the most important and valuable article of export from this district is birds' nest. Probably not less than fifteen or twenty thousand pounds' worth are annually sent to Singapore and China. The nest in size and shape may be compared to the vertical half of a small teacup, and its appearance is that of having been constructed of threads or fibres of gelatine. The best are white and glassy-looking, and may fetch as much as fifty shillings per lb., but the inferior nests contain many impurities, and are perhaps worth not more than two shillings. This curious article of commerce is produced by a small swift of the genus *Collocalia* (*C. linchi* and others), and is used by rich Chinese for making soup. Although a few nests are sometimes seen built against the sea-cliffs in the full glare of the sun, the vast majority occur in caves in the limestone rock, and are often in complete darkness. In such places the birds build in incredible numbers. Thus, the yield from the Gomanton caves is valued at over £5000 annually. The collecting is chiefly carried out by Buludupi Dyaks, who show the most extraordinary skill and daring, obtaining the nests even from the roofs of the caves, which are sometimes three or four hundred feet or more in height. Long bamboos with a candle affixed near the end are used for detaching the lower nests. To obtain the others slender rattan ladders are pegged against the walls, and skeleton stages of bamboo run out in what appear to be utterly inaccessible situations. When it is remembered that the work is carried on almost in darkness and at such dizzy heights, it is only remarkable that there are not more fatal accidents than the few which occur. The first nests are taken in March, and there are generally two, and sometimes three, subsequent collections. The result is arranged according to quality in three classes—the white, medium, and black. About twenty principal caves are known in the North Borneo Company's territory, and there are doubtless many others as yet undiscovered. A large quantity of nests are also exported from Sarawak.

The harvest of the Bornean seas is as little reaped as that of the forests. Shark's fin and *bêche-de-mer* are everywhere to be obtained, especially in the north, and a good deal finds its way, with the birds' nests, to the Chinese market. So also does *kima*—the giant clam (*Tridacna*)—whose shell is used in Europe for the aspersoria or stoups in Catholic churches. Seed pearls are chiefly found on the north and east coast, but the large pearl oyster, which also supplies the mother-of-pearl shell, is not to be obtained in any quantity west of the Sulu group. Tortoiseshell is also exported; but of all these products few are as yet systematically worked by the English, and hardly any by the Dutch.

Much the same may be said concerning the mineral wealth of the country, which is both considerable and widely spread. The coal measures are practically inexhaustible, and have been worked at various places in almost every part of the island, both by Europeans and natives. The results, however, have been almost uniformly unsuccessful; but this failure must be ascribed to the undeveloped state of the country and other causes of secondary importance, and the mines will doubtless be worked with remunerative results in the future. The "Julia Hermina" mine, near Banjarmasin, which promised well, was hardly completed when, in 1859, an insurrection took place, the European staff were murdered, and the works completely destroyed. The Pengaron coal mine, also in the neighbourhood of Martapura, was commenced in 1848, but did not average a larger annual output than about 6000 tons, and was abandoned in 1884, as was also the neighbouring Asahan mine, which had been working fourteen years with much the same results. A mine was also worked in Koti, abandoned, and once more reopened in 1886. In Sarawak the Raja opened a mine on a tributary of the Sadong river in 1880, the prospects of which are promising, nearly 50,000 tons having been raised in 1886. He also purchased, two years later, a concession for the working of the seams at the mouth of the Brunei river. On the island of Labuan is a mine, till lately abandoned, which has caused the failure of three or more companies, but is now being successfully worked; while in Pulo Laut, the large island at the south-east point of Borneo, about 5000 tons are yearly raised by the natives and supplied to Dutch steamers. There is little doubt that petroleum, which has been found in many places, will eventually become a workable and most valuable product.

Antimony is known both from South and West Borneo, but it is only worked in Sarawak territory, chiefly near Bidi. The average amount of ore raised is about 1500 tons annually, but the output seems of late to have fallen off. Mercury, too, occurs in the upper basin of the Sarawak river, existing as cinnabar, and it is mined to an annual value of from £30,000 to £100,000. Platinum occurs, and is obtained in small quantities as a by-product in gold-washing. Lead, tin, zinc, arsenic, copper, and iron have been found in various parts of the island, but none are worked, with the exception of iron, from which the natives make excellent krisses and parangs. A rich vein of silver was discovered in Sarawak near Bau in 1881, and in the following year some 1400 tons of ore, valued at over £13,000, were raised, but the vein rapidly became exhausted.

It is, however, for gold and diamonds that Borneo is most celebrated. There are said to be few rivers in the island which are not auriferous. The metal is obtained almost entirely from river-washing or the drift gravel, and is chiefly worked by the Chinese, who have established themselves in the chief gold district for some centuries, especially about Sambas — this region being now generally known as the "Chinese Districts." Their powerful co-operative unions enabled them to render themselves independent of the native princes, and it cost the Dutch in 1850 a war of four years' duration to subdue them. It is here, in certain places in West Sarawak, in the valleys between the spurs of the Tana Laut range in the south-east and in the basin of the Kahayan, and on the Segama river in North Borneo, that gold occurs most plentifully. But, on the whole, although there must be large fields at present undiscovered, the output of the precious metal is not great, and it chiefly serves as the means of livelihood for large numbers of Chinese. What the actual amount may be is not known, but there is no doubt that it has of late decreased considerably. Diamonds are likewise very widely distributed, but they are chiefly found in the richest gold districts. The yield, like that of gold, is much less than in former years, but in the early part of the century it was considerable. Several diamonds of 60 or 70 carats, according to Dr. Posewitz, have been known to have been found, and many of the Malay Sultans and Rajas possess stones of large size. The art of diamond-cutting has been long known, and is carried on in many places both in South and West Borneo. It is said that Cape stones are largely imported to be sold to the Rajas as the production of the country.

From what has been already written, it may be gathered that the arts and manufactures of Borneo are of a limited nature, and carried on by the Malays and Chinese rather than by the natives, whose industry in this way is chiefly confined to the manufacture of weapons and the spinning and weaving of cotton. In some parts, especially in Northern Borneo, the richer chiefs are in possession of ancient blue jars of large size, which are extremely prized, and valued at ridiculous prices, but these have undoubtedly been imported from China. Potteries exist, however, in various places, and turn out a considerable quantity of coarse ware. Brunei is celebrated for its goldsmiths' work, and for its gongs, which are of very rich tone, due, it is said, to the large admixture of silver. The silk sarongs made in this city are in their way unrivalled, and being often much decorated with gold thread, are very costly. The diamond-cutting industry has been already alluded to.

BRITISH NORTH BORNEO.

In the year 1865 the American Consul then resident in Brunei obtained certain land concessions from the Sultan, which, though not actually co-extensive with the territory now known as British North Borneo, comprised a very large portion of it. The result was the formation of the American Trading Company of Borneo, and a large number of Chinese having been imported, a settlement was founded on the Kimanis river. The venture was a failure, the Chinese settlement was soon abandoned, and the Company practically ceased to exist.

In December, 1877, Mr. Alfred Dent and Baron von

Overbeck concluded negotiations with the Sultans of Brunei and Sulu, by which certain territories were granted to them by the latter in fee simple. A provisional company was formed, and a Royal Charter petitioned for. It was granted, and on the 1st November, 1881, the British North Borneo Company, with an available capital of about £400,000, commenced its existence. Various inland districts and the small Mantanani Islands were acquired later; in 1889 the British Colony of Labuan was placed under the administration of the Company, and finally a British Protectorate, established in 1888, has materially strengthened the position of the country. Brunei and Sarawak being also under British protection, many difficulties with regard to external politics are removed, and trade having steadily improved, the new colony may be said to have a fair chance of ultimately succeeding.

The territory thus acquired has, including the islands, an estimated area of 31,000 square miles. It extends from the Sipitong river in Brunei Bay to Sta. Lucia Bay on the east coast, and its coast-line measures about 1000 miles. It is thus slightly larger than Ceylon. It possesses a number of excellent harbours, the soil is both rich and fertile, and though it is without the numerous navigable rivers of Dutch Borneo, there are in most districts sufficient waterways into the interior to serve for the transport of produce. The central position of the country is likewise in its favour, while its proximity to China, and the marked preference the Chinese have always shown for Borneo, have considerably simplified the labour question.

The Government is administered by a Governor, with whom is associated a Colonial Secretary. There are two Residents and several Assistant Residents. The mode of administration is somewhat similar to that of a British Colony, but the Government require the native chiefs to maintain order and further justice, and with the example of Sarawak before them, have instituted a Legislative Council, composed of the higher European officials and the leading native chiefs. There is no army, but the constabulary, composed chiefly of Sikhs, and numbering about 300 men, preserve order, and act when required as a military force. By its Charter the Company binds itself to forbid the possession of slaves to any stranger, but is not obliged forcibly to put down slavery among the tribes, although it agrees " to discourage to the best of its power, and, as far as may be practicable, to abolish by degrees, any system of domestic servitude existing among the tribes of the coast or the interior."

Although British North Borneo as a colony is still in its earliest infancy, its growth has, so far, been fairly promising. The capital, Sandakan—or, as it was at first named, Elopura—is situated on the northern shore of the bay of that name, which is without doubt the finest in the island. This harbour is completely landlocked, and is clear of dangers; it has a depth of 15 and a breadth of 5 miles, admits the largest vessels, and has 13 rivers running into it. The town is built about a mile from the entrance, and contained in 1891 a population of 6350 persons, of whom 3200, or more than half, were Chinese, and 114 British. Vessels of large draught can lie alongside the pier, and supplies of all kinds are plentiful. A neat Government House dominates the anchorage; there is a club, a hotel, jail, barracks, and hospital, besides numerous stores, and jinrickshaws supply the place of cabs. Yet, little more than a decade ago, Mr. Pryer found the site an uninhabited jungle, and the bay the resort of semi-piratical Bajaus. Kudat, which was

SANDAKAN.

formerly the capital, is the next most important station. It is situated in Marudu Bay, at the extreme north of the island, and has the maritime advantage of being upon the Singapore side of the difficult and dangerous Mallawalle Channel; but its trade is considerably less than that of its rival, and it is no doubt less healthy. The other Government stations are Gaya, Papar, Silam, and Mempakol. The latter is a new settlement, chiefly occupied in consequence of Labuan having fallen under the administration of the Company. Silam, Papar, and Gaya are small stations, the former being chiefly important from its experimental gardens, and Gaya as the port of the chief cattle district.

The British North Borneo Company does not itself engage in trade, but is merely an administrative body, drawing its revenues from a native poll-tax, which can as yet be only very partially levied; from various duties, among which is that of 10 per cent upon all jungle produce; from opium and spirit licenses, which are farmed out; and from stamp duties, etc. The revenue, which was $82,448 in 1884, has steadily risen. In 1887 it was $142,687, and in 1891 $417,028. The expenditure for the same three years was $242,450, $204,343, and $509,535, so that apart from land sales the budget still shows a considerable deficit. The exports—the chief of which are tobacco, birds'-nests, gutta, rattans, and sago—have considerably increased, and in 1891 reached a value of $1,238,277. As yet, of course, only the seaboard of the great area owned by the Company has been at all brought under European influence. The interior is an unknown land which, at the risk of their lives, a few bold explorers have here and there crossed. But it is probable that not many years will elapse before it has been well mapped and its inhabitants rendered partially civilised. The Segama river has been proved to be rich in gold, and an attempt is being made to render its upper basin more accessible by the construction of a road. The development of the tobacco plantations, which has of late been extraordinarily rapid, will no doubt bring considerable wealth to the colony. About ten of these are established, and the value of the export rose in 1891 to nearly $700,000, but the opening up of the interior will depend chiefly upon its mineral resources. In this respect there is no reason to believe that the country will prove inferior to the neighbouring state of Sarawak. A telegraph line connects Labuan with the mainland, and is being carried to Sandakan and Silam.

Two islands of a certain importance lie off the northern point of Borneo—Banguey and Balambangan—both of which are owned by the British North Borneo Company. Banguey is about 22 miles in length by 12 in breadth, and has an area of about 170 square miles. Geologically it resembles Borneo, exhibiting granites, gneisses, and mica-schists, but Banguey Peak is reported to be volcanic. It is inhabited chiefly by Dusun Dyaks. The soil is fertile, and two tobacco plantations have been established on the west side of the island. On the south is a fair harbour formed by three small islands, and here a small settlement—Mitford—has been established by the Company. Balambangan is much smaller, being only forty square miles in area, and is uninhabited, but it is memorable as the scene of a disaster to the English in 1775. When, in the middle of the last century, the Sultan of Sulu was found a prisoner in Manila on the occupation of that city by the British, Admiral Drake obtained from him the cession of Balambangan as a reward for his release. The British flag was accordingly hoisted in 1763, and a post established on the island by the East India Company about the year 1770, which acted in some degree as a check upon the pirates with which these seas at that time swarmed. The garrison at first numbered nearly four hundred men, but the climate had told so severely upon them that only 75 infantry and 28 gunners were fit for duty on the occasion of which we are now speaking. The Spanish were at this time intriguing in Sulu, where opinion was divided among the Datus, some being in favour of the English, while others wished to expel them. Eventually the counsel of the latter prevailed, and on the 5th March, 1775, the place was surprised and taken by a force of 300 Sulu and Illanun pirates under the Datu Tenteng; the whole garrison, with the exception of the Governor and two or three men, slaughtered; and booty to the value of one million Spanish dollars seized. The Sultan of Sulu, although nominally repudiating this act, received a great part of the spoil, and no reparation appears to have been exacted by the English. Some little time later the settlement was re-established, but it was again abandoned in 1803. A few overgrown ruins and traces of old clearings are all that now remain to mark the spot.

Labuan.

The island of Labuan is situated on the north-west coast of Borneo, opposite the mouth of Brunei Bay. It is 12 miles in length, and has an area of 32 square miles only. It was occupied in 1846 by the British, after difficulties with the Sultan of Brunei, and Sir James Brooke was appointed the first Governor. The importance of having some station, especially where coal was obtainable, midway between China and Singapore was partly the cause of its selection, but the island has not fulfilled the expectations formed of it, and in 1889 its administration was made over to the British North Borneo Company.

Labuan, as its name implies, is provided with an excellent harbour, but has few other advantages. It is low, flat, and swampy except at its northern end, and in spite of the greater part of the forest which covered it having been destroyed, the rainfall is excessive; a large portion of the land is unfit for cultivation, and the soil is on the whole poor. The low and marshy ground is, however, suitable for growing the sago-palm, and rice is cultivated. Plantations of the West African oil-palm (*Elæis guineensis*) have been tried with more or less success, but the chief trade is in sago. Factories where the raw product, as used by the natives, is washed and dried into the European commercial article have been established for many years. The flour thus obtained is sent to Singapore for granulation, and forms the principal item in the list of exports. The population in 1891 was nearly 6000, and the greater part of the trade is carried on by Chinese. The existence of the Company in North Borneo materially affected the condition of the island during the period of rivalry, but under the new administration, and especially since the establishment of Mempakol—the station on the mainland—its prospects are better. The coal-mines are now being worked by the new Central Bornean Company, who have steamers running twice a month to Singapore. Their efforts are being directed to the reconstruction of the railway from the mines to Victoria Harbour, which is now nearly completed; and under an improved system of working, the output is expected to be a large one.

Brunei.

The territory of the Sultans of Brunei, whose power in former centuries extended actually over the greater part of Northern and North-western Borneo, and nominally over all the Malay settlements in the island, is now reduced to very narrow limits. It embraces, in fact, very little more than the lower part of the valley of the river Limbang, upon a side branch of which the capital is built. The first visit of the Spaniards in 1522, and the description given by Pigafetta of the court, have already been mentioned on a former page. The Sultan holds his office by right of heredity, and claims descent from the Menangkabo Malays of Sumatra. There is also a hereditary nobility; but the power and glory of the state has departed, the Sultan's palace is little better than a barn, and the titles of his Datus and Pangerangs a barren honour. The city of Brunei, however, still remains in many particulars unchanged from its state as described by Pigafetta. There are, it is true, no batteries of trained elephants, and the number of inhabitants, if his account be correct, is at the present time much diminished, but the manner of life remains the same. Scarcely a traveller has described Brunei without speaking of it as the Venice of the East, and it is, on the whole, a not inapt comparison. The vast collection of houses is built on piles in the water, and placed in the centre of a lake-like expansion of the river 15 miles from the sea, shut in on all sides by hills which, though of insignificant height, are not lacking in picturesqueness. A most striking view is obtained from them of the city. Scarcely an inch of ground is to be seen anywhere, and many of the houses are built in deep water. In what may be termed the main street the larger vessels lie at anchor, while innumerable canoes dart about in every direction, from the Pangerangs' barges propelled by twenty paddles to the little flat "dug-out" with a bare inch of freeboard, manned by a solitary naked native. The market is, perhaps, one of the most extraordinary sights the East has to show. Each stall is a canoe, and it would puzzle the spectator to form any estimate of their number, for the water is covered with craft of all sizes in incessant motion. At one moment there is a dense pack around some Chinaman or other trader, and each vociferates the prices of the produce on sale. At another there is a rush in the opposite direction, and the former buyer is deserted. A continuous onward movement is at the same time taking place, so that in the course of an hour or two the market has floated through a considerable part of the town. As in other countries, the vendors are almost without exception women, each of whom wears a palm-leaf hat of enormous size, which serves the purpose of an umbrella also, for it is large enough to protect the whole body from either sun or rain. Several other towns in the Malay Archipelago resemble Brunei in being almost entirely aquatic; as, for example, Palembang, but they are in nearly every case built close to a river bank, and hence the appearance presented is quite different. The population is estimated at from 12,000 to 15,000.

The trade of Brunei is of no importance. What exists is in the hands of a few prosperous Chinese. The goldsmiths and brass workers are renowned, and the krisses and gold-embroidered sarongs are of beautiful workmanship. Fishing and the cultivation of the sago-palm and rice are the chief occupations of the peasants, who have groaned beneath the burden of an intolerable taxation, and still

s

BRUNEI.

more intolerable extortion, on the part of the *orang kayas*, until they have ended in revolt. Of the ultimate fate of this corrupt and ill-governed state there can be no doubt. Brunei is destined before very long to become incorporated with one or other of the European colonies by which she is hemmed in. It may be said that the large annual payments made in consideration of land grants by the Raja of Sarawak and the British North Borneo Company have alone enabled her to preserve her autonomy so long.

Sarawak.

The territory of Sarawak, on the north-western coast of Borneo, is in many respects one of the most interesting spots in the whole vast extent of the tropical world, for here an English gentleman rules as absolute monarch over a considerable population of Malays and Dyaks, to the complete satisfaction and contentment of both. The English rule has now lasted fifty years, and appears to be firmly established. It has withstood the early machinations of discontented Malay chiefs, an insurrection of Chinese miners, and the death of its founder; but, as it has not relied for support upon either force or fraud, but has always existed for the well-being and through the goodwill of the people governed, it has taken firm root in the soil, and seems likely to endure for many generations, if the wise policy of its founder continues to be the guiding star of his successors. From the career of Sir James Brooke, Raja of Sarawak, lessons of inestimable value in the management of a colony of uncivilised Asiatics may be learnt.

Early in 1839, Mr. Brooke reached Sarawak in a vessel of his own, and finding the country in a state of chronic insurrection, helped its ruler the Raja Muda Hassim to suppress it, partly by an exhibition of force and partly by conciliation. Eventually, on the 24th September, 1841, Hassim abdicated in favour of Mr. Brooke, who thus became Raja of Sarawak, with a territory about 60 miles long by 50 wide. After some trouble and delay, the title was confirmed by the Malay Sultan of Borneo, on the 1st August, 1842, and Mr. Brooke, intensely interested in his strange acquisition, at once set himself to work to consolidate his power, to introduce just reforms, to establish a code of laws, to develop commerce, and to suppress piracy. The condition of the country was such that the work might have appeared hopeless to a less wise and energetic ruler. Complete anarchy prevailed. Malays were fighting against Malays, and Dyaks against Dyaks. The condition of the latter was miserable in the extreme; they were exposed to every exaction, their children were taken from them for slaves, their villages were attacked and often destroyed by piratical tribes from the adjacent rivers, and the destruction of their crops often exposed them to the extremity of famine. To the Malays the Dyaks were people to be plundered in every way, and when it could not be done openly, it was effected by means of tax-collecting and forced trade, against which the poor Dyaks were at first afraid to complain. In a very few years this system was wholly changed; the Dyaks were protected from plunder and imposition so long as they paid the moderate tax levied upon them, and the Malay chiefs obtained their dues with more regularity, and without the need of supporting a crowd of followers who lived on plunder. The Malays who had formerly administered the internal affairs of the district were kept in office, and as no new laws were made without their advice and co-operation, neither their emoluments nor their dignity were seriously interfered with.

The little opposition Mr. Brooke experienced in making these radical changes was largely due to his extremely conciliating and dignified manner, so accordant with the Malay character; and to his having acquired the Malay language by intercourse with the higher classes, and being able to speak it with great purity and ease. He was also tolerant of native prejudices, and had studied the native character so completely that he well knew how to influence it. His personal courage, and the sagacity and boldness with which he detected and put down some of the early conspiracies against his rule, won the better class of chiefs to his side; and the great respect he always paid to the Mohammedan religion, even using the precepts of the Koran as the foundation of many of his amendments of the law, disarmed the opposition of the priests, and enabled him subsequently to introduce English missionaries among the Dyaks without exciting the least animosity.

No less wisdom was shown by the mode in which justice was administered. Three courts were established—a police court, a general court, and a native religious court—the latter chiefly for the settlement of cases relating to marriage or divorce. The police court dealt with the simplest cases, the general court with all other cases, civil and criminal. There were no lawyers, and hardly any forms. The parties in dispute appeared with their witnesses. They gave their evidence and were examined by the judge, assisted by the native chiefs, and by any European residents who chose to be present, and they obtained substantial, cheap, and speedy justice. The Raja had associated with him in the government a small body of Englishmen, carefully selected, who took their tone and manner from him; and every native knew well that if he were wronged he could get redress, and that the wealth or power of his oppressor would avail nothing with his judges.

The success of this system of rule was never better shown than during the Chinese insurrection, when, having narrowly escaped with his life—his friends killed or wounded, his house burnt down, and much of the town destroyed—the whole population, Malay and Dyak alike, rallied round the English Raja, drove out and almost exterminated the invaders, and triumphantly brought him back to rule over them. In what other country shall we find rulers alien in race, language, and religion, yet so endeared to their subjects? And the phenomenon is still more marvellous when we consider that these subjects were themselves of two races—a superior and an inferior, an oppressing and an oppressed; yet both alike joined to bring back the foreign ruler who had introduced equality and had stopped oppression. This example shows us that the art of governing half-civilised races is not so complex and difficult as has been supposed. It requires no peculiar legal, or diplomatic, or legislative training; but chiefly patience, and good feeling, and the absence of prejudice. The great thing is, not to be in a hurry; to avoid over-legislation, law-forms, and legal subtleties; to aim first to make the people contented and happy in their own way, even if that way should be quite opposed to European theories of how they ought to be happy. On such principles Sir James Brooke's success was founded. It is true, he spent a fortune instead of making one; but he had his reward in having brought peace, and safety, and plenty where there was before war, and oppression, and famine, and in leaving behind him, over the whole of Northern

Borneo, a reputation for wisdom, for goodness, and for honour which will dignify the name of Englishman for generations to come.[1]

Since the days of its founder, the State of Sarawak has much increased in extent. For a long time the Bintulu river formed its north-eastern boundary, which was afterwards extended to Baram Point. Later, difficulties occurring with regard to the Trusan river, in the east of Brunei, led to the cession of it to Sarawak, a wedge of territory thus being interposed between the North Borneo Company's land and that of the Sultan of Brunei. The constant revolts of the tribes on the Upper Limbang later brought about a similar result, but in this case the cession, which took place in 1890, was compulsory, not voluntary. On the 14th June, 1888, a British Protectorate of Sarawak was proclaimed.

The territory, which thus hardly allows of much further expansion, comprises a large area of valuable land within easy reach of Singapore, the great market of the Eastern Archipelago. It is rich in minerals and has several navigable rivers. It is progressing steadily, although the development of its resources can be hardly said as yet to have fairly begun. The government is an absolute monarchy, but is in effect very much that of an English Crown Colony. Associated with the Raja is a Supreme Council of two European officials, and four natives of high rank, nominated by the Raja. All ordinary legislative business is thus carried on, but the sovereign can at all times exercise his right of autocracy, though this step is not often taken. In addition to the Supreme Council, there is a General Council of fifty members, which meets triennially, or on special occasions. The country is divided

---

[1] This account of Sir James Brooke's rule is chiefly founded on Mr. Wallace's personal observation.

into districts, each of which is administered by a Resident, who is assisted by European, Eurasian, or native subordinates. He acts as judge, using a modification of the Indian Criminal Code, but in certain cases there is a right of appeal to the Raja.

The State possesses a small standing army in the "Sarawak Rangers," a body of about 300 well-drilled natives, officered by Europeans, and armed with breech-loading rifles. There are forts on most of the rivers, mounting a few cannon only, but sufficiently strong to withstand native attacks. In addition, some twenty or thirty thousand men can be put in the field, the Dyaks of the Batang Lupar, Seribas, and other rivers constituting a reserve force to be called out in times of necessity. These men, who were in old days head-hunters, are far superior to any European troops for the work for which they are needed, being well trained, thoroughly accustomed to forest warfare, and unhampered by commissariat difficulties. In consideration of their services they are exempted from the poll-tax.

The trade of Sarawak shows a slow but steady increase. The chief products are sago, which is exported to the value of about £70,000 annually; gambir and pepper; coal, of which from the Muara mines there is now a large output; various forest products, the most important being gutta-percha, dammar, and rattans; and antimony, cinnabar, diamonds, and gold, the three first of which show a tendency to decrease. Planting has of late been much encouraged. The imports consist mostly of opium, salt, tobacco, cloth, crockery, and brass ware. The revenue is principally derived from the opium farm, i.e. the right to import the drug and control its sale, which is the monopoly of a single individual. Practically, this is a sort of capitation tax on the Chinese, who are almost the sole consumers. It has been found better to make it a private monopoly than to retain it in the hands of the Government. There is also a poll-tax, from which the reserve forces are exempt. The other chief returns are from mining royalties, customs, excise, etc. The revenue for 1890 was $413,112, and the expenditure $362,778.

The tribes and peoples inhabiting Sarawak are various. The Malays proper abound most at the capital, Kuching, with a few settled on the banks of almost every river and creek. The Chinese are also chiefly settled at Kuching, and at the gold mines up the river. Others are at the Marup mines on the Batang Lupar, and they are found as petty traders everywhere. The "Land Dyaks" occupy Lundu and the interior of the Sarawak and Sadong river-basins, while the "Sea Dyaks" inhabit the country eastward. The Milanaus are settled at the mouths of the Rejang, Bintulu, and several of the smaller rivers. Several tattooed tribes known as Kanowits, Pakitans, Pengs, and Punans live inland in the Rejang and Bintulu districts, and beyond them are the Kayans, who have been already alluded to. The population of Sarawak can only be roughly estimated, for some little portion of the country is still unknown, but it is probably between 350,000 and 400,000.

There is both a Church of England and Roman Catholic Mission in Sarawak. The Episcopal See of "Singapore, Labuan, and Sarawak" comprises all the Straits settlements, as well as the protected States of Borneo, and there were in 1892 twelve English missionaries in the Raja's territory, besides Chinese. Large boys' and girls' schools are established at Kuching, and religious and lay instruction is afforded at all the mission stations. Many churches and chapels are already built.

The mission press has issued translations of the Bible in various dialects. The Roman Catholic Mission has only been recently established. As yet, however, only partial success can be said to have attended the efforts of either party, Dyak and Chinese being alike little influenced by religious feeling. No work is attempted among those of Mohammedan faith. It is not considered advisable by the authorities, and if undertaken would be almost certain to result in failure.

Kuching, the capital, is a thriving town of about 20,000 inhabitants, situated about 25 miles up the Sarawak River, which near its mouth is broken up into numerous channels and creeks, as is the case with most Bornean rivers. At the town it is a strong stream, two or three hundred yards in width, and of sufficient depth to admit of the anchorage of British gunboats, but it is much to be regretted that Kuching was not built at the mouth of the river, instead of in its present position, for without good pilots it is somewhat difficult of access. The situation is nevertheless very picturesque, and the shipping and busy life of the Chinese bazaars evince the activity of trade. Everything has the air of being well and solidly established. White battlemented forts overlook the anchorage, and there is a large court-house, barracks, museum, hospital, and prison. The Astana, or palace of the Raja, is a fine castellated house, with a moss-grown tower, and with smooth lawns running down to the river. Good roads lead in various directions, and the bungalows of the Europeans are surrounded by beautifully-kept gardens. The present Raja is Sir Charles Brooke, K.C.B., nephew of Sir James Brooke, and adopted as his son and successor by the Malay chiefs before Sir James finally left Borneo.

KUCHING, SARAWAK.

We may conclude with an extract from a Consular report made by Mr. Ussher upon the condition of Sarawak, which, though written in 1878, is equally applicable to the present date:—"It is not too much to say that Sarawak presents one of the few remaining chances of existence to the enervated and indolent race of Malays. Under such a government, which appears to strive to impress them with a sense of their duty to the State, as well as with a feeling of self-respect, by inducing and encouraging them to take an active part in the administration of public affairs, the Malays of Sarawak ought to prosper; and they have, moreover, continually before their eyes the example of the misgovernment and anarchy existing in the wretched kingdom of Borneo proper, which is apparently hastening to ruin and decay.

"The policy of the Sarawak Government appears to me to be just and equitable towards the native Dyak and other races. It may fairly be assumed to be so, if we take as a test the fact that extensive tribes of savages have been transmuted from lawless head-hunters and pirates into comparatively peaceful agriculturists. . . . One of the principal recommendations attaching in the eyes of the native to European rule in Sarawak is the honesty of its administration, especially in pecuniary matters. The object of the Malay nobles in the olden times, and indeed now in the territories of Brunei, was to squeeze as much as might be from the wretched aborigines; whereas the principal object of the European appears to them to be to solve the problem of how to carry on an effective government at the lightest possible cost to its subjects.

"Another recommendation in the eyes of the native is the possibility of obtaining even-handed if rough justice.

It is not necessary, as they see and admit with satisfaction, that litigants should enter into a pecuniary competition with their opponents to purchase the favour and countenance of their judges.

"The occasions requiring the employment of armed force are becoming rare, and disturbances are strictly local. The real power of Sarawak is based upon the remembrance and gratitude due to the late Raja Sir James Brooke, as well as upon the firm administration and even-handed justice of the present government. No one visiting Sarawak can fail to observe the respect and affection in which the present raja and his family are held by the entire community. The fact is as noticeable among Europeans as among the natives; and I may observe that the European staff is socially on a par with the officials of the generality of our colonies. The mode of life among the European body is quiet and unostentatious, but of hospitality there is abundance, and no visitor leaves Sarawak without pleasant reminiscences of his stay."

This authoritative statement as to the present condition of Sarawak must be highly gratifying to all friends and admirers of the late Sir James Brooke. Under the cautious phraseology of an official report, we cannot fail to see the record of a splendid and almost unexampled success in the art of government—a success effected under difficulties far above the average, and to be estimated by a standard far truer than that of commercial development, namely, the happiness and contentment of the entire population.

Dutch Borneo

The possessions of the Dutch in Borneo are about 750 miles in length from north-east to south-west, and have an average breadth of about 250 miles, thus exceeding in area all the other territories of the island. To the north they are bounded for a great part of their extent by the main, but nameless, range of the island, which runs from north-east to south-west. The seaboard thus extends from Tanjong Datu on the Sarawak border to a point high up on the east coast. The exact boundary on this side was for long a matter of dispute, the British North Borneo Company claiming as far as the Sibuku River in about 4° N. lat., while in their maps the Dutch marked the limit of their territory as extending to the southern horn of Darvel Bay; but the parallel of 4° 10′ has lately been determined as the boundary.

As has been already stated, the acquisition of these large possessions has been an affair of time, dating its commencement from 1606, when the Dutch were first attracted to the coast by the pepper trade. It was not till many years later, at the end of the last century, that they aimed at the possession of something more than sites for their factories. The territory of the Sultan of Banjarmasin was the first to come under their suzerainty in 1785, and from this beginning they have become the owners of more than two-thirds of the island, although their rule in a great part of it is almost nominal. The only districts really settled are, roughly speaking, the basin of the Negara, an affluent of the Barito, and the country lying between Pontianak and the Sarawak territory.

Dutch Borneo is divided for political purposes into two "Residencies"—those of "West Borneo" and "South and East Borneo," of which the latter is considerably the larger. The former comprises the country drained by the Kapuas, and has its southern boundary near Cape Sambur. It is believed to contain about

400,000 inhabitants, and is divided into two chief provinces—Pontianak and Montrado (Menterado). Of the sixteen Government stations, all except one (Sukadana) lie on or to the north of the Kapuas. The Residency of South and East Borneo has Banjarmasin for its capital. There are seventeen government stations, and the population is estimated at over 600,000. This division contains both the wildest and the most settled districts, the country round Amuntai and Negara being as populous and cultivated as many parts of Java, while the far interior, except on the rivers, remains still impenetrable, or at least unpenetrated. North of the Koti River even the coast is little known, though of late the boundary difficulty with the North Borneo Company has resulted in the frequent presence of gunboats, and a Controleur has been for some time stationed at the mouth of the Kayan or Bulangan River. The system of government by the Dutch in Borneo is very much that adopted by them in Sumatra. Unable yet to control any but a small portion of the vast mass of the population nominally under their rule, they are content to await their opportunity, permitting time slowly but surely to accomplish for them what would be less effectually gained by haste and force. Wherever feasible, an Assistant Resident is appointed to the capital of the chief native prince, to act conjointly with him; but in every case the orders are given to subordinates, and the general system of government is carried out by the native ruler. In many instances the official is supported by a small garrison, and in some places, notably in West Borneo, where the Chinese element prevails, and even now occasionally gives trouble, there are a good number of troops.

The city of Pontianak, though not by any means the largest in the island, is sufficiently important from its nearness to Batavia and Singapore, and from being situated upon one of the finest rivers in Borneo—the Kapuas. It is built about 15 miles from the sea, at the confluence of the Tambu, an affluent which rises in Mount Penrisan on the Sarawak border and is noteworthy as yielding diamonds. The buildings are of the usual Malay type, except where owned by Europeans, and the life is semi-aquatic, although in this respect it presents a much less characteristic and curious sight than Banjarmasin or Brunei. Each nation — Dutch, Malay, Chinese, Bugis, etc.—has its own quarter, and the population is variously estimated at from 18,000 to 20,000. Coasting from Pontianak along the southern seaboard, the entrances of innumerable rivers are passed, all of which bring down much forest produce to the villages at their mouths, where it is collected by Bugis and other native traders. All these rivers have been explored almost to their sources by the Dutch, but no officials are stationed on their banks, except at Sampit Bay, and it is not till Banjarmasin is reached that civilisation reappears.

Banjarmasin is the largest and most important city in the whole of Borneo. It contains between 40,000 and 50,000 inhabitants, and lies at the entrance of a most populous district, which has been civilised for centuries, and is rich in mineral wealth, especially in gold, diamonds, and coal. It is built not on the Barito itself, but on an affluent, the Riamkina or Martapura, and its houses occupy the banks for a distance of two miles, while the river itself is blocked, except in midstream, by a dense pack of bamboo rafts, floating houses, pile dwellings, and craft of all descriptions and sizes. Here, in 1700, the English had a factory and fort, the garrison of which were surprised and massacred by the natives seven years later. About 50 miles farther up the river is Martapura, in the neighbourhood of which are extensive coal-fields. It was in this district and the Negara valley that the first settlements of the Javanese were established, and various ruins of temples and other buildings still remain as memorials of Hindu influence, and are especially numerous near Amuntai.

On the east coast, some 50 miles north of Pulo Laut, is Pasir, a small independent state, ruled by a Sultan, who, though under the suzerainty of Holland, has as yet no Dutch official attached to his court. The capital, of the same name, is situated about 40 miles up an estuary, and is said to have 20,000 inhabitants. Among them are large numbers of Bugis from the Celebes coast, who principally carry on the trade, which consists almost entirely of forest produce. The embouchure of the Mahakkam or Koti river is the seat of two or three large towns, and here likewise there is considerable commercial activity. The State is a semi-independent Sultanate, the nominal capital of which, Tangarung, is situated about 60 miles up the river. The real centre of trade is at Samarinda, where the Dutch have an Assistant Resident. Here may be seen the same separation of the inhabitants into special quarters according to their nationality, and the same semi-aquatic life, which is noticeable in many Malay and most Bornean towns. The Bugis are especially strong in Samarinda, having their own laws and chiefs, and ruling the markets. The inhabitants of the upper waters of the Koti and Barito rivers are Kayans, the most powerful and widely-distributed race of all the Dyaks of Borneo.

Three small archipelagoes of islands belonging to the Dutch lie off the north-western point of Borneo—the Natuna, Anamba, and Tambilan groups. They are all

T

inhabited by people of Malay stock, who carry on a trade in coco-nuts, sago, and mats with Rhio and Singapore. Great Natuna is the principal island. It is about 40 miles in length, and has an estimated area of about 600 square miles, most of which is covered with forest. These groups are under the administration of the "Residency of Rhio and Dependencies," but the Dutch have no resident officials on any of them.

The value of the exports from Dutch Borneo in 1890 amounted to £400,000, of which £245,000 was from "West Borneo," and £155,000 from "South and East Borneo." In the former province the following articles head the list:—copra, £90,572; gutta, £77,207; rattan, £35,618; and coco-nut oil, £15,275. In the latter, gutta, £134,975; and rattan, £7568, are the most important items.

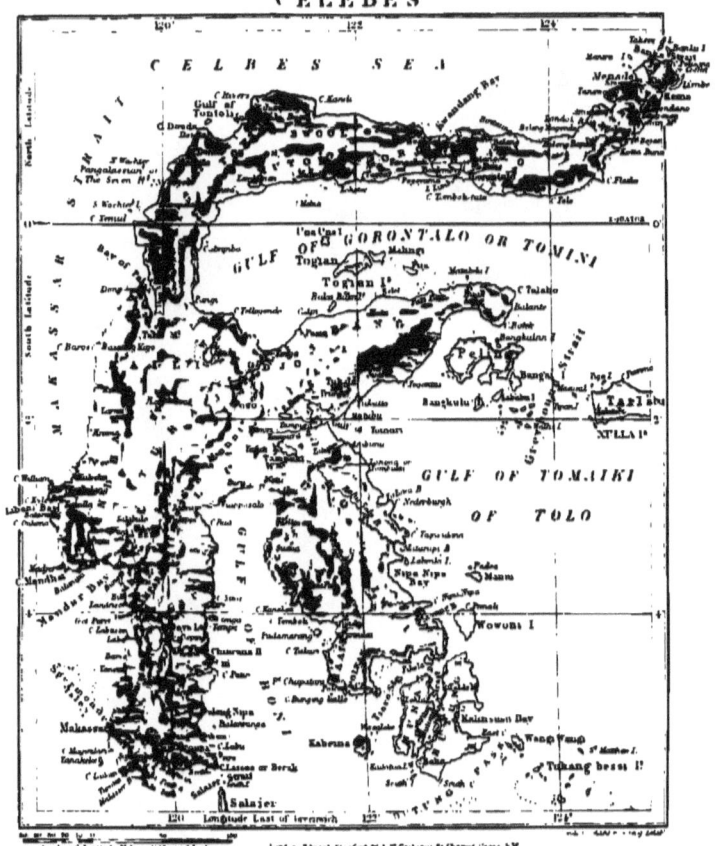

CHAPTER VIII

CELEBES

1. General.

CELEBES is the fourth island in magnitude in the Eastern Archipelago, being surpassed only by New Guinea, Borneo, and Sumatra. It has Borneo—from which it is separated by the Makassar Strait—on the west, and the scattered islands of the Moluccas on the east. On the north it is washed by the Celebes Sea, which intervenes between it and the Philippines, while to the south an island-dotted stretch of ocean of no great depth—the Flores Sea—separates it from the island of that name and others of the Sunda chain. It thus occupies a position midway between the great Malay islands on the one hand and the Papuan group on the other, belonging, as will be seen, to neither of these divisions, but exhibiting zoological and other peculiarities of a most marked and interesting nature, which serve to isolate it in a remarkable manner from every other island in the archipelago.

In shape Celebes is one of the most fantastic and curious islands in the world, although Gilolo to the eastward seems almost a replica upon a smaller scale, and Borneo, as has already been mentioned, must in former ages have closely resembled it, the gulfs having only begun to be obliterated in the Tertiary period. It consists of a central mass, from which radiate four enormous arms forming three deep gulfs on the eastern side, while the western has a curved and nearly even coast-line. The northern peninsula sweeps north and east in a double curve for nearly 500 miles, having an average breadth of not more than 40 or 50 miles. The other peninsulas are shorter and a little wider, and the total area of the island is estimated at 68,200 square miles.

Of this large island, upon which the Dutch have been settled for more than two centuries, very little is known. It is only at the extreme north and south points—in the Minahasa and Makassar districts—that any regular settlements have been formed and civilisation introduced. These are the great coffee districts. Elsewhere, for the most part, the country is a *terra incognita*, where the Dutch have not even native "postholders." Even the coast-line of the three gulfs is very little explored, and only roughly charted. All attempts, then, at estimating the population of the island cannot be otherwise than purely conjectural, although it is known to be scanty. It may roughly be placed at under a million.

2. History.

It is uncertain when Europeans first visited Celebes. It is stated that a few Portuguese found their way to Makassar shortly after the taking of Malacca, but in Ribero's great map, published in Seville in 1529, no trace of the island is to be found, although Gilolo and the Moluccas are delineated. Rebello, writing forty years later, speaks of it in very vague terms as "possessing many kings and cattle and buffaloes and goats," and

it is therefore unlikely that the Portuguese established
themselves on the island at an early period in the history
of the archipelago. All eyes were then turned to the
Moluccas and their spices, and Celebes, as we now know,
yielded few of the products coveted by Europeans except
gold, and for this reason carried on only a restricted
trade. Whether Hindu rites ever came into anything
like general use is unknown, but it is not at all probable,
although sculptured remains indicative of the worship of
Siva are said to exist. Mohammedanism was not introduced until about 1600—a fact which, as has been
remarked by Crawfurd, proves how small until then had
been the intercourse of the western nations of Asia with
Celebes, when it is remembered that Sumatra had been
converted four centuries before. The Dutch commenced
trading with Makassar in 1607, and definitely established
a factory there in 1618. In 1660 a fleet under Van
Dam effected the conquest of the kingdom, sinking six
ships of the Portuguese, then allies of the king, and
taking their fort. The Portuguese ejected, the Dutch
turned their attention to the north of the island, whence
they also expelled the Portuguese seventeen years later,
and in 1703 built a fort at Menado. Little, however,
was attempted in the way of civilisation in this part of
the island until the beginning of this century. In 1822
the coffee-plant was introduced, and in 1849 Menado
and Kema were made free ports. The English occupied
Makassar for a short time at the beginning of the present
century previous to the restoration of the Dutch possessions in 1816.

3. Physical Features.

So little is really known of the interior of Celebes,

that it is not possible to give with certainty even a rough outline of its physical geography. Each peninsula is nevertheless known to have a central mountain chain. In the north and south this has a tolerably continuous elevation, while in the eastern limb it is believed to be for the most part of lower altitude and discontinuous. No active volcanoes are known except in Minahasa, the district at the extremity of the northern peninsula, but there are abundant evidences of their former existence in several places. These chains, which are believed to radiate from a high central mass, of which Mount Latimojong is possibly the nucleus, are found to be largely formed of gneisses and granites wherever they have been examined, and in various districts, but especially in the north, a great deal of auriferous quartz is found. At the southern extremity rises a mass of elevated land, composed of Secondary rocks and distinct from the main range, culminating in the Peak of Bonthain, which is said to be over 10,000 feet in height. The height of the Donda mountain, at the north-western angle of the island, is also stated to be nearly 10,000 feet, but in neither case does the appearance of the mountain justify such an estimate. Mount Klabat a volcano situated at the extreme northern point, has an altitude of 6800 feet. As far as is yet known, these and Mount Tukala (8500 feet), in the eastern peninsula, are the most important peaks of Celebes.

The northern peninsula, rugged and mountainous, and clothed with dense vegetation, terminates in Minahasa, one of the most fertile districts in the archipelago, and it is here only that the volcanic forces are still active which are traceable in other parts of the island. Gunong Sudara (4400 feet), Klabat, the Lokon peak (5240 feet), Saputan (5963 feet), Tongkoko, and others, are all vol-

MOUNT KLABAT, FROM KEMA BAY.

canoes of recent origin, and several have been in eruption in the course of the present century. Other evidences of the character of this region occur in the shape of hot springs, mud volcanoes, and solfataras. Mr. Wallace thus describes some curious phenomena of this nature near Langauan, a little to the south of the Tondano Lake:—"A picturesque path among plantations and ravines brought us to a beautiful circular basin about 40 feet in diameter, bordered by a calcareous ledge, so uniform and truly curved that it looked like a work of art. It was filled with clear water very near the boiling point, and emitted clouds of steam with a strong sulphureous odour. It overflows at one point and forms a little stream of hot water, which at a hundred yards distance is still too hot to bear the hand in." The mud-springs, which are about a mile from this place, are still more curious. "On a sloping tract of ground in a slight hollow is a small lake of liquid mud, in patches of blue, red, and white, and in many places boiling and bubbling most furiously. All around on the indurated clay are small wells and craters full of boiling mud. These seem to be forming continually, a small hole appearing first, which emits jets of steam and boiling mud, which on hardening forms a little cone with a crater in the middle. The ground for some distance is very unsafe, as it is evidently liquid at a small depth, and bends with pressure like thin ice." Hot springs exist also by the Limbotto Lake, and in various other places; and at Tanjong Api—a headland on the eastern peninsula opposite the Togian Islands—jets of inflammable gas are being constantly emitted.

The rivers of Celebes are necessarily small, the largest being the Sadang, which is supposed to rise in the central plateau, and enters the sea on the west coast, some 80 miles north of Makassar, after a course of about 200 miles. The Bahu Solo, which rises in the Tafuti Lake and debouches just north of Nipanipa Bay in the south-eastern peninsula, is hardly more than 120 miles in length. Neither of these are navigable for anything but small craft. The Chinrana, however, which runs into the Gulf of Boni close to the town of that name, admits large native vessels for a distance of 50 miles or more.

Celebes has few of the temporary lakes which are so marked a characteristic of the Philippine Islands and Borneo. It exhibits none of the vast level stretches of low-lying post-Tertiary land which are daily flooded by tidal action as in the latter country. But it has several fresh-water reservoirs, which are in some cases of considerable extent, though not, apparently, of great depth. The largest of these is Lake Poso, in the centre of the island. Lake Tempe is drained by the Chinrana, and is about 20 miles in length. Two other sheets of water, Tafuti and Ranu, each not less than 10 miles long, are situated near the head of the Tomaiki or Tolo Gulf. All these are little known, but the Limbotto and Tondano lakes are in districts long settled, and have Europeans living on their shores. The former is close to Gorontalo, in a plain surrounded by mountains, and was doubtless formerly of much larger area. Now it does not exceed 7 miles in length. It is drained by the Gorontalo River, which has carved its way to the sea through the coast-range by a short but steep gorge. The Tondano Lake, which is of much the same size, lies in the midst of some of the most beautiful scenery in the archipelago, the centre of the fertile and thickly populated district of Minahasa. It has been described as occupying the crater of an ancient volcano, but upon what grounds it would be difficult to say, for there is nothing to support such a theory. The river draining it debouches at Menado, making a descent of many hundreds of feet in its short course, and forming a waterfall of great beauty, the upper plunge of which is about 100 feet in height.

4. Climate.

The central position of Celebes, its shape, and its physical characteristics have combined to render it the healthiest of all the large islands of Malaysia. The violence of the W. monsoon and the abundance of its rains are mitigated by Sumatra and Borneo, while in like manner the parching easterly winds which from April to October blow over the Sunda chain as far as the middle of Java, drying up the streams and causing the trees to shed their leaves, are less felt, and materially affect only the southern and south-eastern peninsulas. The shape of the island is such as to admit health-giving sea-breezes almost to its entire area, while the absence of the low-lying and frequently-inundated plains which form so large a portion of Sumatra and Borneo renders malaria far less common than in those countries. Not that paludal fevers and dysentery are unknown: the great infant mortality afflicting the Minahasa population is no doubt indirectly due to the former of these two maladies. But, on the whole, tropical disorders are far less frequent and severe here than in most other parts of the archipelago.

Owing to the influence of the S.E. monsoon, the climate of the Makassar district differs from that of Minahasa, being divided into a distinct wet and dry season, while the latter region, lying close to the equator, has a more equably distributed rainfall, and though occasionally subject to drought, is perennially verdant.

The average annual rainfall of Makassar is 128 inches, and that of Menado 107 inches.

5. Fauna and Flora.

The botany of Celebes is not yet well known. Recent collections from the northern peninsula indicate a considerable affinity with the Philippine group, and many of the coast plants are identical with those of the adjacent islands, but it is probable from what is known of the flora that it is distinct and peculiar. Of its zoology we have much more knowledge, and we find that its animals—considering the central position of the island—are wonderfully peculiar.

Taking first its mammalia, we find that Celebes differs broadly from Borneo and Sumatra in having no tailed monkeys, no insectivora, no feline or canine animals, no elephant, rhinoceros, or tapir. It has only five large, and eleven or twelve small, terrestrial quadrupeds. The former are—(1) A large black tailless baboon or ape; (2) a deer; (3) a remarkable small wild buffalo, resembling an antelope (*Anoa depressicornis*); (4) a wild pig; (5) the babirusa or "horned pig." The smaller animals are—the tarsier (one of the lemurs); a civet-cat; five squirrels; two rats; and two kinds of cuscus, a marsupial opossum-like creature. These animals may be divided into three groups. Some, as the deer, the civet, and the tarsier, are identical with species of Borneo and the western islands; and, as all are kept as domestic pets by the Malays, they may have been introduced, and have escaped from captivity. Others, as the wild pig, the squirrels, and the rats, are peculiar species, but are allied to those of Borneo and Java, and thus indicate a more distant period of immigration. Others again, as the ape, the anoa, and the babirusa, are altogether peculiar.[1] No animals at all nearly allied to them are to be found in any of the Asiatic islands, or, in fact, anywhere else, if we except an allied form of the anoa which exists in the island of Mindoro in the Philippines; and we are thus led to speculate on their

THE ANOA (*Anoa depressicornis*).

transmission from a very remote epoch, when Celebes formed part of a continent which disappeared before the existing Asiatic islands were formed; for on any other supposition it is most difficult to understand how these

[1] It is true that the former occurs on the island of Batjan, and the babirusa at the N.E. point of Buru, but it is most probable that they have been introduced by the agency of man.

singular animals should have been preserved in Celebes and nowhere else. And, lastly, we have the marsupial cuscus, indicating that the island has received some of its productions from the Moluccas or New Guinea, where alone these animals abound; and we have also two forest rats of the sub-genus *Gymnomys*, which are allied to Australian species.

Turning to the birds, we find facts of equal interest; and, considering how easy it is for this class to pass over narrow seas, even more extraordinary. There are now about 160 species of land-birds known from Celebes, belonging to 124 generic groups. About 90 of these species are peculiar to it and the small adjacent islands; while, of the remainder, about 50 come from the Asiatic and 20 from the Australian side. This is what we might expect, looking at the great extent of the opposing coasts of Borneo, which are much richer in birds than the Moluccas. The peculiar species of Celebes are generally related to birds characteristic of one side or the other, and in this way also we find the Asiatic side preponderating in the proportion of 24 to 15. But if we look at the number of genera of land-birds, abundant in Borneo or the Moluccas, which are absent from Celebes, we find the most striking deficiency on the Bornean or Asiatic side. Thus, 8 important families, and 16 genera which are highly characteristic of Borneo or Java are unknown in Celebes; while of the Moluccan groups of equal importance there are only 1 family and 12 genera absent. These remarkable deficiencies, quite as much as the species it actually possesses, stamp the character of the Celebesian fauna, and give a clue to its past history.

Of the land mollusca we have as yet but scanty knowledge. Such genera as are known are for the most part found also in Borneo and Sumatra, but *Planispira* is a Moluccan form, and *Obba* and *Obbina*, which occur in North Celebes, are purely Philippine. No peculiar genus has hitherto been discovered, but the material is as yet hardly sufficient to form deductions, and taking account

THE BABIRUSA (*Sus babirusa*).

of both mammalia and birds, of which two groups alone we possess sufficiently detailed information, we cannot doubt the great antiquity and extreme isolation of this island from the rest of the archipelago. The two remarkable mammals—the ape-baboon (*Cynopithecus*) and the four-tusked pig (*Babirusa*), as well as a curious bee-eater (*Meropogon*); three remarkable genera of starlings (*Basilornis*, *Enodes*, and *Scissirostrum*); two peculiar magpies (*Streptocitta* and *Charitornis*); and an anomalous kingfisher (*Ceycopsis*), have none of them any near allies in the archipelago, and are only remotely connected with groups now inhabiting the Asiatic or African continents. They appear, in fact, to be remnants of the Miocene fauna, at a period when the ancestors of all the chief types of both the temperate and tropical zones of the Eastern hemisphere were to be found in the Euro-Asiatic continent. The peculiarities of the animal life of Celebes may be best explained by supposing it to be an outlying portion of that Miocene continent, which became detached from it, and has since never been actually joined to any Asiatic or Australian land. It has thus preserved to us some descendants of ancient types, and these have become intermingled with such immigrants from both east and west as were enabled to establish themselves in competition with the ancient inhabitants. To the naturalist, therefore, Celebes is an island of extreme interest. It cannot be said to belong either to the eastern or the western divisions of the archipelago, but to stand almost exactly midway between them; the relic of a more ancient land, and dating from a period perhaps anterior to the separate existence of any of the islands.

The insects, although less perfectly known, offer analogous peculiarities to those presented by the higher animals. They are isolated alike from those of the Sunda Islands and the Moluccas, and present certain specialities of form and coloration not found elsewhere. The details are of too technical a nature to find a place here, but they are such as fully to confirm the general conclusion we have arrived at, as to the long-continued isolation of this remarkable country.

6. Native Races.

From what has been said of the extreme antiquity of Celebes, and the peculiarity and isolation of its animals, it might be expected that some equally peculiar tribes of mankind might be found here, or even some relic of primeval man. But it must be remembered that man is pre-eminently a migrating and an aggressive animal, the higher or more energetic races constantly displacing the lower or less physically powerful; so that his present distribution may have little relation to the ancient history of the countries he inhabits. It is highly probable that a low and primitive race did once inhabit Celebes; but if so, it has, so far as we know, completely disappeared, and the whole island is now occupied by many distinct tribes in various stages of civilisation, but all belonging to the Malayan race. They may be roughly classed into two groups—the Mohammedan semi-civilised tribes, and the Pagans, who are more or less savages. The former read and write, and mostly have peculiar alphabetic characters; they have fixed governments, regular clothing, and are considerably advanced in agriculture and the arts, being, in fact, the equals of the true Malays and the Javanese. The latter are more or less complete savages, without writing or fixed governments, usually with imperfect bark clothing, and without the arts of weaving or working metals.

The most important of the Mohammedan peoples are the Bugis, the Mandars, and the Makassars. The Bugis occupied originally only the district of Boni in the southern peninsula, but have now extended over a considerable area. They are composed of many tribes, of which the Waju are the most powerful, and are governed by independent Rajas, banded together in confederacies. The Bugis are the most advanced of all the natives of Celebes, and would seem, to judge from their language, to have acquired their civilisation mainly from the Javanese. They invented a peculiar alphabetical character, and a calendar, the year consisting of 365 days, divided into 12 months, each with its native name. The development of this people appears to have been of recent date, for they are not even mentioned by the older Portuguese writers. Now they are the greatest maritime people and traders in the Malay Archipelago, navigating from the farthest point of Sumatra to New Guinea. They are, moreover, not only traders but settlers, and have established themselves in most of the large towns in the different islands, dwelling apart in a separate "Bugis quarter," ruled over by their own chiefs under their own laws. These enterprising people are good shipbuilders, constructing praus (*padewakan*) of 50 or 60 tons burden, with which they trade eastward or westward according to the monsoon. Their energy contrasts strongly with the ordinary Malay character, but they resemble that nation in being both proud and vindictive. They are also as passionate as they are brave, and "running amok" is perhaps more frequent in Celebes than in any of the other islands.

The Mandars occupy the western portion of the island, which projects out into the Strait of Makassar, north of Cape Mandar. They speak a distinct language, and are still partly pagan. They are energetic fishermen and traders, and their country produces edible birds' nests and some gold. The Makassars inhabit the southern and western extremity of the southern peninsula. Their chief town and the residence of the Raja is Goa, only a few miles from Makassar, the Dutch capital. Their language is likewise distinct, but contains more introduced words than Bugis. Like Mandar, it is written in

HOUSE OF RAJA OF GOA, S. CELEBES.

the Bugis character, as are also some languages of the northern peninsula and of the island of Sumbawa.

All the remaining inhabitants of Celebes are, or have been until lately, in a state very similar to that of the

Dyaks of Borneo. They are, some of them, head-hunters, and even cannibals. Human skulls ornament the chief's houses, and, when he dies, it is necessary to obtain two fresh human skulls with which to adorn his grave. Some curious burying-places exist in the northern peninsula, near the village of Sawangan, which have been described by the American traveller Bickmore. These are what may be termed vertical coffins, consisting of solid rectangular upright stones, deeply hollowed out at the top, so as to receive the body, and covered with a roof-shaped capstone, adorned with rude carvings of human figures in a sitting attitude, the knees clasped by the hands. This elaborate mode of burial, if correctly described, is, it is believed, unique among savage tribes. These northern people, however, are different from the Dyak-like tribes farther south, and may have affinities with some of the indigenes of the Philippines, or of the islands of Northern Polynesia. In this peninsula the number of different languages is extraordinary. At its extremity, a small tract of country some 60 miles by 20, more than a dozen are spoken. Some of these may perhaps be more or less dialectic, but the majority are said to be quite distinct, and the people of the different tribes cannot make themselves understood except through the medium of Malay, although, perhaps, their villages may be within three miles of one another. The Minahasans have been almost all converted to Christianity, and have become an orderly, industrious, and intelligent people. At Tomoré, on the eastern side of the central portion of the island (and probably elsewhere), the natives make bark cloth, closely resembling the "tapa" of the Polynesians. It is beaten out by wooden mallets till it becomes as thin and tough as parchment; it is then washed with an extract from some bark, which gives it a glossy surface, and renders it capable of withstanding a good shower of rain, so that it becomes a really serviceable article of clothing.

7. The Dutch Settled Districts.

In spite of its being in great part unexplored, the whole of the island of Celebes is claimed by the Dutch, and divided by them into three political departments, of which the "Government of Celebes and its Dependencies" is the most extensive, embracing not only the southern half of the islands, with Salaier and the Butung group, but also the island of Sumbawa and part of Flores. The Residency of Menado includes the greater part of the northern peninsula and the shores of the Gorontalo Gulf, while the country drained by the rivers emptying themselves into the Gulf of Tolo are under the nominal administration of the Resident of Ternate. These divisions are, however, of little practical moment except to cartographers; for, except at Labuan-dede, in Tontoli Bay, and Mendono, opposite Peling Island, there are no Europeans out of the Makassar and Menado districts.

The Makassar District is the part which was earliest known to the western nations, and it was here, after the defeat of the Portuguese, that the Dutch first established themselves, building a fort in 1665. The country round is one of the most important coffee districts in the East, is traversed by good roads, and controlled by Dutch officials resident in fifteen different towns and villages. In the lowlands great quantities of rice are grown. Cotton is also cultivated, and the Makassar and Bugis women make *sarongs*—the skirt or petticoat universally worn by Malays of both sexes—which for durability and permanence of colour are unrivalled, and are highly esteemed over the whole archipelago, those ornamented with gold thread bringing very high prices.

Omitting the cities of Java, Makassar is the most important town in the whole of the Dutch East Indies— the centre of trade of a vast extent of country, a position it owes to the wonderful mercantile energy of the Bugis, a people who are to the archipelago what the Chinese are to Asia proper. Makassar may be said to be the Hongkong of the Dutch, while Batavia is their Singapore. Although an open roadstead, the port affords safe anchorage at almost all seasons. It has good piers, and is frequented by much shipping. The town is low and flat, but healthy, although from December to March the rains are heavy. It contains over 20,000 inhabitants. The business quarter, thick with powdery dust in the dry season, lines the shore for half a mile, and is crowded with Chinese, Bugis, and Arabs. Here are the offices and "godowns" of the Dutch and German merchants, the latter being strongly represented here, as in other Malay towns. Northward is a populous native suburb. The European quarter lies at the south of the town, the villas thickly shaded with trees, and near it is Fort Rotterdam, where the garrison is quartered, strongly built, but now useless against large ordnance. The town is walled, and many of the streets are kept clean by means of narrow canals into which the tidal waters are admitted at high tide and allowed to run out with the ebb. Northward of Makassar, and lining the coast for nearly 50 miles, lies the Spermonde Archipelago, a complex network of countless islands, reefs, and shoals, densely populated by tripang fishermen and covered with coco-palms.

The Menado Residency consists of the volcanic region of Minahasa, about 70 miles long, and an extensive district beyond forming the Assistant-Residency of Gorontalo. The whole of this country was formerly tributary to the Sultan of Ternate, and was inhabited by numerous savage tribes whose habits have already been described. When the Portuguese were expelled in 1677, it was taken possession of by the Dutch, and many of the natives were converted to Christianity. The country, however, did not begin to progress much till 1822, when it was found that the elevated plateau of the interior was admirably adapted to the growth of coffee. Native instructors in the art of coffee cultivation were brought from Java; the native chiefs, under the title of Majors, were induced to encourage the formation of plantations by a grant of five per cent of the produce; and a fixed price was paid for all properly cleaned coffee brought to the Government warehouses. European superintendents of the plantations were appointed to each district, good roads were made, the villages were gradually improved, and schools and churches built. Now there are 125,000 Christians in the district, with excellent schools established in all the villages. The country, moreover, has become a perfect garden. In many of the villages the streets are bordered with hedges of roses, which thrive admirably at from 2000 to 3000 feet elevation, and are in perpetual bloom; the cottages are symmetrically arranged, nicely painted, and embowered in flowering shrubs and fruit trees; while the people are all well dressed and well fed, well behaved and contented, presenting a marvellous contrast to the naked savages of fifty years back who were the fathers and grandfathers of the present generation.

A considerable portion of Minahasa is an uneven plateau, from 2500 to 3000 feet above the sea, with mountains rising to 6000 feet or more. The highest village is Rurukan, 3500 feet above the sea; and here, in the month of June, the thermometer is usually 62° Fahr. in the morning, and rarely rises above 80° during the day. Here oranges thrive better than in the lowlands, bearing abundance of most delicious fruit, and rice produces good crops without irrigation. The scenery is magnificent. Numerous volcanic mountains clothed with the richest vegetation lend grandeur to the prospect, and form a charming contrast to the coffee plantations, the rice fields, the gardens, and the neat cottages that everywhere meet the eye.

The chief towns of Minahasa are Menado and Kema, on opposite sides of the peninsula, the former used as the chief port during the eastern, and the latter during the western monsoon. They are less than twenty miles apart, and are connected by a good road. Menado is the capital town, and the place where the Resident lives. It is a small but picturesque town, and as almost every house stands in a garden and is surrounded by beautiful shrubs, trees, and flowers, it has a very charming effect as compared with the more mercantile appearance of Makassar. Its population is over 4000. An excellent system of roads connects all the chief towns and villages of Minahasa. The district has of late become very populous, and there are now probably not less than 160,000 inhabitants.

The coffee tree was first introduced into the Minahasa district in 1822, and at the end of 1889, 7,767,159 trees were under Government cultivation, without including private plantations. The industry has been the means of converting the country from a wilderness of jungle, peopled by head-hunting savages, into a well-cultivated garden tilled by natives who are almost without exception Christians. Yet this result has been

MENADO, N. CELEBES.

brought about by a system which most Englishmen would condemn untried—that of enforced labour. Any person of the peasant class not having a trade is compelled by law to plant coffee. Each must, if required, plant 25 trees every year, but the number depends upon his last year's production, and is regulated by the Controleur. There are Government plantations in every village, and both the land and the seedlings are supplied by the State. The success of the industry is in great measure due to the equable rainfall, the north of Celebes herein differing greatly from Java, which is exposed to a long-continued drought during the easterly monsoon and excessive rains in the wet season. The berry is of particularly good flavour, and finds its market chiefly in Russia, bringing a far higher price than that produced in Java. All the coffee thus grown by the natives has to be sold to Government at a fixed price. It is divided into two qualities, for which fourteen and seven guilders are respectively paid per picul of 133 lbs. This price is, however, not the actual cost to the Government, since presents have to be given to the head-men and "Majors," and as the crop is bought on the plantation, the cost of conveyance to the coast is considerable. Should a Dutchman wish to plant coffee, he is permitted to do so, the system being only a Government monopoly so far as the natives are concerned. He is allowed to take up land at a rental of one guilder per bouw ($1\frac{3}{4}$ acre), and pays a head-tax of a dollar on his coolies. The wages of the latter are six guilders, or rather less than ten shillings, a month, and a catty ($1\frac{1}{3}$ lb.) of rice per diem. Every adult male is, however, compelled to give thirty-six days in the year to the service of the Government for road repair and work of a like nature, or else to provide a substitute.

The effect of the Dutch "culture-system" is perhaps better seen in Minahasa than in Java, and no one could visit the district without being struck with the example of prosperity and happiness it affords. Some years ago Mr. Wallace pointed out that it is only by some such means that the gulf between savagery and advanced civilisation can be bridged, and that the experiment of introducing free trade and free labour among a childlike and irresponsible people must inevitably be fraught with disaster. Twenty years later Dr. Guillemard found the Minahasans "a contented, happy people, among whom drunkenness and crime were almost non-existent; the land highly cultivated, and the villages neater and cleaner than in any part of the civilised world," and was constrained to agree with Mr. Wallace. A still later traveller, the naturalist Dr. Hickson, who resided in Northern Celebes for a year in 1885, thus speaks of the *corvée* in Minahasa:—"The system of *heerendienst* has been very severely criticised by many well-meaning persons as tyrannical and unjust, but I cannot help thinking that every one who is really acquainted with the circumstances of these colonies and the character and condition of the people must admit that it is a service which is both necessary and just. The Dutch Government has brought to the people of Minahasa not only the blessings of peace and security, but also the possibilities of a very considerable civilisation and commercial prosperity. The natives are now able to sow their rice in perfect confidence that they will gather the harvest in due season; they are able to send their corn, their chickens, and other produce to the markets without fear of being plundered on the road, and without experiencing the horrors of war and bloodshed; they pass their lives in peace and quietude from the cradle to the grave. In return for this it is only just that every able-bodied man should be compelled to lend a hand in maintaining this happy condition of affairs. In a land where the necessities of life are so easily obtained, and the wants of the people are few, poverty is inexcusable and starvation unknown. Under such circumstances it would be impossible for the Government to obtain a sufficient number of men to labour on the roads at a reasonable wage, and in consequence they would be either neglected or extremely costly to maintain. The *heerendienst* is, then, the only system by which the roads can be kept in a proper state of repair without over-burdening the exchequer or increasing the taxation of the people beyond their capabilities. If it is true that some of the Dutch officials have occasionally used the *heerendienst* for their own personal service, it is the abuse of the system we should deprecate, not the system itself."

West of Minahasa is Gorontalo, which gives its name to the great gulf intervening between the peninsula and the rest of the island. The district, which is inhabited by native tribes under chiefs or rajas, is administered by a Dutch Assistant-Resident. Most of the people here are of a markedly different type from the short, light-coloured, and amiable-looking Minahasans, being taller, darker, and with crisper hair, but nevertheless showing no sign of Papuan blood. Many are Mohammedans, but the greater number pagans, as are almost all the tribes farther west, except on the coast, where are some settlements of Bugis and Mandars who trade with the people of the interior. The town of Gorontalo is situated close to the Limbotto Lake, and contains about 3000 inhabitants. Its chief exports are copra and copal. The Dutch have been settled here from the seventeenth century, and remains of an old fort still exist, with walls

10 or 12 feet high, which is said to be of Portuguese construction. The country is in many places comparatively bare of vegetation; it is of granitic formation, and gold is widely distributed, although as yet no very rich quartz has been found. The natives of Pogoyama and Pagoat, westward of Gorontalo, pay tribute to the Dutch in gold dust.

8. Trade and Products.

The total value of the exports from Celebes in 1890 is officially stated at £564,058. This includes Sumbawa, but the trade of this island is of very little importance. By far the most valuable product is coffee, of which 4110 tons were exported, valued at over £300,000. Of this the Menado district yields about one-eighth only. In the Makassar district the Government have no plantations, the industry being entirely in private hands, but of the Menado crop about three-fifths belongs to the State. The coffee of Minahasa is considered to be the best-flavoured in the world, and is chiefly sent to Russia.

The chief exports of Southern Celebes after coffee are dammar (£53,000) and tripang (£40,000), this latter Chinese edible being a special product of the surrounding seas, as is tortoiseshell (£12,000), no other part of the archipelago producing anything like the quantity. Nutmegs are also grown largely, the export being valued at nearly £13,000, an amount which is exceeded only by Banda and the west coast of Sumatra. The exports of Northern Celebes apart from coffee differ a good deal from those of the Makassar district, the most important being copal (£23,000), rattan (£15,000), tobacco (£8000), and nutmegs and copra (each about £10,000). The vanilla orchid is grown in small quantities, and cacao promised well until lately, when many of the plantations were ruined by disease.

The mineral products of Celebes are comparatively unimportant, although it is possible that further knowledge of the country may reveal gold-fields of value. Coal is found in various places in the Makassar district, but is of poor quality and is not worked. Iron and copper are obtained in small quantities by the natives. The gold mines are chiefly in the northern peninsula, in the native states of Buül, Mutong, and in the neighbourhood of Pagoat, but the methods employed are primitive, and, the output passing into the hands of native traders, no satisfactory statistics are available.

9. Islands belonging to Celebes.

Celebes is rich in islands, which are for the most part situated at or near the extremities of the four great peninsulas of which it is composed. Thus, from the north, the Banka, Talaut, Tulur, and Carcaralong groups form a series of stepping-stones, as it were, to the southern end of Mindanao in the Philippines. Around Balante, the eastern promontory of Celebes, are the Togian, Peling, and Xulla groups. Off the end of the south-eastern peninsula lie the large islands Muna and Butung (Boeton), while between the south promontory and Flores the sea is covered with a multiplicity of reefs and islands, of which Salaier only is of importance.

Of all these, the chain of islands to the north are the most interesting in every way. They have scarcely ever been visited by Englishmen, but Dr. Hickson's visit to them in 1885 has added considerably to our knowledge of them. They were first seen by Europeans in 1521, when the two remaining vessels of Magellan's squadron sailed southward for the Moluccas after the death of their leader. As early as the sixteenth century the Portuguese missionaries laboured in Siau and Sangir, building churches whose ruins are still to be seen. The Spaniards also established themselves, but were driven out, as were the Portuguese, by the Dutch, who came formally into possession in 1677. The islands are now administered by Controleurs resident in Great Sangir and Salibabu,[1] and there are three or four European missionaries stationed among the people. An attempt has been made at instruction by native teachers, but on the whole the people are in a state of semi-savagery, although peaceable among themselves and not ill-disposed to Europeans.

It is uncertain whether the Salibabu group are volcanic, although the Nanusas, lying beyond them, are so. The main chain of islands, however, exhibits volcanoes almost throughout its length, and many of these are active. From the paucity of soundings, it is not known as yet whether a very deep channel does or does not exist in the submarine bank which is presumed to connect Northern Celebes with the Philippines, but the sounding of 930 fathoms obtained by H.M.S. *Flying Fish* in the Banka Passage indicates that the connection, if any, must have been at a comparatively remote period. It is probable that a still deeper channel exists a little to the south of the Philippines, for the zoology of the Sangir chain appears to be far more Celebesian than Philippine. Taking the islands in order from the south, Talisse is the site of the coco-nut plantations of a Dutch

---

[1] There is considerable confusion in the nomenclature of the groups to which these islands respectively belong, the names Tulur and Talaut having been applied to both. To avoid misapprehension, they are accordingly spoken of here as the Sangir and Salibabu groups.

company, and the neighbouring island of Banka was once a noted resort of pirates, but is now only inhabited by a few fishermen. About 35 miles N.N.E. lies Ruang, an active island-volcano about 2200 feet high, which, though of insignificant size, has been the scene of several eruptions, the most important in 1871, when 400 persons lost their lives, chiefly from a seismic wave which was said to have been over 80 feet in height. Siau Island, 20 miles to the north, is about 10 miles in length, and has four volcanic peaks, the most northern, 6000 feet high, being active. The Rajas of this island were in former days very powerful, sharing the rule of the Salibabu group with the Rajas of Sangir. We next come—passing over a number of small islands—to Great Sangir, the most important of the chain. It produces considerable quantities of copra, which is chiefly shipped by Chinese traders from Taruna, the capital, which is the residence of the Controleur, and a port of call for the Netherlands India S.S. Company's steamers. This island is about 25 miles in length, and has many extinct craters, and more than one active, the most important being Awu, which has an altitude of about 5000 feet, and has been one of the most formidable volcanoes in the archipelago. In 1711 its eruption caused the death of 2000 people, and in 1856 nearly 3000 perished. On the 7th June 1892 a destructive eruption took place, which appears to have caused the loss of many lives, for within four days of its cessation the Controleur had recovered 300 bodies.

Dr. Hickson describes the Sangir people as consisting of nobles, freemen, and slaves—a race of sailors, building excellent praus. A good cloth of banana fibre is made, and coco-nuts largely grown. The language is peculiar, the marriage system matriarchal. North-east of Sangir, and some distance from the main chain of islands, is the

Salibabu group, peopled by a timid, inoffensive race of semi-pagans, with a language closely allied to Sangirese. They live in large communal houses like the Dyaks of Borneo, practise circumcision, and are little acquainted with the metals, their weapons even being made of wood. At the time of Dr. Hickson's visit they were suffering from some form of malaria, which, aided by total neglect of sanitary laws, had then killed 3000 out of the 9000 inhabitants. The largest island in the group is 35 miles in length.

Due east of Celebes, beyond Peling Island, is the Sulla or Xulla group, consisting of two large islands, Xulla Tarlabu and Xulla Manggala, stretching in an east and west direction for about 100 miles, divided only by a narrow strait about the centre, with a smaller island, Xulla Bâsi, to the south. The western island is scantily inhabited by a race allied to those of the eastern peninsula of Celebes and the island of Bangaai; the others appear to have no indigenes, but to be colonised by the Malays from Ternate with their Papuan slaves, which has given rise to the report that these islands were inhabited by a people of Papuan race. Xulla Bâsi is much the most important island. It is about 26 miles long, is well cultivated, and produces much wax and honey. At Sanana Bay is a Dutch resident official, and a small fort has been built. Coal of an inferior quality is found on the island. The whole group is nominally subject to Ternate, but both geographically and zoologically the islands belong to Celebes. They are inhabited by babirusas and deer, while their birds, which are tolerably well known, resemble those of Celebes much more closely than those of the Moluccas. The Peling and Togian groups are inhabited by tripang and turtle fishermen, and very little is known of them.

Off the S.E. promontory we come to the large islands of Muna and Butung (Boeton). The latter is over 100 miles long, and is composed chiefly of coralline limestone, although it is said to have an extinct volcano at its northern extremity. The united population of the two islands exceeds 20,000, and large quantities of cotton are grown.

The island of Salaier, off the southern point of Celebes, is 40 miles in length, and is densely peopled, the population of the entire group being over 50,000. The Dutch have a small settlement and a fort here, and have planted the teak tree with success. This completes the enumeration of the islands of any importance belonging to Celebes. The whole western and northern coast after leaving Makassar, for a distance of more than 800 miles, presents not a single island of the slightest importance. A deep sea everywhere approaches close to the shore, and probably indicates that on this side the land has undergone little change, either of elevation or of subsidence, for a very long period.

CHAPTER IX

THE MOLUCCAS

1. General.

THE term Moluccas, or Maluco Islands, was originally applied to the five small islands which are situated on the west side of Gilolo, or Halmahera, as the island is more properly termed, and in which alone the precious clove was produced. Now, it is extended so as to include almost all the islands which lie directly between Celebes and New Guinea. The three large islands which are considered geographically to form the most important portion of the Moluccan group are Gilolo, Ceram, and Buru; but between and around these are a vast number of islands of various sizes, so connecting the Moluccas with the New Guinea and Timor groups that it is very difficult to define accurately what islands should be included in the one or the other.

As we have already considered the Sangir and Salibabu islands to be extensions of Celebes, we have no difficulty in fixing on Morti or Morotai, to the north of Gilolo, as being the first island of the group in this direction. In like manner, having taken the Xulla islands as belonging to Celebes, we have the Batjan group, Obi, and Buru as the western limits of the Moluccas. To the

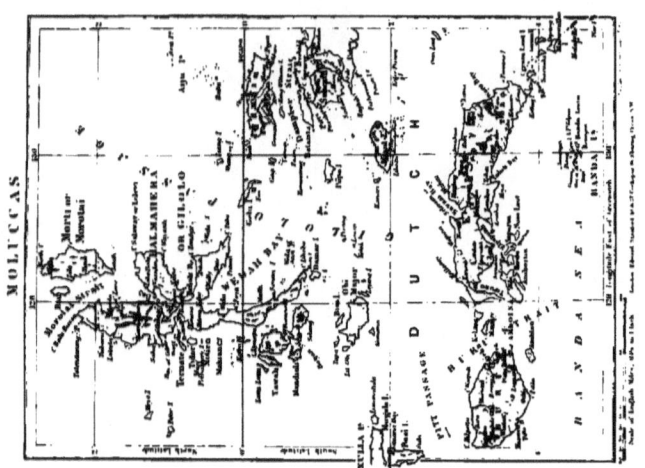

east there is more difficulty. Waigiu and Misol are inhabited by true mop-headed Papuans and by birds-of-paradise, and therefore undoubtedly belong to New Guinea, with which country, moreover, they are connected by a shallow sea-bottom. It will be well, therefore, to take the 100-fathom line as the boundary of the Papuan group, and we shall thus have the small group of Siang, Gebi, Gagi, and Popa as belonging to the Moluccas. Beyond the east end of Ceram we have a number of small islands leading on to the Ké group; and as these agree with all the other islands we have been considering, in being forest-clad, while their productions ally them more to Ceram and Banda than to the Aru Islands, we shall take these as the farthest extension of the Moluccan group to the south-east. It is true that the Timor Laut group is not much farther to the south, but these islands begin to be bare of forest, and thus belong naturally to the comparatively arid Timor group. Thus limited, the Moluccas, or Spice Islands, as they are sometimes called, extend about 600 miles from north to south, and about 500 from east to west, but they fall naturally into two subdivisions—that of Gilolo on the north, and that of Buru and Ceram on the south. Situated on both sides of the equator, and far enough removed from Australia to be unaffected by the arid winds which blow from it, these islands are all clothed with a magnificent vegetation, and enjoy a climate which, by its equability of temperature, combined with moisture, and tempered by perpetual breezes, is perhaps unsurpassed in any part of the tropics. For nearly two centuries they were the scene of ceaseless and sanguinary struggles between the Spaniards, Portuguese, and Dutch for their possession. At the present time their value is no longer what it was, but a certain amount of trade is still carried on at Ternate, Amboina, and Banda. All the islands are in the possession of Holland, but the two largest, Gilolo—or Halmahera—and Ceram, are as yet comparatively little known.

2. Geology and Natural History.

The great volcanic belt passes through the whole length of the Moluccas, and gives them their distinctive character, yet several of the islands are entirely without volcanoes, either active or extinct, and some appear to be wholly non-volcanic in structure. Beginning with Banda on the south, the line of volcanic action passes through Amboina to Buru, where a volcano is said to exist in the western part; it then turns northward through Batjan, where there are boiling springs, to the line of active volcanoes running from Makian to the northern extremity of Gilolo, where are several volcanic peaks. In the vicinity of the volcanic districts there are usually abundant signs of upheaval, in the form of raised coral reefs or masses of coral limestone far inland. At the extreme north, the island of Morti is coralline and volcanic, but has no volcano. The centre and most of the southern peninsula of Gilolo is composed largely of coral rock. At Amboina we find a base of crystalline rocks, with abundance of coralline limestone, forming hills of considerable elevation and very rugged, the hollows being filled with red clayey earth, probably decomposed volcanic ashes. Farther east, the small islands of Goram, Manowolko, and Matabello consist wholly of coral reefs raised to a considerable height, while Great Ké Island is also very largely composed of the same rock. The large island of Ceram, however, appears to offer a contrast to the rest of the Moluccas. No volcanoes are known in it, and the rocks, so far as observed, appear to be ancient stratified deposits of a highly crystalline character, though limestone occurs at its eastern extremity. The great central mountain, Nusa Heli, is said to be nearly 10,000 feet high, but no European has ever visited it.

The vegetation of the Moluccas is exceedingly rich and varied, and would well repay systematic exploration. Here is the native country of the most precious of spices, the clove; and here are also wild nutmegs, cardamoms, the kanari nut, and the cajuput-oil tree. Palms and pandani are very abundant, dammar pines grow in the forests, while ferns, creepers, and flowering shrubs in endless variety clothe the forest glades and the rocky beaches with exquisite drapery.

The animal life is much better known, and enables us to decide that it belongs generally to the Australian type, and more particularly resembles the fauna of New Guinea. A few of the Asiatic forms of mammalia, resembling those of the western islands, are still found here; such as the deer, which abounds in all the larger islands, and even in several of the smaller ones, since it occurs in Ternate and Tidor, in Banda, and in Ceram Laut. The species is almost, if not quite, identical with one common in all the great Malay islands, and it may very well have been introduced by the Malay colonists. None of the islands have any monkeys, except Batjan, in which is found the tailless baboon-ape of Celebes; while in Buru alone is found the babirusa, another of the peculiar forms of that island. Both of these are considered by Mr. Wallace to have been introduced by human agency. Pigs are abundant in all the islands, and some of them are believed to be peculiar species. The only carnivorous animal is the common civet-cat (*Viverra tangalunga*); and as the Malays often keep these creatures for the purpose of obtaining the perfume, of which they are very fond, it has probably been introduced by them. The only other quadrupeds are bats, which are abundant, a shrew, and several marsupials

MOLUCCAN CUSCUS (*C. ornatus*).

of the genus Cuscus, as well as a small flying-opossum resembling those found in Australia. If, therefore, we leave out of the list those species which there is reason to think may have been introduced by man, we find an excessive poverty of mammals, hardly to be equalled anywhere else in the world under similar conditions.

Birds, on the other hand, are tolerably abundant, and are in many respects interesting. Their essentially Papuan character is indicated by the fact that out of the 78 genera in which the Moluccan land-birds are classed, no less than 70 are characteristic of New Guinea, while only six are peculiarly Indo-Malayan. The species, however, are to a great extent peculiar, more than 140 being entirely confined to these islands out of a total number of about 200 land-birds. A most remarkable feature is the immense preponderance of the three groups—parrots, pigeons, and kingfishers. These together form *one-third* of all the land-birds, while in continental India they only form one-twentieth. As these groups are rather above the average of size, and contain an unusual proportion of gaily-coloured species, they give to the birds of the Moluccas an air of special brilliancy. Among the most beautiful are the crimson lories, the racquet-tailed kingfishers, and the green fruit-doves; and there are also some brilliant ground-thrushes and fly-catchers. In the islands of Batjan and Gilolo, and possibly in Obi, there is a peculiar species of the bird-of-paradise family—*Semioptera wallacei*, discovered by Mr. Wallace in 1858—the only one yet found beyond the Papuan region. Very curious, too, is the occurrence of the great wingless bird, the cassowary, in Ceram, distinct from the numerous species that inhabit New Guinea and the adjacent islands. The mound-building birds of the genus *Megapodius* are especially abundant in the Moluccas, being found even on the smallest islands and uninhabited islets.

Regarded from the point of view of their land Mollusca, the Moluccas fall into two distinct groups—the northern comprising Ternate, Gilolo, Batjan, and Obi; and the southern consisting of Buru, Ceram, Amboina, and

WALLACE'S BIRD OF PARADISE (*S. wallacei*).

the chain of islands east of it. The former shows a closer relation with New Guinea than does the latter group. Thus it exhibits seven species of the markedly Papuan genus, *Papuina*, as against one in the southern group. Again we find certain distinct points of connection with Celebes in the latter, which do not exist in the other. No distinct Australian influence is noticeable, although in the Ké Islands the one *Limnæa* and two out of the four species of *Isidora* are common to North Australia.

Equally splendid as the birds are the insects of these islands, which in some particulars surpass those of any other part of the world. Here are butterflies of the largest size and most vivid colours—some of the most intense metallic blue, as *Papilio ulysses*, or the richest silky green, as *Ornithoptera priamus*; while others exhibit golden yellow or the most vivid crimson hues, displayed in an endless variety of patterns on a velvety black ground. The beetles also are remarkable for size or beauty, the wonderful long-armed beetle of Amboina (*Euchirus longimanus*) being one of the giants of the insect world.

3. Inhabitants.

In the Moluccas at least three native races encounter each other and intermingle—the Malays, the Papuans, and the Indonesians or pre-Malays; and with the very imperfect knowledge we at present possess it is not always easy to disentangle the one from the other, or to determine which are pure races and which the results of a more or less complex intermixture. People of Malay race and Mohammedans in religion inhabit the small islands of Ternate and Tidor, each under a native sultan, whose rule extends over a number of adjacent islands. They speak distinct but closely allied languages, which are widely different from any of the western Malay tongues, and are probably compounded of some aboriginal dialects spoken by the indigenes and that of their conquerors. These are the most important of the Malay States of the Moluccas, but other tribes with a great variety of languages are found on the coasts of Ceram and in the smaller islands of Goram, while tribes of pagan Indonesians in a lower state of civilisation inhabit parts of Buru. The great island of Ceram, however, is inhabited by people who are perhaps of partly Papuan race, having frizzled hair and prominent features, with a darker skin and more lengthy limbs than the Malays. They are utter savages and head-hunters. Most of them are still in a state of absolute freedom in the mountains of the interior, but some have been collected in villages on the coast, and have become converted nominally to Christianity, while others are equally nominal Mohammedans. In Buru occurs a similar race, and also in some parts of Halmahera; but in the northern peninsula of the latter island, and having their headquarters at Galela, there is a very interesting race, as light in colour as Malays, but tall and well made, with handsome prominent features, curly hair, and bearded. They resemble Polynesians in many respects, and may perhaps be a remnant of the early Caucasian immigration referred to on a former page, intermixed with the Papuan aborigines. They speak a highly peculiar language. They are good boat-builders, and wander all over the northern part of the Moluccas, collecting tripang and turtle-shell, hunting deer and pigs, and smoking the meat. They also make settlements on any uninhabited spot that suits them, cut down the forest, plant maize or rice, and seem altogether a more enterprising and energetic people than those around them.

Besides these, we have in all the chief towns of the Moluccas a number of the descendants of the early Portuguese settlers. These go by the name of "Orang Sirani," or Nazarenes. They speak Malay with a considerable intermixture of Portuguese words, but owing to their having been under Dutch rule for several centuries, they have become Protestants, and are altogether ignorant of their own origin.

In addition to these sources of ethnological confusion, we must remember that slavery has long prevailed in these islands, and that, as already stated, by means of the piratical fleets, slaves have been brought from the remotest parts of the archipelago. The Ternate and Goram people are great traders to New Guinea, and Papuan slaves are very common. Again, we find in most places a considerable number of Chinese and Arab merchants, who all have native wives. For more than a century after the first discovery of the Spice Islands by the Portuguese, the ships of all nations—Spanish, Dutch, and English especially—crowded into the eastern seas to obtain a share in the traffic in spices, which was in those days as alluring as the search after gold, and even more profitable. Among the crews of these vessels there would be men of every race, and many of them would become temporary, and some permanent, settlers in these sunny isles, and leave behind them descendants who would add to the diversity of type among the apparently native races which is here so puzzling.

4. History and Political Divisions.

From the remotest times the spices of the Moluccas have been known to the civilised nations of the West. The clove is mentioned by Pliny, for the "cariofilum" or "gariofilum" of that author, which he describes as growing in an Indian grove, is hardly likely to be anything else. It was known to the Arabians and Persians, through whose hands it doubtless passed on its way to Europe; but it was not until the Portuguese reached the Indies that any definite knowledge of the position of the Moluccas was obtained. Sequeira, visiting Malacca with his squadron in 1509, found the spice-laden ships in that port; but some three or four years previously both Banda and Ternate (or Tidor) had actually been visited by the Italian Varthema, who probably gave a full account of them to Albuquerque before he returned to Europe and published his voyages. Immediately after the fall of Malacca, a small fleet of three vessels was despatched thither under Antonio d'Abreu, and visited Buru, Amboina, and Banda. The loss of one of the ships resulted in Francisco Serrão, the captain, being brought to Ternate, where he remained until his death. He found the islands in the possession of Mohammedan Malays, who had conquered them about half a century before. For ten years the Portuguese seem to have made no further effort to acquire the islands; but in 1522, a few months after the visit of the two remaining ships of Magellan's fleet, Antonio de Brito arrived with a squadron of seven vessels and established Portuguese rule, which for more than 60 years was characterised by the most atrocious cruelty and treachery. At the end of that time it was practically terminated by a rising of the islanders. Meanwhile, the Spaniards, in spite of having agreed in 1529 to renounce all claim to the Moluccas for the sum of 350,000 ducats, had not only intrigued against the Portuguese in the islands, but had even fitted out expeditions against them. In 1606 a squadron from Manila succeeded in taking both Tidor and Ternate, but no garrison appears to have been established. The Dutch now came upon the scene, and in 1613 contrived to conclude a treaty with the Sultan of Ternate by which the latter agreed that the trade in cloves should be the exclusive property of Holland. Under the pretext of the infraction of the terms of the agreement, the various islands were soon reduced. Little by little the Moluccas thus passed into the hands of Holland, and though many revolts occurred, the intervals between each became longer, and in 1681 the last expiring effort was made, and made in vain. Thenceforward there have been no events worthy of record except the temporary occupation by the British at the period of the Napoleonic difficulty.

The Residencies of Ternate and Amboina share the administration of the islands at the present day. The former comprises a larger area of territory than any other residency in the Netherlands India, extending from the middle of Celebes to the eastern boundary of Dutch New Guinea, a distance of nearly 1500 miles. Such a division appears at first sight most unfitting and arbitrary, but it is not so in reality, for the territory thus united represents (together with the Amboina Residency) the ancient kingdoms of Ternate and Tidor. The Sultans of these two insignificant islands were in bygone days the most important in the archipelago, the Sultan of Ternate ruling southern Mindanao, the Sangir group, the greater part of the eastern half of Celebes, the Timor, Buru, and almost all the Ceram group; while the Sultan of Tidor's possessions lay chiefly to the east, and comprised half Gilolo and Ceram, and the whole of western New Guinea and its islands. It is thus in virtue of their treaties with the Tidor potentate that the Dutch claim sovereignty over New Guinea up to the 141st degree of east longitude.

The Resident of Amboina administers not only Buru and Ceram, but Banda, Ké, the Aru and Timor Laut groups, and all the small islands west of the last named up to, and inclusive of, Wetta.

5. Halmahera.

The island of Halmahera or Gilolo, although almost as large as Ceram, is comparatively unimportant. It is of peculiar shape, very much resembling that of Celebes upon a smaller scale, and consisting of four peninsulas radiating from a small central mass, and divided by three deep gulfs on the eastern side. With the islets close to its coasts, it has an estimated area of 6500 square miles; but it is very thinly peopled, owing to the prevalence of piracy until lately, and the entire population probably does not exceed 125,000. It is very mountainous and rugged, and has many volcanoes, especially in the northern peninsula. Four are situated close to the western coast, the most important perhaps being Gamakora. Tolo, at the northern extremity, has also had several eruptions, as has the little peak of Tarakan (620 feet) near the town of Galela. The highest point is stated to be 6500 feet. But, although not much is known of its geology, it is probable that the island is in the main of ancient formation, judging from zoology. The interior of the northern peninsula seems to be the only part possessing an indigenous population, and here we find the people with crisp hair, taller than Malays, and with prominent noses; of Papuan type, but evidently far from pure as a race. Other Papuan affinities occur in the ornithology of the island, which may thus be said to be the meeting-ground of the races and fauna of these two sub-regions. The Galela district is highly cultivated, producing large quantities of rice. Here and at Patani, at the extremity of the south-east peninsula, are "Post-holders," and at Sidangoli in Dodinga Bay half a dozen native soldiers are stationed, but these are the only places in the whole extent of the island where representatives of the Dutch Government are to be found. Morti Island is practically uninhabited.

6. Ternate.

As far as regards magnificence of scenery, Ternate is perhaps the finest harbour in the Dutch Indies, for it is formed by two volcanic islands whose peaks are nearly 6000 feet in height, and of wonderfully graceful outline. That of the island of Tidor, which shelters the anchorage to the south, rises majestically from a mass of wild and gloomy-looking hills, but Ternate consists of the volcano alone, which leaves little room for the town to nestle at its foot. Eastward, across a wide strait, are the rugged blue mountains of Halmahera, terminating towards the north by a group of three lofty volcanic peaks.

The island of Ternate is nearly circular, is about 5 or 6 miles in diameter, and has an area of about 25 square miles. It is remarkably healthy, and although rain falls on an average during 216 days in the year, the weather is very bright and sunny except during December and January. Owing to the position of the land, the monsoons become deflected, and blow from the north and south chiefly—from the former point during the first three months of the year, and from the latter from May to October. April, November, and December are the months of variable winds.

The volcano is about 5600 feet in height, and constantly emits smoke. Between 1608 and 1840 there

COCO-NUT GROVE, TERNATE.

have been as many as fourteen eruptions, many of them severe. A few miles to the east of the town a black, scoriaceous, rugged tract, called by the natives "Batu-angas" (burnt rock), marks the lava stream which descended to the sea during a great eruption about a century ago. The last great earthquake occurred on 2nd February, 1840, at midnight, during the festival of the Chinese New Year, a circumstance which prevented much loss of life, since all the inhabitants were up feasting, and seeing the processions and amusements. The shocks continued all night and part of the next day, throwing down every stone building, and more or less wrecking almost all the rest, and they did not wholly cease for a fortnight. Earth-waves moved along the streets like rollers on the sea, the earth opening and closing again; but the line of disturbance was very narrow, the native town, a mile to the east, not suffering at all. It travelled from north to south through the islands of Tidor and Makian to Batjan, reaching the latter place, 100 miles distant, at four in the afternoon of the following day, so that the wave was propagated at the rate of only six miles an hour. Everywhere in the suburbs of the town may be seen ruined walls, and gate-pillars with the stones twisted on each other, and the remains of massive stone and brick buildings, gateways, and arches, showing the greater magnificence of the old town, till sad experience taught the superiority of wood and thatch as building materials in an earthquake-tortured country.

Ternate is a free port, and is still a place of some importance. The population is about 9000, of whom 350 are Europeans, 300 descendants of the Portuguese and natives, 500 Chinese, and 100 Arabs, the remainder being Malays of this and surrounding islands. There is a garrison, quartered in "Fort Oranje," a strong fortification with fosse and drawbridge, built, it is said, on the foundations of an old Portuguese structure. At the south end of the town, overgrown with jungle, are the remains of a small fortress, with beautifully laid courses, which is possibly that erected by De Brito in 1522. The trade has lessened of late, but Ternate is still the market of the northern Moluccas and some parts of New Guinea. The chief exports are gum-dammar and tobacco (each about £11,000), nutmegs (£7600), and gum-copal. A few birds-of-paradise are exported, but most of these are taken straight from the Aru Islands and the MacCluer Gulf to Makassar. Cloves, the ancient product of the true "Malucos"—Ternate, Tidor, Motir, Makian, and Batjan—now form no part of the commerce; they are now grown chiefly in Celebes, Amboina, and Java. The early Dutch rulers extirpated the tree here in 1652 in order to secure the monopoly, which they endeavoured to do by restricting its cultivation to the island of Amboina, of which they had exclusive possession There is now no Government monopoly, and the total annual export is about a quarter of a million lbs. for the entire archipelago. Slavery was abolished in Ternate and Tidor in 1879.

7. Tidor and the Lesser Moluccas.

Immediately south of Ternate, which forms the northern link, runs a chain of small islands, parallel with and close to the west coast of Halmahera, which are sometimes termed the Lesser Moluccas. Three of these, like Ternate, are true volcanoes, while Maré is formed of upraised volcanic materials, and the Kaioa group, farther to the south, are raised coral reefs. All the islands are inhabited by Mohammedan Malays, each with their peculiar language, the island of Makian having two.

PEAK OF TIDOR FROM TERNATE.

Tidor is the largest and most important, its Sultan having in past times ruled over a large territory in the archipelago. It was here that the *Trinidad* and the *Victoria*, the two vessels of Magellan's squadron, were so hospitably received, and obtained their cargoes of cloves, the first brought from the islands by a European ship. The peak of Tidor is about 5900 feet in height, and of exceedingly graceful shape. Although there are hot springs at its base, it is now extinct, and there are no records of any eruption. The Dutch have a few soldiers upon the island, but no civil authority. The population is about 8000.

Maré, known as Potbakker's Island, from the useful clays found on it, is not otherwise of importance. Motir, with a peak 2800 feet in height, which was the scene of an eruption in the last century, has also few inhabitants. The next island, Makian, at one time most productive in cloves, is at present chiefly given over to the cultivation of tobacco, and is thickly populated. Its cone was formerly thought to be extinct, but in 1646 a great eruption blew it up, leaving a vast crater, with a huge rugged chasm on one side of it, and destroying the greater part of the population. Then for two centuries it was quiet, the people who had escaped came back, houses were built, and twelve villages were formed on its shores. But on 29th December, 1862, it again burst forth with as great violence as before, and destroyed nearly the whole population. Over 4000 perished, the greater number from drowning, overcrowding the praus in their frantic efforts to escape. The sand and ashes thrown up by the volcano reached Ternate, thirty miles off, the next day, and formed a cloud so dense as to darken the air, and make it necessary to light lamps at midday. They fell to the thickness of three or four inches over that island, and even to a distance of fifty miles, destroying all the crops, and doing great injury to shrubs and fruit-trees.

Still farther south, but in the same north and south line, lie the two distinct and compact groups of Batjan and Obi. In ancient times the former constituted an independent Sultanate, surrounded in every direction by the vast domains of the Sultans of Ternate and Tidor. The island has other reasons to be considered distinct, as, although volcanic in its northern portion, it is in the main composed of ancient rocks, as is also the Obi group. In length it exceeds 50 English miles, and the great mountain mass of Labua, at the southern end, is 7150 feet in height, and is believed to be non-volcanic. The interior is uninhabited, or nearly so, and the small littoral population, two or three thousand only in number, is composed of Ternate Malays, Galela men, and immigrants from the west coast of Celebes. The clove is said to grow wild. The black Celebesian monkey, *Cynopithecus nigrescens*, is found—the most eastern point of the distribution of the Quadrumana—but, as before stated, it is considered by Mr. Wallace to have been most probably imported by man. Here, too, is the beautiful and curious bird-of-paradise, Wallace's Standard-wing (*Semioptera wallacei*), the only representative of the Paradiseidæ found in the Moluccas. The Dutch have a Controleur and a small garrison stationed at the village of Batjan, on the west coast, and the present fort—Fort Barneveld—was built as long ago as 1615 upon the site of one erected many years before by the Portuguese. Near Batjan are some coal-mines which have been worked intermittently, though to no great profit, for nearly half a century; and gold and copper are also found in small quantities. A Dutch company has established plantations of coffee and cacao, which have been only partly successful. Mr. Wallace considers that the island is one which would perhaps repay the researches of a botanist better than any other in the whole archipelago. It contains a great variety of surface and of soil, abundance of large and small streams, some of which are navigable, alluvial plains, abrupt hills and lofty mountains, and a grand and luxuriant forest vegetation. Moreover, having no savage inhabitants, every part of it can be visited with safety. The other islands of this group are practically uninhabited.

Obi Major, the chief of the Obi group, is a fine island about 45 miles in length by 20 in breadth. The mountains of the interior reach a height of 5000 feet or more, but appear to be clothed with forest to their summits, as, indeed, is the whole island. It is well-watered, and is apparently both fertile and healthy. Yet, strangely enough, the group is totally uninhabited, the only instance of the kind in the whole of the archipelago, and this, too, in spite of its central position. Now and then it is visited by fishermen from Batjan, who build huts and occupy themselves in curing fish or catching turtle; but no permanent settlement exists, and it does not appear that any people of Papuan race ever established themselves here, as was the case in Halmahera to the north, and probably in Ceram to the south. Among the Ternate natives Obi bears the reputation of being haunted, which may perhaps account for the absence of population. It was inhabited in former times, and Dr. Guillemard found old sago and nutmeg plantations on the western side of the island, where are the ruins of an ancient Dutch fort. Obi is probably in no part volcanic, but appears to be composed of the older crystalline rocks. Coal and lignite exist, and probably gold, but no explorations have been made, and the existing charts of the island are extremely inaccurate.

8. Buru.

We now come to the southern Moluccas, which are under the administration of the Resident of Amboina, one of the largest of which is Buru, an oval island about 90 English miles in length, with an area of 3380 square miles. Although a volcano is said to exist at the western extremity, the island is believed to be largely composed of the older stratified rocks. It is, in parts, of great elevation, Mount Tumahu (8530 feet) being, apart from those in Ceram, the highest peak in the Moluccas, while others exceed 7000 feet. The elevation is highest towards the western end, while at the north and east it is comparatively low. Surrounding Kajeli Bay is a vast, circular, and level plain, which occupies nearly one-fourth of the island. In the north the country is somewhat bare, and much covered with coarse lalang grass, but the greater part of the rest of the island is forest-clad. The villages round the coast are inhabited by semi-civilised Mohammedan Malays from the various surrounding islands, who have intermixed with the older inhabitants; and a tribe of mild light-coloured people of Malay type, apparently allied to the natives of Eastern Celebes, occupy the northern and western parts. The interior is peopled by a peculiar race, which, according to some authorities, is of Papuan type. If this be true, these "Alfuros" must have lost the chief characteristics of that race, judging from the description of Mr. H. O. Forbes, the only naturalist who has visited the heart of the country. He describes them as averaging 5 feet 2 inches in height, of a brown or yellowish-brown colour, weak in build and somewhat effeminate, and very timid. They live for the most part in isolated houses, and slavery is non-existent. The characteristic Papuan nose, which overhangs at the tip, is never seen, and there is very little hair on the face and body. Even the hair, though crisp or wavy, is not frizzled. There is therefore an absence of all the chief Papuan characteristics, and the connection, if any, must date from a very remote period.

Buru contains deer and the babirusa. The presence of the latter animal is difficult to account for, and it is especially remarkable that it should be confined, as far as is known, to the eastern extremity of the island. The Waikolo Lake, near the centre, is 1900 feet above the level of the sea, and, though some miles across, possibly occupies the site of an ancient crater. There are two resident Postholders, one at Kajeli Bay, and the other at Masareti, on the south-west coast. The former place is far the most important, large quantities of cajuput oil being manufactured. This product is obtained from the leaves of *Melaleuca kajuputi*, and is exported to the value of about £10,000 annually. The town is low and unhealthy, and the land here appears to be gaining rapidly on the sea. Fort Defensie, built in 1778 close to the water, now stands nearly half a mile inland. The population of Buru is estimated at about 60,000.

9. Ceram.

Ceram is 216 English miles in length, and has an estimated area of 7000 square miles. It is therefore one of the great islands of the archipelago, but its importance is by no means in proportion to its size. It lies with its long axis east and west, and is traversed from end to end by a very fine range of mountains, which give it a grand and massive appearance from the sea.

The highest of these is Nusa-heli, the height of which has been found to be 9612 feet, and there are at least four other peaks exceeding 6000 feet. None of them are believed to be volcanic, and the mass of the island where it has been examined is found to be composed of plutonic and sedimentary rocks. Coal exists, but of what period does not seem clear. The only evidences of active volcanic forces are hot springs and the rather frequent occurrence of earthquakes. There is not a single good harbour in the whole island except at Amahai on the south coast, and there are no navigable rivers. Towards the western end two deep bays, nearly opposite each other, reduce the width of the island to about 15 miles. Here a native path crosses from shore to shore, and this is almost the only part of the interior known to Europeans.

The coast villages, as is generally the case in these islands, are inhabited by a mixed Malay people, and in the neighbourhood of the Amboina group many are Orang Sirani, or so-called Christians, of whom a considerable number can read and write. In the interior live a race who are perhaps of mixed Papuan descent, split up into different tribes, speaking different languages, and little, if at all more civilised than the pure Dyaks of Borneo. They are head-hunters, living in large villages, and cultivating sago, bananas, and a little rice. The whole island is densely covered with forest, and in all the swampy valleys the sago-palm grows wild, supplying the chief food of the inhabitants, as well as an article of trade, sago cakes being the provision with which every native boat is supplied for a voyage. The Dutch have four stations on the island, and an " Aspirant Controleur " lives at Wahai on the north coast, where there are European coffee and coco plantations. The people are, however, poor, for little trade is carried on, and the abundance of sago gives them no inducement to cultivate the soil. There is hardly any part of the East where the traveller finds it so difficult to procure the usual tropical fruits and vegetables, or any food fit for the consumption of civilised beings. The population in 1878 was supposed to be about 226,000.

10. The Amboina Group.

The Amboina group consists of the main island, Ambon—or, as it is known to the English, Amboina—and three smaller islands lying to the east—Haruku, Saparua, and Nusa Laut. It was hither that the Dutch in the middle of the seventeenth century brought the clove cultivation, having extirpated the tree in its native islands of Ternate, Tidor, and Makian; and, although this industry is no longer a monopoly, and the spice exported in much reduced quantities, the good roads on the smaller islands, and the size of the capital, testify to a long-existent civilisation, which has affected all the native inhabitants.

The main island is about 30 miles in length, and is so deeply indented by two bays on opposite sides that it forms practically two islands, the narrow, sandy, connecting isthmus being only 30 yards wide. Across this—the "Paso"—the native praus are dragged, the passage between the town and the smaller islands being by this means greatly shortened. The total area of the island is about 260 square miles, and the population 32,000, of which rather more than half live in the town. The size of these Molucca towns thus falls far short of that of the populous cities of Java, Sumatra, and even Borneo, although their trade has been renowned for centuries.

The island was originally one vast, unbroken forest, and is so still, except around the town. The highest peak attains an elevation of 4010 feet. In the north-west of the island is a volcano, which has been in eruption many times between 1674 and 1824, but since that date it has been so completely quiescent that most of the inhabitants will not believe that any volcano exists. They are supported in this opinion by the fact that no one now knows exactly where it is, there being no lofty cone, and nothing to distinguish it at a distance from the forest-clad hills which surround it. Neither is Amboina now much subject to earthquakes, although many have occurred, and may any day occur again. While Dampier was here in 1705 there was a great earthquake, which lasted two days, and did great mischief, the ground bursting open in many places, and swallowing up entire families in their houses. The ground swelled like a wave of the sea, and the massive walls of the fort were rent asunder in several places.

Amboina was first known to Europeans in 1511, in which year Serrão, one of the commanders of the fleet of d'Abreu, who had been sent by Albuquerque to discover the Moluccas, landed with his crew, having been shipwrecked on some reefs to the south. The town was taken from the Portuguese by the Dutch in 1609. It is celebrated as having been long the residence of the botanist Rumphius, who died here in 1693, and of Valentijn, the historian of the Dutch Indies. The inhabitants of the island, as might be surmised from its having been so long under foreign dominion and a centre of trade, are a mixed race, formed chiefly of Moluccan Malays and indigenous Ceramese. They inhabit a number of villages round the coast, speak several different languages, and are all professedly either

Mohammedans or Christians. The latter, the Orang Sirani (Nazarenes), strike the traveller at once on landing, dressed as they are from head to foot in black. Even the garments are altered, the Malay sarong being discarded for trousers, and the costume is utterly unsuited to the climate. These people, at all events in the town, are in many respects inferior to the Mohammedans, being lazy, proud, and untruthful, and their religion appears hardly better than a modified fetichism. "It seems," writes Mr. Forbes, "to lie on them like an awesome thraldom." Otherwise, they are much superior in point of civilisation to the ordinary coast natives of the islands, although a species of mild Mafia exists—the Kakian society—which seems to include persons of all nationalities and colour.

The town of Amboina is situated on the south side of the western inlet, about ten miles from the open sea. It is a free port, carrying on trade over a wide area. It is well laid out with regular and broad streets and a wide green *plein*, and the red laterite roads and abundant flowers and foliage give it an attractive appearance. There is an imposing Government House, and Fort Victoria, originally built by the Portuguese, but enlarged and strengthened by the Dutch in 1609, is a massive building which has managed to survive the earthquakes, and still protects the large storehouses in which in former days the cloves were kept. Amboina may be regarded as, primarily, a military station. Here, too, are the headquarters of the mission staff and schoolmasters. Amboina is celebrated for its shells, collections of which have been made by the natives ever since the days of Rumphius two centuries ago, and there is, perhaps, no one locality in the world where so many beautiful varieties are to be easily obtained, the traders bringing them from New Guinea and many distant islands. From here they are sent in large quantities to Singapore. The celebrated Amboina wood, much esteemed for cabinet work, is obtained from the knotty protuberances formed on certain forest trees growing in Ceram. The true seedless bread-fruit, very rarely found out of the Pacific Islands, grows in Amboina and the smaller adjacent islands.

The island exhibits an extraordinary climatic abnormality, the period of the west monsoon, from October to April, being the fine season. At this time the monthly average of rainy days is 13 only, and the rainfall 8 inches, while during the remainder of the year 21 days out of every month are wet, and the monthly rainfall 27 inches. The total annual rainfall is thus 191 inches, and with the steady high temperature prevailing it might be imagined that the island would be particularly trying to Europeans, but this does not appear to be the case.

The trade of Amboina is not large, as most of the Bugis who visit New Guinea and the remoter islands now carry their produce direct to Makassar or even to Singapore. Numbers of small native vessels, however, continually visit it, bringing the produce of the surrounding coasts and islands. In 1890 turtle shell to the value of £5050 was exported, and 107,107 lbs. of cloves, valued at £3179, these being the chief exports from the islands. On the giving up of the monopoly of cloves, a tax was imposed upon the heads of families of the native population. In 1893 this was changed into a tax which is levied on the whole male population above sixteen years of age.

11. Banda.

The Banda group, though small in extent, is important

as having long been the exclusive nutmeg-garden of the world, and it is still the place where this beautiful tree grows in the greatest perfection. Omitting the small islets, it consists of six islands, situated about 60 miles south of Ceram and 130 miles from Amboina. Of these only three are of any importance: Banda Nera, upon

BANDA VOLCANO.

which the town is situated; Banda Lontar, the site of the chief nutmeg parks; and Gunong Api, the volcano. The largest is Banda Lontar, $7\frac{1}{2}$ miles long, and of semilunar shape, having the other two islands in its concavity, while two islets projecting from its eastern horn form with it nearly half a circle, the only portion now remaining of what was at one time a gigantic crater.

From its now submarine floor the present active peak of Gunong Api has risen as a secondary crater, which, though of small size, has been terribly destructive. It rises straight from the sea as a steep and almost perfect cone, 1858 feet in height and two miles in diameter at its base. Excepting close to the sea, where there is a little bush and some coco-nut palms, it is almost entirely bare of vegetation, and its dark gray mass of scoriae and ashes is only marked by the furrows of water-courses, and, on its summit, by large deposits of sulphur. It is perpetually smoking, and its periods of activity have not only been numerous but prolonged. During the last three centuries eruptions are recorded at fifteen distinct periods, some of them lasting several months, and being generally accompanied by destructive earthquakes. On six occasions earthquakes have occurred unaccompanied by eruptions, the last great one being in 1852, when a wave swept over the islands and destroyed many acres of the nutmeg plantations. In 1690 and 1691 there was a succession of eruptions and earthquakes, which so devastated the place that many of the inhabitants emigrated to Amboina and Celebes to escape destruction, and it was said that but for the firmness of the Resident the islands would have been utterly abandoned. These eruptions have been frequently followed by severe epidemics, which have been even more fatal. Although the islands are over 1700 miles distant from Krakatau, the appalling eruption of that volcano made itself felt even here as a small seismic wave which rushed through the harbour from the westward, but did no damage.

A narrow creek—the Zonnegat—only navigable by small craft, separates Gunong Api from Banda Nera. It is on this island that the town is placed, the cool-looking white houses covering the whole length of its southern shore, and forming one of the neatest and cleanest settlements in the whole of the Dutch Indies. In the western outskirts live the Chinese traders, dealers in and exporters of the varied products of New Guinea and the surrounding islands. In the middle of the town is Fort Nassau, built by the Dutch in 1609, and a ruined fortress built by the Portuguese more than 350 years ago stands at the eastern extremity of Lontar; but the most important and largest—the most conspicuous building on the island both from its size and position— is Fort Belgica, pentagonal in shape and very massive, placed on a small plateau above the town. It was commenced in 1611, and has remained unharmed through the many earthquakes it has experienced, so solidly has it been constructed. Behind it rises an abrupt jungle-covered rock, 800 feet in height, from which there is a beautiful view of the town, the volcano, and the nutmeg gardens, which cover most of the larger island.

The nutmeg trees are here grown, as they grow in their native forests, under the shade of lofty forest trees; the tree used here being the kanari, which grows to a great height, its nuts producing a valuable oil. The light volcanic soil, the partial shade, and the constant moisture of these islands, where it rains more or less every month in the year, seem highly favourable to the nutmeg tree, which here reaches a large size, produces abundance of fruit, and is quite free from those diseases which have led to the practical abandonment of nutmeg-growing in Singapore. The nutmeg tree was a native of Banda, and man's cultivation has followed the method of nature, without attempting to force her to an unduly rapid production. The Government monopoly has long since been given up, and every one is permitted to plant and sell as he pleases, but the industry is chiefly in the hands of large proprietors. The trees are in fruit and blossom during the greater part of the year, and bear the

NUTMEG FRUIT, SPLITTING AND SHOWING MACE.

peach-like fruit at the end of the shoots. The fleshy exocarp is thrown away, the mace is removed and dried in ovens, and the nut is kept to dry slowly, enclosed in its shining outer shell, until ready for export. The fruits are devoured whole by certain large pigeons of the genus *Carpophaga*, which consequently fell in early days under the ban of the Dutch, who were endeavouring to restrict the tree to the Banda group, and feared that the birds would be the means of conveying it elsewhere. It is a very singular fact that the nutmeg—like the clove—is not, and does not appear ever to have been, used by the native races, and it is difficult to explain how they can have become known to civilised nations at so early a period in the world's history, especially in the case of the clove, where the product is so largely artificial.

The Banda Islands were first visited by Varthema in about 1505, who, rather inaptly, speaks of them as being most wretched and gloomy in appearance. Six years later, Antonio d'Abreu reached them with his fleet of three vessels and brought a cargo of nutmegs back to Malacca, but some years elapsed ere the Portuguese fairly established themselves. They did not hold them long, being ejected by the Dutch in 1609. On this occasion the natives opposed the new-comers, and succeeded in killing the admiral and sixty-five of his men. The result was a war of extermination; 3000 were killed and over 1000 taken prisoners, and the rest fled the islands. The plantations, or "parks," as they were called, were divided among the conquerors, whose descendants—the "Perkeniers"—much mixed in blood, held them as freehold on condition that they delivered the entire produce to the Government at a fixed rate. The Bandanese having been exterminated, it became necessary to get other labour, and this was done by a wholesale system of slave-catching in the less known islands, Siau in the Sangir chain supplying a large number. Later, when the carrying trade in slaves was abolished, the "parks" were worked by convict labour.

The exports of Banda being incorporated in the official publications with those of Amboina, no exact details of the produce of the islands can be arrived at. From the latter port in the year 1890 nutmegs to the value of £36,000 and mace to that of £42,000 were sent to Europe, the greater part, if not all of which was grown in Banda. The population of the settlement is about 7000, and the inhabitants are a miscellaneous assemblage of all the races found in the far east.

12. Islands East of Ceram.

East and south of Ceram are a number of small islands forming a series of stepping-stones to the more important and larger Ké group. First we have great and little Keffing close to the main island, and a little farther, but still connected by shoals and islets, Ceram Laut. North-west of the latter are two singular islands, Gisser and Kilwaru. The former is of annular shape, with a narrow entrance to the lake-like harbour. It was formerly a veritable nest of pirates, but has now been converted into a coal depôt by the Government. Kilwaru corresponds to Dobbo Island in the Aru group, to which reference will presently be made, in being a great native market or bartering-place for the products of all the islands round. Hither come the Bugis traders from Celebes in the west monsoon, meeting the traders in pearls, tortoiseshell, dammar, etc., from the New Guinea coast, and the paradise-bird collectors, whose wares also include live birds and animals of every kind, cassowaries, brilliant lories, crowned pigeons, and other rare and beautiful species. The village is built around a small sand-bank, the houses standing on piles half in the water, and quite concealing the land, so as to give the place a most singular appearance from a distance. Its eastern portion is under a native raja, and the western in Dutch hands, separated from the other by a strong stone wall, which also surrounds the island.

About 30 miles farther on we come to the Goram group, consisting of the two islands of Goram and Manowolko, and the smaller island of Suruaki. These are governed by a native raja, and the inhabitants are generally known as Goram men. They are Mohammedans of Malay type, with a slight infusion of Papuan blood, who speak a peculiar language, and are probably derived from a mixture of Bugis with Moluccan Malays. They are a race of traders and ships' pilots, making voyages every year to the Ké and Aru islands, and to New Guinea, selling their produce to Bugis traders, who take it to Makassar or Singapore. Although a Dutch postholder is resident here, money is unknown to them, and the chief barter is cotton twist. These islands consist of raised coral reefs, with cliffs and terraces rising two or three hundred feet high. In Manowolko there are no streams, but there are some in Goram, which probably has a substratum of harder rock. Goram is surrounded by an encircling reef, entirely under water except at the lowest ebb tide, but affording excellent anchorage and smooth water within.

Twenty miles farther to the south-east are the small Matabello islands, of coral rock raised to a considerable height, and with a closely encircling reef leaving a narrow but secure passage for native boats within it. The rugged hills of these islands are covered with coco-nut trees, and the natives get their living by making coco-nut oil, which they sell to the Bugis traders. The only water here is obtained from a few small wells near the beach; and as the people live high up on the hills, they rarely, if ever, use water for any purpose but for drinking. They are brown Papuans with frizzly hair, and are pagans, but from much association with the Bugis and Goram traders have obtained some small tincture of Mohammedanism.

Tior, the Nusa-tello, and Tionfoloka islands complete the chain between Ceram and the Ké group. They appear to be inhabited by a mixed race chiefly Papuan in character.

13. The Ké Islands.

This small but compact little archipelago lies between 5° and 6° S. Lat., and consists of three chief islands—Nuhu Ju-ud or Great Ké, Nuhu Roa or Little Ké, and Ké Dulan. They came formally into the possession of Holland as far back as 1665; but so little were they explored up till 1886, when they were surveyed by Captain Langen, that not only their outline, but even their number, was unknown. Their entire surface is covered with the densest jungle, and they are tolerably thickly peopled as compared with many islands in these seas. Though there are no active volcanoes, old craters have been found both on Ké Dulan and Ju-ud, and severe earthquakes have occurred. The islands differ considerably. Ju-ud or Great Ké is long, narrow, and elevated; in shape like a club or bludgeon, its head lying to the north. Although 64 miles in length, its average breadth is not more than from 1 to 3 miles. It is said to be composed of sandstones and granites, but its northern peaks—the highest of which is 2200 feet—are probably volcanic. A long and narrow channel, apparently of deep water, separates this island from the others, which are massed together to form a labyrinthine archipelago of over thirty islands, beset with reefs and shoals. These are evidently of much more recent origin, the highest point of Nuhu Roa attaining an altitude of 200 feet only, and being formed of coralline limestone and shells. Ké Dulan is celebrated for its harbour, which was visited by the *Challenger* in 1874. Here, at Tual, resides the Controleur and a small colony of Germans who are engaged in the timber trade. The islands have no season of drought such as is experienced by those farther to the west, the ultimate links in the great Sunda chain. The west monsoon brings a considerable amount of rain, with stormy and unsettled weather, but from April to October, when the easterly monsoon prevails, the weather is settled and fine. The average rainfall is 102 inches.

Captain Langen, who has resided for a considerable time on the group, divides the natives into three classes —the aborigines, the Papuans, and the immigrant Malay people, who are of varied nationality. He describes the true Ké natives as tall and strongly built, with well-shaped but large noses and high cheek-bones, with black and brown coloured beard, and long, wavy, but finely curled black hair, mixed with several lighter or darker shades of brown, reaching to the shoulder and projecting all round the head. The skin is in colour midway between the Papuan and Malay. True Papuans were at one time established in several places, but especially on a small island which still bears the name of Pulo Papua; but constant warfare existed between the two races, and the Ké people eventually succeeded in driving them out. They had nevertheless intermarried for many generations, and as a consequence a mixed semi-Papuan race is found in all parts.

The total population in 1887 was 20,030, of which about 6000 were Mohammedans. In 1886 and 1887 smallpox carried off at least 3000. The islands are ruled by eighteen Rajas, whose title is hereditary, and who hold the silver or gold-mounted sticks which the Dutch confer upon the princes or chiefs subject to them throughout the archipelago. Villages are very numerous all round the coast of Great Ké. They are surrounded by stone walls, and the houses, which are here as elsewhere pile-built, are family, not communal, as in Borneo and New Guinea. A certain amount of uncultivated land belongs to each village, the boundaries of which are established by the chiefs; and here, according to Captain Langen, the native may cut sago-palms or timber, but the coco-nuts are regarded as general property, and are under the guardianship of the chiefs, who on certain days permit them to be gathered, the nuts being divided among the people in proportion to their rank.

The Ké islanders exhibit the artistic skill of the Papuans, showing especial taste in carving, and understanding the rudiments of drawing—a rare accomplishment in Malaysia. On the face of some sea-cliffs on the north-west coast of Nuhu Roa are coloured, incised drawings of animals, praus, etc., which, if not ancient, are at all events not of recent date, and are looked upon by the natives as the work of spirits. But the industry in which they most excel, and for which they are celebrated throughout the archipelago, is shipbuilding. In this they are wonderfully clever, for the vessels are built not only with very simple tools, but without the use of iron, the solid planks being secured together by pegs and fastened to the ribs by rattan. So truly do they work, that planks 20 or 30 feet long are fitted to each other on the curved sides of a vessel with such accuracy as to require very little caulking. Every plank is cut out of the tree with an axe, each tree producing two only. In this manner craft of all sizes are made, from the smallest canoe to schooners of 150 tons, the latter being brought for sale to Banda and other places, or acquired by Bugis traders for the Aru trade and pearl-fishing. All the tools necessary for the work are constructed by native blacksmiths, who are almost without exception from the island of Teor, some 80 miles north-west of the group.

There is little trade in Ké excepting in timber; the most important tree is a species of ironwood. *Marinda citrifolia* gives a yellow dye from its bast, of which 80 to 100 tons are annually exported. The fauna of the group is hardly known, but appears to be of Papuan type, and one of the small tree kangaroos (*Dendrolagus*) is found.

CHAPTER X

THE TIMOR GROUP, OR LESSER SUNDA ISLANDS

1. General.

FROM the east end of Java a chain of important islands stretches in a straight line for about 800 miles, till it seems to be turned aside by encountering the large island of Timor, and is then continued by a series of gradually diminishing islands for about 400 miles farther. From the eastern extremity of Timor another series extends to Timor Laut. Between the western end of Timor and Sumbawa the islands of Rotti, Savu, and Sumba, or Sandalwood, form a kind of loop-line to the principal chain. A volcanic belt, with many active volcanoes, runs in a direct line from Java to the east end of Timor, and thence through Timor Laut to the Ké group. Sumba Island and the western half of Timor appear to be non-volcanic.

The whole group of islands we are now considering have a very different aspect from most other parts of the Malay Archipelago, and especially from the Moluccas, being deficient in verdure, for the most part without forests, and often absolutely barren. This deficiency of forest-covering begins even in Bali, so close to luxuriant Java, and increases as we go eastward, till, in the great island of Timor, such forests as are found in Borneo and the Moluccas are quite unknown, and are only represented by dense thickets of thorny shrubs, scattered trees of eucalyptus, euphorbia, casuarina, and sandalwood, and patches of more luxuriant woods in some of the moister ravines. The country, in fact, resembles Australia much more than the Moluccas. Some of the purely volcanic islands near Timor, of which Wetta is an example, are bare in the extreme, reminding the traveller more of the burnt hills of Aden than the luxuriant vegetation of the Spice Islands. We can hardly err in tracing this remarkable aridity to the vicinity of the heated interior of Australia, directly to the south-east of the islands of this group. It is well known that this arid continent exercises a disturbing effect on the meteorology of all the surrounding countries, diverting the monsoons from their due course, and by its ascending currents of heated air preventing the deposition of moisture that would otherwise take place.

The island of Bali is connected with Java by a very shallow sea, and has no doubt once formed part of that island, with which its vegetable and animal productions closely correspond. The strait separating Bali from Lombok is, on the contrary, very deep; and directly we cross it we come among a new set of animals, and appear to have left Asia for Australia. We at once meet with those singular birds the mound-builders (*Megapodiidæ*), brush-tongued lories, as well as friar-birds (*Tropidorhynchus*) and other honeysuckers, cockatoos, and many other groups found only in the Australian region; while a number of animals, found in the larger Asiatic islands, suddenly disappear. We have no longer any elephants, rhinoceroses, tapirs, or tigers; none of the carnivora but a common civet-cat (*Viverra*); none of the insectivora but the small shrew (*Tupaia*); none of the numerous rodents but one or two squirrels, and even these do not extend as far as Timor. We thus have the Sunda chain divided distinctly and definitely into an Asiatic and an Australian portion, the dividing line coinciding with the deep-sea channel existing between Bali and Lombok. This boundary is now universally known as " Wallace's line."

The chain is also somewhat sharply divided between the two great races of the archipelago, the Malays and Papuans, although the boundary occurs at a different point, the former people extending as far east as Sumbawa, while from Flores through all the other islands the latter prevail.

2. Bali.

The two islands of Bali and Lombok are the only portion of the Malay Archipelago in which the old Hindu religion still regularly maintains itself, though Hindu Rajas also exercise rule in the Ké Islands.

Bali is almost 90 statute miles in extreme length, and of irregular shape, with an area of about 2075 square miles. It is separated from the eastern extremity of Java by a strait hardly more than a mile wide, and like that island, is mountainous throughout, excepting a small portion in the south, the main chain running from west to east in apparent continuation of that of Java. There are several active volcanoes, the most important of which, perhaps, is Batur (whose height has been estimated by different observers at 3940 and 6400 feet), which is in constant activity, and caused great destruction by an eruption in 1815. Batu Kau (9600 feet) is also active, but Abang (7500 feet) and Agung (10,500 feet) the latter the highest peak in the island—are believed to be extinct, although Agung, or Bali Peak, as it is called by mariners, broke into eruption in 1843. There are no navigable rivers, although small streams are numerous, and in many cases are entirely utilised for purposes of irrigation, an art which is brought to great perfection. Many become dried up in the east monsoon. A number of small lakes exist, some at considerable elevations, and formed either in old craters or in depressions caused by volcanic disturbances; and these too are largely used as

ROYAL PALACE, BALI.

reservoirs to supply water for irrigation, the plains and lowlands being highly cultivated and exceedingly fertile.

Bali has been well described as an old-fashioned Java. The manners and customs of that island as they existed a couple of hundred years ago are here preserved almost unchanged. The people are scarcely to be distinguished from the Javanese in appearance, excepting that they are perhaps a little taller and more sturdy in build. They live in villages surrounded by clay walls, and their houses have also walls of clay with a thatch of grass or palm leaves. Their agriculture is very perfect, and owing to the fertility of the volcanic soil and the constant supply of water for irrigation, their fields produce a continual succession of crops, giving the country the appearance of a vast and highly-cultivated garden. The chief export is coffee, of which £43,750 worth was shipped in 1890. Tobacco, cattle, and copra to the amount of over £10,000 each were also exported, but there is not otherwise much trade, and these figures also include Lombok.

The Balinese are fair handicraftsmen, especially in gold and iron, making excellent weapons with the rudest tools and appliances, including even long-barrelled guns with flint locks, used in war and for shooting wild cattle. The language, though written in the Javanese character, and, like it, having two different forms or dialects— the high and low Balinese — is quite distinct. The ancient Kawi language, extinct in Java, is still used by the priests and in legal business. There is a written code, both civil and criminal. Literature was abundantly represented in almost all its branches, but a period of decadence has set in, and the Balinese are no longer the cultured race they were in former days. The religion prevalent is a mixture of Buddhism and Brahmanism, but numbers of the coast people are Mohammedans. The people are divided, as among the old Hindus, into four castes—priests, soldiers, merchants, and labourers, and there is also a Pariah class; the second order, that of soldiers, includes almost all the rajas, gustis, and governing classes. Caste prejudice and laws are still very strong, and the burning of widows and slaves on the death of great men is apparently still practised, although the victims usually stab themselves before the fire is lighted.

Bali and Lombok together form a separate Residency, the seat of government being at Buleleng on the north coast of the former island. There are still seven kingdoms or districts ruled over by native princes, who are in many cases practically possessed of despotic power, though all are more or less subservient to European rule. The two Dutch provinces are Buleleng in the north and Jembrana in the west. The population of the island is very dense, a late estimate placing it at 802,930, or 386 to the square mile, which nearly equals that of the densely populated parts of Java.

3. Lombok.

Lombok is thus called only by Europeans, from a village on the northern shore of the island. The Malay traders call it Tana Sasak, or the Sasak country, from the name of the people who inhabit it. To the Balinese, the conquerors of the island, it is known as Selaparang.

The island is divided from Bali by the Lombok Strait, which, though only 23 miles in breadth, is of great depth. Larger and more compact than Bali, being of a sub-quadrangular shape, it is about 55 miles long by 45 broad, and has an area of 2090 square miles. Two mountain ranges traverse it from east to west, the northern volcanic and of great height, the southern of recent calcareous formation and low, but the chains are nearly joined by a lateral secondary range which divides the intervening valley into two. The eastern part of the northern chain is composed of the giant volcanic mass of Gunong Rinjani, better known to Europeans as the Peak of Lombok. Its height has been variously given between the limits of 8000 and 14,000 feet, but Crawfurd, apparently on Dr. Zollinger's authority, fixes it at

12,375, which measurement, since it coincides very nearly with one taken by Lieutenant R. ff. Powell, R.N., during the voyage of the *Marchesa*, may be considered tolerably accurate. This volcano is, like all the others in the island, practically extinct, although a thin line of smoke is sometimes seen issuing from near the summit. It has never been ascended by any European.

As in Bali, there are numerous lakes, mostly formed in extinct craters or depressions caused by volcanic action, and they are similarly used for irrigation purposes. The largest, Segara-anak, or the "Baby Sea," is at an elevation of nearly 9000 feet, but is of no great extent. The rivers are also small but numerous, and are unfit for navigation, but in the rainy season they bring down vast volumes of water, and are at all times used to irrigate the land by a system as elaborate and careful as that obtaining in Bali, if not more so. There are few places in Java so highly cultivated and tended as the fertile valley which occupies the middle of the island. Large crops of maize and rice are grown, the latter being exported in considerable quantity. Coffee, cattle, and horses are also represented in the exports. The handicrafts are not equal to those of Bali, the Sasaks being especially an agricultural people, but excellent krisses and other weapons are made, and a large quantity of cottons are woven. Chinese copper money is the only coin current with the natives of the interior.

Lombok is less known and less civilised than Bali. The Sasaks—apparently the original inhabitants, for there is no trace of an earlier race—are a Malay people allied to the Javanese and Bugis, but speaking a peculiar language akin to that of West Sumbawa, and written in the Balinese character, which, with a few minor differences, is the same as the Javanese. They are Mohammedans, though very lax in the practice of their tenets, and about a century ago were conquered by a prince of Karang-Asam in Bali, whose descendants now rule over the whole island—a solitary example of Hindus having conquered and still keeping rule over Mohammedans. The Dutch have no civil representatives on the island, but there are a few Europeans resident at the towns of Ampanam and Labuan Tring. A number of Balinese are settled in the capital city of Mataram, and these are all of the Hindu religion. Mataram is only three miles inland from Ampanam, the chief port of Lombok, which consists of four kampongs or villages, inhabited respectively by Sasaks, Balinese, Bugis, and Malays. Many whalers come here to obtain rice and provisions. The lading of ships is, however, very dangerous, owing to the heavy swell that breaks upon the steep beach, even in the calmest weather. Boats are continually upset and lives lost here, and the inhabitants often speak of the sea as a hungry monster, ever trying to devour them. When there is a little wind from the south or south-west, bringing in a swell from the Pacific, the rollers rise to an enormous height, breaking close to the beach, on which they fall with the noise of thunder, and occasionally rush up with such fury as to render it very dangerous to walk near the high-water mark.

The Balinese appear to govern in Lombok with some skill and moderation, but the laws are very severe, theft being punished with death, while any one found in another's yard or house at night is lawfully stabbed and his body thrown into the street, when no inquiry takes place. The Raja has a well-armed and drilled force of some thousand men. In the city of Mataram none but the ruling classes may ride on horseback, and every native on meeting a chief gets off his horse and sits on

the ground till he has passed. Here, as in Bali, the
women are the chief traders; and the market of
Ampanam, held under a magnificent avenue of fig trees,
is an interesting sight, where all the chief products of
the country and the many races that inhabit or frequent
it are to be found collected together. A few miles
inland the Raja has a park and pleasure-house called
Gunong Sari, where there are handsome brick gateways
with Hindu deities in stone, resembling those of the
ruined cities of Java; fish-ponds stocked with fish, which
come to be fed on the striking of a gong; and deer which
will come out of the woods to take bread from the
visitor's hand. There are also fantastic pavilions, grotesque statues, and groves of fruit trees,—altogether a
very pretty place, though now much neglected, but still
serving to show that these Rajas of Bali had once some
love and admiration both for nature and art.

The population is estimated at about 540,000, which
is at the very high proportion of about 258 to the square
mile. Of these about 30,000 only are Balinese, and
about one-fifth of that number Bugis and Malays. The
Sumbawa eruption of 1815 was the cause of the death
of many thousands, the island being buried in ashes to
the depth of 18 inches, and of late smallpox and cholera
have also been very fatal.

4. Sumbawa.

Crossing the Allas Strait from Lombok, only 10 miles
in width, we come to the much larger island of Sumbawa,
which is 170 miles long, and exceedingly irregular in
shape, being almost cut in two by the deep and wide
Sale Gulf. Its area is estimated at about 5300 square
miles, or a little greater than that of Jamaica, and it is

surrounded by numerous small islands. Although the Dutch have had a footing on it for more than two hundred years, it still remains but little known.

Like Bali and Lombok, Sumbawa seems to have its mountains ranged more or less in two lines, running from west to east, the volcanoes for the most part occupying the more northern portion. Of these, both active and extinct, there are many. The most important are Ngenges (5560 feet) and Lante (5413 feet), in the western half of the island; the gigantic Tambora (9040 feet), occupying the northern peninsula; Dende (5151 feet), Soro Mandi (4553 feet), and Aru Hassa (5568 feet), grouped together on the western side of Bima Bay; and Sambori, Lambu, and Massi at the eastern end of the island. Gunong Api or Sangeang Island, off the north-east coast, is an active island-volcano of striking appearance, rising to a height of over 6000 feet from a base of only about 7 miles in diameter. The land in the south of Sumbawa is of lower elevation, and some of the mountains and hills, notably Tafelberg, at the extreme western end of the island, appear to be of sedimentary formation. Of the volcanoes above-mentioned, that of Tambora is incomparably the most important, causing, as it did in 1815, one of the most awful eruptions ever recorded in history. It is said that previous to this catastrophe the peak was more than 13,000 feet high. Now it is variously estimated at from 8600 to 9040 feet, so that the apex for a height of about 4000 feet must have been blown into the air. That this may well have occurred is evident from the fact that the crater, as it at present appears, has a diameter of over 7 miles. The following account of the occurrence is taken chiefly from Sir Charles Lyell's *Principles of Geology*:—

The great eruption began on 5th April, 1815, was

most violent on the 11th and 12th, and did not entirely
cease till the following July. The sound of the explosions was heard at Benkulen in Sumatra, a distance of
over 1100 miles in one direction, and at Ternate, a distance of over 900 in a nearly opposite direction. Violent
whirlwinds carried up men, horses, cattle, and whatever
else came within their influence, into the air; tore up
the largest trees by the roots, and covered the sea with
floating timber. Many streams of lava issued from the
crater and flowed in different directions to the sea,
destroying everything in their course. Even more
destructive were the ashes, which fell in such quantities
that they broke through the Resident's house at Bima,
more than 60 miles to the eastward, and rendered most
of the houses in that town uninhabitable. On the west
towards Java, and on the north towards Celebes, the
ashes darkened the air to a distance of 300 miles, while
fine ashes fell in Amboina and Banda, more than 800
miles distant, and in such quantity at Brunei, the capital
of Borneo, more than 900 miles north, that the event is
remembered and used as a date-reckoner to this day.
To the west of Sumbawa the sea was covered with a
floating mass of fine ashes two feet thick, through which
ships forced their way with difficulty. The darkness
caused by the ashes in the daytime was more profound
than that of the darkest nights, and this horrid pitchy
gloom extended a distance of 300 miles to the westward
into Java. Along the sea-coast of Sumbawa and the
neighbouring islands, the sea rose suddenly to the height
of from 2 to 12 feet, so that every vessel was forced
from its anchorage and driven on shore. The town of
Tambora sank beneath the sea, and remained permanently
18 feet deep where there had been dry land before.
The noises, the tremors of the earth, and the fall of ashes

from this eruption extended over a circle of more than 2000 miles in diameter, and out of a population of 12.000 persons who inhabited the province of Tambora previous to the eruption, it is said that only 26 individuals survived. The mountain is now quiescent, and few signs of the catastrophe remain, save that the course of the lava-streams may be traced by the inferior height of the jungle now covering them. The little island of Setonda, which is situated a mile or two to the northwest, is a secondary crater of Tambora, and, like it, appears to be extinct.

Sumbawa has its coast-line broken in two or three places with curious fjord-like bays, of which the most important is Bima. The narrow entrance, barely 400 yards in width, and guarded by two old and ruined forts, opens into a spacious harbour surrounded by mountains, which is the only port visited by ships, and the sole point of contact between savagery and western civilisation. The Sale Gulf is little known. Here, and about the island of Mayo, pirates are said still to lurk, taking praus and making occasional descents on the villages, so that the shores of the gulf are more or less deserted for some distance inland, where the natives live in stockaded towns. The land south of the gulf is very low, and not more than nine or ten miles broad, and the monsoon blowing across it from April to October as a strong south-easterly wind parches the entire country, so that the trees shed their leaves, and the ground is thick with a very fine, powdery dust. The difference between the seasons becomes more marked as we progress eastward in the Sunda chain, the drought being here more severe and the rainfall heavier than in Bali.

The people may be divided into three groups—the Sumbawans proper, the Bugis and Makassar immigrants,

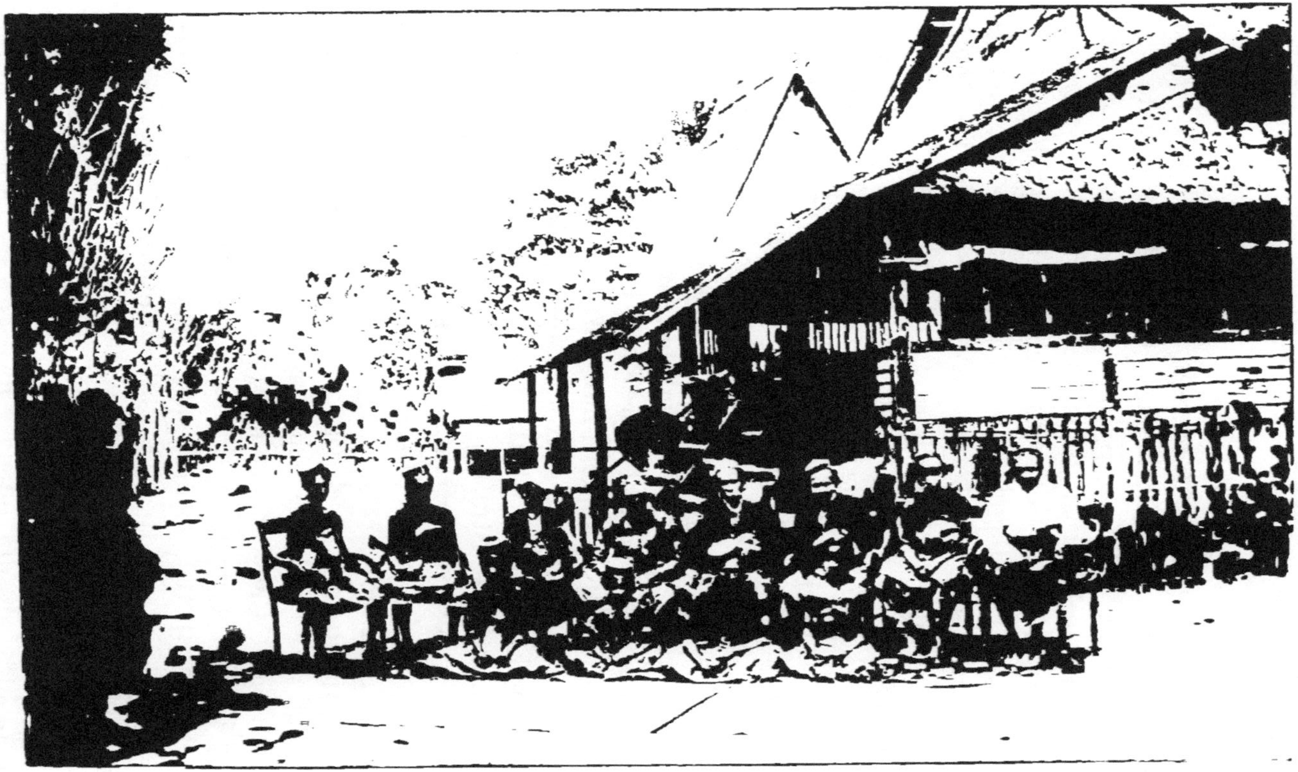

SULTAN OF BIMA AND HIS SUITE, SUMBAWA.

and a race of people of whom almost nothing is known, and who may possibly represent the original inhabitants of the island. Of the first-named the affinities do not appear to be satisfactorily made out: they are of sub-Malayan stock, with linguistic peculiarities pointing rather to a connection with Celebes than with Bali or Lombok. The Buginese and Makassar people immigrated in large numbers a few years after the great Tambora eruption, which is said to have caused the death of some 70,000 of the islanders. They are chiefly confined to the western portion of the island. Five distinct languages are spoken, and most of the people are Mohammedans, except the wild tribes above-mentioned, who are pagans. There are two Sultanates—Sumbawa and Bima. The Sultan of Bima's dominions extended not only over the eastern half of the island, but over Banta, Komodo, and the western part of Flores, and formerly over Sumba also. The Dutch rule is, however, acknowledged, and a Controleur and small garrison are established at Bima, the island, together with the western part of Flores, being under the administration of the Resident at Makassar. There is, however, no direct jurisdiction, such authority as is exerted being carried out through the medium of the native rulers.

Agriculture is much less advanced in Sumbawa than in Bali and Lombok. There are no natural reservoirs of water, and the streams are often precipitous, and run dry in the summer, so that irrigation would be difficult even to expert agriculturists. Some of the valleys are very fertile, and the frightful eruption of 1815, which for some little time after rendered the land unfit for cultivation, had as its eventual result a very greatly increased fertility when the volcanic ejecta had become thoroughly disintegrated. Rice is very largely grown, and forms the staple, for neither the sago nor coco-nut palm is suited to the climate. The export trade is very small. Ponies are the most noteworthy feature of it, many being sent to Batavia, while every year a shipload is despatched to Mauritius. The animals are considered the best in the whole archipelago, and, though very small, are of good shape and powerful. In Dr. Zollinger's time the Sultan of Bima was said to own over ten thousand. Almost every native rides, and carries his spear even if at work in the fields. The mineral resources of the island are as yet unexplored, but gold and arsenic are known to exist, as well as petroleum. The island has been conjectured to have a population of about 150,000; it is at all events thinly peopled as compared with Bali and Lombok. The towns of Bima and Sumbawa have each about 5000 inhabitants. There are hardly any Chinese settlers, but some hundreds of Klings are resident in or near Bima.

5. Flores.

Passing eastward from Sumbawa, the Sapi Strait is first crossed. It was at one time much used by vessels, but now the Allas Strait is preferred, being both wider and easier. The small island of Komodo, which is of volcanic formation, is said to be practically uninhabited, being only temporarily used by fishermen. Next comes the Strait of Mangerai, which is almost unknown, and swept by tremendous currents, as are most of the passages through this great island barrier. Its eastern shores are formed by another small and uninhabited island, Rindia, which abounds in wild buffaloes and horses, and is separated from Flores by a narrow and reef-beset passage.

Flores is 232 miles long and from 10 to 35 miles

wide, having an estimated area of about 6300 square miles. Its eastern part was, until 1859, claimed by the Portuguese, who had small settlements, protected by forts, at Larantuka, Ende Bay, and other places. It is very mountainous, and has numerous active and extinct volcanoes, but the older rocks would also seem to be represented, although to what extent is uncertain, for the interior is a *terra incognita* to Europeans. The highest peak is Romba, near the middle of the south coast, with an elevation of 9187 feet. Rokka, about 15 miles west of it, is also a fine volcano, reaching a height of 6562 feet. At the east end of Ende Bay, Gunong Api runs out as a promontory into the sea, and is in a state of constant activity, as also appears to be another peak a few miles eastward. At the eastern end of the island three fine volcanoes dominate the Flores Strait; at the southern entrance is Lobetobi, 7425 feet in height, a twin peak of which the lower crater is active; at the northern narrows rises Illimandiri (5170 feet), which appears extinct, but has hot springs at its base. Katabelo occupies the middle promontory, facing another volcano on Solor Island, and is 3600 feet high only. The island of Palani or Rusa Raja, lying five or six miles seaward from the middle of the north coast, is also a volcano, the height of which has been found to be 4593 feet. These are the chief mountains at present known, but an exploration of the island would no doubt result in the discovery of others.

On the coasts of the island, especially on the northern side, we find the usual intrusive foreign population. In 1847 a colony of Bima natives were settled in Bari Bay to serve as a check on the pirates who used to resort thither, and they are now found some distance inland and along the coast. A mixed race of Bugis people also form a large proportion of the littoral population, but according to Dr. Weber the true Buginese are hardly seen except at Maumeri, where they construct the large trading praus for which they are so famed. The aboriginal inhabitants thus occupy the interior. They are totally distinct from the sub-Malayan peoples of the coast, and are by most observers considered to be of Papuan origin. They are tall and strongly built, with somewhat of the unreserved and noisy manners of the New Guinea savage. The teeth are filed to points; the nose is large, rather prominent, and finely cut; the skin dark, or, according to some travellers, sooty-black. The hair is frizzly and abundant, but waved, and less resistent than in the true Papuan; and altogether the Flores aboriginals may perhaps be said to be most nearly allied to the Timorese. They are not very friendly even near Larantuka, where Europeans have been long settled, and a Dutch expedition attempting to explore inland from the south coast in 1889 was attacked and driven to retreat, the leader and two Government officials having been wounded. These people are pure pagans, their creed being apparently a form of nature-worship. The earth is considered holy, and to be disturbed as little as possible, so that in the dry season they will only dig for water in the river-beds as a last resource. The coast dwellers are mostly Mohammedans, but the Portuguese made some converts during their tenure of the island, and a good number, especially of the mixed race of Portuguese blood in Larantuka, still call themselves Christians, and are said to be visited by the priests from Timor. There is also a Dutch Catholic mission at Maumeri and Sikka. The people inhabiting Rusa Raja Island are pagans of the same race as those of the interior.

There is not much trade in Flores, but Larantuka is visited in the westerly monsoon by the praus of the Celebes traders, who ship rice, birds' nests, tortoiseshell, wax, and so forth, and bring Butung sarongs in exchange. Sandalwood and cinnamon are also exported in small quantities, and a few ponies. The forests produce various dyes, such as sapan wood and another known as " kayu kuning" by the Malays, yielding a yellow dye. The thickets near the coast are rendered dangerous by the presence of a very poisonous shrub, probably one of the *Euphorbiaceæ*, whose juice causes severe wounds and fever, and even blindness when it touches the eye. Copper, gold, and iron are known to exist, and tin is worked by the natives on the south coast, but the mines have never been visited by Europeans.

Larantuka is the chief town, situated just within the northern entrance of the Flores Strait. It gives its name to the eastern portion of the island. The name Flores is seldom used in the archipelago in common parlance, the natives speaking of Mangarai, Ende, or Larantuka, according as they wish to refer to the western, central, or eastern part. The whole population of the island has been roughly estimated at 250,000. Flores falls under the administration of the Resident of Timor, and besides the sub-Controleur at Larantuka, there are two Postholders on the island, one at Maumeri on the north coast, and another at Ambugaga in Ende Bay.

6. The Solor and Allor Groups.

Between Flores and Timor lie the five smaller islands comprised in these two groups—Solor, Adenara, and Lomblen forming the first named, and Pantar and Allor (or Ombay) the Allor group. Solor and Adenara lie nearly north and south of each other, being separated by the narrow Solor Strait. Omitting this, there are thus five breaks between Flores and Timor in this vast island chain—the Flores, Lamakwera or Boleng, Allor, and Pantar Straits, and the broad and profound channel known as the Ombay Passage. The latter is most used by vessels, but all are navigable, though more or less dangerous from the terrific currents which sweep through them, and at times render ships quite ungovernable. Their strength may be realised from the fact that mariners are cautioned in sailing along the islands not to approach within 12 miles of the mouth of the Straits, lest their ship should be drawn in. A vessel has been known, while experiencing strong southerly winds at the northern entrance of the Komodo Strait, west of Flores, to be drawn in at the rate of *eleven miles an hour.* Yet these currents are most uncertain, and vessels are sometimes not only days, but weeks, endeavouring to pass through. In March, 1868, some twenty or thirty sailing ships had been in vain trying to get eastward through the Ombay Passage, with the result of always losing by day what was gained at night. At length the captains of two ships resolved to try the Lamakwera Strait. In two days the entrance was reached, and in two and a half hours they had passed through.

All these islands are inhabited by a race similar to the people of the interior of Flores—dark, tall, and frizzly-haired, and little known to Europeans—while on the coast are settled a few Bugis or other Malays. They are nominally under the jurisdiction of the Residency of Timor, and there are Postholders at Terong in Adonara and Allor Ketjil in Ombay. The entire population of the two groups is believed to be about 125,000 inhabitants.

Solor is the smallest of the five islands, and the

natives are said to be very hostile in parts. The Dutch as early as 1613 drove the Portuguese out of a small settlement they had established here. Adonara is more populous and larger; its highest peak, the volcano Mount Wokka, attains a height of 4882 feet. Lomblen or Kawella is 55 miles long, and has an area of about 400 square miles. The coast is high, bold, and barren in appearance, and at least four volcanic peaks exist, of which Lamararap (5800 feet), at the southern extremity of the island, is the most lofty. It was through this group that the *Victoria* — the last remaining ship of Magellan's squadron — passed, most probably by the Flores Strait, and the islands are mentioned by Pigafetta. Pantar is about 28 miles long, and is said to be sparsely populated by natives who are not to be trusted. Ombay or Allor is the largest of the five islands, being about 65 miles in length by 15 in breadth. It is almost all high land, especially at the east end, and, unlike many others of the chain, is covered with high trees to the summit of the mountains. The *Victoria* refitted here in 1522, and Pigafetta speaks of the natives as cannibals, and even at the present day they are said to be head-hunters in the interior.

7. Wetta and the Serwatti Group.

East of the Ombay Passage lies Kambing, a small island about 12 miles long, which is noteworthy as belonging to the Portuguese, although it is in no way connected with Timor, being separated from it by a channel nearly 2000 fathoms deep. It has a mountain 3273 feet in height, at the summit of which are numbers of small mud volcanoes, exhibiting eruptions at regular intervals. Wetta is a considerable island, 70 miles in length, high and barren, the north-west coast formed by arid mountains about 4000 feet high. The country seems absolutely bare of trees, looking like a recent volcanic product. The inhabitants are akin to those of Timor, and are said to be harmless and timid. There are a few Bugis settled on the coast, and the principal product is beeswax. The population is believed to be about 8000.

The appellation Serwatti Islands includes the scattered groups which intervene between Wetta and Timor Laut. They have, however, no geographical unity, though ethnographically they are connected by the fact that they are for the most part inhabited not by people of Papuan or sub-Papuan race, as might be expected, but by natives of Malay stock, numbers of whom are nominally Christians. In the last century the Dutch had small settlements on many of the islands, and the individuals then converted became, as a result of their education, the ruling class. Although many of the Dutch posts were given up, the islands relapsing into a *terra incognita* which has only of late been re-explored, this curious state of things has persisted, and the people are industrious and peaceable instead of being head-hunting savages.

Following the chain of the Lesser Sundas onwards, we come to Roma, a compact island about 10 miles in diameter, with an area of 150 square miles. It has a single high peak, and is surrounded by a number of small islands, the exact position of which is not yet known. The soil is very fertile, and the inhabitants of whom there are over 1000, are professedly Christians. About 80 miles farther to the north-east lies a very similar group, the central and most important island of which is Damma, where, at the village of Wulur, a Postholder is stationed. It has an active volcano 3000 feet in height, and a fair harbour. The nutmeg is said to have grown here at one time, but to have been extirpated by the Dutch. About 70 miles farther in the same direction is Nila, with a small volcano which has been active in recent times. Finally, the chain terminates with Serua; or possibly Manok Island, a small and isolated volcanic peak in 5° 33′ S., may be the ultimate link.

The remainder of the Serwatti islands form a chain connecting Wetta with the Timor Laut group, though whether situated on one and the same raised submarine bank is unknown, the soundings in these seas being few in number. Kissa is the most western, and is densely populated, for, though possessed of an area of less than 40 square miles, there were in 1886 nearly 10,000 inhabitants. The Dutch formerly had settlements in two or more places on the island, but have now abandoned them, chiefly, it is said, owing to the droughts which so frequently occurred. In spite of the barren and mountainous character of the land, the soil is very fertile, and passing ships obtain provision abundantly and cheaply. The inhabitants are a tall and good-looking race of Christian Malays, who are good agriculturists. Pura-pura, a village on the south-west coast, is the principal port of the Serwatti islands, and two miles inland is a walled town of some size, with a large church. The Letti group, of which Moa is the largest island, is peopled almost as thickly with a similar race. Many cattle are raised. The Karbau peak on Moa attains a height of 4100 feet, but the remainder of the island is flat and coralline. The group contains 11,000 inhabitants, and a representative of the Dutch Government resides on Letti. Sermata, about 40 miles eastward, is little known. Leaving this Malayan oasis, we come again, at the Baba group, to a dark Papuan race, who bear a rather bad character.

The islands are no longer bare, but covered with thick forest, and there is little cultivation. The Dutch have a small coal-depôt here, at Tepa, on the west coast of the main island.

8. The Timor Laut Group.

The Timor Laut or Tenimber Islands are a large and rather closely packed group situated about midway between Timor and Aru. They extend north and south over nearly 2° of latitude, and consist of three main islands—Larat, Yamdena, and Selaru, with thirty or more of lesser area and importance. Such knowledge as we have of the soundings in the neighbourhood seem to point to the existence of deep water around the group, though not to the great depths which appear to isolate Timor. Until 1882 almost nothing was known concerning this little archipelago. The Bugis and Goram traders visited a few villages occasionally, and obtained trepang, tortoiseshell, and other products, but previous to Mr. H. O. Forbes's visit no European had ever remained upon the group, and very few had even landed. In 1882 this enterprising naturalist, accompanied by his wife, was landed at Ritabel in Larat, and remained there for a period of three months. It is to his observations that we are indebted for what little knowledge we possess of the islands.

The chief island, Yamdena, is about 75 miles in length by 15 in breadth. Selaru is 30 miles long, and Larat not quite so large. The islands are all low, and apparently all composed of recently upheaved coralline limestone, with the single exception of Laibobar Island, which attains a height of about 2000 feet, and is most probably a volcano. There are absolutely no inhabitants in the interior, but along the coast, especially in the north, the villages are numerous. Mr. Forbes regards the natives as a mixed race of Papuan, Polynesian, and Malay blood. They use the fork-like hair-combs of the Papuans, and are very clever carvers of wood and ivory, the latter substance being brought as tusks from Singapore and Sumatra by Buginese traders. Drunkenness is rather common, the spirit used being distilled from the sap of the coco-palm. Tobacco is only grown for chewing. The constant tribal or village wars which appear everywhere to exist oblige the people to live in stockaded towns, set about with sharp-pointed bamboo stakes, and agriculture suffers in consequence, and not the less from a dearth of water. Maize is the staple, but sweet potato, manioc, and sugar are also grown. Neither rice nor sago appears to be cultivated, but the natives are industrious fishermen.

Mr. Forbes found characteristic Australian trees conspicuous by their absence. Eucalyptus, casuarinas, and phyllode-bearing acacias were not seen, but urostigmas, sterculias, and myrtles formed a conspicuous feature of the flora. The avifauna is markedly Papuan, with a slight Timor element, and this Timorese affinity is also shown by the Lepidoptera. There are no deer, and the tree kangaroo (*Dendrolagus*), a striking Papuan form, has not been found, though existent, as we have seen, in the Ké Islands. On Yamdena large herds of buffalo have run wild.

9. Sumba, Savu, and Timor.

Sumba, the little island of Savu, and the group of which Timor forms the main island, are in no way connected with the great Sunda chain just described. They form a group apart, but whether connected with each other by submarine banks is as yet unknown, although this is improbable. Between them and these eastern Sunda islands very deep water is known to exist. In the Ombay Passage, separating Timor from Ombay, the depth of water probably averages about 2000 fathoms, while between Sumba and Flores such soundings as have been taken show it to be about 700 to 900 fathoms. This separation is borne out by geological evidence, Timor consisting mainly of slates, schists, and sandstones, with limestone rocks of carboniferous age at the western extremity, thus differing considerably from the chain of volcanic islands which run from Java to Banda. Moreover, Timor is not only washed by deep water on its northern but also on its southern shores, for the great bank of soundings, which runs out for a vast distance from Northern Australia, suddenly ends about 90 miles from Timor, and gives place to great depths of from 1000 to 2000 fathoms. It might thus be expected that an isolation so long continued as these facts imply should be manifested by great singularity in the fauna and flora. This does not, however, appear to be the case, although collections are perhaps as yet too scanty to permit a judgment, except possibly as far as regards the botany of the island.

Timor, which lies with its long axis in a N.E. and S.W. direction, is almost exactly 300 miles long, and of tolerably regular outline, being for a great part of its length about 60 miles wide. It is therefore considerably larger than Ceram, and has an estimated area of 11,650 square miles. It is mountainous throughout, and its surface exceedingly broken and rugged. The ranges do not, however, often rise higher than 5000 or 6000 feet, and they are generally bare or thinly wooded, and often exceedingly sterile, especially on the Australian side.

The most important mountains are chiefly in the northern part, but Mount Alas, which has the greatest altitude, is situated about the middle of the island near the south coast, and is stated to reach the height of 12,250 feet. Another fine peak is Kabalaki, about 10,000 feet, not far from Dilli. The chief mountain in Dutch territory is Lakan (6500 feet). It was for long supposed that Timor was without volcanoes, but this is not the case, and there have been recent eruptions both in the eastern and western parts of the island. Mr. Scrope in his work on volcanoes speaks of Timor Peak as a mountain of great height, continually active before the year 1638, when it was blown up during an eruption and the peak replaced by a crater-lake. Before this occurrence the mountain was said to be visible 300 miles off, which, if true, would imply that it was the loftiest in the archipelago. Earthquakes are rather frequent, and mud volcanoes exist in Semang and Landu islands.

Mr. Forbes speaks of the country at some distance inland from Dilli as presenting the most bizarre and fantastic appearance from the limestone formation prevalent in that region. Superimposed clays make landslips extraordinarily frequent, and he regards road-making as almost impossible in many places for this reason. The paths are deep ditches along which the ponies pass in single file, now ascending, now descending the abrupt ravines which are so marked a feature of the island. Iron occurs, as well as copper and gold, the two latter probably being abundant, and coal and petroleum are also found. The rivers are numerous but not navigable, and from the excessive drought of the dry season and the porous nature of the soil many at that time of year do not reach the sea. No lakes of any size are known.

From a passage in Pigafetta's diary, it appears possible that the Portuguese may have reached Timor before the visit of the Spaniards in 1522, but we have no definite record of any such occurrence, or of when they became established on the island. They were driven out of Kupang by the Dutch in 1613, and the two nations were engaged in frequent warfare during the eighteenth century. In 1859 the boundaries were settled by treaty, leaving, roughly speaking, the south-western moiety to the Dutch and the north-eastern to the Portuguese. The latter government, however, also own two small districts within their neighbour's territory. The Dutch capital is Kupang, a neat little town near the southern extremity of the island, with a mixed population of about 7000, consisting of Malays, Chinese, Arabs, and natives, besides a considerable number of Dutch, living in well-built houses. The Resident administers the government of Sumba, Savu, and the Solor and Allor groups, in addition to the many native "kingdoms" into which Timor is divided. The town is a place of some trade, and whalers, as well as many merchant ships, call here for provision and water. Trade is still carried on chiefly by barter, the most prized article of exchange, according to Mr. Forbes, being a species of bead of an ochreous red colour, the place of manufacture of which is quite unknown. A small string eight or nine inches long has a value of about £12.

The Portuguese have their chief settlement at Dilli, a miserable town of hovels, half ruined and deserted, the houses and even the church being only of clay and thatch, without any attempt at decoration or even neatness. With the exception of the Governor, officials, and soldiers, there are hardly any Europeans, and the entire population is not above 3000. It is, moreover, very unhealthy, especially from November to April, when the westerly monsoon brings an abundant rainfall. There are not five miles of road in any direction, and the fine hills that rise at the back of the town have not even decent bridle-paths to make them accessible. A good force of police is required, as street robberies are frequent. The condition of the colony appears wretched, and a Portuguese writer to *As Colonias Portuguezas* complains that there are neither funds nor men to keep it going. Omitting the Dutch steamers, which touch regularly at the port, hardly any vessels visit it. In the year 1885 only twelve entered it, and of these seven were Dutch. The export trade in coffee has fallen off, although the berry is exceedingly good. The exports, which in 1888 amounted to the value of £110,000, had fallen in 1890 to £72,000. Of this latter sum coffee represented almost the whole, its value being given at £67,000; the remainder was practically confined to beeswax and sandal-wood. What trade exists is chiefly in the hands of Macao Chinese.

Mr. H. O. Forbes describes Timor as portioned out into small kingdoms ruled over by independent chiefs. In Portuguese Timor there are forty-seven such kinglets. Each kingdom is in turn divided into districts or *Sukus*, ruled over by Datus. Most if not all of these native princes pay some sort of tribute, and it is said that each kingdom has a different language, or at all events a widely different dialect. Under an energetic government, and with some outlay in the construction of roads, the island might be prosperous, for wheat and potatoes of excellent quality are grown on the hills, and might be cultivated in sufficient quantity to supply the whole European population of the archipelago. Sheep also thrive on the hills, and though wool-bearing varieties have not been introduced, the mutton is very good. In the Dutch part, coffee is not grown for export, and there is very little trade, ponies and sandalwood forming the only items of any importance.

The inhabitants of Timor are regarded by almost all travellers in that country as a very mixed race, in which the Malay, Polynesian, and Papuan elements are blended. It is impossible to find a typical Timor native, so much does individual differ from individual. On the whole, they somewhat approach the Papuan type, but the hair is much less frizzled and the features less prominent. There is also a marked tendency to yellowness in the colour of the skin. The Timorese have never invented writing, as have the Sumatran tribes, and in point of civilisation they are not more advanced than the Dyaks. They weave cotton cloths of a peculiar pattern, make curious wallets of cloth, and form ingenious umbrellas from palm-leaves. They carry signal pipes by which they can communicate with each other at great distances across ravines. They do not live in villages, but in scattered huts, or family hamlets, thus differing from almost all the peoples we have hitherto considered. The practice of *tabu* is in full force, and almost every settlement has a *Luli* house or temple, the most important object in which is the *Vatu-luli*, or sacred stone, on which offerings are made to an indefinite deity or spirit. A species of nature-worship exists, and there are sacred groves wherein no branch may be broken or stone turned. The natives are still head-hunters in many parts, but the custom of sacrificing slaves at the interment of their chiefs and on other occasions has been checked to a certain extent by European rule. Some tribes have become Christian, or nominally so. Rice is grown to some extent, but the staple food of the natives is Indian corn. The population of the island can only be conjecturally estimated. By Señor Vaquinhas that of Portuguese Timor is thought to be over half a million, and of the Dutch possessions about 250,000.

Semao or Semang Island is only important as forming a Dutch coaling station. Rotti, distant only 8 miles to the south-west—for Landu is a peninsula, and not an island as usually represented—has an area of 655 square miles, and is chiefly of limestone formation with elevated coral-reefs, and is nowhere more than 800 feet high. The population is probably about 60,000, and the people of Malay origin, being short, smooth-haired, and brown-complexioned. They are very peaceable, and are ruled by eighteen Rajas, who are all under Dutch authority. A few are Christian, but the majority pagan. Rice, sugar, tobacco, and cotton are grown, and the miniature ponies of the island are renowned throughout the archipelago for their excellence.

Though only about 20 miles in length and 185 square miles in area, the small island of Savu is thickly populated, and contained in 1884 over 20,000 people. Judging by some of the chiefs seen by Mr. Wallace in Timor, they are of a very superior type, resembling Hindus or Arabs rather than Malays, and having fine, well-formed features, with straight, thin noses and clear brown complexions. A Dutch postholder resides at Seba or Laipaka on the north-west coast, and a school has been established here. Large numbers of ponies are bred, some of which are exported.

Sumba or Sandalwood Island is of considerable extent; containing about 4000 square miles, and having a length of 130 and a breadth of some 30 or 35 miles. It appears to be surrounded on all sides by very deep water, although the strait separating it from Flores is only 27 miles wide. It is believed to be chiefly composed of the sedimentary rocks, and no volcanoes are known though they may quite possibly exist, as our knowledge of the island is very scanty. The northern coast is very high, forming precipitous, wall-like cliffs, which are about 1200 feet high, and remarkably uniform. The south-eastern portion is a level plain covered with grass and isolated trees. The people are very numerous, although the estimate of 400,000 which has been given is probably much exaggerated. They are of Malayan race, and possessed of a certain civilisation. Their religion appears to be a vague nature-worship with some traces of Hindu influence. The country is well cultivated, rice and Indian corn are grown, and goats, buffaloes, and ponies bred. Of the latter, 1496 were exported, chiefly to Java and Mauritius, in 1889. Birds' nests are found in large quantities, and some beeswax and tortoiseshell, but sandalwood is almost unknown. The trade is carried on by Bugis, who visit the island regularly in their praus, and a few Arabs settled at Nangamessi—known to the Dutch as Waingapu—on the north coast.

MELANESIA

CHAPTER XI

NEW GUINEA AND THE PAPUANS

UNDER the name of Melanesia we comprehend all the islands and groups of islands stretching from New Guinea in the west to Viti or Fiji in the east; that is to say, the domain chiefly occupied by the Papuan race. The series begins with New Guinea and its surrounding islands, and the Admiralty Isles, New Britain, and New Ireland, to the north-east. Proceeding still eastwards, or rather to the south-east, we meet with the Solomon Islands, the Santa Cruz or Queen Charlotte group, the New Hebrides, the French settlements of New Caledonia and the Loyalty Islands, and lastly, considerably farther east, the Fiji Archipelago.

The present chapter treats of New Guinea, and the islands which are joined to it by a shallow sea, and have evidently, at no distant period, formed with it one extensive land.

1. General.

The great island of New Guinea or Papua stretches in a N.N.W. and S.S.E. direction, beyond the Moluccan

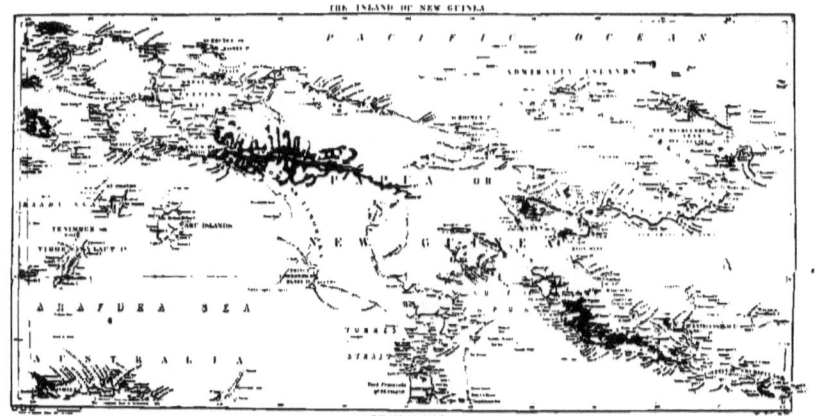

and Arafura seas, thus forming a barrier between the Malay Islands and the Pacific. Directly to the south lies the continent of Australia, separated from it by the shallow waters of Torres Strait, which is only 80 geographical miles wide. It lies wholly to the south of the equator, extending between 0° 19′ and 10° 42′ south latitude, and between 130° 57′ and 150° 52′ east longitude. Its extreme length, according to present knowledge, is 1490 miles, and its greatest breadth about 410 miles. Its area is about 300,000 statute miles, so that it is very considerably larger than Borneo, which has generally been thought to exceed it, and undoubtedly holds the first place among the islands of the globe. The form of New Guinea is very irregular, but it has a large compact central mass, with great prolongations at both extremities. Its extensive north-western peninsula, formed by the deep inlet of Great Geelvink Bay on the north, is again almost cut into two portions by the deep and narrow MacCluer's Inlet on the west coast. The western extremity terminates in English Cape, near the large island of Salwatti. The southern extension is somewhat more elongated, and bifurcates to form Milne Bay, the terminal promontory being East Cape. Generally the outline is tolerably even, but there are a good many inlets, bays, and harbours in various parts of its extensive coasts. The best known are Dorei Harbour, Humboldt Bay, Astrolabe Bay, Finschhafen, Huon Gulf, Dyke Acland Bay, Collingwood Bay, and Goodenough Bay, on the north; Milne Bay at the south-eastern extremity; Orangerie Bay, Port Moresby, Redscar Bay, Hall Sound, and the estuary of the Fly River to the east of Torres Straits; with Triton Bay, Kamrau or Arguna Bay, Patippi Bay, and Segaar Bay on the west coast of the northern peninsula. There are also numerous islands all round the coast, which afford shelter, and to some extent supply the want of harbours. Beginning at the Moluccan side, we have Waigiu, Batanta, Salwatti, and Misol, all grouped round the western promontory, and, in the case of the two last-named, connected with the mainland by innumerable islands, islets, and reefs. Wessel's or Adi Island protects the entrance of Arguna Bay, and farther south is the Aru group, which, though at some distance from New Guinea, is connected with it by very shallow soundings. Frederick Henry Island almost forms a portion of the mainland, being cut off from it only by the narrowest of channels. We pass through the reef-beset Torres Strait and reach the south-eastern promontory without meeting with anything more important than scattered rocks, but at this point are closely packed together countless islands, which a very slight elevation would join to the mainland. The Louisiade Archipelago forms with Rossel and Sudest Island the terminal point, and to the north lie Woodlark Island, the Trobriand group, and the more important D'Entrecasteaux islands. Coasting the northern seaboard and passing New Britain and New Ireland, we find a long chain of islands fringing the shore, and at no great distance from it, all of small size, and almost all volcanic, the craters of some being still active. The final group are those situated in Geelvink Bay, the Schouten Islands, Nufur, and Jobi Island, of which the latter, with a length of over 100 miles, is the most considerable.

2. Physical Features.

New Guinea appears to be divided into a northern and a southern mountainous portion, with a vast extent of low country in its central part, though whether these lowlands extend quite across to the Pacific Ocean is still uncertain. The massive peninsula north of MacCluer's Inlet appears to be everywhere mountainous, a continuous series of range behind range extending along its north coast. The most lofty peak of the Arfak range of this series was found by Lieutenant Powell, during the cruise of the *Marchesa*, to be 9046 feet, but it is possible that farther inland still higher altitudes may be reached. The Wa Samsum river, which enters the sea near Cape Spencer, probably rises in the Arfak Mountains. It has not been visited by Europeans, but the necessary shortness of its course precludes its being of any great size. In the narrow isthmus at the head of MacCluer Inlet there is a ridge about 1200 feet high. The seas approach each other very closely here. They are known to be in one place only a few hundred yards apart, and it is not yet absolutely certain that this supposed peninsula may not prove to be an island. Lately its insularity has been reported to be proved, but to all intents and purposes it forms part of the mainland, and will be thus described in these pages. South of the inlet lies another land-mass of almost equal size—the Onin Peninsula—and this also appears to be mountainous. When we pass into the great central mass of land to the south and east of Geelvink Bay, we find the ranges of still greater altitude. The Charles Louis Mountains, beginning close to the coast with Mount Lakahia (4526 feet), increase to the eastward till, at about long. $136°$ E., they reach a height of 9500 feet. They thence stretch farther inland in the same uniform direction, and their summits have been seen from the sea in fine weather, apparently covered with snow, and have been estimated to attain an altitude of from 16,500 to 17,500 feet. They are thus the loftiest known peaks in the whole archipelago, and even in the whole area between the Himalayas and the

Andes. This great range appears to run approximately along the 4th parallel of latitude, and it may possibly be continuous with the lofty ranges in German New Guinea. That it does not extend farther south is proved by the fact of the Fly River having been ascended more than half-way across the island in a low country with but very small hills. Everywhere on the south of the island, west of Torres Straits, the coast is low and swampy, and no hills are visible. Passing Torres Straits and reaching the eastern side of the Gulf of Papua, we find hilly ground, which soon gives place to fine mountains. From about 8° S. to the terminal south-east point of the island the country inland rises in an almost unbroken series of magnificent ranges, from the Albert Mountains in 146° E. long. to the Stirling Range, which ends at East Cape. The chief feature of these highlands is the Owen Stanley Range, which according to present measurements exceeds 13,000 feet. Many peaks exceed 9000 feet, six are between 10,000 and 11,000 feet, three between 11,000 and 12,000, and two over 12,000. Most of them are, however, not isolated mountains, but the culminating pinnacles of ranges. The scenery is here very grand, the country being extremely broken and rugged, and cut up by deep gorges.

The northern shores of British New Guinea are for the most part bold, but the great ranges are not here so conspicuous, being situated closer to the southern than to this side. As the boundary between the British and German possessions is passed the mountainous character of the interior becomes increasingly marked, and at no great distance inland from the Maclay Coast are three separate ranges of great height, of which one—the Bismarck Range—is reported to be snow-covered, while the peaks of the others do not fall far short of 12,000 feet.

Farther, in lat. 4° S., the Kaiserin Augusta River debouches, the only stream of value for navigation in this territory. From Humboldt Bay—the German-Dutch limit—onwards to the entrance of the Great Geelvink Bay, the same high coast prevails, except at the most northern point, where it is broken by the vast delta of the Amberno River. This stream has not yet been explored, but it is known to be of considerable size. Each of the three divisions of New Guinea—Dutch, British, and German—is thus provided with a single large river—the Amberno, Fly, and Kaiserin Augusta respectively.

3. History.

The existence of New Guinea was probably known to Albuquerque after his conquest of Malacca in 1511, and when the *Victoria*, the only remaining ship of Magellan's squadron, completed the first circumnavigation of the globe and returned to Seville in 1522, she brought skins of the bird-of-paradise, obtained from the natives of Tidor in the Moluccas, which must have been procured from the mainland or some of the islands of Papua. Yet this region does not appear to have been visited, or even sighted, by Europeans for some years later, although it is frequently and erroneously mentioned as having been seen by d'Abreu in his Moluccan voyage in 1511. Don Jorge de Meneses, the Portuguese commander, was the first to discover it, accidentally overrunning his distance in voyaging from Malacca to Ternate in 1526. He appears, as far as can be gathered from scant details, to have reached Waigiu Island, and to have stayed there some time. In 1528, and again in 1529, Alvaro Saavedra undoubtedly visited the north coast, and sailed along it for a great distance on the occasion of his second visit, probably nearly as far as Astrolabe Bay. The natives were at that time known both to the Spaniards and Portuguese as "Papuas," a name given them by the people of the Moluccas, Galvão tells us, "because they are black, with frizzled hair." Another Spaniard, Ynigo Ortiz de Retes, in the ship *San Juan*, also sailed along the north coast in 1546, anchored in several harbours, and was the first to give the country the name of New Guinea, from the resemblance of the people to negroes. In 1606 Luis Vaz de Torres passed through the straits which still bear his name, and sailed along the south coast, taking possession of it in the name of the king of Spain. In the same year the Dutch began their explorations in these seas, visited the Aru and Ké islands, and sailed along the west and south coasts of New Guinea; and from that time, for more than two centuries, almost all the exploration of the coasts was made by this nation; and we find their voyages commemorated in numerous Dutch names, as Geelvink Bay, Schouten's Islands, and MacCluer's Inlet. In 1700 our countryman Dampier sailed along the north coast, touching at many points, naming many capes and islands, and discovering the strait which bears his name. Thus a considerable knowledge of the coast was obtained, but not a single attempt was made to penetrate the interior. In 1827 a small Dutch settlement was attempted at Triton Bay, on the south-west coast, but it was soon given up, and no attempt at exploration appears to have been made. Mr. Wallace was informed by a Dutch gentleman at Makassar that the officer in charge of this settlement, finding the life there insufferably monotonous, killed the cattle and other live stock, and reported that they had died, and that the place was unhealthy and the natives intractable. Had a naturalist been chosen for the post, there is every reason to believe a very different result would have been obtained.

Although until quite recently New Guinea was an almost complete *terra incognita*, many naturalists and travellers have of late years visited and explored it. Even now, however, no land journeys of any length have been made into the interior, which is only known by the ascents of the Fly and Kaiserin Augusta rivers. It would be beyond the scope of this volume to refer in detail to the work of each explorer, but some of the most important points may here be given. After what may be termed the middle period in the history of discovery —that of Cook in 1770, of D'Entrecasteaux in the *Recherche* in 1793, of Duperrey in 1822-25, and of Dumont d'Urville, who explored the northern coast in the *Astrolabe* in 1827—the work was again taken up by Englishmen, and in 1843 the Fly River was discovered by the ship of that name. From 1846-50, H.M.S. *Rattlesnake* surveyed the coasts and islands to the south, and it was the officers of this vessel who viewed and named the lofty Owen Stanley peaks. But it was not till 1873 that Captain Moresby, in the *Basilisk*, determined the form of the south-eastern extremity, which had previously been totally unknown, and thus completed our knowledge of the external form and dimensions of this vast island.

We may pass now to the various attempts to penetrate the interior and investigate the fauna and flora of this most interesting island. In 1858 Mr. Wallace visited Dorei, on the north coast, and remained there with four Malay servants for three months and a half. This was the first time that any European had ventured to reside alone, and practically unprotected, on the mainland of this country. In missionary enterprise the Rev. J.

Chalmers must be mentioned as one of the early pioneers on the south coast. Visiting the Gulf of Papua in 1877, he, later, established himself at Port Moresby, and has done much to elucidate the ethnology of the Papuans, as has his co-worker Mr. Lawes, and also Mr. van Hasselt in Dutch New Guinea. The naturalists Bernstein and Von Rosenberg had previously investigated the north-west peninsula, and in 1871 the Russian Miklukho Maklai resided for fifteen months upon the coast which now bears his name ("Maclay Coast"), under conditions of great hardship. In 1872, Signor d'Albertis, an Italian naturalist, succeeded in ascending part of the Arfak range, and returned with rich collections of the insects and birds; but this exploit, successful as it was, was eclipsed by his exploration of the Fly River four years later, which he ascended for over 500 miles, thus penetrating to the very heart of the country. Meyer in 1873, and Beccari in 1875, collected in North-Western New Guinea, the former paying special attention to the exploration of Geelvink Bay, and crossing, or nearly crossing, the island at its two narrowest points. Two years afterwards Mr. Wilfrid Powell made a hazardous voyage along the coasts of New Britain in a small vessel of only 15 tons burden, mapped a large area until then unvisited, and also visited the north coast as far as Humboldt Bay; and in 1883 Mr. Kettlewell's yacht *Marchesa* cruised for some time in the waters of Dutch territory, visiting most of the great islands, and obtaining very large collections of birds and insects. The Swiss collector, M. Léon Laglaize, made several expeditions to the north-western peninsula about this period, and was the first to penetrate the country of the Karons.

In 1884 the eastern portion of the island was annexed by Great Britain and by Germany, and since then expeditions have been very numerous in the territories of both powers. The most important are those of Captain Everill, who ascended the Strickland River—the great tributary of the Fly—in 1885; of Mr. H. O. Forbes, who in the same year penetrated some distance towards the Owen Stanley range, but did not reach its summit; of Mr. Cuthbertson, who partly ascended Mount Obree; and finally of the Administrator, Sir William Macgregor, who, in addition to tracing the Fly River to its sources and making innumerable minor expeditions, succeeded in 1889 in gaining the summit of Mount Owen Stanley, the highest peak of the range of that name. In German New Guinea the work of geographical exploration has also been energetically undertaken, notably by Baron von Schleinitz in 1886, who investigated a great part of the coast; by Captain Dalmann, to whom our knowledge of the Kaiserin Augusta River is due; and by others too numerous to mention.

4. Geology.

In such an extensive country, with lofty mountain ranges, we may be sure that a large variety of sedimentary and igneous rocks occurs. As yet, however, the geology of the island is very insufficiently known. It was for long supposed that no volcanoes existed on the mainland, but it is now known that this is not the case. Mount Victory, on the shores of Collingwood Bay, opposite the D'Entrecasteaux group, having been seen in a partly active state. Mount Cyclops, near Humboldt Bay, is possibly a volcano, and craters have been reported to exist in the Arfak range. In some of the ranges of the southern portion of British territory, basaltic rocks occur, and volcanic breccias superimposed on talcose schists and slates. It is quite possible that in the northwest of the island, where earthquakes are frequent and at times severe, and where there are signs of upheaval over wide areas, further knowledge of the country may reveal the existence of active craters. There is no lack of evidences of volcanic action, both past and present, in the islands from the Louisiades to Humboldt Bay. Beginning with the D'Entrecasteaux group, all appear to be volcanic, the focus of action being now centred in Ferguson Island, where, on the west coast, over an area of eight or ten square miles, are numerous boiling springs, geysers of hot mud and saline lakes, and thousands of fumaroles, with considerable deposits of sulphur. The long chain of islands from New Britain to the Schouten group, which have already been alluded to, have a similar origin.

The recent superficial deposits occupy an enormous area, at all events in the British territory. The whole of the coast line of the Gulf of Papua and the vast basin of the Fly River is thus composed, and probably the area south of the Charles Louis range also. Upraised coral reefs are a marked feature of St. Aignan and other parts of the Louisiades, of the peninsula forming the northern limit of Goodenough Bay, of the Stirling range, where they are found at a height of 2000 feet or more, and of many parts of the German territory, especially in the neighbourhood of Finschhafen. At Dorei Bay they are well marked. In most of the islands and localities examined by Mr. A. G. Maitland of the Queensland Geological Survey, these elevated reef-masses, when viewed from a distance, present the appearance of vertical walls and level terraces, stretching often for considerable distances, and the faces of these cliffs are sometimes covered with vegetation to such an extent as to present the appearance of a huge wall of foliage. The

"Port Moresby Beds," which consist of sandy limestones and fine-grained calcareous shales, seem to be the most widely evident rocks of the Tertiary period on the southern coast of British New Guinea. The mountainous regions in the interior of this territory appear, with the exception of the district around Mount Yule, to be composed of metamorphic rocks, principally of schists, becoming more highly metamorphosed as the higher altitudes are reached. These slates and schists of undetermined age are very conspicuous in the D'Entrecasteaux and Louisiade groups, in which islands the only "payable" gold yet found in New Guinea was discovered in 1888. The igneous rocks, as already mentioned, occupy a considerable area, but that they are not necessarily of any very great age is shown by the fact that they rest in many instances on the most recent strata. The formations in the interior from Cape Buru (long. 135° E.) are believed to be jurassic limestones and dolomites.

Of the useful minerals in New Guinea not much is as yet known. Various causes have rendered exploration and prospecting a matter of great difficulty. The Germans appear, like the Dutch, to have paid little attention to the resources of their great possessions in this respect, and our knowledge is chiefly confined to the work of a few geologists and prospectors in British territory. Although traces of gold are obtainable in most of the rivers of the south coast, no reefs have been discovered. In 1888 the gold-fields of Sudest Island were opened, and in a few months about 800 Australian diggers were engaged. The diggings were all alluvial, and although some thousands of ounces of gold were won, the field was worked out in a few months. A little later St. Aignan was found to yield paying gold, but the same result occurred. It is very probable that further exploration will reveal rich fields on the mainland. The only other minerals known are sulphur, iron, plumbago, and mercury, of which the first-named is alone to be remuneratively worked. The mercury occurs as cinnabar on Normanby Island.

5. Climate.

The size and position of New Guinea are such as to interfere considerably with uniformity of climate. Thus in the neighbourhood of the Arfak Mountains, which lie almost under the equator, the rainfall is very heavy, and few days in the year are absolutely dry, while in parts of the British territory at the other extremity of the island the influence of the proximity of Australia and other causes are sufficient to bring about periods of drought, though these are never of the severity and regularity of the dry seasons of the Lesser Sunda Islands. Roughly speaking, it may be said that the easterly monsoon brings rain not only in the Moluccas but in New Guinea, except in most parts of its south and west coasts, and the high ranges of the latter country, condensing the rain-clouds of the Pacific breezes, act as a sort of umbrella to the north coast of Australia and Timor at this season. Thus Finschhafen, near the Huon Gulf in German New Guinea, receives its greatest rainfall with the south-east trades from June till October, while at Port Moresby, on the opposite side of the peninsula, the weather is very dry at this period, and the heavy rains fall with the westerly monsoon from January to April. Local peculiarities, however, cause certain exceptions to this rule. Thus Konstantinhafen, though distant only about 150 miles westward of Finschhafen, has its rains at precisely the opposite season—a result brought about by the great mountain masses of the Bismarck and Finisterre ranges, which intervene between the two ports; and Hatzfeldthafen, still farther west, is protected in like manner. Konstantinhafen has an annual rainfall of about 120 inches, which exceeds considerably that of the other German settlements. At Port Moresby the mean is 72 inches. No European settlements exist in Dutch territory, and we have thus no records, but the rainfall of Dorei and the north-western peninsula most probably exceeds any of these figures.

At Port Moresby the grand mean temperature in 1892 was found to be 83° Fahr., the highest maximum 96°, and the lowest minimum 72°. In the German territory temperature is lower, the mean annual of Hatzfeldthafen being registered at 78°, and the lowest minimum at 66° Fahr., but the north-west extremity is no doubt the hottest, as well as the wettest, portion of the island. Although these recorded temperatures are greatly exceeded in many parts of Australia, the heat of New Guinea, owing to the superabundance of moisture, is far more trying to Europeans, and the climate cannot be regarded as otherwise than very unhealthy. Nor is this unhealthiness confined to Europeans. Between the years 1873 and 1887, 201 Polynesian teachers were employed in the various missions in British territory, and of these no less than 95 died. The chief disorders affecting foreigners are the various forms of malarial fever and ulcers of the leg. Elephantiasis and leprosy are common among the natives, but still commoner is a form of ringworm, which, though found in many islands from the Moluccas far into the Pacific, has its chief focus in New Guinea. Spreading from various centres, it covers the skin with circles of curious accuracy of outline. In time these meet, and the whole body may become covered with the marks, ring forming within ring, the patterns thus made giving at a little distance the effect of tattooing. In some villages quite half the population are affected. The exanthemata are at present unknown.

6. Flora and Fauna.

The soil in New Guinea is almost everywhere exceedingly fertile, and the country covered with dense virgin forests, although in a few localities, especially on the south coast—of which Port Moresby is one—we find treeless tracts of barren soil. In German New Guinea are stretches of park-like country not unlike those met with in the neighbourhood of Kina Balu in North Borneo. Though small tracts occur here and there, no large areas of the worthless lalang grass, such as those in Java and Sumatra, are known. In the forests the trees, which are perhaps on the whole less lofty than those of Bornean and Celebesian forests, are covered and matted together with creepers and rattans, the dense foliage shutting out the sun's rays, and causing in most places a lack of the smaller herbaceous plants. It is probable that the total number of vascular plants existing in the island is not far short of 4000 species. Omitting the vegetation of the littoral, which has a considerable similarity throughout the Malay Archipelago, and that of high altitudes, to which special reference is necessary, and taking that only of the intervening region for consideration, we find it to be eminently Malayan in character, though perhaps more so generically than specifically. Yet that a strong Australian element is also present is shown by certain species of *Drosera, Eucalyptus, Grevillea, Clerodendron, Leptospermum,* and phyllode-bearing Acacias; and, in the mountains, of *Epilobium, Galium, Myosotis, Gaultiera,*

Araucaria, Styphelia, etc., which are found only in Australia and New Guinea. The island may, however, be said to have a well-marked individuality in its plants, as it has in its birds. Baron von Müller, reporting on the highland species gathered during Sir William Macgregor's expedition to the summit of the Owen Stanley range, records that of the eighty plants obtained in the highest altitudes nearly half the number seem to be endemic. Of these nineteen are of Himalayan type (Rhododendrons, Vacciniums, etc.) Two represent new genera—one allied to the exclusively Italian *Nananthea*, the other to the Australian and chiefly alpine *Trochocarpa*. Four plants are identical with species found on Mount Kina Balu in Borneo. Certain species occurring in England, yet not cosmopolitan, were also found, among them *Taraxacum officinale, Scirpus cæspitosus, Lycopodium clavatum, Hymenophyllum Tunbridgense*, and the common male fern. Arboreal vegetation was found to cease at 11,500 feet. On Mount Douglas and other mountains of the range a cypress (*Libocedrus Papuana*) constitutes the principal forests. The Arfak Mountains have yielded a very similar flora. What the lofty summits of the as yet unascended Charles Louis range will afford the botanist is one of the many interesting problems of New Guinea, but it is possible that the 5000 feet by which they are supposed to exceed the Owen Stanley Mountains may yield much that has not been found on the latter. In Northern New Guinea the Australian connection is very little marked. Thus the Germans have not yet recorded any species of eucalyptus, though this genus is known in Misol Island; and only one acacia, one of the most marked of Australian forms.

The zoology of New Guinea is at present far better known than its botany, and is exceedingly interesting;

because the island is evidently the centre from which most of the animals of the surrounding islands and many of those of North Australia have been derived.

Mammalia are very scarce. The largest and almost the only placental mammal is the wild pig, of a peculiar species; and there are also a few peculiar mice. All the rest are marsupials, the most remarkable being the small tree kangaroos forming the genus *Dendrolagus*, while some of those which are terrestrial are yet more allied to the

SPINY ANT-EATER (*Proechidna*).

last than to the Australian kangaroos. Seven other genera of marsupials belonging to the families *Dasyuridæ*, *Peramelidæ*, and *Phalangistidæ* inhabit New Guinea, and of these, four do not inhabit Australia and one more is only found in the adjacent northern territory. The Monotremata are represented by spiny ant-eaters (*Proechidna*) of two species, allied to the echidna of Australia.

In birds the richness is as conspicuous as is the poverty in mammals. Already more than 400 species of land birds have been discovered, and they comprise a larger proportion of beautiful and gorgeously coloured species than are to be found in any other country. About forty species of birds-of-paradise are now known, and an immense variety of kingfishers, parrots, and pigeons, including the most beautiful and remarkable of their respective families. About forty genera of landbirds are exclusively Papuan, as are considerably more than 300 of the species; and we may be sure that the great mountain ranges still contain many treasures for the ornithologist. The birds-of-paradise are without doubt the chief feature of the Papuan ornis. With the sole exception of Wallace's Standard-wing (*Semioptera wallacei*), which occurs in the Moluccas, no species is found except in New Guinea and its islands. Although differing considerably from each other in form, all have one characteristic in common—the development of abnormal plumage of striking form and brilliant colouring. Thus in *Paradisea* we find magnificent sub-alar plumes of great length, and in colour ranging from deep red to lemon yellow, according to the species. *Parotia* has stiff and wire-like barbs, terminated by a spatulate expansion, springing from above the eye, and tufts of metallic silver at the forehead and occiput. In *Epimachus* the tail is of extraordinary length, and large curved plumes of the richest violet stand out above the thigh. Still more curious are some species of *Diphyllodes*, with the two middle feathers of the tail prolonged and coiled like a watch-spring. In *Lophorhina* a fan of velvet-black feathers springs from the occiput and reaches beyond the tail, while the breast is adorned with a pointed shield of metallic emerald green; and the brilliant red king-bird (*Cicinnurus*) has delicate shoulder-tufts and the discshaped ends of the tail decorated with the same vivid colour. Other genera have similar and not less extraordinary characteristics. Allied to the well-known Australian bower-bird are several species of *Amblyornis*, some of which construct playing or coursing grounds of so remarkable a nature that, were not the facts attested by well-known naturalists, they would be almost incredible. One (*A. Musgracianus*) builds a raised ring

BOWER OF AMBLYORNIS (*A. Musgracianus*).

around a small tree, this miniature circus being about two feet in height and provided with a parapet, the whole having the appearance of a marble fountain, while small sticks placed in various positions on the tree resemble jets of water. But singular as is this bower, it is eclipsed by that of another species (*A. subalaris*). This bird, also selecting a small tree as the centre of its building, forms around its base a bank of moss, which it decorates by inserting flowers. The ring or circus is

round this bank, and the whole is protected from the
sun or rain by a domed construction which completely
covers and surrounds it, except for an entrance at one
side.

The brilliant and singular racquet-tailed kingfishers
(*Tanysiptera*) are almost as much Moluccan as Papuan,
but the same cannot be said of the brush-tongued lories,
which, of many species and varied coloration, have their
true home in Western New Guinea. The parrot family
is here extraordinarily rich in genera and numerous in
species, and includes the great black cockatoo (*Microglossus*), and the pigmy parrots (*Nasiterna*), some of
which are under four inches in extreme length. The
absence of predatory mammalia has permitted the
cassowary—unlike most of the *Ratitæ*—to live in the
forests, and for the same reasons we find stately ground
pigeons (*Goura*), as large as small turkeys, to be exceedingly abundant.

Reptiles on the whole are not very numerous, either
specifically or individually. The widespread *Crocodilus
porosus* abounds in the southern part of the island, but is
seldom seen in the north. The fresh-water tortoises
are for the most part either allied to or identical with
Australian forms, although the recently-discovered
Carestochelys—a species with the paddle-shaped feet of
the oceanic turtles and without the usual horny plates of
the carapace—is peculiar and distinctly un-Australian.
Of the Monitors—a widely-distributed family, but perhaps
attaining their greatest development in Australia—there
are six species, of which half that number are peculiar.
Of other lizards there are about fifty species, the Agamas
being especially well represented. But here, as among the
Chelonians and the Snakes, a foreign element is present
in the genus *Goniocephalus*, which may be regarded as

Indian. About thirty kinds of snakes are known, but only six or seven of these are dangerous. Mr. de Vis classes them in seventeen genera, of which all but four are Australian—a proportion which strongly suggests community of origin in former ages. "But on the other hand," he writes, "when we descend to species we find that fewer than a third of these are Australian as well as Papuan, and that these few include the fresh-water and tree snakes, which have exceptional means of spreading from one land to another. . . . The process of transformation has, therefore, been carried on for a considerable time, but has not endured long enough to effect more than specific changes, save in one instance. So that we are led by the testimony of the snakes to the same conclusion as that gathered from a review of the lizards, namely, that New Guinea was separated from Australia at no very modern period."

Although perhaps scarcely equalling those of South America, the insects of New Guinea offer a great variety of strange forms and gorgeous hues. Conspicuous among the butterflies both for size and colouring are the green and gold Ornithopteras of the *O. priamus* type, the female of which exceeds seven inches across the wings. Still more beautiful is *Papilio penelope* with its metallic blue colouring—a common species, and, like the first, of Moluccan type. Beetles are hardly less conspicuous and interesting. The class, however, is as yet only partially known, and is less to be relied upon to throw light on the former connections of the island than any other.

The Molluscan fauna, on the other hand, is of great assistance in this respect. It is the richest, and by far the most original, of all the Australasian region. To quote the words of Mr. A. H. Cooke, "We find ourselves, almost in a moment, in a district full of new and singular forms. New Guinea may be regarded as the metropolis of the rich Helicidan fauna which is also characteristic of the northern group of the Moluccas, of N.E. Australia, and of the Solomons and neighbouring groups. Here abound species of *Papuina* and *Insularia*, among which are found, if not the largest, certainly the most finished, forms of all existing *Helices*. *Obbina* and *Physota*, genera which culminate in the Philippines, here find their most eastward extension." Considerable traces of a Polynesian element are found, especially in the eastern part of the island (*Partula, Tornatellina, Thalassia*). The land operculates are feebly represented as compared with the true Pulmonata, and are mostly of marked Polynesian type. Not a single *Cyclophorus* occurs, and *Lagochilus*, *Alycæus*, and all the tubed operculates, so characteristic of the Indo-Malay fauna, are conspicuous by their absence. A single *Perrieria* is a very marked feature of union with Queensland, where the only other existing species occurs, and a solitary *Phytida*, so far the only representative of the group of carnivorous snails, emphasises this union still further. Little is known of the fresh-water molluscs, but on the whole the relations appear to be Australian rather than Indo-Malayan.

7. The Papuan Race.

We now come to the consideration of the peoples inhabiting the vast area just described. Whatever opinions may be held concerning the place of origin of the Papuan, there is no doubt that New Guinea—and, still further to restrict, the north-western portion of it—is now the focus of that race. Further, no other race inhabits this area, unless, as is held by some ethnologists, the Karons be of Negrito stock. For as long a period as Europeans have been acquainted with the country, that is to say from the beginning of the sixteenth century, its inhabitants have been known by the name they now bear, the derivation, according to Crawfurd, being from the Malayan *papuwa* or *puwah-puwah*, "woolly-haired." Although the pure race appears to be confined to the north-western part, and perhaps to the interior, the Papuan of mixed blood is found from Flores in the west to Fiji in the east, though his range in point of latitude is not great, and is, roughly speaking, limited by the equator and Torres Strait.

Professor Keane speaks of the Papuan as "one of the most strikingly distinct types of mankind," and the description would probably be acknowledged as just by most travellers acquainted with the pure race. In southern and eastern New Guinea the natives differ widely from the type, and differ also much among themselves in many ways—a fact that has led some observers to the conclusion that the Papuan cannot be regarded as a distinct race. The typical individual nevertheless exhibits such marked characteristics, both physically and mentally, that he forms an extraordinary contrast with his neighbour, the Malay, and it is impossible for any one who has studied the latter people on the one hand, and the Australians and brown Polynesians on the other, to doubt that any such conclusion is erroneous.

The typical Papuan may be described as follows:—He is decidedly tall in stature, much surpassing the Malay in this respect, and being equal, and even superior, to the average European. He is strongly built, but the legs are thin and weak, and he is usually more or less "spur-heeled"; but the hands and feet are large, and contrast greatly with the Malay fineness of bone. The colour of the skin varies from a deep chocolate or sooty-brown to a shade which is not far from black, although never

A PAPUAN OF DUTCH NEW GUINEA.

reaching the true black of some of the African peoples. The skull is dolichocephalic, the jaw prognathous. The lips are full, but never like those of the negro, the face somewhat oval, the brows very prominent. The most characteristic feature is the nose, which is large, somewhat curved, and high, but depressed at the tip. It is thick at the base and the nostrils are broad, and, owing to the *ala nasi* being attached at a higher level on the cheek than in Europeans, a large portion of the septum is left exposed. This is generally transfixed by a nose-bar of bone or shell, which fact is alone sufficient to show to what extent this condition obtains. The hair, dry, frizzly, and rough to the touch, acquires a considerable length, forming a very large, crisp, and mop-like mass, which in its fullest development much resembles a guardsman's bearskin in size, and is the pride and glory of the wearer. The hair is curiously stiff and resilient, so much so that if the hand be laid on one of these compact and elaborately tended coiffures, it meets with almost as much resistance as it would if pressed against a short-clipped European beard. The face is without much beard, but the chest, legs, and forearms are usually more or less hirsute, the hair being short and crisp.

Nor does the Papuan appear to differ less from the Malay in his mental qualities than in his figure and features. Impulsive and demonstrative in speech and action, he gives expression to his emotions and passions in cries and laughter, in ejaculations, and boisterous leaps and gestures. Women and children take part in all their dealings, and seem little disconcerted by the presence of strangers or Europeans. In estimating the intellectual powers of the Papuan, Mr. Wallace places him above the Malay, attributing his actual inferiority to the absence of the deeper influences of more highly-cultured races with whom the Malay has been repeatedly brought into contact. "It appears," he says, "that

whether we consider their physical conformation, their
moral characteristics, or their intellectual capacities, the
Malay and Papuan races offer remarkable differences and
striking contrasts. The Malay is of short stature, brown-
skinned, straight-haired, beardless, and smooth-bodied.
The Papuan is taller, is black-skinned, frizzly-haired,
bearded, and hairy-bodied. The former is broad-faced,
has a small nose and flat eyebrows; the latter is long-
faced, has a large and prominent nose and projecting
eyebrows. The Malay is bashful, cold, undemonstrative,
and quiet; the Papuan is bold, impetuous, excitable, and
noisy. The former is grave, and seldom laughs; the
latter is joyous and laughter-loving; the one conceals
his emotions, the other displays them."

The native of New Guinea usually goes naked save
for a breech-cloth of bark for the men and a fringed girdle
or short petticoat of this or woven grass for the
women. In some places on the northern coast both men
and women go entirely naked. He pays great attention
to his hair, which, though sometimes kept short, is
generally worn in the enormous mop already described,
or partly shaved in front and drawn backwards, or grown
into tassels arranged stiffly around the head, or in a
variety of bizarre fashions too numerous to mention, of
which not the least singular is the training of the hair
through one or more short cylinders of bamboo and
letting it expand into a large ball above, so that the
head looks as if planted with small cabbages. While
those of Malay race seem to have little desire for
personal adornment, the Papuan evinces a great taste for
it, especially on festal occasions. The hair is decorated
with the brilliant flowers of the Hibiscus, or with plumes
of the bird-of-paradise. Through the septum of the nose
is thrust the nose-bar, which is sometimes of shell or

bone, sometimes of wood, and in Eastern New Guinea two boar's tusks are often worn in this fashion, with their tips turned upwards. The comb, especially among the purer race, is one of the most characteristic features of his decoration. It is made of a long piece of bamboo split at one end into prongs, while the other projects beyond the forehead of the wearer to a distance sometimes of a couple of feet or more, and is transfixed with feathers of the parrot or other birds, or by splinters of bamboo bearing discs of pith. Necklaces are worn in almost every part, generally of small shells, teeth, or bones; they often bear a large valve of the pearl-oyster or the snowy *Ovulum ovum* as a pendant. *Conus millepunctatus* and other shells are ground down into bracelets and armlets, but grass or fibre is also much used for arm-bands, and these serve in lieu of pockets, beneath

PAPUAN OF DOREI BAY.

which to tuck any small article. The western Papuan does not paint himself much, but is fond of decorating his breast and arms with raised scars produced by the frequent use of the moxa. Elsewhere the painting of the face and body with various colours—black, white, yellow, or red—is common.

Papuan architecture is in many ways remarkable. The houses are in all cases built on piles, as indeed are those of nearly all Australasian peoples, but communal houses are a marked feature. They exist also in Borneo, as we have seen, but in Papua they are of much larger size. Buildings of this nature, containing many families, are not infrequently over 500 feet in length, and some have been measured over 700 feet. The roofs are often "turtle-back," but in the eastern part of the island ridge roofs and rising gables are seen. Club houses, of the same nature as the "balais" of Sumatra, are found in most villages all over the island, at all events on its seaboard. The very peculiar "dobbos" are apparently more or less confined to British territory. These are houses built in high trees, their use being chiefly that of an acropolis in times of danger, but some tribes who are especially harassed by warlike neighbours appear to live entirely in them.

The Papuan is only a very indifferent seaman. While the Bugis of Celebes think little of voyaging 1000 miles across the Banda Sea to the Aru Islands, the natives of the Papuan Gulf creep along its shores in their "lakatois" with considerable mistrust, usually anchoring at night if they can. The Papuans of Salwatti Island form an exception to this rule, and construct good sea-going praus, which they manage with skill. On the whole the race may be described as agricultural, especially in the eastern portion of the island, where the ground is everywhere cultivated—sweet potatoes, yams, bananas, and sugar-cane being grown, and the fields fenced as a protection against wild pigs. The coco-nut palm is here seen in abundance, but it is far less common in Dutch territory, where agriculture is not so much pursued, sago and fish forming the principal diet. The domestic animals are the pig, dog, and fowl, all of which are eaten. They also eat the cuscus, kangaroos, lizards, fish, and molluscs, as well as many kinds of large insects; and in places where they have no communication with Malays or Europeans they use salt-water for cooking as a substitute for salt. In some parts of German New Guinea they make an intoxicating kava by chewing, as in the Pacific: but this is unusual, and in most places they have no intoxicating drink, and are unacquainted with the art of fermenting either palm-sap or cane-juice.

Among the Malays of the islands we have hitherto considered, the spear and the kris—or some weapon of the same nature as the latter—are the characteristic arms. Here, in New Guinea, we find these more or less supplanted by the bow and arrow and the club. Spears are used, tipped with hardened bamboo or bone; and a kind of whirl-bat of hard wood elegantly carved, knives of obsidian, and axes of jade or greenstone ground to an edge are also met with, the latter resembling those of the stone age found in Europe. Altogether peculiar to the Papuans are the bamboo blow-pipes, which were perhaps used for signalling, perhaps with the object of intimidation, by means of dust blown into the air. These do not appear to have been noticed by travellers since the voyage of Lieutenant Kolff in 1828. The practice was first observed by Captain Cook on the south-west coast, where also the Dutch found it, and the more probable explanation seems to be that it was an attempt to imitate the smoke of firearms, and has been given up now that its uselessness has been discovered.

Although a few of the coast people have adopted a nominal Islamism, and the English missionaries have laboured hard, as have a handful of their Dutch brethren in Geelvink Bay, to win converts to Christianity, the vast bulk of the Papuans are pagan. Their religion, if such a term can be used, consists mainly in a sort of nature-worship—a belief in spirits of the woods and rocks and the sea, almost all of which are of a malevolent disposition. The spirits of the dead wander restless until some abiding-place is prepared for them; hence on the death of any person the relatives proceed to make a wooden image as an earthly habitation for his ghost. This image, or *korowaar*, as it is termed by the Nufoor Papuans, is often carved

KOROWAAR.

with considerable artistic skill, and on its completion a dance is always held. A kind of ancestor-worship is found in Dorei Bay and other places, large temples with caryatid piles being constructed to hold the images of the *Mon* or "first people," and a very similar custom is found in New Britain. Definite notions of a future state are widely held, and the next world believed by some tribes to be beneath the earth, by others above the clouds. Very curious are the strict rules of *tabu* existing in some parts; in some cases these correspond almost exactly with forms of *hlonipa* among the Zulus; thus, for example, the bride and her near relations must avoid the sight of the bridegroom and his people until the marriage. Feasts are celebrated on various occasions, such as marriages, burials, and the like, and are accompanied by singing and dancing. Dancing is, in fact, a leading feature in Papuan life; it is frequently indulged in two or three days, or rather nights, in succession, and barns are sometimes especially built for this amusement on the occasion of great feasts. Cannibalism, though not a general custom, exists in many parts; the Karons of the north-west indulge in the practice, and it is not uncommon among the tribes of the Gulf of Papua.

Foremost among the characteristics of the Papuan are his love of decoration and his sense of form, the latter of which is specially shown in his aptitude for carving. While the West African exhibits an almost entire want of proportion in his work, together with crudeness of design and lack of finish, the carving of the Papuan—especially when it ·is remembered that it is most frequently executed without iron tools—is singularly good both in plan and execution. The pillows or head-rests, formed of two conventional monsters placed back to back and supporting the scroll-work upon which the smooth semi-lunar bar rests, are remarkably good in design, and no two are ever alike. Scroll-work is much used, the *korowaar* figures being usually carved with a hand resting upon a shield of this nature. The praus also are frequently adorned with a figure-head of fretwork, and some of these are of designs which would be creditable to a pupil in a school of art. The carving of the caryatid piles of their temples is less good, and probably intentionally grotesque.

In the islands of the great Australian Archipelago which we have hitherto considered, the tribes and nations inhabiting them have been, as we have seen, for the most part monarchical in their form of government. We find in Java, Brunei, and elsewhere, sultans and princes of more or less power, with a court and nobles. In all, or almost all, there have been, if not rajas or kinglets, at least greater or lesser chiefs to whom the people render some sort of obedience. But in New Guinea we find a totally different state of affairs. Throughout the length and breadth of the island, so far as is known, no system other than that of the most primitive form of socialism exists. Chiefs are unknown. Certain individuals by force of character, or by virtue of their known prowess in war, have more influence than others in their tribe, but this influence seems to be at best but slight, and each person is obedient to himself alone or to some unwritten code of public opinion. It is this fact perhaps more than any other which has so greatly hindered not only the civilisation of the people, but our knowledge of the country. Each handful of people has always lived in a state of perpetual warfare with its neighbours. The Dutch, in their annexations in the Malayan islands, had but to gain this or that Raja by diplomacy or force, and no further question presented itself. In New Guinea European administration is attended by far greater difficulties, since the equal distribution of authority—or rather the want of any authority—renders agreement upon any subject no very feasible matter. It is to this system that is due the formation of innumerable offset tribes, and hence we find that languages or dialects are equally innumerable, and add still further to the obstacles that missionaries and officials encounter in their endeavours to introduce Christianity and civilisation.

The preceding general account is intended to apply to the typical Papuan. A considerable margin must, however, be allowed for individual and local peculiarities. The tint of the skin, the stature, the habits, and even the character, vary considerably, but the best observers agree in considering that such variations imply no difference of race. The people of New Guinea, like all others, have undoubtedly intermingled with many surrounding peoples. Malays have settled on their western and northern coasts, Australians have probably mixed with those living on the shores of Torres Strait, while the brown Polynesians have undoubtedly occupied some portion of the south-eastern promontory. But in every part of New Guinea one physical character remains nearly constant—the frizzled hair—and this alone would suffice to refute the opinion of those who have hastily declared the people of the south-eastern extremity to be undoubtedly Malays.

8. Mission Work in New Guinea.

In Dutch territory Dutch and German missionaries have been at work in Dorei since 1856, and of late two or three additional stations have been established, all of which are in Geelvink Bay. Twenty-eight years from this date the entire result of the work and the sacrifice of many lives was only 16 adult and 26 child converts, so that the mission has not fulfilled the expectations formed of it. The Papuan is bold, self-reliant, and almost entirely devoid of the feelings of reverence and respect,

and no rapid conversion to Christianity, as has been the
case in some of the Pacific islands, is ever likely to take
place in New Guinea.

The missions in British territory have been more
successful. Here native teachers have been largely
employed, chiefly Tongans, Samoans, and Fijians, the
last being found to be the best workers. The field has
been wisely apportioned between the different missions
employed, so that they in no way interfere with each
other's sphere of action. The Wesleyan Mission, established in 1891, occupies the Louisiade and D'Entrecasteaux groups, and the mainland from East Cape to
Cape Ducie; the Anglican Mission, also established in
1891, the whole of the north-east coast from Cape Ducie
to the northern boundary; and the London Missionary
Society all the south coast, excluding the parts occupied
by the missionaries of the Order of the Sacred Heart.
The latter, under the charge of Bishop Verjus, has its
headquarters in Yule Island, and stations on the adjoining coast. The London Missionary Society is under the
management of Mr. Chalmers and Mr. Lawes, who have
both rendered great service to science by their numerous
explorations and careful researches in ethnology. It has
been established for many years, and has done a vast
amount of work. In 1889 it possessed a staff of 10
European and about 100 native workers, and the
stations occupied were over 50 in number. Church
members—that is to say, adults who, having been in the
catechism class for at least a year, and having given
satisfactory evidence of character, have been baptized—
numbered about 500. The children attending school
were 3500. The Colonial Office Report describes the
success of the mission as clear and incontestable. "One
acquainted with the native race and condition of the

country," it continues, "cannot without admiration see what has been accomplished by the veteran members of the mission. So far as one can judge, the Papuan has not, as yet, been deeply impressed by the truths of the Gospel. To religious fervour they are strangers. They cannot be said to be devotees of the Church, or to be otherwise than indifferent to her teaching. But if striking outward manifestation of the working of religious feeling be rare among those under the influence of the mission, it can be said without reserve that the labours of the missionaries have to such an extent modified the ways of thinking and the social relations of the natives, that the good they have done is incalculably great."

Missionary enterprise is not so manifest in the German territory, but the Wesleyans have 3 European and nearly 50 Fijian workers in New Britain and New Ireland, each with a station of his own, and there are said to be numerous converts. Missionaries of the Order of the Sacred Heart are also working in the Gazelle Peninsula.

9. Political Divisions.

Dutch New Guinea.—The extent of the dominion of the Sultan of Tidor in ancient times has already been mentioned. The submission of that monarch to the Dutch gave the latter the suzerainty of the "Raja Ampat," or the "territory of the Four Rajas." This included a large part of Western New Guinea, the exact boundaries of which were undefined. Eventually the 141st parallel of east longitude came for a time to be accepted as the limit. In 1893 the boundary was further altered. Starting from the mouth of the Reusbach River in 141° 1′ 48″, this longitude is followed to the Fly River. The boundary then follows the Fly

River until the longitude of 141° is reached, when this meridian is taken as the limit. The territory thus acquired, although it will be long before Holland can develop it, must be regarded as the most promising of the three portions into which the island has been divided. That of Germany labours under the disadvantage of remoteness, while British New Guinea consists very largely of low, flat, unhealthy land, which is not adapted for European residence or cultivation. The Dutch have an abundance of good harbours and fertile highlands; and a certain amount of trade, which is capable of considerable development, has for over three centuries been carried on with the Moluccas. Their portion forms part of the system of the Netherlands India, and offers fewer difficulties to administration and settlement than does the rest of the island to their neighbours. As yet, however, there are no settlements in any part of the territory, if we except those of the few missionaries in Geelvink Bay. In 1827, as before mentioned, a small fort and garrison was established in Triton Bay, but it was soon abandoned.

The Malays, who trade in paradise-birds, pearl-shell, and a few other natural products with the natives of Dutch Papua, recognise certain subdivisions of the country. The two great north-western peninsulas go by the name of Papua Onin, the northern being called Onin dibawa or Lower Onin, and the southern Onin diatas or Upper Onin. The natives of the western coast of this part have a bad reputation, and the Bugis and Goram men who trade with them never go unarmed, and say that if they cannot agree on a bargain they have to fight. Of all the places in Dutch New Guinea, Dorei is the most important. It was here that Mr. Wallace lived in 1858; and various explorers, Beccari, D'Albertis, Meyer, and others made it their starting-point on their expeditions. It is the focus or capital of the Nufur Papuans, a people of some importance. The typical race has here become rather mixed, as at all trading centres. Westward of them live the Karons, a people who have been described—perhaps on hardly sufficient grounds—as of Negrito stock. The southern shores of Geelvink Bay are known as Wandammen, and are inhabited by a tall race of fine physique. On the coast opposite Jobi Island, which is called Tana Aropen by the Malays, the natives go quite naked. A little beyond, the Amberno River debouches by numerous mouths, forming a very large delta. It was ascended in part by Mr. van Braam Morris, who reached shallow water sixty miles from the sea, and considered that the river is of no great size. It is probable that the main stream was not found, for the size of the delta, and the fact that the water is discoloured and brackish for some distance out to sea, render it probable that the river is really of large size. Humboldt Bay is the limit of Dutch territory on the north coast. It was visited by the *Challenger* on her celebrated voyage. The natives here are very little known, and untrustworthy.

Returning to the south side of the island, the most known and frequented part is the southern shore of MacCluer Inlet, where at Patippi and Segaar Bays a certain amount of Malay trade is carried on, and a rare Netherlands India steamer touches. South of the great Charles Louis range the country becomes flat and marshy. Between Prince Frederick Henry Island and the British boundary are the headquarters of the Tugere tribe, who are the pirates of New Guinea, raiding in large expeditions, and keeping the people of a considerable extent of country in a perpetual state of terror.

German New Guinea.—The remaining half of the

island from the 141st parallel eastward is again subdivided into two nearly equal portions, of which, by an agreement with Great Britain in 1886, Germany possesses the northern, together with New Britain and New Ireland, and the various small islands in the neighbourhood. To this territory the name of Kaiser Wilhelm Land has been given, and, in defiance of the rules of geographical nomenclature, the names of New Britain and New Ireland have been altered to Neu Pommern and Neu Mecklenburg. All this group, including the Admiralty Islands, is collectively known as the Bismarck Archipelago.

This dominion is administered by the New Guinea Company, who exercise the rights of sovereignty delegated to it by imperial letters patent, except where such functions are, in virtue of a special agreement, undertaken either partly or wholly by officials appointed by the home Government. The Commissioner is selected by the Government from the Board of Agriculture, and is supreme; the head of the Company is known as the "Landeshauptmann," and under him are various judges, residents, and other officials. The Company received the imperial authorisation on 17th May, 1885. No arms or spirits are permitted to be sold, and the labour traffic is forbidden except for German plantations. There are five districts — Finschhafen, Konstantinhafen, Stephansort, Hatzfeldthafen, and Mioko — the latter in the Bismarck Archipelago.

Finschhafen, the most important settlement, is situated a few miles north of Huon Gulf. It has a good harbour, and the land in the neighbourhood is especially good, though thickly populated. The scenery is remarkably pretty. Though wooded near the sea, the country immediately inland is hilly and dotted with clumps of trees, presenting the appearance of an English park. The settlement itself, which is far from healthy, shows evidence of much care and order in its well-kept paths and pretty gardens. There are horses, cows, fowls, turkeys, pigs, and many sorts of European vegetables, and all produce is to be had at cheaper rates than in Australia. A hospital, shops, a small police force, and other elements of civilisation exist, and there is steam communication with the other stations. At one time the Queensland steamers ran to Finschhafen, but the Australian immigrants having declined to settle under the Company's laws, they have been taken off. Fever is very prevalent here, and mosquitoes and flies are in some seasons almost a plague. Earthquakes, which are numerous, form another drawback. The natives are friendly, and now that the aims of the Company are better understood, are ready to embrace the trade advantages thus brought to their door. They are essentially an agricultural people, and great numbers of coco-palms are grown. North-westwards from Finschhafen to Cape King William, a distance of 30 or 40 miles, a beautiful series of terraces extend, which are specially suited for cultivation. These are three in number, and are remarkably regular in appearance. They are upraised coral beaches, but nevertheless run no risk of drought, the land being irrigated by countless streams of excellent water. Large native plantations of bananas and yams exist at Fortification Point and other places, and Mr. Wilfrid Powell considers that no better place for a settlement could be found in the tropics than Cape King William. The natives are very clever at irrigation, using bamboo tubes joined with resin, and the houses are built with sides of pandanus-leaf mats, which are rolled up to let in the air and light as the occupier desires. Much pumice is found along the coast, and the cliffs opposite Rook Island are of basaltic formation, and reach a height of 1000 feet.

Between this point and Astrolabe Bay lies the "Maclay Coast," so called after the Russian explorer Miklukho Maklai. It is thinly inhabited, and is believed to have no good harbour. The entire country between Huon Gulf and Astrolabe Bay is composed of much elevated, broken, and precipitous land, and comprises three ranges of great altitude. The most northerly are the Finisterre Mountains, whose eastern peaks culminate in Mount Disraeli and Mount Gladstone, both of which are over 11,000 feet. The summits of the Krätke range, lying immediately to the south, vary from 11,000 to 12,000 feet, and these are believed to be again surpassed by the Bismarck range, which lies not far from the Anglo-German boundary, and is reported to be snow-covered. Some of its peaks are known to exceed 15,000 feet.

Astrolabe Bay contains the two stations Konstantinhafen and Stephansort, which are about 10 miles apart, the latter lying at the head of the bay. Konstantinhafen was badly chosen, having neither protection nor anchorage. It was in this bay in 1871 that Miklukho Maklai built his house and lived among the natives for more than a year. He found them tolerably peaceable, but in as low a state of civilisation as any race on the globe. Numeration often did not extend beyond the number one, iron was unknown, and the old men of the tribe spoke of fire as having only been recently introduced. Even then they were unable to make it, and if by any chance their hearths became simultaneously extinct, which from the smallness of the villages seems to have been a not unfrequent occurrence, they had to journey to the next settlement to relight them. The number of inhabitants in the bay is about 4000. Although fond of hunting, they are chiefly an agricultural people, growing yams, sweet potatoes, and bananas ; but a good deal of the cultivation is done by the women. Maklai introduced maize among them with much success.

From the head of Astrolabe Bay to Hatzfeldthafen, the next station, is a distance of about 100 miles. The coast is bold and precipitous, and without reefs, and the land much elevated, though, as far as is known, without ranges of very great altitude. The development of the station has not been so much pressed as at Finschhafen and in the Bismarck Archipelago, and occasional difficulties have occurred with the natives. A certain amount of planting has nevertheless been undertaken with fair success. Inland from Hatzfeldthafen to the north-west the country is promising, with wide valleys and open tracts of lalang grass alternating with the forest. There is a good deal of native cultivation, and more or less trade among the villages. Sixty miles farther to the north-west, the mouth of the Kaiserin Augusta River is reached, its fresh water colouring the sea for some miles from shore. It is without a delta, and has no bar interfering with navigation, and may be thus considered almost as important a waterway as the Fly River. It has been ascended to a point distant 380 miles from the mouth, at which spot it had still a depth of 10 feet. It is a river which thus affords access to a considerable extent of country, and its value is still further increased by its navigability for large ocean-going steamers for a distance of over 100 miles. The banks are high, but are periodically overflowed during the rainy season. From the Kaiserin Augusta north-westwards towards the Dutch boundary the land is much flatter, these low elevations apparently being continuous with the vast flats of the Fly River basin; but near the source of the latter, and not far from the junction of the boundaries of the three territories, rises the very rugged and precipitous Victor Emmanuel range. It has not yet been visited, but when sighted from the south by Sir William Macgregor, appeared to consist of two distinct chains, of which the northern is the higher, probably attaining an elevation of from 10,000 to 12,000 feet. No settlements have been made by the Germans between the Kaiserin Augusta and their boundary at Humboldt Bay.

The so-called Bismarck Archipelago has been known longer than the coast of the neighbouring mainland, and German traders have had posts on the Duke of York group, which lies between New Britain and New Ireland, since 1878. The two last named islands are the most important in the archipelago, but are still very little known, and the focus of German influence and exploration is chiefly centred in the coasts and islands of the narrow St. George's Channel which separates them. The headquarters of the New Guinea Company were until recently at Mioko, on one of the small islands of the Duke of York group, but owing to the unhealthiness of the site, and for other reasons, it has been removed to Blanche Bay in the north of New Britain. Although a more or less deep sea separates the Bismarck Archipelago from New Guinea, and they are thus, strictly speaking, not Papuan islands, except from an ethnological point of view, they will, for the sake of convenience, be presently described under this heading.

The aims of the New Guinea Company have been chiefly agricultural. Tobacco, cotton, coffee, and cacao have all been grown with tolerable success, especially the two first named. In Konstantinhafen 13,224 lbs. of cotton are said to have been obtained from 25 acres. At all the stations yams, mountain taro, mandioca, and sweet potatoes are cultivated in sufficient quantities to support the natives employed on the plantations. It has not always been found easy to procure labour, nor is the Papuan at first a good labourer, but after patient instruction he greatly improves, if away from his home. Many of the men are drawn from Mioko in the Bismarck Archipelago and from Rook Island, the Company assigning labourers to private settlers. The hire varies from 4 to 10 marks per month. In spite of the limited number of hands available, the introduction of Chinese and Indian coolies has been opposed by the Company. Hitherto copra has proved the most lucrative article of trade, but there are various valuable natural products which have been little exploited, among them massoi-bark and phosphate of lime, the latter being found in some quantity on the Purdy Islands, which lie between the mainland and the Admiralty group. Of the introduced vegetables, pumpkins, beans, tomatoes, and maize have been very successful, the latter being remarkably productive, and greatly valued by the natives. At Ralum, in New Britain, there are 500 acres under coffee and cotton cultivation, the owner being a half-caste Samoan; and at Mioko the Hamburg Plantation Company also grow coffee, apparently with success. Nevertheless, it cannot be said that the outlook is very promising. The difficulties which such experiments must always meet with are still further increased by the remoteness and insalubrity of the country.

British New Guinea.—The British flag has been hoisted at various times and in various places in Eastern New Guinea without further steps having been taken towards actual possession. A more formal act of incorporation with British territory in Australasia was, however, performed on 4th April, 1883, when Mr. Chester, acting under the instructions of the Premier of Queensland, took possession of the eastern part of the island in the name of the Queen. The home Government, nevertheless, did not see fit to confirm this annexation, and it was annulled; but difficulties having subsequently arisen with regard to the action of Germany in Papuan waters, it was resolved in 1884 to make the south-eastern portion British, and in November of that year Commodore Erskine proclaimed it a protectorate. Sir Peter Scratchley was appointed Special Commissioner, but fell an early victim to the effects of the climate, and it was not until 1886 that the Anglo-German boundaries were finally agreed upon. On 4th September, 1888, the protectorate was constituted a colony under an Administrator, subordinate to the Governor of Queensland; this colony, Victoria, and New South Wales guaranteeing £15,000 per annum towards the cost of administration. The area of territory thus acquired is believed to be about 63,000, and with the islands 86,000, square miles. The laws of Queensland have, with a few slight alterations, been instituted. The sale of firearms, powder, and intoxicants is prohibited; no alienation of land from the natives is permitted, and until 1892 the labour traffic as it formerly existed was forbidden, the removal of natives from their own district being contrary to law; but from this date, under certain restrictions, the natives can be hired for labour in any part of the possession. Under the Administrator is a small Executive Council of not less than two persons, and there is an armed constabulary composed of natives, Solomon Islanders, and Fijians. The capital and seat of Government is at Port Moresby, in the central district; the western division is administered from Mabudauan, which is situated almost opposite Cape York; the eastern from Samarai, an island in China Strait; and the Louisiades from Nivani, a small island lying south-west of St. Aignan. At all these settlements courts are held. There are also two stations — Rigo and Mekeo — under Government agents, the former on the coast about 40 miles south of Port

NATIVE OF BRITISH PAPUA (HEATH ISLAND).

Moresby, the other some distance up the St. Joseph River, which reaches the sea in the vicinity of Yule Island.

Broadly speaking, British New Guinea may be divided into two portions, the physical characters of which are in marked contrast—the western low, flat, and marshy; the eastern much elevated, and exceedingly rugged. Beginning at the western boundary, we find the former characteristics strongly apparent. In some places the land is so little elevated that the foreshore left exposed at low tide is as much as 10 miles in width. From here to the Fly River the country is very sparsely inhabited, owing chiefly to the ravages of the Tugere tribe, a cannibal people of nomad, raiding habits, who have their headquarters in the neighbourhood of Prince Frederick Henry Island. The Fly has an enormous embouchure in about 8° 30′ S. lat., with Kiwai Island in its centre. This island is about 36 miles long, and has a population of quite 5000, the people being well disposed, living by fishing and agriculture. In this district the large houses characteristic of New Guinea are especially noticeable, many being 500 feet or more in length, and accommodating some hundreds of people.

The Fly River was first ascended in 1876 by Signor d'Albertis, who explored it for a distance of over 500 miles, and it has since been visited and charted by several English travellers. Sir William Macgregor reached in 1891 a point 605 miles distant from the mouth, beyond which it was impossible for his boats to proceed. It was found that the tidal influence extended to a distance of 150 miles from the sea. Here the river was 600 yards in width and 40 feet in depth, and was estimated to send down 180,000,000,000 gallons of water in the 24 hours, or enough to supply 120 gallons per diem to the entire population of the globe. In lat. 7° 30′ S., that is to say, at about the middle point of its course, the Fly receives its largest affluent, the Strickland, which was explored nearly to its source in 1885 by Captain Everill. The next tributary met in ascending is the Alice, 460 miles from the mouth. Between the junction of these two rivers the course of the Fly forms for some distance the British boundary. Its sources were found, as far as could be judged, to be in the southern outlying ranges of the Victor Emmanuel Mountains. Though affording an excellent waterway to the heart of the country, this fine stream is not of such value as might be expected, for the land it traverses is almost everywhere unfitted for cultivation, and probably very unhealthy. Many of the tribes appear to be of nomad habits, perhaps for this reason, and those of the upper part of the river are not much given to agriculture, living on sago and the produce of their bows and nets. In this part gold was discovered by the Administrator's expedition, but nowhere in payable quantity.

Beyond the mouth of the Fly the coast of the Gulf of Papua appears to be a dead level for a vast distance, intersected by innumerable mangrove creeks and labyrinthine delta-channels of small rivers. The land then rises rapidly as we proceed eastward, until we find ourselves in the high and exceedingly rugged portion of the possession of which mention has already been made. The greater part of the interior of the south-eastern part of the island may be described as mountainous, a more or less continuous range forming the backbone of the country from Mount Yule to Milne Bay, and to this the name of Owen Stanley Range was given by the officers of H.M.S. *Rattlesnake*.[1] The most northern peak of any importance is Mount Yule (10,046 feet), a more or less isolated mass, of volcanic formation, whence the St. Joseph River takes its rise. To it succeeds the group of which Mount Owen Stanley—the highest peak of British New Guinea—is the highest summit.[2] These form a

[1] The extent of this range has been wrongly limited by some writers and cartographers to the mountain mass of which Mount Owen Stanley forms the highest point.

[2] Sir William Macgregor's new name for this peak (Mount Victoria) cannot be retained, the mountain he ascended being without doubt identical with the Mount Owen Stanley of the *Rattlesnake* survey.

wide mass of mountain and ravine, which is described as bristling with peaks and pinnacle-like rocks, and containing hundreds of inaccessible crags and precipices. The most important secondary heights are Mount Albert Edward (12,550 feet), Mount Scratchley (12,250 feet), Winter Height (11,882 feet), Mount Douglas (11,796 feet), and Mount Knutsford (11,157 feet). The whole of this range was explored and Mount Owen Stanley (13,121 feet) ascended by Sir William Macgregor in 1889. This portion of the country is drained by the Vanapa River, across which suspension-bridges of rattan and bamboo, beautifully constructed and of considerable length, are built by the natives. The remaining important peaks of the Owen Stanley range are Mounts Obree (10,246 feet), Brown (7947 feet), Clarence (6330 feet), Suckling (11,226 feet), Dayman (9167 feet), and Simpson (9972 feet).

About 25 miles south of the Vanapa River, which discharges its waters into Redscar Bay, is Port Moresby, the capital and seat of Government, and the headquarters of the London Missionary Society. It has been established since 1873, but is still a very small settlement, containing few European houses except those of the Mission, the Government offices, the jail, printing-office, etc. It is fairly healthy, but the land around is treeless and barren. The rains fall from January to March, but the rest of the year is very dry. From May to October the south-east winds blow strong and regularly, and during this period the Owen Stanley range is generally obscured by cloud. East of Port Moresby, and between the Goldie and Kemp-Welch rivers, lies a broken mountainous country unconnected with the main range, and apparently of volcanic formation. From here almost to the end of the island the interior is practically unknown. There are no rivers of importance, and no settlements of any kind even on the coast except one or two solitary mission stations. Near the southern horn of Milne Bay, on Samarai, a small island in China Strait, is the Government station for the eastern division—an unhealthy and unsuitable locality which will in all probability be eventually abandoned. The north-east coast of the possession is imperfectly known, and has no European settlements. It is a remarkable fact that no lakes are known with certainty to exist in any part of New Guinea, though one has been reported to lie westward of Mount Yule, and another in Dutch territory near Etna Bay.

As yet, not much has been done in the way of agriculture and planting by Europeans. Such trade as exists is almost entirely in natural products, and is carried on only with Cooktown and other Queensland ports. Pearl-shell, timber, tripang, and copra are the chief articles exported. In 1892 tripang to the value of £3400 passed the customs, and copra to £2084. The latter trade is capable of much development, and may possibly become important. A plantation of coffee in Milne Bay is reported to give fair promise of success.

The population of New Guinea has been variously estimated at from one half to two millions, but it is probable that it even exceeds the latter figure. In many places it is very dense. The number of native inhabitants in British territory has been roughly placed at 350,000. Of Europeans there are about 150.

10. The Islands of New Guinea.

The Dutch islands of New Guinea are numerous, and in some instances of considerable size. Beginning at the southern boundary, the first of any importance is Prince Frederick Henry Island. Although 90 miles in extreme length, it is low, perfectly flat, and marshy, and is only separated from the mainland by a narrow channel. It thus partakes of the nature of a delta island, and is of little or no value. To the north-north-west lies the Aru group, a vast congeries of islands, the nearest of which is not less than 70 miles distant from the mainland, yet the intervening sea is so shallow as everywhere to be fished for pearls by the native divers, and the presence of cassowaries, kangaroos, and birds-of-paradise shows the islands to be purely Papuan. The group is compactly massed, and is about 130 miles long by 50 broad, consisting of one island—or, more accurately, land mass—of large size, the Tana besar of the Malays, and innumerable other islands. This Tana besar is divided by numerous narrow channels, resembling rivers, the origin of which it is difficult to explain, the more so as in some cases these marine rivers, as they may be termed, are *culs-de-sac*. Herr Ribbe and another German naturalist resided on the islands for more than a year in 1882, and records that rain fell on 250 days in 12 months' observations. This rainfall, however, was considered unusual, and the islands sometimes suffer considerably from drought. The natives are undoubted Papuans, although they do not cultivate the large mops of hair usually worn by that race. Every family has its peculiar totem, which is carved over the doorway of the house, and the houses are of remarkable construction, built on piles sunk in the solid rock, and consisting of two rooms only, the one surrounding the other. The people are apparently divided into two brotherhoods or confederations— the Uli-luna and the Uli-siwa—which are more or less at enmity with each other. An altogether separate tribe are the

Korongo-eis, a people who dwell in the interior, and have never been seen by Europeans. They are described as having white skins and light hair. On the west coast some of the villages are nominally Christian, and the Malays have also introduced Mohammedanism. For at least three centuries and a half, and probably much longer, trade has been carried on with the Moluccas in bird-of-paradise skins, and as a consequence the natives have long been acquainted with the useful metals, ivory, cloth, and so forth, and ardent spirits. These products, however, pass through many hands, and civilisation has not accompanied them, so that the people are almost everywhere perfect savages, and in many places go entirely unclothed. Agriculture is in a very primitive condition, and sago is the staple food. The land appears to consist entirely of raised coral rocks, covered with dense forest and impassable swamps, and though there are a few hills of about 1000 feet, it is on the whole but little elevated above sea-level.

Mention has been made upon a former page of the little island of Kilwaru, east of Ceram, as one of the great trading centres between the rude savagery of New Guinea and the semi-civilisation of Western Malaysia. We have in the Aru Islands a similar example, except that the trade is more important. The little island of Dobbo, on the west of the larger mass, is the seat of a temporary town or fair during the season, which lasts from January to July or August. The permanent residents are very few, but there are whole streets of houses belonging to the traders who annually flock here. These are Chinese, Bugis, and men from Makassar, Goram, and Java, who come here in native praus as soon as the west monsoon has set in, and open stores for the purchase of the produce of the surrounding islands, of which pearl-shells, tripang, and tortoiseshell are the most important, with edible birds' nests, pearls, birds-of-paradise, and ornamental timber in smaller quantities. The return of the praus is determined by the advent of the east monsoon. The trade many years ago was estimated at £18,000 per annum, and is now probably much greater, and during the height of the season there are between 4000 and 5000 people collected, representing all the chief races of the archipelago. The Dutch are represented by a Postholder here, but no other European resides on the islands, which are remarkable for their unhealthiness.

Misol is the next island we come to, lying 50 miles north of Ceram, but divided from that island by a very deep sea, while, though almost as far distant from New Guinea, the intervening water is very shallow. It is of a compact sub-triangular form, about 50 miles long by 20 wide, mountainous and forest-covered. It contains kangaroos and birds-of-paradise, and the usual characteristic Papuan fauna. The inhabitants of the interior are true Papuans, but on the coast are a mixed Malayo-Papuan race, who are Mohammedans, and are ruled over by a raja tributary to the Sultan of Tidor. This island is seldom visited, and very little is known about it.

Salwatti, Batanta, and Waigiu are three large islands off the north-west extremity of New Guinea. Salwatti, of a roundish form, and about 30 miles across, is separated from the mainland by the narrow Galewo Straits. Batanta, divided from the last-named island by Pitt Strait, is long, narrow, and mountainous. Thirty miles northward we come to Waigiu, nearly 80 miles long by 20 wide, but much cut up by deep inlets, which penetrate from the south almost to the north coast. This island is very rugged and hilly, but with no very lofty

VIEW IN WAKIU ISLAND.

mountains. In the north are hard crystalline rocks, but the south is mostly coral limestone, fissured and worn into many fantastic shapes. The whole is covered with dense forest. Batanta and Waigiu are remarkable for possessing two peculiar paradise-birds, not found in any other island—the Red bird-of-paradise and Wilson's bird-of-paradise. Batanta is almost uninhabited, but in Waigiu the people of the coast live under petty rajas, subordinate to the Sultan of Tidor, to whom they have to pay an annual tribute of paradise-birds, tortoise-shell, and sago. In this island there are "Alfuros" or wild tribes in the interior, as in Salwatti.

Passing eastward to Geelvink Bay, we find two islands at its mouth, the Willem Schouten or Misore group, the easternmost of which is known as Biak, the other as Suk, or Supiori. They are scarcely ever visited, and the interior is quite unknown, but it is believed that no birds-of-paradise exist, though the rare and beautiful crown-pigeon, *Goura Victoriæ*, which is also found on Jobi Island, occurs in abundance. Jobi, or Jappen as it is sometimes called, is of considerable size, being 110 miles long and 10 to 15 in breadth. The village of Ansus on its southern coast carries on a certain trade with Dorei, but the natives, although not so treacherous as those of the Willem Schouten group, are not entirely trustworthy, and are constantly at war with the people of the interior. Dr. Guillemard was told in Ansus that there were seven tribes of "Alfuros" in the island, of which the Natawoi and Roba speak the same language, as do also the Papuma and Arowaba. Those of the Marau, Aiomi, and Ariwawa are distinct, and there are thus five languages exclusive of that of the coast dwellers, all of them sufficiently dissimilar to be incomprehensible to persons of another tribe. The coast people are probably mixed with, or a branch of, the Nufur Papuans—a tribe of considerable importance about the region of Geelvink Bay, who believe Mafur Island to have been their place of origin. Nufur, or a patois of it, is largely used as a *lingua franca* on the coasts of north-west New Guinea, where it takes the place of Malay. Jobi contains four different species of paradise birds.

The Papuan islands belonging to Germany are separated by a wide stretch of sea from those both of the Dutch and English. They are collectively known as the Bismarck Archipelago, and—omitting those of no importance—consist of the Admiralty group, New Hanover, New Ireland (Neu Mecklenburg), the Duke of York group (Neu Lauenburg), New Britain (Neu Pommern), and a chain of volcanic islands bordering the mainland.

The Admiralty group is composed of one large and numerous small islands; the former is distant about 180 miles from Hatzfeldthafen, the nearest point of New Guinea, and is about 60 miles in length by 20 in average breadth, with mountains rising to the height of about 3000 feet. These are believed to be extinct volcanoes, but the greater part of the island seems to consist of raised coral rocks. The Admiralty group was first visited in 1767 by Carteret, whose boats were attacked by the natives, but no Europeans appear to have actually landed until the visit of the *Challenger* in 1875. The people are mop-headed Papuans of the usual type, fond of ornaments, and habile carvers of wood. A peculiar ornament is a circular white plate ground out of a Tridacna shell, on which is cemented a plate of tortoise-shell, cut out into a great variety of beautiful designs, no two being alike. The islanders are ignorant of tobacco and make no fermented drinks, and the metals are unknown to them, their tools and weapons being of stone, shell, or obsidian. They differ from most Papuans in having no bows and arrows, clubs, or shields; and their architecture is also peculiar, the houses in size about 20 by 10 feet— being built on the ground, of an elongated beehive shape, with low walls sometimes made of billets of wood. These and other characteristics probably indicate a mixed origin at a remote period, due to the influx of immigrants from islands to the north and east. The language has some peculiarities which ally the people with the Caroline Islanders rather than with those of New Guinea.

Under the name of the New Britain group are comprehended the remaining islands of the Bismarck Archipelago, which form an enormous horse-shoe with the concavity turned to the west. At the extremity of the northern arm lies New Hanover, and at that of the southern is Dampier Strait. New Britain and New Ireland are by far the largest of the group, around which are scattered a number of smaller islands and reefs. Although their existence has been known to Europeans since the time of Schouten and Le Maire, these lands were little visited up to the establishment of the German protectorate, and for a long time were believed to form part of the mainland of New Guinea. It was not until Dampier sailed, in 1700, through the strait that now bears his name that this supposition was proved to be incorrect. He described them as "mountainous and woody, with rich valleys and pleasant fresh-water brooks," while the small volcanic islands in the strait "vomited fire and smoke very amazingly," as they do at the present day. The whole group, indeed, forms an area of great volcanic activity, of which the Gazelle Peninsula of New Britain may be said to be the centre.

New Hanover is probably about 40 miles by 20 in area, but its coast-line is unsurveyed and the interior practically unknown, the natives being very hostile. It has high mountains, and is apparently very fertile, with many rivers, rich valleys, and plains. The people are said to be of the same race as those of New Ireland.

New Ireland was thought by Dampier to be part of New Britain, but Philip Carteret proved its insularity in 1767. The island is long and very narrow, its length being 240 miles and its width on an average about 15 only. The western end is low and flat, but proceeding eastward the land rises, until, both on the north and south sides, the coast is very bold and abrupt, with mountains of some height in the interior. A neck of low land now succeeds, after which mountains again occur, reaching in about lat. 4° S. a height of 7000 feet. Their summits are very jagged and precipitous, but to what extent these and the other ranges are volcanic is uncertain. In the mountains in the middle of the island chalks and sandstones lie in alternate strata. The shape and conformation of New Ireland preclude the existence of anything but small streams; yet the population is largely agricultural, and in many parts very dense, although the people chiefly live by the seashore. From Count Joachim Pfeil's account it seems as if an immigration from the Gazelle Peninsula to the middle part of New Ireland had taken place, which inserted itself like a wedge between the aborigines, for in appearance, language, and customs the people of that district resemble those of New Britain, and differ from the natives of the rest of the island. The latter are small men, neatly built, lively and cunning, while the inhabitants of the Gazelle Peninsula and central New Ireland are tall, powerful, and full-bodied. Among the peculiar

customs thus imported into New Ireland, and similar to
a practice prevailing among certain Australian tribes, is
the division of the inhabitants of each village into two
classes—the *maramara* and *pikalaba*—marriages within
these groups being strictly prohibited, and punishable
with death in the case of the woman, and heavy fines for
the man. While with the New Britain people the dead are
either buried in the houses or thrown into the sea, the
aborigines of New Ireland burn the corpse and preserve
the ashes. Cannibalism is general; the flesh of the pig
and of man is cooked, but everything else is eaten raw.
Both men and women go absolutely naked. The houses
are small, low, isolated huts about 8 feet by 5, beehive-
shaped, and surrounded by bamboo palisades; the sort of
courtyard thus formed is kept very clean, and serves
as a kitchen and dining-room. There are also larger
common houses for the young unmarried men. Cultivation is fairly advanced. Taro is the chief plant grown,
together with immense numbers of coco-nut palms, but
bananas and sweet potatoes are generally found.

The chiefs have very little authority, the equality of
the individual being as marked a feature here as in New
Guinea. There is no tattooing, but circumcision is practised. Polygamy is general. Very remarkable is the
custom of immuring young girls of six or eight years of age
in cages of palm-leaves like huge extinguishers, out of
which they are not allowed to come until they are to be
married. Some are so shut up for five years, old women
attending them. These cages are placed inside large
houses set apart for the purpose, and the girls are only
taken out once a day to wash, but they never leave the
house. The house itself is surrounded by a reed fence,
so that there is little ventilation within the cages, yet
the girls do not seem to suffer in health. A somewhat

similar practice, to which reference has been made, occurs in some parts of Borneo.

New Britain is 350 miles in length, and like New Ireland very narrow, but more irregular in shape. Its northern coast-line is still very imperfectly known, and is beset by many outlying islands; the south coast is bold and abrupt throughout its entire extent. The north-eastern end of the island terminates in the Gazelle Peninsula, and here the evidences of volcanic activity are most marked. Commanding Blanche Bay, at the very extremity of the island, are the peaks known as the Mother and Daughters, two of which are active. In May, 1878, a volcano suddenly arose in the bay, and close by is a hot-water river, up which a boat can be rowed for several hundred yards, the water in many places being actually boiling. The district is nevertheless very thickly inhabited, and there are small European settlements on Matupi Island and the mainland, as well as at the neighbouring Mioko on the Duke of York group. Here are the stations of the New Guinea Company, the Deutsche Handels und Plantagen Gesellschaft, and an American firm, while a dozen or so of individual traders lead a struggling existence in this and neighbouring localities, copra being the chief export. The Administration owns three steamers, and there is a six-weekly communication with the Netherlands India ships at Batavia. The New Guinea Company and the Wesleyan and Roman Catholic missionaries have exercised a certain amount of influence upon the people in this district, who now begin to be ashamed of their cannibal habits, and themselves attempt in a certain measure to put down crime, bringing in the delinquents for judgment to the Germans; but the bulk of the natives are complete savages—a race of totally naked cannibals. 'They are dirty, and, unlike most Papuans, unskilled in carving and the making of pottery; but fair agriculturists, holding markets at the German stations, to which the people of the interior come. They have a fixed monetary system, the currency consisting of strings of cowries (*dewarra*), plates of shell ground thin, and tobacco. The principal weapons are slings, which are used with great accuracy and force, and spears. The natives are exceedingly clever fishermen, constructing basket and other traps of considerable ingenuity.

In addition to the volcanoes already mentioned and two other active craters to the south of Open Bay—the Father (4000 feet) and South Son (3000 feet)—the greater number of the outlying islands on the north side of New Britain, such as Gicquel, Raoul, Du Faure, Willaumez, and others, are believed to be volcanic, and Duportail is known to be partly active. Cape Gloucester, the extreme west point of New Britain, is a complete nest of volcanoes, which were found by Mr. Wilfrid Powell to be in a state of violent eruption in 1877; a hundred or more craters, large and small, vomiting fire and smoke and fine ashes, the light produced by the eruption at night being sufficient to enable a book to be read. Tupinier Island was at the same time in eruption. From the western end of New Britain extends a series of islands for a distance of about 400 miles along the coast of the mainland, and these also are volcanic. On the 13th March, 1888, Volcano Island was almost engulfed by the sea, producing a tidal wave which caused great damage, and killed the two German explorers Herr von Below and Herr Hunstein, who were at the time on an expedition to the west coast of New Britain.

Although the natural history of the New Britain group shows a close affinity to that of New Guinea, no paradise-birds are yet known to inhabit the islands, and it is probable that none exist. Both the cassowary (*C. Bennetti*) and the white cockatoo are found in New Britain, but, curiously enough, neither exists in New Ireland. Apart from the bats, which are numerous, some thirteen or fourteen kinds being known, the mammalia are limited to about six species, among them being a small kangaroo.

The British islands of New Guinea, although perhaps as numerous, are by no means so important as those belonging to Germany. The Louisiade Archipelago appears to be a continuation of the eastern promontory of the mainland, while to the north of the latter a rough triangle is formed by three groups—the D'Entrecasteaux, Trobriand, and Woodlark islands. A large and thickly-packed mass of islands are grouped round the same promontory, and form the eastern boundary of China Strait. These, with the exception of Samarai, on which is the Government station, are of no great importance.

The Louisiades were probably discovered by Torres as long ago as 1606, but though contributions to our knowledge of them were made by D'Entrecasteaux and Bougainville, it is only quite recently that any details have been obtained of this labyrinth of reefs and islands, and Captain Moresby, during his survey of 1873-74, was the first to make his way through the barrier of reefs at Teste Island. Rossel Island occupies the terminal position in the group. It is 21 miles in length, densely wooded, and composed of stratified rocks rising to a height of 2750 feet. It shows traces of gold. The people are cannibals, and are remarkable as not infrequently exhibiting the very singular dental abnormality of macrodontism, several teeth being joined together. Sudest is the largest and most important of the group, being 45 miles long by about 7 broad. Like Rossel and St. Aignan islands, it is composed of the older rocks, and has produced a considerable amount of gold, but the field is now worked out. When the rush was at its height in 1889, some hundreds of diggers were at work, and the island is in consequence completely explored. St. Aignan is 25 miles long, and has an area of over 100 square miles. It differs from all the islands of the group in having no protecting reef, and the natives are not expert fishermen as are the other inhabitants of the Louisiades. It rises to a height of 3400 feet, and is extraordinarily broken and rugged, being intersected by numerous very deep and narrow gorges. The mass of the island is apparently composed of schists and slates, and a gold-field was opened after the failure of Sudest, but met with a similar fate, the metal being rapidly exhausted. The natives are head-hunters, but apparently not cannibals.

The D'Entrecasteaux Islands are three in number—Normanby, Fergusson, and Goodenough—none of which are surrounded by reefs. All are peopled by head-hunters, and the last mentioned island is conspicuous as the only one where fairly amicable intertribal relations exist. Normanby is 45 miles long, irregular in shape and mountainous, its highest peak 3600 feet. It is thickly populated, as are the others. Traces of gold and tin have been found. Fergusson, the central island, is about the same length, but much larger, having an area of over 500 square miles. It is volcanic, very fertile, and well inhabited. The highest peak, Mount Kilkerran, is believed to be about 5000 feet. A description of the solfataras and hot springs which abound on the western side of the island has been given on a previous page. Goodenough Island, though not more than 23 miles in length, is traversed by a fine mountain range whose bare summits reach an altitude of 8500 feet. They are most probably of volcanic origin. The scenery is described by Captain Moresby as grandly picturesque. The sides of the chief peak—Mount Goodenough—are cultivated to a height of about 2000 feet, and an abundance of mountain torrents dash down its ravines. The natives are clever agriculturists, constructing terraces and building stone walls four feet or more in height round their gardens— the only instance of the kind known in British New Guinea.

The Trobriand group lie about 30 miles north of the D'Entrecasteaux Islands. They are low, coral islands, and densely inhabited, the population probably being not less than 20,000. The natives have undoubtedly a strong admixture of Polynesian blood, and are well disposed. The soil is exceedingly fertile, so much so that the islands have been termed the gardens of British New Guinea. Woodlark Island, though unproductive, is also well populated.

Before leaving the subject of New Guinea, we may glance for a moment at the conditions the country presents with regard to European administration and settlement. The Dutch portion affords various advantages which are not shared by either the British or the German possessions. It is the most easily accessible from the larger centres of civilisation; has carried on a certain amount of trade with the Malays for three or four centuries; is in close proximity to the Moluccas, and can be easily served by the same line of steamers; is only an extension of a vast possession of practically unbroken boundaries; and, finally, has a coast with few reefs, but a number of good harbours. Not only is the German territory far distant from any other possession of that nation, but it is likewise remote from civilisation, and is without doubt very unhealthy.

PAPUAN HOUSE, DOREI BAY.

British New Guinea has the advantage of propinquity with Australia, but it is to be feared that from an agricultural point of view the possession is of little value.

The western portion is a vast extent of flat, sour land and marsh, quite unfit for European population, and unsuitable for the growth of most things except the sago-palm, while the eastern part is nearly everywhere so broken and precipitous as to form an almost hopeless barrier to general cultivation.

The policy adopted by each of the three nations is quite distinct. Holland, rich in the possession of an enormous area of neighbouring land still undeveloped, has been content to let her territory remain untouched. Here and there, in this or that village or island, she has erected her coat-of-arms; and semi-Malay rajas, hardly more advanced in civilisation than the Papuans, hold her insignia. An occasional visit from the Resident of Ternate serves to keep up in the larger coast villages the remembrance of their dependence, but little else is done, and there is not even a Postholder in the whole 150,000 square miles which are believed to constitute her possessions. Germany, on the other hand, has set about her administration with all the ardour characteristic of a nation as yet unversed in the art of colonisation. Ruling through a commercial company, the line adopted has been more or less commercial, and the chief aim is the furtherance of agriculture. Hitherto her efforts have not been as successful as might be desired. England has sought first of all to establish her authority and to introduce order and civilisation. In course of time she will look to the development of the abundant natural products of the country, but cannot now, if ever, hold out hope of success to the European planter. The discovery of gold, by no means an improbable event, would do much to develop the resources of the country, but New Guinea is as yet too uncivilised for such a discovery to be dissociated from a vast amount of suffering and disorder. Meanwhile the progress made has been considerable, and it is claimed by the Administrator that a very large proportion of the coast tribes understand that a Government has been established. Hundreds ask for Government interference when they get into trouble with their neighbours, and over a great part of the coast line a shipwrecked crew would now not only escape murder, but receive assistance. The great obstacles to the progress of civilisation in the island are the non-existence of chiefs or rulers of any kind; the ever-prevailing state of intertribal warfare; and the innumerable languages resulting from this isolation of tribes. The establishment of peace and order cannot be otherwise than a lengthy and difficult task.

CHAPTER XII

THE SOLOMONS, SANTA CRUZ, NEW HEBRIDES, AND NEW CALEDONIA

1. The Solomon Islands.

THE Solomon group consists of a double row of islands extending south-eastward from the Bismarck Archipelago for a distance of about 700 miles. It comprises seven chief islands, all of which are, roughly speaking, of much the same size and shape. In the north-eastern row are Bougainville, Choiseul, Ysabel, and Malaita; and in the south-western New Georgia, Guadalcanar, and San Cristobal. The three first-named are within the sphere of German influence, the remainder were annexed by the British in 1893. The islands are volcanic and mountainous, the mountains being arranged more or less in conformity with the axis of the group.

Bougainville, the most northerly of the group, is the largest, being nearly 140 miles long and 35 broad. It contains also the highest mountain, Mount Balbi (10,170 feet), and two volcanoes in a state of constant activity. Guadalcanar is scarcely less mountainous, though of inferior height, Mount Lammas, the highest point, not exceeding 8000 feet. Savo, a small island lying between it and Ysabel, has a dormant crater, but the volcanoes of

New Georgia and San Cristobal are now apparently extinct. The latter island is largely composed of much altered and sometimes highly crystalline volcanic rocks, which Mr. T. Davies regards as having been formed at considerable depths, and indicating great geological age. In many parts there are evidences of upheaval on a vast scale, such as to lead Mr. Guppy to the conclusion that the islands have not at any time been connected with New Guinea. But on the whole the fauna has such marked affinity with that country that it can hardly be accounted for by such a theory, although the remarkable specialisation of some forms leads to the conclusion that the islands must have been long separated.

The Solomons were discovered, and many of them named, by the Spaniard Mendaña in 1568. For two centuries their position remained unknown, the journals of the voyage having been suppressed; but Carteret reached them in 1767 and Bougainville in the following year. Subsequently they were frequently sighted or touched at by navigators; but the treacherous and bloodthirsty character of the natives always prevented much intercourse. Of late years traders have frequented the islands, and in 1847 a mission was established. Several of these pioneers were murdered, however, and even now travel in most parts is impossible owing to the savageness and treachery of the natives. When Europeans become more familiar to them it is probable that these frequent murders will cease, but at present there is no doubt that the Solomon islanders are more dangerous than any other natives of Melanesia. There are now, nevertheless, not less than thirty white men either resident on the islands or permanently engaged in trade with their inhabitants.

We are indebted to Mr. H. B. Guppy and Mr. C. M. Woodford for the greater part of the information we possess of the group. The islands are nearly everywhere covered with fine forests, the vegetation being described as unusually luxuriant and beautiful, even as compared with the other islands of the Pacific. The forest-trees are magnificent, and tree-ferns of 30 or 40 feet high abound. Besides sandal-wood, ebony and lignum-vitæ grow, and from the fruit of *Parinarium laurinum*, one of the Chrysobalaneæ, a resin is obtained which is everywhere used for the caulking of canoes. Thirteen palms are known, of which no less than six are Arecas. The Banyans are equally well represented. The islands form the limit of many of the peculiar animal forms of New Guinea. Mammals are few. The common Cuscus is the only marsupial, but there are seventeen bats, of which six are peculiar to the group. There are four indigenous rats, of which two discovered by Mr. Woodford are of extraordinary size, being nearly two feet in length. In the avifauna the paradise-birds are wanting, but many distinctly Moluccan and Papuan genera occur, such as *Lorius*, *Nasiterna*, *Geoffroyus*, and *Eos* among the parrots, *Dicæum*, *Graucalus*, *Centropus*, *Macropygia*, and others. Of seventeen species of lizards, seven are peculiar to the group, and five of eleven snakes; but this individuality is perhaps best exhibited in the frogs, of which of thirteen species no less than eleven are peculiar. Among them is the enormous *Rana guppyi*, which attains a weight of between 2 and 3 lbs.; and the group is otherwise remarkable as affording a new family—the Ceratobatrachidæ—peculiar in having both jaws toothed. Such distinct forms prove the insularity of the Solomons to have been established at a very remote period.

The natives of the Solomon Islands exhibit considerable variation both in physical characteristics and customs, the people of Bougainville Island, for example, differing considerably from those of the eastern portion of the archipelago. The preponderance of the Papuan type is, however, unquestionable. Mr. Guppy describes the typical native as of a deep brown colour, with a loose frizzled mass of hair forming itself into a bushy periwig. The nose is short and generally straight, but often arched; the lips prominent, the chin receding. The average height of the men does not exceed 5 feet 4 inches, but the Bougainville people are taller and sturdier, and of deeper colour. The hair is often stained light brown by lime, or of a ruddy or magenta tinge by various coloured earths. It is cut as a sign of mourning. The beard is very variable: in some instances fully developed, but in most scanty or almost absent. The dress is of the slightest, at most a T-bandage, but in many cases, and almost invariably among the inland tribes, the men go entirely naked. In San Cristobal the unmarried women are completely without clothing, and the married women nearly so. The lobes of the ears are often greatly distended, and the septum of the nose pierced as among the New Guinea Papuans, whom they also resemble in their excessive love of personal adornment. The Solomon islander loads himself with bracelets, nose and ear ornaments, necklaces, and girdles, in the construction of which he shows great ingenuity. He makes circular or crescentic plates of pearl-shell, overlaid with open tortoise-shell work, like those of the Admiralty islanders, these being used as pendant ornaments for the chest. The snowy *Ovulum ovum* is also much worn. The necklaces are of small shells, porpoise, dog, or other teeth, and beads. Bracelets ground out of the huge valves of the *Tridacna* are favourite ornaments, and of late traders have introduced imitations of these made in white china. On festal occasions the flowers of the scarlet hibiscus are used for adorning the hair, or are tucked beneath the armlets. Tattooing is less common than the patterns produced in raised scars by the use of the moxa.

Dug-out canoes, and the system of outrigging so widely used in the East Indian Archipelago, are not very frequently seen, the boats being usually built of planks. The large war-canoes, 40 or 50 feet in length, are highly decorated with carving, and with inlaid shells, paint, and tassels of dyed pandanus leaves, and have very high upturned prows. The houses vary much in construction, but most are of small size with a gable roof. Those of the chiefs are larger. As a rule they are not built upon piles. The "*tambu*-house" is a sort of club, corresponding to the large houses for young men in New Guinea and some parts of Sumatra. The war-canoes are also kept here, and the ashes of the chiefs; the bodies of most of those of that rank being cremated, while ordinary persons are generally buried at sea.

Hereditary chiefs exist in almost every tribe. Head-hunting is general, and cannibalism is widely practised. Captain Redlick in 1872 saw a human body cooked whole, and Mr. Perry, an English resident at Makira, told him that he had seen twenty such ready to be served up at one time. Polygamy prevails, and some chiefs have as many as eighty or a hundred wives. The people are agricultural, cultivating the banana, taro, and sweet potato. They are also good fishermen, and not only make good nets, but have many exceedingly ingenious methods of taking fish. The weapons in use in the group are bows and arrows, clubs, spears, and tomahawks, and the wicker shields which are carried are often beautifully ornamented with shell-work.

It will thus be seen that the Solomon islanders closely resemble the New Guinea Papuans, both in manners and customs and physical appearance. The use of kava, however, together with the existence of chiefs, the custom of tattooing, the construction of small houses, and plank-built boats, are non-Papuan characteristics, and point distinctly to the existence at some period of a Polynesian influence.

2. The Santa Cruz Islands.

Lying about 200 miles east of the southern islands of the Solomon group, and about the same distance from the nearest of the New Hebrides, are the Santa Cruz or Queen Charlotte Islands, scattered in their distribution, and none of them of large size. They were discovered by Mendaña during his second expedition in 1595, and they were not again seen by Europeans until 1767, when Captain Carteret rediscovered them. They have since been visited by many exploring expeditions, and have become memorable as the scene of more than one tragedy. Here La Pérouse's expedition came to a sudden and disastrous termination, and Commodore Goodenough and Bishop Patteson were murdered by the natives. All the islands are volcanic, and there are no atolls and few fringing reefs except at Vanikoro.

The group is composed of the Duff Islands to the north-east, the Matema or Swallow Islands, Santa Cruz (Nitendi), Tupua, Vanikoro, Tinakula or Volcano Island; while to the south-east are the small and isolated islets, Tukopia, Cherry Island (Anuda), and Mitre Island (Fataka). Santa Cruz, from which the group takes its name, is about 16 miles long, is densely wooded and well watered, but the natives until recently bore the worst of characters. Here Carteret lost his pilot and boat's crew by the treachery of the people, and Commodore Goodenough was murdered in 1875. Five years later Bishop Selwyn succeeded in ingratiating himself with the natives, and a missionary station was established. Vanikoro is the most southerly of the main group. Its highest peak, Mount Kapogo, has an altitude of about 3000 feet. The island is scantily populated, is covered with dense forest, and is said to be very malarious. On the reefs off the south-west part of the island were lost the two ships of La Pérouse in 1788. Their fate remained a complete mystery for nearly forty years, until Captain Dillon, guided by the discovery of certain relics on Tucopia Island, eventually found the remains of the vessels in 1827, and a cleared spot on the neighbouring beach, where, as he was informed by the natives, the survivors built and launched a vessel from materials obtained from the wrecks. A further search by Lieutenant Bénier of the *Fabert* in 1883 resulted in the discovery of other relics, including a bronze cannon. Volcano Island, or Tinakula, as it is called by the natives, although small and hardly exceeding 2000 feet in height, is remarkable for the constant state of eruption of its crater, which has been apparently active since its discovery nearly three centuries ago. The Swallow or Matema Islands are chiefly noteworthy as the scene of the murder—on Nukapu—of Bishop Patteson, in 1871.

The Santa Cruz Islands are inhabited by a dark-skinned and frizzly-haired people, who bear the marks of the intermixture of two or more races, and may be described as of sub-Papuan stock. They are mostly monogamists, and live under chiefs, and are a fishing rather than an agricultural people, constructing well-built and large canoes, and navigating boldly to long distances. The villages are neat and carefully kept, and often surrounded by stone walls, but the pile-built dwellings so characteristic of the Malay and the Papuan are seldom seen. The people are keen traders, and apparently good-natured and well-disposed, but they are still not to be trusted, in spite of the establishment of mission stations, and anthropophagy still continues. The inhabitants of the Duff Islands, as well as those of Tucopia and Cherry Island, differ entirely in appearance, speech, and customs from those of the rest of the archipelago, and are undoubtedly Polynesians.

3. The New Hebrides.

These islands extend for a distance of over 500 miles in a direction roughly north and south, midway between the Santa Cruz and Loyalty groups. Quiros discovered them in 1606, and, believing them to be a part of the supposed antarctic continent, gave them the name of Australia del Espiritu Santo. It is to Captain Cook, however, who visited them in 1774, that they owe their present name. Many of them are still little known, the character of the natives preventing exploration of the interior. The climate is also inimical to Europeans, malaria and dysentery being common. The entire population is conjectured to be about 70,000, and there are about 120 white residents, of whom about half are French.

The New Hebrides may conveniently be divided into two sections, a northern and a southern. The southern comprises five islands, of which the chief are Aneitium, Tanna, and Erromanga. The first named has had white residents for over fifty years. Although of small size, being hardly more than ten miles long, the island is said to have had at one period a population of 12,000, but this number is now reduced to 1500. Mission stations of the Presbyterian Church have been established in all the five islands, but they have been especially successful in Aneitium, where the natives are all converted to Christianity, and can all read and write. More than forty schools are in existence. There has been no murder on the island for many years, and crime of any kind is almost unknown. Tanna is about 30 miles long by 10 wide, well wooded, and with mountains of 3500 feet. It is exceedingly fertile, and is highly cultivated, and European plantations have been formed on it for some years past. The natives are about 8000 in number. Formerly cannibals, they have now almost abandoned the practice, but intertribal warfare is still very common. The island contains the most formidable volcano in the group—Mount Yasowa. Captain Cook described it as discharging a column of heavy smoke like a vast tree, whose crown gradually spread as it ascended; and it is still active at the present day, Mr. F. A. Campbell stating that the noise of its eruption is distinctly heard upon Aneitium, 40 miles away. The height of this volcano is less than 1000 feet, but the crater was found by Admiral Markham to be 600 feet in diameter. The island is visited by frequent and severe earthquakes, which in 1878 destroyed the harbour of Port Resolution. Erromanga Island is the largest of the southern group, and is high, rocky, well wooded, and in some parts highly cultivated. The natives bear a bad name, and five missionaries have been murdered by them at different times, but this sacrifice of life has not been in vain, for the character of the people has much improved of late, and out of the population of 2500 over 1000 are said to be Christians. Sandal-wood was at one time plentiful on the island, but no system having been adopted for the proper preservation of the species, it is now verging upon extinction. Copra is the chief product of all the islands, but coffee, sugar-cane, nutmegs, and sago have been grown with more or less success.

The northern group of the New Hebrides is more compact, and is composed of about thirty-five islands, some of which are of considerable size. At the north are the Banks Islands, forming a separate group, and memorable as having been discovered by Bligh during his passage to Timor in the open boat in which he was set adrift by the mutineers of the *Bounty*. Of this group the two chief islands are Vanua Lava and Santa Maria or Gaua Island. The natives are for the most part of a friendly disposition, and differ in many ways from those of the rest of the New Hebrides. The New Caledonian Company has stations on some of the islands, and coffee, maize, nutmegs, and pepper are grown; but the most valuable product is rosewood, which appears to be very plentiful. The population is supposed to be about 5000. These and the islands to the south as far as Ambrym form the field of the labours of the Anglican Melanesian Mission.

The islands constituting the main mass of the archipelago lie directly south of the Banks Islands, and are of considerably larger size. Espiritu Santo, the largest, is nearly 80 miles long; Mallicolo comes next, with a length of 55 miles; and Aurora, Pentecost, Ambrym, Api, and Vate or Sandwich Island are, roughly speaking, about equal to each other in size, having perhaps an average area of about 250 square miles. Espiritu Santo is heavily wooded, and has mountains of 5000 feet, and broad and fertile valleys watered by numberless streams. Its beauty and fertility are indeed most striking, and were greatly extolled by Quiros in his report to Philip III. It was on this island, at the head of St. Philip Bay, that he established his settlement "New Jerusalem," on the banks of a stream to which he gave the name of the "Jordan." It was foredoomed to failure, and his settlers had soon to fly to save their lives from the malaria and the spears of the natives. Near Cape Cumberland, the northern extremity of the island, are some very curious ruins, the origin of which is still involved in mystery. The buildings are apparently of great size, monolithic pillars, ruined walls, and masses of cemented masonry being scattered over a plain of about three miles in extent. A second and apparently similar site occurs at a place about five miles distant. These ruins have been by some attributed to the Spaniards, but probably on quite insufficient grounds, and it seems more reasonable to suppose that, in common with the remains on the Ladrones, Carolines, and other islands, they were constructed by some pre-existing race, who have left no other trace behind them, but who may have been, conjecturally, an early immigrating Caucasian people from Indo-China. Of the remaining islands, Vate is perhaps best known to Europeans. It has large plantations, some of which are the property of French companies formed in New Caledonia.

All the New Hebrides are volcanic, but there are a few small outlying coral-reef islands. Numerous extinct craters exist in all the islands, but the peaks of Ambrym and Lopevi, and Mount Yasowa in Tanna, are active, and Vanua Lava sub-active, with thermal springs. Captain Cyprian Bridge describes the southern islands as being the most varied in scenery, Erromanga and Sandwich having step-like terraces faced with precipitous bluffs of coralline limestone, and stretches of open grass land. Good harbours are scarce in the archipelago, which is a drawback to their settlement, as from November to April the weather is often unsettled, and hurricanes not uncommon. The fauna is little known, but there appear to be no indigenous terrestrial mammals except rats, and the variety of the birds is far less than in the Solomon Islands and New Caledonia. The exploitation of minerals has not been taken in hand, but copper, iron, and nickel have been found.

The inhabitants of the New Hebrides vary very considerably from island to island, and show distinctly the hybridism of the race. In some places—as, for example, Pele and Vele, two small islets close to Sandwich Island, and in Aoba or Lepers' Island—there are true Polynesians, tall, light-coloured, and with almost straight hair; but the rest of the natives are dark-skinned and woolly-haired people, who, although without the pronounced Papuan features, are undoubtedly of that stock. Many of the customs are purely Papuan. They use bows and arrows, pierce the nostrils, enlarge the ear lobes, paint their faces in stripes, use the moxa, and have "gods" with the features identical with similar carvings in New Guinea. In character they are excitable and treacherous, and cannibalism, though now less frequent, was at one time a universal practice. The houses vary much in construction, some being round like those in New Caledonia, others consisting of a roof only, coming down nearly to the ground. The villages are often fortified with stone walls, and in some places each house also, thus forming a network of palisades. A curious series of gigantic drums are used in some islands, these instruments being formed from hollowed tree-trunks of various heights and sizes, with a narrow longitudinal slit down the front. They are carved in the shape of human beings, and implanted in the ground, and are used on the occasion of great war-dances and other ceremonies. There are at least twenty quite distinct languages spoken in the archipelago. In the small island of Tanna alone there are no less than six, all mutually unintelligible.

The New Hebrides formed at one time the almost sole recruiting-ground of the labour traffic, the natives being taken away in large numbers— often by force or fraud— to work on the plantations of Queensland, Fiji, and New Caledonia. There is much difference of opinion as to the effects of this traffic. Mr. A. Trollope, who has seen the natives at work in Queensland, thinks it must be beneficial; that the islanders learn lessons of civilisation and that work produces property; that they learn to sow, dig, plant, and to clothe themselves. Mr. F. A. Campbell, who has studied the returned labourer in his native place, gives a very different picture. He declares that the New Hebrideans are not in the least improved, but rather injured, by their three years' labour. Whatever goods they bring home are at once distributed among their friends and relations; they throw off their clothes, paint themselves, and resume with eager delight all the savage practices they have so long been deprived of. The only accomplishment they bring back, and of which they are proud, is the facility of swearing in English. They not only relapse into their old ways, but become more degraded, if that be possible, and certainly more vicious; for the plantations turn out some of the most accomplished specimens of savage scoundrelism imaginable — men who have engrafted on their originally depraved nature the vices of civilisation but none of its virtues. On the whole, there can be little doubt that, viewed in every aspect, there is an overwhelming preponderance of evil in this modified slave trade. The absolute savage cannot be improved by taking him away from his natural surroundings and placing him under totally new conditions and in the midst of a civilisation utterly beyond his comprehension.

The ownership of the archipelago was for a long time a *vexata quæstio*. Owing to various disturbances, for the most part the outcome of the raids of "black-birding" schooners, detachments of French marines were sent from New Caledonia to Mallicolo and Sandwich in 1886. This brought about the Anglo-French treaty of the 24th October, 1887, by which the two powers agree conjointly to safeguard the interests of colonists. Many of the latter are French, the "Société Calédonienne des Nouvelles Hébrides" now being landowners to the extent of 1,750,000 acres. It is this connection with New Caledonia which has given the islands the advantage of steam communication with the outside world, French vessels running from Noumea and calling at the chief ports at regular intervals. An inter-insular steam service was also established in 1890.

4. New Caledonia and the Loyalty Islands.

New Caledonia is the most southerly of the Melanesian islands. It lies in a north-west and south-east direction just within the Tropic, and is distant about 700 miles from the nearest point of Australia. It is 250 miles long, and lies in an almost perfect straight line, having a very uniform average breadth of 35 miles. Its area is estimated to be about 6500 square miles, and it is almost entirely surrounded with coral reefs, which, being situated at a distance of from 5 to 18 miles from the shore, afford ample protection except in very heavy weather. The north-eastern coast is almost straight, but on the opposite side of the island the shore is penetrated by bays and inlets, forming a number of excellent harbours. New Caledonia is very mountainous, exhibiting two parallel ranges which extend, roughly speaking, throughout the length of the island, separated by a main valley, but united in many places by secondary chains. These mountains are rather uniform in height, but while in the north they are continuous, in the southern part they form more or less isolated masses springing from level and marshy plains. An unnamed peak in the north-east reaches the highest altitude (5570 feet), and close to it is Mount St. Panie (5390 feet). In the southern part of the island, about 25 miles north of Noumea, Mount Humboldt rises to the height of 5360 feet. There are no active volcanoes, but there are evidences of old volcanic action, and thermal springs occur. The only river of any importance is the Diahot, which reaches the sea in Harcourt Bay at the northern extremity of the island, and is navigable for 25 miles.

Captain Cook discovered and named New Caledonia on the 4th September, 1774, but did little towards its exploration. It was examined in detail by D'Entrecasteaux in 1791, who lost here his able captain, Huon Kermadec. In 1843 the French hoisted their flag, but owing to the pressure of the British Government this action was disavowed. A few years later the massacre of the survey officers of the *Alcmène* led to reprisals, and Admiral Ferrier-Despointes formally took possession of the island in September, 1853. It was first used as a penal settlement in 1864, and after the Franco-German war large numbers of Communists were sent there. In 1878 a serious revolt of the natives occurred, and many colonists were massacred and plantations destroyed. In its suppression over 1000 Kanakas were killed and great numbers sentenced to penal servitude.

The geological formation is chiefly sedimentary, consisting of schists, limestones, serpentine, and gneiss, with ancient plutonic rocks. The metals are numerous, and in many cases of widespread occurrence, and it is probable that further exploration will show that in this respect a promising future is in store for the colony. Gold, antimony, mercury, silver, lead, copper, nickel, cobalt, and chrome have all been obtained, as well as coal of various kinds. Of the metals named, the five last alone occupy an important position on the list of exports. Gold has been found in many places, but as yet nowhere in quantity except on the left bank of the Diahot river, whence from 1871-75 about £30,000 was obtained. Near the same locality lead occurs, and antimony was worked for some time at Nakety near Kanala on the north-east coast. The copper mines of most importance were at Balade, near the Diahot river, where more than 50,000 tons of very rich ore were raised, but they were given up in 1884. Much copper is, however, produced from the smelting works at Pam. In 1890 the mining of the silver lead ores was energetically resumed. The nickel deposits are of especial value, as the metal is almost everywhere else found in small quantities, there being but few places in the world where it can be worked with profit. The most important mines are those of Kanala and Ballarod, and the smelting furnaces of Thio have lately been in great activity. The coal-beds are believed to occupy a very large area. Of late the Government has charged itself with their exploration, and they are about to be worked; but hitherto they have produced nothing for want of capital and proper labour. It is estimated that the coal, which is said to be of good quality, can be sold at Noumea for as low a price as 12s. per ton. The official report for 1891 gives the value of the year's export of these metals and their ores as follows:—Nickel, £143,804: silver lead, £26,145; cobalt, £11,338; chrome, £11,336; and copper, £6219.

New Caledonia differs from all the other islands of Melanesia in its drier and cooler climate. It is said to be healthier than France, and the weather has been described as a perpetual spring with a moderately hot summer of four months' duration. The rainy season is irregular and ill-defined, but the rains fall chiefly during the first six months of the year. The average annual fall at Noumea is 70 inches. On the east coast, where the mountain slopes are exposed to the prevailing wind, the rains are more frequent and heavier. Cyclones occur, but fortunately not often, as they cause enormous damage to the plantations. The flora is rich and peculiar, over 1100 dicotyledons being known, but the character of the vegetation differs very much according to the locality. Much of the island is bare and arid-looking, or partially clothed with bushes and mast-like pines (*Araucaria Cookii*). In the north only, and on some of the mountain sides, is there any extent of forest country. The sandal-wood, once plentiful, has almost disappeared, but there are many fine timber trees, among them the kauri. The aromatic niauli (*Melaleuca viridiflora*) is closely allied to the cajuput-yielding tree of Buru, and affords a similar valuable oil.

The fauna shows great deficiency in mammalian life. A single *Pteropus* is found, but terrestrial mammals seem to be confined to a rat, which is probably an introduced species. Reptiles are very few. The affinities of the group are not very evident. Mr. E. L. Layard considers that the connection is on the whole greater with Australia than with New Zealand. The avifauna certainly shows this; the genera *Trichoglossus*, *Artamus*,

Graucalus, Lalage, Pachycephala, Myzomela, Glyciphila, and others, point markedly to a western origin, but on the other hand the land-shells differ entirely from those of Australia, not a single *Helix* of the Australian type being found. The most abundant genus is *Placostylus*, which is entirely wanting in Australia.

The natives are a well-made race with frizzly hair, dark skins, and pronounced features, distinctly Papuan in origin, though now much intermixed with Polynesians. They are divided into numerous tribes under chiefs, and the various tribes are bound together by alliance into two main bodies, after a system similar to that mentioned as existing in the Aru Islands. They pierce and distend the ear lobes, wear the scantiest possible clothing, are great lovers of dances, and have large images sculptured in wood in every village. They are firm believers in forest-haunting demons, and until the advent of the French were all anthropophagists. In these and other characteristics the influence of their Papuan ancestry is plainly to be traced. In other respects they do not show this influence. Thus the houses are circular, well and strongly built, and with a high extinguisher-like conical roof, surmounted by an elaborately carved finial, which varies in the chiefs' houses according to their rank. The heads of the children are often artificially malformed, and the use of the bow and arrow is unknown in warfare. Constantly engaged in intertribal fights, the people are far from contemptible opponents, and offered a brave resistance to the French. In the art of agriculture they are superior to every other race of the Pacific, building elaborate aqueducts and irrigating their land with almost as much skill and care as the Balinese. The languages, which are numerous, do not appear to differ from each other so much as in the other Melanesian islands. A

NATIVES OF NEW CALEDONIA

curious feature is the use of the plural by the chiefs in speaking to the people, and by the people in addressing them.

About the middle of this century the population of New Caledonia was estimated at 60,000. It is now known to be 22,000, and there is no doubt that the Kanakas, as the natives are called, are disappearing no less rapidly than the natives of other islands of the Pacific wherever they have come into either friendly or hostile contact with the white man. Internecine warfare, intemperance, and domestic and foreign vices have combined to accelerate the process. Abortion is practised, and the female births are far less numerous than the male, and by many authorities the entire extinction of the people is regarded as near at hand. "Reserves" are apportioned to them in the same way as to the Indians in America, in which no land is permitted to be alienated to whites. Missionaries labour among them, and the pacification of the island is the aim and object of the "Administrateurs." Yet the relations between the Kanakas and their masters is not entirely satisfactory, and probably never will be, for each is mutually suspicious of the other.

Agriculture in New Caledonia is more successful in the hands of the small native farmer than the white colonist, who is much hampered by lack of labour, to remedy which natives from the New Hebrides were largely introduced, as well as a few coolies and Chinese. Maize and taro are the staple native products; rice was until lately hardly at all cultivated, so that as much as £10,000 worth had to be annually imported, but it is now being grown in considerable quantity. Sugar-cane is much grown, and there are several sugar-mills in the colony, but no sugar is exported, and the cane is to a great extent used for the manufacture of the "tafia" spirit, which, sold at the low price of 5d. the litre, does much to demoralise the Kanaka. Cotton has been tried with only partial success, but fairly large quantities of copra and coffee are exported. The growth of wheat was at first believed to be impossible, but later experiments with Australian kinds have proved successful, a return of 42 bushels per acre having been obtained. It is estimated that there are about 120,000 cattle upon the island, and these do well. Sheep are few, the principal obstacle to their success being a species of lalang grass known to botanists as *Andropogon austrocaledonicum*, the prickly seed of which, penetrating the skin of the animal, buries itself in the subcutaneous tissues and eventually causes death.

The imports for the year 1888 amounted to £366,878; the exports to £119,269. The corresponding figures for 1890 are £443,660 and £285,622. Both exports and imports sank after the year 1882, the latter from the reduced number of convicts, the former from the temporary inactivity of the mining industry, but in 1890 a great improvement was manifest in the affairs of the colony. About one half of the total imports are on account of the penal administration. Most of the trade of the island is carried on with New Zealand and Australia in British vessels.

New Caledonia is a colony administered by a Governor, in whom is vested the entire military authority. In the control of civil matters he is aided by a Privy Council. The territory is divided into five arrondissements, which (with the exception of Noumea, which is under the Governor) are controlled by "Administrateurs." There is a Chamber of Commerce and a Chamber of Agriculture, and public instruction is provided by a college and 44 schools, which are attended by over 2000 pupils. A "Conseil Général" elected by universal suffrage has powers nearly corresponding to those of France. The island returns no Député, but is represented in France by a delegate to the Colonial Office.

The penal establishment is the chief feature of the island. There are five classes of convicts, arranged partly in conformity with the French law, which enacts that those condemned to penal servitude for eight years or over are kept for life upon the island, while those of shorter sentences are not permitted to return to France immediately on the expiration of them, but have to undergo surveillance for a further period of three years. The first class, or *libérés*, are practically free, and have either small farms or act as household servants, etc. The second class are employed on farms and public works, and receive regular wages. The

NEW CALEDONIAN FLUTE-PLAYER.

third class are kept at hard labour on road-making and like employments, and are unpaid, but receive very liberal rations. The fourth class are under strict prison discipline, and the fifth are the habitual criminals and incorrigibles. By diligence and good behaviour the convict can raise himself from class to class. Political prisoners are now almost non-existent, the many thousand Communists of 1872 having nearly all returned. There are now about 10,000 persons under the management of the penal establishment, of whom about one quarter are *libérés*, but only 200 women. The Government permit the immigration of women desirous of becoming the wives of *libérés*, and they are entrusted to the care of Sisters of Charity, but there are as yet, comparatively speaking, few families, and the descendants of the convicts are never likely to become a large class as in Australia. Numerous penitentiaries are established near Noumea, while others exist in various parts of the island. Of the latter the most important from an agricultural point of view is Bourail, a town situated in the centre of the south-western seaboard, where the concessions granted to the *libérés* have now become rich plantations. The garrison maintained on the island is composed of 2000 marines and a battery of artillery; and a large force of gendarmerie act as police. The works carried out by convict labour have enormously improved the settled parts of the island. Public buildings, forts, and lighthouses have been erected, hills levelled and swamps filled up, quays constructed, and an excellent supply of water brought to the capital. The means of communication have also been greatly improved. A network of telegraph lines connects the chief towns of the island, and excellent roads have been made. Recently a railway has been laid connecting the capital with Kanala on the north coast by way of Paita, Tomo, and Nakety. Much of the island service is carried on by steamers, and various lines afford regular communication with France, Australia, Fiji, and New Zealand.

Noumea, the capital, is the only town of any size in the colony. It has a population of about 7000, and is beautifully situated. The harbour, formed by Nou Island and the Ducos peninsula, both of which are the sites of penitentiaries, is both safe and roomy. The entire population of the island is probably about 44,000, of whom about 22,000 are natives, 10,000 convicts, 6000 officials and soldiers, 2000 imported labourers, and the rest settlers.

The Isle of Pines, which lies 30 miles from the southern extremity of New Caledonia, is a raised coral island about 8 miles across, which has long been used as a penitentiary by the French. At one period over 3000 Communists were there imprisoned. It is now used for native convicts and the *relégués* or those condemned to life transportation.

The Loyalty Islands,

a natural dependence of New Caledonia, form a small chain parallel to it at a distance of about 70 miles. They are all upheaved masses of coralline rock, and comparatively sterile, but at one time abounded in sandalwood, which is now becoming extinct. They consist of three principal islands, Uea to the north, Lifu, and Mare. The population a few years ago was estimated at 19,000, but is said to have diminished. The natives closely resemble those of the New Hebrides, and thirty years ago were a race of savage cannibals. Now they are, especially in Mare, the most civilised of any Melanesians, except perhaps those of Aneitium. Many missionaries, both Catholic and Protestant, have worked in the islands. There is in all a great dearth of water, and the juice of the coco-nuts forms the usual drink of the inhabitants. Uvea or Uea, the northern island, is the smallest but most fertile of the group. Lifu, occupying the central position, is the largest, and is about 35 miles long by 15 wide. Its town, Chepenehe, is the capital of the Loyalty group and the residence of the French Administrateur. It has a population of about 8000 natives, who are industrious and harmless. The majority of the men wear no dress of any kind. On Mare most of the people are Christians; they build good houses, work, trade, and save money.

In the northern part of Uea there is a regular colony of Polynesians, who are said to have come only two or three generations back from an island of the same name west of Samoa. A similar migration of the dark race seems to have occurred from Mare to Maer or Murray Island in Torres Straits, the name also having been transferred. The resemblance of the people of this latter island to the natives of the Loyalty group was noticed by Jukes.

CHAPTER XIII

THE FIJI ISLANDS

1. General.

FIJI, or more correctly Viti, is a British colony consisting of a rather compact mass of reefs and islands lying about 1900 miles north-east of Sydney, and 1200 miles due north of New Zealand. It is situated between the New Hebrides and Tonga groups, and its centre is crossed by the antipodean meridian and the 18th parallel of south latitude. It is composed of two large islands, Viti Levu and Vanua Levu, several of smaller size, and a large number of insignificant islets whose number has been placed at 250. About 80 are inhabited. The total area of the group amounts to 7421 square miles, so that it is about equal with Wales in size. Viti Levu claims about half of this area, and is thus larger than Corsica. The islands are of volcanic origin, well wooded, and very fertile; the south-eastern or weather side being the most luxuriant, owing to the heavier rainfall. Here the country is covered with a dense jungle, unbroken except by the clearings necessary for plantations, but on the lee side their aspect is very different, and we find open grassy country, here and there dotted with casuarinas and screw pines. Most of the islands are high and mountainous, and rise abruptly from the sea. There is nowhere much level land; hills and lovely valleys succeeding each other from the shore towards the interior, while lofty peaks rise in every direction, and numerous ridges and spurs branch off in endless complexity. Considering their size and rocky nature, the islands are wonderfully well watered, and the two larger have numerous streams, many of which are navigable by boats for a considerable distance inland. The scenery in many of the valleys is very grand, abounding in precipices and gorges, and the soil is everywhere fertile, consisting of decomposed volcanic or coralline formations. In the opinion of Mr. J. Horne, government botanist in Mauritius, there is hardly any land that is not capable of profitable cultivation.

Viti Levu and Vanua Levu, the largest islands, occupy the north-western part of the archipelago. The former, oval and regular in outline, is about 90 miles in length by 65 in width, and has an area of 4112 square miles. It contains the largest rivers and the greatest extent of level land. On its southern coast, with a good and easily accessible harbour, is the town of Suva, now the official capital of the group, the old capital Levuka in the island of Ovalau having for various reasons proved unsuitable. The Rewa, on the banks of which are numerous sugar and other European plantations, debouches near the eastern extremity of the island; it is the largest river in the group, and can be ascended by flat-bottomed steamers for a distance of over 50 miles. Vanua Levu lies to the north-east of Viti, and is of very irregular shape, and though nearly 120 miles long, is not much more than half the size of the latter island, its area being 2432 square miles only. It is traversed from end to end by a range of mountains, the

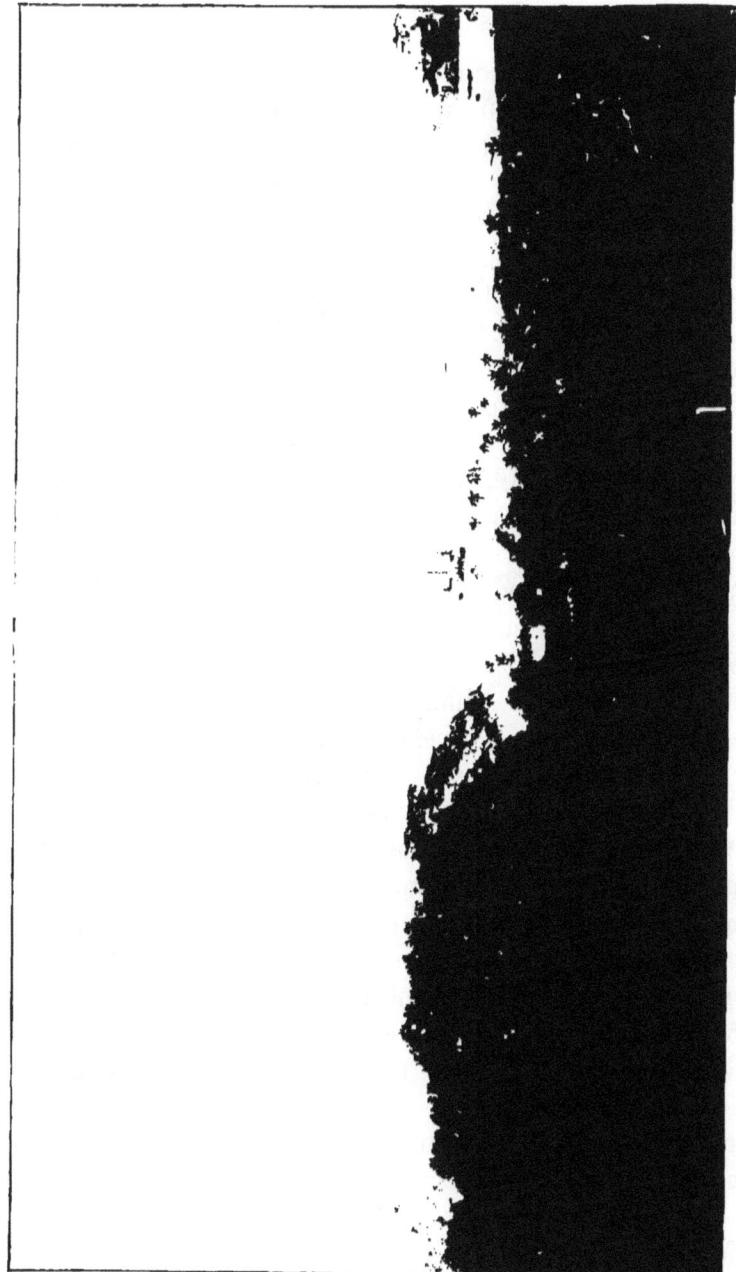

SIVA HARBOUR, IFU

longest slope of which is towards the north-west, with peaks between 3000 and 4000 feet in height. These are covered with dense forests along the watershed, which intercept the south-east trade winds, and, while giving rise to numerous streams, leave the greater part of the island to the north and west subject to long-continued drought. On the south coast, in Savu-savu Bay, are the hot springs of Waikama, which have a temperature within a degree or two of boiling-point, and are used by the natives to cook their food. Taviuni, the third island in point of size, has mountains of 4000 feet, whose slopes are well adapted for agriculture, and many Europeans are consequently established there. Kandavu, the south-westernmost of the group, is thickly populated, and long celebrated for its forests of kauri pine, from which numbers of the large Fiji canoes were built. Another island of some importance is Ovalau, the chief town of which—Levuka—was until recently the capital of the archipelago. It is nearly circular in form and about 7 miles across, and is very mountainous, rising to an elevation of more than 2000 feet, and presenting in this small area of 43 square miles all the features of a great mountain system, with numerous ranges and spurs, beautiful valleys, and narrow gorges. Levuka consists of one long street extending along the beach and occupying almost the whole of the level ground. The dwelling-houses are perched on the rocky mountain-side above the town, and are approached by steep winding paths or steps over rocky slopes. The site was incapable of extension, so that the removal of the official capital to Suva, where there is ample space for a considerable town and suburban population, and ready access to the interior of a large island, was fully justified.

2. History.

Fiji was a discovery of the Dutch, Tasman having passed through the group from east to west in the celebrated voyage in which he made himself famous by the still greater discoveries of Tasmania and New Zealand. From this date—1643—the islands remained practically unvisited for more than a century and a half. Cook anchored off the outlying and southernmost island in 1773, but only for a single night, and Bligh passed the group in 1789 while on his memorable boat-voyage to Timor after the mutiny. Dumont d'Urville was the first to make, in 1827, a detailed reconnaissance of the archipelago, and he was succeeded in 1840 by the American Exploring Expedition under Captain Wilkes, who made a tolerably complete survey. Since then Sir E. Belcher and other English naval officers have filled in the necessary hydrographical details, and land-surveys of the principal islands have been carried out by Government surveyors.

Early in the present century a number of escaped convicts from New South Wales established themselves on Viti, and being men of reckless character and provided with firearms, managed to acquire a considerable amount of power among the murderous cannibals by whom they were surrounded. Partly through their assistance, it came to be recognised that a lucrative, if somewhat dangerous, trade was possible to the adventurous, and schooners soon visited the archipelago in some numbers to obtain *bêche-de-mer*, sandal-wood, and other products. A few years later a small colony of Australians of a rather more reputable character settled in Levuka, and received fresh additions from time to time, especially on the waning of the Californian goldfields. Almost at the same date as this settlement, namely, about 1835, the Wesleyan missionaries began work in the islands, aided by Tongan teachers. The Tongan power had always been dreaded by the Fijians, and had made considerable conquests in the group, and the missionaries, taking the former people as their allies, were able to make the abolition of cannibalism and the adoption of Christianity compulsory on the natives who fell under Tongan rule.

In 1859 King Thakombau, who, in consequence of some alleged injuries inflicted upon an American subject, had been fined a sum of £9000 by that nation, formally offered to cede the islands to Great Britain at the price of the settlement of this claim, but the offer was not accepted, and Fiji remained for some years in an unsettled state as regards its government, an attempt at a Constitution in 1871, which vested almost all the power in the hands of the European planters and traders, having failed. In 1874 Mr. Layard and Commodore Goodenough were sent to report upon the advisability of annexation, and as a result the islands were unconditionally ceded by Thakombau to Great Britain on the 30th September of that year. The little island of Rotuma, about 300 miles north of Fiji, was annexed by the British in 1880.

3. Geology and Climate.

The formation of the group appears to be almost purely volcanic, and everywhere tuffs and basalts, both compact and scoriaceous, give evidence of past eruptive action. At the present time, however, there are no active volcanoes, although extinct craters are numerous, as in Kandavu, the Ringgold Islands, and others. The most striking of these, perhaps, are Totoya, and Mango. The latter, in the southern part of the archipelago, is 6 miles in diameter, and is shaped in the form of a ring, broken towards the south, at which point the sea has burst through what was formerly the lip of a large volcano and filled the crater, forming a circular lake 3 miles across, with fine surrounding peaks and pinnacles, the summits of some of which are over 1000 feet above sea level. The decomposed volcanic rocks have in almost all the islands formed a peculiarly rich and fertile soil, which affords nourishment to a most luxuriant vegetation. The eruptive action must be of considerable antiquity; no traces of recent outbursts are to be found, and no streams of lava or solfataras, though hot springs exist in Viti Levu, Vanua Levu, and Ngau. Earthquakes are of infrequent occurrence. They are said to be most numerous in the month of February: but though several shocks may follow rapidly on each other, they are seldom severe.

Situated as isolated land-masses of no great size, exposed to the constant and beneficent action of the trade winds, the Fiji Islands are on the whole very healthy. Although on the weather side the atmosphere is humid and the vegetation profuse in growth, while on the lee side the air is drier and the soil more or less barren, there is no great corresponding difference in temperature. From observations made at Suva, the absolute maximum and absolute minimum may be placed at almost 90° and 63° Fahr. respectively, and the daily mean at 79. February and March are the hottest months, with a mean of 83°, and July and August the coolest. From June to the end of October is the period of least rain, the heavier rains falling in the hot season, a great advantage from an agricultural point of view; but the rainfall is uncertain and variable both as regards time and quantity. The total annual rainfall at Suva probably averages about 110 inches, but it is undoubtedly much greater in other parts, and may be considered heavy even for a tropical country. Since 1862 the thickly-wooded hills around Levuka have been cleared, as they afforded shelter to mountaineers who in those days often plundered the town, and in consequence the number of rainy days, though not the total rainfall, has been materially reduced. Formerly the rain came in gentle showers which sank into the ground and refreshed the vegetation, whereas it now descends in torrents, and runs off the ground, carrying away the loose soil and doing great damage to both soil and vegetation. It is to be hoped that the Government will strictly regulate the forest growth of these islands, and thus avoid the irreparable deterioration both of soil and climate which has been caused in many parts of India and Ceylon by indiscriminate clearings. The easterly winds are fairly steady from April to November, but during the remainder of the year north and north-west winds frequently blow. A drawback to the islands, much dreaded by the planters, are the cyclones, which are most severely felt in the western part of the group. They occur generally either in January or February, and are sometimes accompanied or followed by a "tidal wave," causing considerable damage, though never productive of the appalling results characteristic of similar phenomena in the Philippines.

The Fiji Islands afford a world-famous example of the virulence which may be acquired by a disease when transplanted to a virgin soil. In 1875 measles was accidentally introduced for the first time into the country by H.M.S. *Dido*, and in a short time about 40,000 of the natives are believed to have perished. The health of the European planters and other residents is very good, the average death-rate being under 16 per thousand. Malarial fever is not common. Dysentery occurs, but is usually not of a severe type. The condition of the natives is not so favourable, civilisation being followed here, as in so many other islands of the Pacific, by the introduction of new diseases, and a corresponding increase in the mortality, and the annual death-rate probably averages over 40 per thousand, the infant mortality being especially great. Nor is this compensated by a correspondingly large birth-rate, the latter, as far as can be gathered, not much exceeding 36 per thousand. These figures, however, are only approximate, owing to the difficulty of obtaining accurate returns.

4. Flora and Fauna.

The dense vegetation of the islands is thoroughly tropical in character. On some of them grow millions of coco-nut palms, of which the Europeans own numerous plantations. The sandal-wood, the chief object of the trader's search in earlier days, is now practically non-existent as an article of trade, being confined to a few localities in the south-western parts of the two larger islands and to gardens. There are various conifers allied to species found in New Caledonia, and from the dakua or Fiji pine (*Dammara vitiensis*) a good deal of resin was at one time obtained; but this tree, like the sandal-wood, is now becoming more or less scarce. The vesi (*Afzelia bijuga*) and dilo (*Calophyllum inophyllum*) are much used for boat-building. In some of the more open parts the vegetation has an Australian character, owing to the presence of phyllodineous acacias, two casuarinas, and several kinds of *Metrosideros*. On the mountains above an elevation of 2000 feet we find hollies; myrtaceous, melastomaceous, and laurinaceous trees; epacridaceous and vaccinaceous bushes, with bright-coloured orchids and delicate ferns and mosses; but no true alpine vegetation exists.

Omitting the Chiroptera, the mammals seem to be confined to three or four different species of rat, of which one is possibly peculiar to the group. Among the birds, which do not differ greatly from those of the Tonga and Samoa groups, are no remarkably specialized forms.

The islands are rather rich in land-molluscs, which show a distinct connection with the Australian molluscan fauna. Most of the shells of the Tonga and Samoa islands are found, but in addition the genera *Placostylus*, *Nanina*, *Diplommatina*, *Pupina*, and *Lagocheilus*; the first-named, as in New Caledonia, being strongly represented. The genus *Succinea*, which is widely diffused throughout the Pacific, has not yet been discovered. Mr. A. Garrett in a recent list enumerates 146 species as known from the group, of which 85 are peculiar to it.

5. People.

The Fijians are a dark-coloured, frizzly-haired, bearded race, reproducing in the east the tall and muscular bodies of the finest of the western Papuans, but much superior to them both in regularity of feature and in degree of civilisation. They exhibit, however, in some parts, signs of intermixture with the Polynesians of Tonga and Samoa, who long ago established colonies in the

Fiji Islands, and have to some extent modified both the customs and the language of the indigenes. Yet they remain undoubted Melanesians, and differ from their eastern neighbours not only in their scanty dress, which is hardly more than that of the savage New Hebrideans, but in using the bow and arrow as a weapon, and in making pottery, both arts being foreign to the true Polynesians.

The people had a regular system of government under chiefs of tribes, of whom there are twelve or more. The tribe, or *matanitu*, is composed of an association of clans, these being termed *galis*, and each *gali* consists of numerous families, or *matagalis*. The manners and morals are in many respects those of a civilised people, yet perhaps nowhere in the world has human life been so recklessly destroyed, or cannibalism been reduced to such a system, as here. Human flesh was, till a generation ago, the Fijian's greatest luxury, and not only enemies or slaves kept for the purpose, but on rare occasions even relatives and friends were sacrificed to gratify it. At great feasts it was not uncommon to see twenty human bodies cooked at a time, and on the demand of a chief for "long pig," which was their euphuism for a human body, his attendants would rush out and kill the first person they met, rather than fail to gratify him. No less horrible were the human sacrifices which attended most of their ceremonies. When a chief died a whole hecatomb of wives and slaves had to be buried alive with him. When a chief's house was built, the hole for each post must have a slave to hold it up and be buried with it. When a great war-canoe was to be launched, or to be brought home, it must be dragged to or from the water over living human beings tied between two plantain stems to serve as rollers. Stranger still, and altogether incredible, were it not vouched for by independent testimony of the most satisfactory character, these people scrupled not to offer themselves to a horrible death to satisfy the demands of custom, or to avoid the finger of scorn. So firm was their belief in a future state, in which the actual condition of the dying person was perpetuated, that, on the first symptoms of old age and weakness, parents, with their own free consent, were buried by their children. A missionary was actually invited by a young man to attend the funeral of his mother, who herself walked cheerfully to the grave and was there buried. In Erskine's *Journal* it is related that a young man who was ill and not able to eat was voluntarily buried alive, because, as he himself said, if he could not eat he should get thin and weak, and the girls would call him a skeleton, and laugh at him. He was buried by his own father; and when he asked to be strangled first he was scolded and told to be quiet, and be buried like other people, and give them no more trouble; and he was buried accordingly.

The weapons of the Fijians consist of spears, slings, clubs, short throwing-clubs, and bows and arrows. Most of these are larger and heavier than those of other Pacific islanders, corresponding to the more warlike character and greater strength of the people. Their towns are often fortified with one or more earthen ramparts faced with stones, and surmounted by a fence of bamboo or coco-nut trunks, the whole surrounded by a deep moat. The houses of the coast people are oblong, 20 to 30 feet long, well built, and with doorways on the two sides 4 feet wide, and only about the same height, but rich men and chiefs have much larger houses.

The doors are of mats, and the floor at the ends is raised a little, and covered with mats for sleeping on. In the mountain districts the houses are square with a central

A NATIVE OF FIJI.

post. Their canoes are well built, of the usual outrigged type, but sometimes more than 100 feet long, double, and of unequal size, the smaller serving as a powerful outrigger. Their agricultural implements were digging-sticks and hoes made of turtle-bone or flat oyster-shells, now replaced by iron. They are skilful in basket, mat, and net making.

The Fijians are cleanly in their habits, and very particular about their personal appearance. They do not load themselves with ornaments, like the more savage Melanesian tribes, and the women only are tattooed. Although so scantily dressed, they are essentially as modest as the most civilised nations, and any public indecency would be severely punished. They have learned many arts from their intercourse with the Samoans and Tongans, but it is the opinion of some that in intelligence they are superior to these people.

6. Religion and Education.

Until the advent of Europeans, the religion of the people consisted in a sort of ancestor-worship. They had priests and temples, a complex mythology, and a firm belief in a future state. The priests were possessed of great power, being much consulted as soothsayers. Circumcision was practised. The temples were of rather elaborate construction, their roofs in the form of a high truncated pyramid surmounted by a large beam with carved and pendent finials; they were surrounded by a walled enclosure, and sometimes built on stone terraces. Human sacrifices were offered. Now the Fijian reads handbooks of theology and the *Pilgrim's Progress*, as well as his Bible, and there is not a single professed heathen in the group.

This great change was mainly effected by the Wesleyan missionaries, who commenced work in Lakeba in the eastern part of the archipelago in 1835. The successes of the Tongans in their invasions of the islands much facilitated their task, and Christianity followed in the wake of the spear and club. But so treacherous were the natives, and so addicted to cannibalism from mere appetite, that the struggle was a severe one, and numbers of the missionaries laid down their lives for the cause. King Thakombau, himself a confirmed cannibal, was at length converted, and human sacrifices abolished, and at the present time there is a church and school in nearly every village. It is not to be supposed that this Christianity is of a very high standard; in a vast number of cases it is no doubt little more than a name, but taking the previous state of things into consideration, the progress made is wonderful, and it is probable that in no place has missionary effort been more successful, and its fruits more apparent, than in Fiji. The Wesleyan missionaries work largely by means of native teachers and ministers, the time of the European staff being chiefly occupied in training and instructing these. All the children go to school, and almost all can read and write. The native clergy are fluent, and often really eloquent, speakers, and make good schoolmasters. In 1891 there were 914 chapels, and 3600 native teachers and ministers, under the management of 11 European missionaries, and the sect claimed over 100,000 adherents. The Roman Catholics have also a numerous following under an Apostolic Prefect and 19 French missionaries, the mission having been established in 1844. There are 178 native teachers, and the education of both native and European girls is attended to by 20 European Sisters. The total number of Roman Catholics in 1891 was returned as 10,500. The Church of England has two churches, one in Suva and one in Levuka. There are three primary schools for the education of European children, with a united average attendance of 250, and the Government Technical School at Yanawai in Vanua Levu instructs about 70 native youths in agriculture, boat-building, and other industries.

7. Agriculture and Trade.

The Fijians have always been good agriculturists, managing their crops with skill and industry, and showing considerable cleverness in their system of irrigation, which is carried out by means of built watercourses and bamboo pipes. They cultivate tobacco, maize, sweet potatoes, yams, kava, taro, beans, pumpkins, and other vegetables, and not a little of their produce is exported. The taxes are often paid in kind. Living in so genial a climate and having so few wants, the Fijian does not of course labour with the persistence and energy of the European, but he is by no means an habitual idler, although he does not bear a good character as a worker among the whites. His independence and the high value he puts upon his services prevent his employment to any great extent in the plantations. The labour question has, indeed, been always more or less a difficulty in the archipelago. In 1879 the first batch of Indian coolies was imported, and since the establishment of the sugar industry many more have been brought into the country, until at the beginning of 1892 there were domiciled over 8000. The coolie works for 1s. per diem, binding himself to his employer for a term of years, the employer having to defray the cost of his passage both ways, which amounts to about £20. The experiment has proved successful on the whole, though crime has considerably increased in consequence, and the propensity of the Indian to go to law on every possible occasion is a further drawback. Recourse is also had to what is officially and incorrectly termed "Polynesian labour"—by which is meant the natives of the New Hebrides and Solomon Islands, and of these there were 2500 in the colony in 1892. In the coco-nut and banana plantations they are preferred to coolies, but for work in the sugar-fields the latter are almost exclusively used. There are no Chinese in the islands.

Fiji has three main exports—sugar, green fruit, and copra. Of these, the first named is by far the most important, over 20,000 tons, valued at £325,525, having been exported in 1891. Eleven sugar mills were at work, and the greatest output is from the Rewa river district. Bananas and pine-apples are sent in great and increasing quantities to Australia, where they find a ready market; and this industry is the second in importance, the value of the export in 1891 reaching £61,000, but a disease affecting the former plant threatens to destroy the plantations. The export of copra was to nearly the same value. Shortly after the British annexation, coffee, cotton, and maize were the chief exports, but the leaf disease ruined the former, and it is no longer grown, while copra and sugar proved more lucrative than the latter. Pea-nuts to the value of £6000 annually leave the islands, and turtle-shell, tobacco, and *bêche-de-mer* in tolerable quantity. Tea, which promised well, is now little grown. It is to be regretted that the cultivation of rice is not more encouraged among the natives, for its success has been proved, and at present more than £10,000 worth has to be annually imported to supply the needs of the population. In the various islands about 40,000 acres of land are under cultivation by Europeans. Of late years the prospects of the colony have not been very good, but in 1891 a great increase in trade manifested itself. In that year the value of the total imports was over £253,000, and of the exports over £727,000, an increase on the preceding year of 22 per cent and 30 per cent respectively. The trade is almost entirely confined to the colonies of New South Wales, Victoria, and New Zealand.

8. Government, Revenue, etc.

The Fiji Islands form a Crown colony administered by a Governor and an Executive Council of three official members. The laws are regulated by a Legislative Council of twelve members, six of whom are heads of departments and six unofficial, nominated by the Governor and appointed for life. The native village and district councils are recognised, and the archipelago is for purposes of native administration divided into twelve provinces, ruled by the same number of salaried native chiefs under the Governor's supervision—an imitation of the Dutch system which has been found to work fairly well. The head of a *Matanitu* or province is termed a *Roko*, and has under him the various *Bulis* or chiefs of the *galis*. While the smaller officials have more frequent meetings, the *Bulis* hold a quarterly court, and the *Rokos*, who are alone responsible to the Governor, meet the latter in annual conclave for the discussion of native affairs. The code in force, although the Acts of the New South Wales Parliament were primarily adopted as the laws of the colony, is arranged to meet the special exigencies of the country, and has been in many ways simplified. It is asserted, indeed, by those qualified to judge, that the legislation of Fiji might afford a model to many older and richer countries.

The colony was started in 1874 by an Imperial grant-in-aid of £115,000, and the Public Debt further comprises a loan of £150,000, bearing interest at 4½ per cent, of which £18,700 only has been redeemed. The revenue rose from £40,000 in 1876 to £91,522 in 1884; in 1891 it was £71,249. The expenditure in the two last-mentioned years was respectively £98,467 and £67,819. In 1888 the revenue first showed a balance over the expenditure, a condition which has been since maintained. It is derived in great part (to the extent of £21,000 in 1891) from native taxation, but chiefly from Customs dues (£31,000).

9. Population, Communications, etc.

That the natives of Fiji have decreased in number to a very considerable extent there is no doubt. In 1859 it was estimated that they formed a population of 200,000. On the 5th April, 1891, the census returned them as only 105,800. The frightful epidemic of measles in 1875 is said to have carried off over 40,000; but apart from this unusual mortality, there has apparently been a steady decrease for a long period. Whether it still continues at the present moment, and if so, to what extent, is not easy to ascertain, for the returns are believed to be not very accurate, and though a decrease of near 9000 was shown by a comparison of the two censuses of 1881 and 1891, it is thought by the authorities to be erroneous. The vital statistics seem to be equally untrustworthy, but the probability is that the Fijians form no exception to the general rule which obtains in so many parts of the world, but more especially in the islands of the Pacific, that the native races are sooner or later inevitably doomed, if not to actual extinction, at all events to something approaching it. The last census gave the entire population of the group as 121,180. Of these 105,800 were natives, 7468 Indian coolies, 2267 "Polynesians," 2036 Europeans, and 2219 natives of Rotuma.

Various lines of steamers connect Fiji with the other British Australasian colonies, running to the ports of Auckland, Sydney, Melbourne, and other places. Inter-insular communication is carried on by small steamers and numerous sailing craft. Carriage-roads are few, but bridle-roads intersect the islands in every direction. In addition to the Government gazettes, two newspapers are published, one at Suva and one at Levuka. There are numerous hotels and banks, a Literary Institute, a Planters' Association, jails, hospitals, and a lunatic asylum. The police consists of an armed native constabulary. A Botanic Experimental Garden has been established for the introduction of species likely to prove of value, and the general furtherance of economic botany. The number of live stock in the colony at the beginning of 1892 was about 10,000 horned cattle, 6000 sheep, and 1000 horses.

Rotuma, a small island of volcanic origin lying about 300 miles north of the Fiji group, was annexed by the British at the expressed desire of its chiefs in 1880. It is about 8 miles long by 2 wide, and is rather thickly populated by friendly natives of mixed sub-Papuan stock, who are said to number about 2500. About the same number have settled in Fiji. All are Christians, having many years ago been converted either by the Tongan Wesleyans or the Roman Catholics. The island is described as being suitable for the cultivation of sugar and cotton, but there are at present no planters, and the natives are a race of sailors rather than agriculturists.

POLYNESIA

CHAPTER XIV

THE FRIENDLY AND OTHER ISLANDS

1. Extent and Component Groups.

POLYNESIA comprises a number of distinct archipelagoes, together with a few smaller groups and scattered islands, distributed over a vast area of the Pacific which may be roughly described as included between the Tropic of Cancer and the Tropic of Capricorn, and bounded on the Australian side by the 180th degree of longitude. Of the larger groups, the westernmost is the Tonga or Friendly Archipelago, with Samoa a little to the north-east. Between these are a few scattered islands, and north of Samoa the small Tokelau group, with the Phœnix group still farther to the north, at no great distance from the Equator. East of Tonga, and in the order named, lie the Hervey or Cook group, the Society Islands (Tahiti), with the Austral or Tubuai Islands to the south of them, and finally the enormous and widespread cluster of islands which are known collectively as the Paumotu or Low Archipelago. The Marquesas are situated almost due north of these, and between them and the Phœnix group already mentioned are several small islands, widely separated, which are of little importance except for the guano yielded by them. The last Polynesian archipelago is that of the Hawaii or Sandwich Islands, situated far away on the northern tropic, with a long chain of smaller islets stretching towards the north-west. Finally, isolated from all other lands by a vast expanse of sea, we have Easter Island, lying about midway between the Low Archipelago and the coast of South America.

2. The Polynesian Race.

As all the Polynesian Islands are inhabited by one race, which differs very little in the several islands, we will give here a brief general description of this interesting people, the Tongans and Samoans being taken as typical examples, except when other islands are specially referred to.

The Polynesians, according to the universal testimony of travellers and residents, are one of the very finest races on the globe. Lord George Campbell, in his description of the voyage of the *Challenger*, says—"There are no people in the world who strike one at first so much as these Friendly Islanders. Their clear, light, copper-brown coloured skins, yellow and curly hair, good-humoured, handsome faces, their *tout ensemble*, formed a novel and splendid picture of the genus *homo;* and, as far as physique and appearance go, they gave one certainly an impression of being a superior race to ours." Captain Erskine, speaking of the same people, says—"The men were a remarkably fine-looking set of people, and among them were several above six feet high, and of Herculean proportions. One stout fellow attracted attention as soon as he crossed the gangway, and I found that

NATIVE OF TONGA ISLANDS.

his arm measured above the elbow $15\frac{1}{2}$ inches, whilst that of one of our forecastle men, probably the stoutest

man in the ship, was but 14 inches." And again—
"The manly beauty of the young men is very remarkable; one in particular, who had decked his hair with the flowers of the scarlet hibiscus, might have sat for an Antinous. Their features are often beautiful, although the nose is somewhat flatter than with us; but this, I believe, is done by the mothers in the children's early youth as an improvement to their appearance." This practice broadens, and to our eye disfigures, the nose, which is naturally rather long and somewhat arched, as shown by portraits, and can hardly differ in its normal state from that of good-looking Europeans. The hair is dark-brown or black, smooth and curly, totally unlike either the frizzled mop of the Papuan or the perfectly straight black hair of the true Malay. They have little beard generally, though sometimes it grows pretty freely. Their average stature is fully equal to that of Europeans. The form of their heads is broad, high, and flattened at the back; the latter feature may, however, be artificial. In character they are cheerful and joyous, fond of dancing and song, and a variety of amusements. Although ceremonious and stately in many of their customs, gloom and moroseness are contrary to their nature. They are very cleanly in all their habits, and have a taste for neatness and order such as never exists elsewhere among people in a barbarous state. Though without written language, they have an abundance of songs and traditions, handed down from one generation to another, as among the ancient bards of our own country.

Although entirely without metals, their native manufactures are very beautiful. They make mats of extreme delicacy, and bark cloth, beaten out to the thinness of fine paper, joined together in rolls sometimes hundreds of yards long, and ornamented with graceful patterns in various colours. Bowls and plates of wood are also manufactured, and cups and bottles of coco-nut shells, beautifully carved and polished. The handles of their implements, clubs, and paddles are carved with a marvellous elaboration, and with great taste, their only tools being formed of stone or shell. Their canoes, sometimes more than a hundred feet long, take many years to build, and are marvels of ingenuity and constructive skill, the planks accurately fitted and fastened together by strong cords, so as to resist the strain of voyages of many hundreds of miles in the open ocean. Their houses are of an oval form, supported on two lofty central pillars, and resting on a row of dwarf posts, the roof strongly formed of rafters and thatch. Their weapons are few and simple, and the art of making pottery is unknown; yet, as they are undoubtedly in a far higher state of civilisation, and far superior in mental capacity to many savage races who possess that art, it is a proof that we cannot measure the status of human advancement merely by proficiency in the mechanical arts. Having no vessels to boil water, their cooking is entirely performed by baking, generally in holes in the ground, a method which, although rude in appearance, is really so satisfactory that we cannot wonder at their not seeking for any other.

Their clothing is simple, consisting of the ordinary T-bandage for the men, and for the women a neat girdle or petticoat formed of dracæna leaves. Sometimes the women use also a garment like the Peruvian poncho to cover the upper part of their bodies, and on state occasions the men drape themselves in voluminous folds of the beautiful *tapa* cloth. The men are usually tattooed in a variety of tasteful patterns from the navel to the thigh, and often around the mouth and eyes also, so that the body looks as if covered with a close-fitting garment of delicate lacework.

These people show how far they have advanced beyond the savage state in nothing more than in their treatment of women, who are no longer beasts of burden or slaves, as among all Melanesian and many Malay tribes, but companions and equals, carefully protected from severe labour or anything that might impair their grace and beauty. The Polynesian women devote themselves solely to household work, making mats and *tapa* cloth, and plaiting ornamental baskets, and they engage only in such light out-door employments as fruit-gathering and fishing, which in their delightful climate is pastime rather than labour.

The Polynesians have for the most part a regular government of chiefs, and a rude religion kept up by priests as the interpreters of the will of their numerous gods, to whose honour lofty temples were raised on mounds of earth. They are warlike, but have none of the savage thirst for blood of the Fijians. They are great orators and undaunted sailors. Their ceremonies are polluted by no human sacrifices; cannibalism with them has never become a habit; they are kind and attentive to the sick and aged, and unlimited hospitality is everywhere practised. The chiefs work as well as the common people, and think it a disgrace if they do not excel in all departments of labour. When first visited by Europeans the people appear to have been remarkably healthy, and the islands were very populous. Captain Cook estimated that the Society Islands then possessed 1700 war-canoes, manned by 68,000 men. Now, the total population of the group is believed to be about 15,000 only! Such has been the effect of contact with European civilisation on a people declared by our great navigator, Cook, to have been "liberal, brave, open, and candid, without either suspicion or treachery, cruelty or revenge"; while the naturalist, Forster, who accompanied him, declared that he "never saw any of a morose or discontented disposition in the whole nation"; and that "they all join to their cheerful temper a politeness and elegance which is happily blended with the most innocent simplicity of manners." It must ever be a subject for regret that a people with so many admirable qualities should be exterminated before our eyes by the relentless march of our too imperfect civilisation.

The traditions of the Polynesians point to Savaii, the largest of the Samoan Islands, as the home of their ancestors, and many peculiarities in language and local nomenclature indicate that the various branches of the race, from the Sandwich Islands to Tahiti, and even to New Zealand, have migrated from this centre. Raiatea, 120 miles west of Tahiti, is another mythological centre to which many traditions refer; as well as Rarotonga, almost midway between Tahiti and Samoa. These may be real indications as to the process of dispersion of the race, but are of little value in determining their origin or first entrance into the Pacific, which must be far too remote an event for legend to afford any trustworthy indications. The antiquity of the people is proved by language and by customs. The languages of all the brown Polynesians are dialects of one common tongue; and because many Malay and Javanese words occur in all these dialects, it has been hastily assumed by many writers that the Polynesians are really Malays, and came direct from the Malay Archipelago, passing by the islands inhabited by the fierce Melanesians till they found unoccupied lands farther to the east. But a more careful study of their language shows, as Mr. Ranken and others have proved, that it is radically distinct from the Malay, in grammatical structure no less than in vocabulary, and that the Malay words after all do not exceed three or four per cent, and are, besides, mostly modern words, not modified roots—a clear indication of their recent origin.

Some evidence of the very remote antiquity of the Polynesians is perhaps to be found in the absence of the art of making pottery among the whole of the race; for it may possibly imply that they left the continent or the western islands before that art was known, its practice being so simple, and at the same time so useful, that, once known, it would probably never have been lost. But on all the great continents and continental islands this is a universal and a very ancient art. There is not a single tribe in the whole Malay Archipelago which does not possess it; and there is evidence in many parts of the world that it dates far back into prehistoric times, and even into the polished stone age. In Eastern Asia, where it attained a high development much earlier than in Europe, it is certainly of extreme antiquity. It may be, however, that during a long process of migration over small coral islands, a process which would probably extend over scores or hundreds of generations, the art of making pottery became lost owing to the want of suitable materials.

We have already seen that their tall stature, their curly hair, their well-formed and rather prominent features, their joyous and laughter-loving dispositions, all separate these people widely from true Malays. Yet they have many characteristics of an Asiatic race, and it seems probable that they came originally, but at a very remote epoch, from some part of Southern Asia. Savaii would be the first lofty and luxuriant island of considerable area that they would meet with, and here they would remain till an overflowing population drove them to seek fresh lands farther east. The slight mixture with the higher class of Melanesians which has occasionally taken place has tended to produce the tall and bulky bodies, the pronounced features, and the slightly curly or wavy hair which distinguishes them from all Mongolian tribes; while it has never been sufficient materially to affect the general lightness of their colour, which has, moreover, been favoured by the preference for the fairest women which they invariably show.

Although the use of the word "Polynesia" as a collective name to include all the islands we have already mentioned has been sanctioned by general custom, it must be borne in mind that the title expresses a purely arbitrary division, founded upon no geographical, national, racial, or linguistic basis. For if it were desired to take the connection of land as our guide, we should have no reason to exclude the Carolines and other islands of Mikronesia. Nationally, Polynesia has never formed a unit, for from the remotest times the people have been split up into innumerable tribes—the inevitable result of the small area and scattered distribution of the islands they inhabit. So, too, with regard to race or language. The Maoris of New Zealand are of the same stock as the Samoans, and the Motu, Kerapuno, and other tribes of Southern New Guinea speak dialects of the same widespread linguistic family. The name, therefore, of Polynesia must be taken only as a convenience to enable us to express certain islands and groups of islands in the Pacific which are inhabited by people of the same stock and linguistic family, but which do not by any means comprise the entirety of this people within their limits.

The peculiarities of the languages of this Mahori

race, as it is termed by Mr. Ranken, have been described by Professor A. H. Keane. Those most remarkable are, he says, as follows :—

1. Their limited phonetic system, consisting of fifteen letters only, five vowels and ten consonants; 2. The absence of *s* in all except Samoan and its direct offshoots Tokelau and Ellice; 3. The great predominance of vowels over consonants, no two consonants ever combining, and no word or syllable ever ending with a consonant, and hence the remark that these are languages "without a backbone"; 4. Their wonderful homogeneity, far exceeding that of the Semitic and all other linguistic families; 5. The almost total absence of inflexion, relations being expressed by *separate particles* preceding and following the unmodified root; 6. Their imperfect differentiation of the parts of speech; 7. The curious practice of "tabooing" words, such as those forming part of a chief's name, either during his lifetime or after his death; 8. Unaccountable and apparently capricious interchange of consonants, such as the universal substitution of *k* for *t* (*kama* for *tama*, etc.) now actually going on in the Samoan group. They agree with the Malayan family chiefly in the possession of a common stock of roots and of certain relational elements. The essential difference between the two consists in their different degrees of development, the Mahori occupying an intermediate position between the isolating and agglutinating, the Malayan having already fully reached the agglutinating state. It is also to be noticed that the literary Mahori, which has grown up of late years, does not always convey a clear idea of its primitive simplicity. The translators of the Bible and other works, partly through necessity, partly through ignorance of its real genius, have introduced a number of neologisms, phrases, idioms, and even grammatical forms, resulting in a new language now currently spoken, especially in Tahiti, which Jules Garnier describes as "si différente de l'ancienne que les vieillards peuvent s'entretenir dans le langage de leur jeunesse sans que leurs fils les comprennent." (*Océanie*, p. 332.) Under such influences it is easy to understand how rapidly Mahori might develop into a perfectly agglutinating tongue.

3. The Tonga or Friendly Islands.

South-east of Fiji lie the Tonga or Friendly Islands, which are divided into three groups—the Tongatabu, Namuka, and Vavau—by two tolerably clear channels. In all they comprise about a hundred islands and islets, of which not more than ten can with justice be placed in the former category. Tongatabu is considerably the largest, being over 22 miles long. Vavau and Eua are next in importance, and there are seven or eight others not less than 5 miles in length. The rest are mere islets. The group is surrounded by dangerous coral reefs, and though the soil is very fertile there is a lack of flowing streams. Most of the islands are low, and consist of raised coral, but there are also a number of volcanic peaks of some height, among which several are active. Kao (5000 feet) has had more than one eruption in modern times; Tufoa, to the west of Hapai, is always smoking, and a considerable eruption took place in 1885. Latte, south-west of Vavau, is sub-active, as is Amargura to the north-west, and there are several other extinct cones. The last-named island was almost destroyed by a violent eruption in August, 1847, the explosions of which were audible 160 miles away. Ashes fell in large quantities on ships 600 miles to the north-east. Previous to this eruption the island was fertile and populous, but it is now barren and treeless and without inhabitants. The people escaped, warned by the violent earthquakes which preceded the eruption.

The Tonga Islands were discovered by Tasman in 1643, and were next visited by Cook in 1773, and again in 1777, on which occasion he stayed three months. The natives belong to the fair Polynesian race, and surpass all the other South Sea islanders in their mental

TONGAN WOMAN.

development, showing great skill in the structure of their dwellings and the manufacture of their implements, weapons, and dress. The Wesleyan Mission was established in 1826, and the people are now all Christians. Almost every one can read, and there is a regular and efficient government under a native king, the treaty between England and Germany in 1886 assuming the autonomy of the group. " It is to the credit of the new State," writes Captain Cyprian Bridge (*Proc. Roy. Geog. Soc.*, 1886), " that its public expenditure is small, that it has been for years perfectly orderly, and that there are in the group probably five times as many miles of carriage road as there are in our own colony of Fiji." These latter are mostly made by prison labour, and the Tongans have always excelled in their construction. At the time of their conquest of Samoa, more than two centuries ago, they made numerous roads in those islands, the traces of which remain to the present day. The people are also admirable boat-builders and sailors, visiting all the adjacent islands in their fine canoes. Latter-day civilisation has introduced cricket, of which they are very fond, and they have become good riders, horses having been introduced for some years. The Tongan dialect is harsher than the Samoan, and is supposed to have been influenced by contact and admixture with the Fijians. The population has been variously estimated at from 23,000 to 30,000, and it does not seem clear whether it is diminishing or increasing, for while in 1839 the estimate of the missionaries placed it at only 18,500, it was conjectured in 1847 to be between 40,000 and 50,000.

Tongatábu, of which Ninkalofa is the capital, is the most important and most visited island, although of no great size. Its area is 128 square miles, its dimensions being about 22 by 8 miles. It is very low, and its surface almost a dead level, its highest point being only

60 feet above the sea. Although purely coralline, the soil is remarkably fertile, though not very deep. The products are chiefly copra, sugar, cotton, coffee, and arrowroot, of which the first-named is the most important export. The trade is mostly in the hands of the Germans, but lately the English have settled in some numbers. The total value of the exports in 1888 surpassed £66,000. In the southern part of the island there is a remarkable monument, consisting of two perpendicular rectangular blocks of stone of great height, deeply morticed to support a large slab across the top, which at one time was surmounted in the middle by a large bowl of the same material. Its history is entirely unknown. A figure of this most interesting monument is here given. Bearing in mind the numerous other stone monuments scattered widely over the islands of the Pacific, from the Carolines to Easter Island, it may be safely concluded that some race, with a different, if not a higher civilisation, preceded that which now exists.

The Tonga group suffer from a somewhat unhealthy climate, the rains being excessive, while both earthquakes and hurricanes are frequent. In October, 1885, a violent submarine volcanic eruption took place about 48 miles N.N.W. of Niukalofa, resulting in the emergence of an island nearly three miles in length by one in width.

4. The Samoa or Navigators' Islands.

North of Tonga some 350 miles is situated the Samoa group, first discovered by Bougainville in 1768, and called by him the Isles des Navigateurs; and visited nineteen years later by La Pérouse, who lost here by massacre De Langle, commandant of the *Astrolabe*, and eleven others. By the Treaty of Berlin of 1889 the autonomy of the

TRILITHON AT MAU'I, TONGA ISLANDS.

islands is guaranteed by Great Britain, Germany, and America, but their future is still uncertain. Owing to the intrigues of foreign adventurers, the government has been very unsettled; a chronic native war has prevailed since 1875, and in 1893 a crisis occurred which added still further to the political difficulties which harass the little State. Under a settled government there is very little doubt that the islands would become prosperous enough. Samoa has been described as one of the loveliest, most agreeable, and productive of all the South Sea groups, and the fertility of the soil is such that the cultivation of tropical plants yields abundant returns, and the means of subsistence are perhaps more easily obtained than in any other part of the world.

For all practical purposes Samoa may be described as consisting of four islands: two small—Tutuila and Manua; and two of considerably greater area—Savaii and Upolu. All are volcanic, and for the most part surrounded with fringing reefs, but the intervening seas are quite free from dangers; and the presence of good harbours, and the fact that the islands lie in the steamer track between Sydney and San Francisco, render the group of importance. The total land-area is estimated at 1100 square miles. Savaii, the largest island, is compact and quadrangular in shape, with a length of about 40 miles and an area of 657 square miles, or more than half that of the entire group. It is nevertheless the least fitted to support a large population, having been so recently subject to volcanic action that much of its surface is absolutely sterile. It has many extinct craters, chief among which is the peak of Mua, which rises to a height of 4000 feet, and another of 5413 feet in the centre of the island. Going inland from the district of Aopo, the traveller passes over a tract of country thickly strewn with scoriæ and ashes, which are evidently of very recent origin, so that the native tradition of the last eruption having taken place only 200 years ago is probably correct. In the north-west of the island are also many miles of lava-plains, but little altered; and in the east there is an older and larger lava-bed partly decomposed and covered with a scanty vegetation. In spite of a considerable rainfall, Savaii possesses only a single river, owing to the porous nature of the vesicular lava, which offers a large extent of heated surface, so as to evaporate the greater part of the moisture, while the remainder sinks down and appears as springs near the coast. The mountainous interior is thus entirely waterless and barren, so that even the natives cannot traverse it. It is a solitude destitute of animal life, alternately parched by a tropical sun and deluged by fierce rain-storms, and affording neither food nor permanent water. The narrow belt of fertile soil which in places extends between the mountains and the sea is, however, exceedingly beautiful, covered with a luxuriant vegetation, and with lofty groves of coco-nut and fruit trees. It supports a population of about 12,000.

Upolu, the next island to the eastward, is the most important of the group. It is extremely fertile, and contains the capital, Apia, which is the residence of numerous Europeans. A range of small mountains, 2000 feet in height, runs through its entire length, the peak of Tafua, at the western end, forming a perfectly rounded lava-cone, with a crater filled with dense forest. Another, Lauto, forms a crater-lake. The island is forest-clad to its highest point, and the scenery of the southern shore is magnificent. The town of Apia contains numerous stores, chiefly German and American; various schools and churches, hotels and other buildings. It is, in fact, a European town, having a municipal government distinct from Samoan legislation secured to it by treaty. A few miles to the west is the village of Malua, where the Training College of the London Missionary Society has been established for nearly fifty years. Here are trained the native missionaries, who are afterwards sent to every part of the Pacific. The college is almost entirely self-supporting, a large estate being farmed by the students, of whom there are generally not less than 100.

Tutuila is chiefly noteworthy as the scene of the *Astrolabe* tragedy, and as possessing one of the finest harbours in the South Sea Islands, Pango-pango, which by a treaty in 1878 was conceded to the United States as a naval and coaling station. Manua, and its two satellite islands, Ofu and Olosenga, form the easternmost limits of the group, but are of no importance.

The Samoan Islands are very subject to hurricanes, which occur generally between December and April. In April, 1850, Apia was almost entirely destroyed by one, and on the 19th March, 1889, three German and three American men-of-war, together with several merchant vessels, were wrecked, and many lives lost, in one of these cyclones, H.M.S. *Calliope* being the only ship in Apia harbour which escaped. Earthquakes are also frequent, but not at all severe, and they do little damage owing to the elasticity and strength of the buildings, which are entirely constructed of posts and light rafters securely lashed together. Evidences of volcanic activity, long past or recent, are abundant. In 1866, a submarine volcano came suddenly into eruption near Olosenga Island, vomiting forth rocks and mud to the height of 2000 feet, killing the fish and discolouring the sea for miles round.

The fauna, like that of most of these oceanic groups,

SAMOA

is exceedingly limited. An indigenous rat of small size is said to exist, and there are four species of snakes. Among the birds is one most remarkable species— *Didunculus strigirostris*— a ground pigeon of metallic greenish-black colour, with bright chestnut back and wings, and a beak of extraordinary shape, which forms a link between the living African *Treronince* and the extinct Dodo. It is now found only upon the island of

DIDUNCULUS.

Upolu, where it is very rare, and will probably soon become extinct.

The Samoans are said to be the fairest of all the Polynesian races, and although not so much advanced in the arts and manufactures as some of their neighbours, surpass them all in many of the characteristics of a true civilisation. Captain Erskine remarks that they carry their habits of cleanliness and decency to a higher point than the most fastidious of civilised nations. Their public meetings and discussions are carried on with a dignity and forbearance which Europeans never equal, while even in the heat of war they have shown themselves amenable to the influences of reason and religion. The former warlike and rapacious character of the Samoans has in fact undergone a complete change since the year 1836, when the archipelago became a chief centre of missionary zeal. All, or almost all, are nominally Christians, chiefly owing to the efforts of the London Missionary Society, who have over 200 native missionaries in the group; but the Roman Catholics and Wesleyans are also well represented.

The political dissensions of the last few years have gradually reduced agriculture to a very low ebb. The Consular Reports of 1893 state that the Samoans have almost entirely neglected all cultivation of the soil, and are so indolent that they actually buy from traders the dried kava root to make their national beverage, sooner than take the trouble of planting a few kava shrubs near their huts, although when once planted the tree requires no trouble or attention. Coolies' wages vary from three to six shillings per diem, and labour is hard to obtain, although to supply this want natives of the Carolines and Marshall Islands have in recent years been frequently introduced. The imports and exports, which in 1883 were £93,607 and £52,074 respectively, sank in 1890 to £43,626 and £20,509, and there has been only slight improvement subsequently. Almost every tropical product seems to succeed, but few are apparent in the list of exports. Copra to the value of £25,000 was exported in 1892, and about £2000 worth of cotton. A little fruit is sent to the Australian market, and cacao has recently been planted. The carrying trade is chiefly in German hands, that of 1892 being £40,000, as against £22,000 shipped by British vessels; but, on the other hand, the imports from the British colonies of

Australia and New Zealand—for there is little or no direct trade with England—were nearly $2\tfrac{3}{4}$ times greater in value than those of any other nation. The population is probably about 36,000, of whom about 300 are Europeans. Steam communication exists with Australia, New Zealand, San Francisco, and Tahiti, the latter island, like Samoa, being a great emporium of South Sea trade.

5. Savage Island.

Savage Island, or Niuë, situated nearly midway between the Tonga and Samoa groups, is a small and very fertile island, about nine miles long, of raised coral rock, and interesting as having a population of mixed Samoan and Melanesian blood. They speak a Samoan dialect, and say their ancestors came from that island, and found a black population, with whom they have intermixed. They are now wholly converted to Christianity, and are found to be a very intelligent, mild, and interesting race, and by no means the dangerous savages they were long supposed to be. Their numbers in 1864 were over 5000, and they are said to increase at the rate of $2\tfrac{1}{2}$ per cent annually. If this be true, we may probably attribute it to the fact that the island is too small to attract any visitors other than the missionaries; and it becomes most valuable evidence that Polynesians may be civilised without being exterminated, if they are only protected from the rude competition, the vices, and the diseases which free intercourse with the ordinary class of Europeans invariably brings upon them. The population in 1892 was, however, said to number 5070, so that, unless emigration has taken place, this report of increase is incorrect. In Mr. Brenchley's *Voyage of the*

Curaçoa, is a most interesting account of this island and the condition of its population in 1865.

6. The Union and Ellice Islands.

The little Tokelau or Union group lies about 350 miles N.E. of the easternmost of the Navigators' group, and consists of three small islands, inhabited by a Christianised people closely resembling the Samoans, and speaking an allied dialect. The population is about 500, and the islands produce little but copra.

The Ellice group, lately annexed by Great Britain, is about 700 miles N.W. of Savaii, and consists of a number of low coral islands and atolls, arranged in nine clusters, extending over a distance of 360 miles in a N.W. by N. and S.E. by S. direction, which axis is common to most of the groups of this part of the Pacific. The population numbers about 2500, and almost all are Christians, mission posts having been established on many islands. All can read, and most write. The inhabitants of Nui speak the language of the Gilbert Islanders, and have a tradition that they came from that group. All the others speak a dialect of the Samoan language, and say they came from Samoa thirty generations back. They have a very ancient spear or staff, which they claim to have brought from Samoa, naming the particular valley they came from. This valley was visited by a missionary, to whom they lent this spear, and he found there a tradition of a large party having gone to sea and never returning, and, moreover, that the wood of which the spear was made was of a kind that grew there. We have here proof that traditions of migrations among the Polynesians may be trusted, even when so remote as thirty generations, or 600 years. In 1863 three-fourths of the population of the island of Nukulailai were kidnapped by Peruvians, under the pretence that they were expected missionaries from Samoa. All these islands are coralline atolls of only a few feet elevation, covered with coco-nuts, and supplying only these, pandanus fruit, and yams in the way of food.

7. The Hervey Islands or Cook's Archipelago.

South-east of Samoa about 700 miles is the scattered Hervey or Cook Archipelago, consisting of nine islands, either volcanic or coralline, and rendered difficult of access by dangerous reefs and the absence of harbours. Rarotonga, the largest, is volcanic and hilly, with fertile and well-watered valleys. It is about 30 miles in circumference, and its peak has an altitude of 2900 feet. It is inhabited by people who have legends of their migration from Samoa, and speak a closely allied language. They say they found black people on the island; and the fact that they have more pronounced features, more wavy hair, and are darker and more energetic than the Samoans, is quite in accordance with this statement. In Mangaia, farther south, this Melanesian type predominates, the people being dark brown, with wavy or frizzled hair, and well bearded. They have still more prominent features than the Rarotongans, and wilder manners, and forty years ago were fierce man-hunters and cannibals.

The natives of this group are now in an advanced state of civilisation. They all read the Bible, dress after the European fashion, and live in stone dwellings grouped in little townships under separate chiefs. They number at present scarcely more than 11,000, of whom 3500 are in Rarotonga alone. They petitioned in 1864 for annexation to Great Britain, and a protectorate was established in 1888. The islands produce coco-nuts, bread-fruit, bananas, coffee, cotton, arrowroot, and tobacco. Many of the natives go as plantation coolies to Tahiti.

8. The Society Islands.

We now come to a group of islands of some importance, which form the chief possession of France in the South Seas. This nation has acquired not only the Society group, but also the Paumotu or Low Archipelago, the Marquesas, the Tubuai or Austral Isles, and the Wallis and Gambier groups. She also claims Manahiki, and taking into consideration New Caledonia and the Loyalty Islands, the land area of her possessions in the South Pacific is probably as great as, if not greater than, that of any other European power.

The Society Islands, eleven in number, and forming a chain in the direction from north-west to south-east, are amongst the best known in the South Sea, and are divided by a wide channel into the Leeward and Windward groups. Amongst the former are the so-called four kingdoms of Huahine, Raiatea, Tahaa, and Borabora, where the natives, aided by the white settlers, for long maintained a spirit of independence, keeping aloof from the rest of the confederacy that earlier accepted the French protectorate. The eastern group includes Eimeo or Moörea in the west, Maitea in the east, and Tahiti in the centre, this last famous for its enchanting scenery. All together have an area of 650 square miles, with a population of 18,000 souls. They were discovered by Quiros in 1606, but for a long time lost sight of, to be rediscovered by Wallis in 1767. Cook gave them the name by which they are now known, and it was on Tahiti that the transit of Venus was observed by him in

1769. From this and other observations the position of the island has been ascertained with as great or greater accuracy than that of any other point in the Pacific. The Windward group came formally into the possession of France in 1880: the Leeward Islands were not ceded till 1888. The islands form one of the earliest posts of the London Missionary Society, who began work here in 1797.

The French administration combines all the groups of islands above mentioned. The Governor resides in Tahiti, and has under him five chief officials, of whom the Ministers of the Interior and of Justice, together with two others nominated by the Governor, form the Privy Council. There is also a General Council of eighteen members elected by universal suffrage. The religion is chiefly Protestant, but there are a good number of Roman Catholics, and a small colony of monogamous Mormons, who have built themselves a temple in the mountains of Tahiti.

Tahiti,

the Otaheite of Cook, is the principal member of the group. It is 35 miles long, has an area of over 600 square miles, and is populated by about 11,000 persons. It presents the appearance of two nearly circular islands united by a very low and narrow neck of land, each of which is of volcanic origin and very mountainous, rising in a succession of bold circular terraces towards the central peaks, and having a broad plain all round the seaboard, which is practically the only inhabited part. Its delightful and healthy climate brings to maturity all the products of the tropics, which are nowhere found in greater fulness and perfection than here. The wayfarer is soothed by the fragrance of sweet-smelling flowers, and delighted with the abundance of oranges, bananas, bread-

VIEW IN TAHITI.

fruit, and coco-nuts which supply perennial food to the natives. The guava, introduced at the beginning of this century, has run wild in such abundance as to have become almost a pest. The beauty of the island has been extolled by almost every traveller who has visited it. In Captain Cook's description, he says:—" Perhaps there is scarcely a spot in the universe that affords a more luxuriant prospect than the south-east part of Otaheite. The hills are high and steep, and in many places craggy; but they are covered to the very summit with trees and shrubs in such a manner that the spectator can scarcely help thinking that the very rocks possess the property of producing and supporting their verdant clothing. The flat land which bounds those hills towards the sea, and the interjacent valleys also, teem with various productions which grow with the most exuberant vigour, and at once fill the mind of the beholder with the idea that no place upon earth can outdo this in the strength and beauty of vegetation."

Tahiti is entirely formed of lavas and other volcanic products, but it is so very ancient, and has suffered so much denudation, that its craters have entirely disappeared, enormous valleys have been excavated, and a wide belt of excessively fertile soil been formed around its base. The American geologist Dana considered it to present the most wonderful and instructive example of volcanic rocks to be found on the globe. The fantastic shape of these is no doubt due largely to sudden upheaval and disruption. Remains of plants and insects similar to those now living in the country are found under some of the ancient lava flows, showing that the formation, as well as the denudation, of the island is, geologically, a recent phenomenon.

This terrestrial Eden is peopled by one of the finest races in the world, whose slightly veiled, or even fully displayed, symmetrical proportions did not fail to excite the admiration of the first European discoverers. Recent opinions, however, are less enthusiastic on the subject, and Von Popp, amongst others, remarks that if we now look in vain for the gigantic race described by Captain Cook, their deterioration is due, partly at least, to civilisation and brandy; notwithstanding which the natives of Tahiti are still a fine, well-proportioned people, tall and robust, with dark-brown complexion, broad nose, slightly protruding lips, beautiful teeth, black and mostly curling hair, but with slightly developed beard. With Christianity some restraint has been introduced amongst the islanders, who formerly indulged in unbridled licentiousness. At present we must visit the remoter villages to see, in their original forms, the seductive dances of the native women, gaily decked with flowers. But all this will soon vanish, with the people themselves, who, like the Sandwich Islanders, are decreasing with alarming rapidity. The idyllic scenes of former days have already mostly disappeared under the influence of the missions; the short and picturesque national garb has been lengthened and rendered unsightly; the Sunday songs and dances have been prohibited; and to harsh treatment, intemperance, and epidemics thousands have fallen victims.

One chief cause, probably, of the decreasing numbers of these people is the prevalence of habits of intoxication, in which they indulge as a substitute for the dance and song and varied amusements so injudiciously forbidden by the missionaries. A recent French traveller, M. Jules Garnier, informs us that the Tahitians now seek the mere sensual pleasure of intoxication, unenlivened by the social enjoyments of their ancient festivals. Most fatal gift of all, they have been taught to ferment the juice of the orange, so abundant and delicious in their island home, and thus produce a liquor with which to obtain the pleasures and the penalties of intoxication, which men, women, and children alike enjoy and suffer. The orange has been for these people as the forbidden fruit of the garden of Eden—the tree of good and of evil.

In the Society Islands, as in many other places in the Pacific, are to be found a number of buildings which testify to the existence in former times of a people of a higher development. They are generally in the form of terraces or platforms, placed in elevated spots, and formed of hewn blocks of stone which are often of great size. In the centre is placed a sort of massive altar. A very large building of this kind exists at Papawa in Tahiti. From a base measuring 270 feet by 94 feet rise ten steps or terraces, each about 6 feet in height. The object of these *morais*, as they are termed, is not very clear. They were in many cases no doubt of a monumental, if not sepulchral, nature; but sacrifices were apparently offered upon them in some instances, and it seems that they also served on occasion as forts or strongholds.

The natives themselves only cultivate sufficient to supply their daily wants, and sell the surplus produce of their orange and coco-nut groves; but on the southern side of the island, in the district of Atimano, a large plantation belonging to an English company was established some years ago. It possessed 10,000 acres of rich land, and imported 1600 Chinese coolies to cultivate it. The forest was cleared away, and the land planted with sugar-cane, cotton, and coffee, while broad roads bordered with plantains and fruit-trees traversed it in every direction. The establishment of this gigantic farm formed a small town picturesquely situated near the sea, and the undertaking promised to be very successful, but reckless speculations caused its failure, and the land now lies waste. Attempts have been made by the French authorities to induce the natives to engage in agriculture, but in vain. Imported labour has not hitherto succeeded, owing to the regulations not giving the planter sufficient hold over his men, and on the whole the agricultural outlook is not promising. The immigration of coolies from Tonquin is contemplated. The French have apparently done all in their power to remedy the state of affairs. The Government even receives the produce of the small cultivators and exports it for them, so as to do away with the profits of the middlemen.

The chief export is pearl-shell, the value of which in 1890 was nearly £60,000. That of copra is not much less. Cotton (£10,000), vanilla (£3000), and oranges (£2000) are the only other noticeable products.

Papeete, capital of Tahiti, is a little city of the most violent contrasts. All the races here settled are represented by a total population of about 5000, of whom about 1000 are Europeans. The "Rue de Rivoli," with its "Palais de Justice," "Trésor Colonial," etc., leads by Government House and the Royal Palace to the "Place de la Cathédrale." The "Rue de la Pologne" shows the bright and dark sides of this little Paris of the antipodes, while a row of Chinese "stores" and "tea-shops" recalls the Chinese quarter in San Francisco. Papeete is the emporium of trade for the products of the South Sea Islands east of 160° E. longitude. Small schooners of from 20 to 50 tons burden bring the produce of the various groups to Tahiti, whence they are shipped direct for Europe either by Cape Horn or the Cape of Good Hope, according to the season of the year. These schooners, of which about twenty fly the Tahitian flag, take back portions of the cargoes of vessels arriving from Europe for sale or barter amongst the islands. The harbour is good, and a despatch boat and four small gunboats form the local force, and Tahiti is also the centre of the French Pacific squadron. The garrison is composed of a small force of infantry and artillery.

PEAK OF MOOREA, SOCIETY ISLANDS.

There is an arsenal, slip, barracks, cathedral, market, hospital, and other adjuncts of civilisation, as well as a botanic, or rather experimental, garden. A good carriage road leads all round the twin islands, only interrupted in one place by the precipices of the S.E. coast. A railway is even proposed, but is not at present likely to be constructed. Tahiti is in communication with Auckland, New Zealand, by means of steamers sailing every six weeks.

The other windward islands are Maitea, an extinct volcano, which forms the eastern limit of the group; and Eimeo or Moörea, also volcanic, but of larger size and very fertile, and extraordinarily rugged and broken as regards its surface.

The chief leeward islands are Huahine, Raiatea, and Borabora. All are mountainous and rugged. The first-named has a good harbour and a population of about 1300. Raiatea and Tahaä resemble Tahiti in being twin islands, but, although surrounded by the same coral reef, they are not in actual contact. Raiatea rises to a height of 3385 feet, and is well watered and very fertile, producing a considerable amount of cotton and copra. Its population of 2300 are all Protestants; there are good schools and a native missionary college, and the island is the residence of the Administrator of the Leeward group. A well-preserved *morai* exists, built of enormous coral blocks. Borabora was formerly renowned for its warriors, but the natives do not now number more than 800. It has a large and good harbour, and its shapely cone, though only 2380 feet high, renders it a striking object from the sea.

9. The Austral Islands and Low Archipelago.

The Tubuai or Austral group is seldom visited even by the French. It consists of four chief volcanic islands, surrounded by coral reefs, and situate almost on the tropic. The climate is thus very healthy, but, owing to the high latitude, the bread-fruit does not flourish. The population does not exceed 1000; it was at one time very much larger, but of late has apparently been stationary. Rapa or Oparo is an outlier to the S.E.—a very picturesque island about 7 miles long, with remarkable needle-like peaks 2000 feet high. The crater of an extinct volcano forms a good and fairly roomy harbour; the climate is delightful, and it is said that, in spite of its unprotected situation, the island is at almost all seasons free from dangerous surf. Coal, or rather lignite, exists. The population, at one time over 6000, sank to 110 a few years ago, but it is now over 200. There seems little doubt that Easter Island—which is known as Great Rapa—was peopled from here. Little known before, the island became important in 1867 as a coaling-station for the steamers of a Panama-Australia line. It was perhaps in consequence of this that it was visited by a French frigate in the same year, the captain of which, it is related, bought the island from the king for a gallon of rum and a suit of clothes. The most remarkable feature of Rapa is the existence of very curious buildings on the summits of the highest hills. Their exact nature seems to be uncertain, whether forts or *morais*—the Polynesian monuments to their illustrious dead. There are terraces and walls constructed of well-shaped blocks, weighing as much as two tons, and joined accurately by cement. Whatever may have been their use or meaning, they are evidently akin to the raised terraces in Easter Island.

The Paumotu, Tuamotu, or Low Archipelago forms a cluster of about eighty islands, of which about sixty are inhabited. Originally discovered by Quiros, they have apparently been peopled from the Marquesas. They are scattered over a vast area, the major axis of which is considerably over 1000 miles in length, and will never be able to do much more than support the small population—less than 6000 souls—which inhabits them. Cocoa-nuts and pearl-shell are almost their only product, and the latter is in many localities beginning to fail. All, or almost all, are lagoon islands.

The Gambier Islands form the S.E. prolongation of the preceding. They consist of five high volcanic islets inhabited by Roman Catholic converts, whose numbers were increased in 1878 by the immigration of the bulk of the inhabitants of Easter Island, 300 in number. The most important is Mangareva or Pearl Island.

Pitcairn Island, celebrated as having been colonised by the mutineers of the *Bounty*, lies at the extreme south-eastern limits of the Low Archipelago, and far out of sight of any other land. It is only two miles in extreme length, and three-quarters of a mile wide, with a fertile volcanic soil, but rocky and mountainous, rising to a height of 2500 feet, so that much of its surface must be too precipitous for cultivation. It is situated in 25° 3′ S. lat., or just beyond the southern tropic, and has a fine climate, producing many tropical fruits and vegetables. It was in 1790 that nine British sailors, six Tahitian men, and twelve women arrived at this speck in the ocean. By discord and murder they were reduced in ten years to one man—an English sailor named Adams—the Tahitian women, and nineteen children. The story of how this ignorant English sailor suddenly rose to the responsibilities of his position, and trained up this little community to habits of industry and morality, and the practice of true religion, is one of the most wonderful and encouraging episodes in the social history of mankind. The little colony was first discovered in 1808 by an American ship, the *Topaze*, which brought the news to

England. They were afterwards visited by two frigates, the *Briton* and the *Tagus*, and in 1825 by Captain Beechey in the discovery ship *Blossom*, who found a community of sixty-six persons living in a state of uninterrupted peace and harmony, and in a veritable "garden of Eden." Groves of coco-nut and bread-fruit trees clothed the rocks down to the water's edge, while in the deep valleys tropical fruits and vegetables flourished luxuriantly. The village stood on a platform of rock shaded by plantains and fig-trees, and surrounding an open square covered with grass. It was encircled by palisades to keep out the hogs and goats which roamed over the island and, with fowls, supplied abundance of animal food. The houses of the islanders were clean and comfortable. Their clothing, entirely made from the bark of the paper-mulberry, was neat and graceful. They all lived as one united family, and crime, or even dissension, was unknown.

Injudiciously, as we think, this intensely interesting social experiment was brought to an end by the interference of well-meaning people. The Pitcairn Islanders were removed, first to Tahiti, then back again to Pitcairn Island. Then in 1856 they were all removed to Norfolk Island, far inferior to their own in climate and soil, though somewhat larger. In 1858 some of them returned to Pitcairn, where, in 1869, they were visited by Sir Charles Dilke, and were doing well. In 1873 Commander K. H. A. Mainwaring found seventy-six inhabitants on the island, and he remarks that epidemic or endemic diseases were unknown among them. In September, 1878, they were visited by Rear-Admiral A. F. R. De Horsey, who found them to have increased to ninety, all in good health, and quite happy; and he adds, that Captain Beechey's testimony to their good qualities, given fifty-three years ago, holds good to this day, since they still continue "to live together in perfect harmony and contentment; to be virtuous, religious, cheerful, and hospitable; to be patterns of conjugal and parental affection, and to have very few vices." Admiral De Horsey concludes by saying, that no one acquainted with these islanders could fail to respect them, and that they will lose rather than gain by contact with other communities.

Although the island was quite uninhabited when the mutineers of the *Bounty* arrived there, many remains show that a considerable population must once have lived on it. Burial-places, large flat paving-stones, stone spearheads and axes, round stone balls, and even stone images, sufficiently prove that this remote speck of land had not only been visited by stray savages, but had been the settled abode of a considerable population, who yet had time to devote to the carving of stone images with tools of the same material.

10. The Marquesas.

North of the Low Archipelago, and about 900 miles from Tahiti, are situated the Marquesas, consisting of eleven chief islands, of which seven are inhabited. They are divided into two groups—a north-westerly, comprising Uapu, Uahuka, Nukahiva and Eiau; and a south-eastern, of which Tauata, Fatuhiva, and Hiva-oa are the chief. They have a total area of some 500 square miles, and a population which has been very variously estimated, but is probably over 6000. They were first seen by Mendaña in 1595, but the N.W. group was not discovered till nearly 200 years later.

The Marquesas, which are all of volcanic origin, resemble the Navigators' group in their general appearance and the outline of their coasts. The interior is steep and hilly, most of the islands being about 3000 feet in height. All the coasts are free of coral reefs, with the exception of a somewhat extensive chain of rocks lying at no great distance from Uahuka. The islands abound in inlets, often forming havens, the approach to which is, however, frequently imperilled by the sudden gusts of wind from the hills.

The soil is, on the whole, less fertile than that of Tahiti, and accordingly bears a less exuberant vegetation. On Nukahiva and Tauata the basalt towers to considerable heights, or at least crops out on the summits of the hills, thus often forming abrupt and jagged walls of imposing appearance. The ground is for the most part rocky, and only sparingly covered with humus, though still sufficient to produce a rich tropical vegetation. The climate is hot on the coasts, but as we ascend to the higher grounds this tropical heat gives place to a perceptible coolness, so that we might almost fancy ourselves at times transplanted to some upland valley of our mountain districts. In other respects the climate is salubrious, giving rise to little sickness either amongst the natives or strangers. None of the volcanoes are active, but there are thermal and mineral springs.

The aborigines of the Marquesas are usually described as the very finest of all the South Sea islanders, and are said to surpass even the Tahitians in physical beauty. Their complexion is of a pure healthy yellow, with a soft ruddy bloom on the cheeks. According to Cook they excel, perhaps, all other races in their symmetrical proportions and the regularity of their features. Few of them remain, however, to enable us to judge of their characteristics. European vices and customs have done their work. The population of Nukahiva was estimated by Krusenstern in 1804 as 18,000, and about eighty years later was said to be under 500. Captain Jouan of the French navy considered that the mortality was in part due to the revolting custom which until lately obtained of shutting up widows for days or even weeks with the putrefying corpse of their husbands; but the unbridled immorality of the people and the introduction of intoxicants have no doubt also greatly contributed to the result.

In their habits and religious practices the natives of the Marquesas resemble the Tahitians in many respects. They formerly worshipped a number of gods, for whom a *morai* was set up in every district, on which swine were sacrificed, for, although cannibals, they never offered up human victims. They were extremely hospitable, which, however, did not prevent them from indulging in sanguinary feuds among themselves. The efforts of the missionaries to evangelise them were long fruitless; recently, however, the majority of the natives are said to have adopted the Roman Catholic form of Christianity. Nevertheless, according to Von Popp, they still remain perfect savages, nor have they yet altogether renounced cannibalism.

The principal island in the Marquesas group is Nukahiva, formerly a French penal settlement. It is about 14 miles long by 10 broad, and is famous for the magnificent cascades which pour over its sea-cliffs. Here is the small but animated port of Taiohai, where resides the French Commissioner of the Marquesas, under whose protection several traders have here founded commercial houses. The islands are well adapted for the growth of cotton, but the people are worthless as agriculturists, and labour is exceedingly difficult to obtain. Moreover, long droughts are not uncommon, lasting as much as ten or even fourteen months, and the Marquesan cultivates little beyond his taro. In the island of Hiva-oa there is another French official, but the progress made towards civilising the natives is not very great.

The Marquesas and Society Islands being the most easterly groups of non-coralline islands in the Pacific, it is interesting to notice the extreme poverty of their animal life. Indigenous terrestrial mammals are quite unknown; neither are there any snakes, and only one lizard. Birds are much less numerous than in the more western islands, no less than twenty-five genera of the Fiji and Samoan groups being wanting, and there is only one new form to supply their place—a peculiar fruit-pigeon (*Serresius galeatus*), which inhabits the western part of Nukahiva. Insects, also, are extremely scarce. This striking diminution of the forms of life indicates that the islands have been peopled by emigration from the west, and do not contain the relics of an ancient continental fauna, as is sometimes supposed; for in that case there would be no reason why the number of genera and species of birds, reptiles, and insects should regularly decrease from west to east as they undoubtedly do.

11. Manahiki, Phœnix, and other Islands.

North of the Society group lie several widely scattered islets very seldom visited, several of which have been annexed by Great Britain. Caroline or Thornton Island, Manahiki, Penrhyn or Tongarewa, and perhaps Suwarrow, may be regarded as forming the Manahiki—or, as it is by some called, the Penrhyn—group. North of these are Starbuck and Malden, both of which are British. Crossing the Equator, we come to another set of islets, lying between lat. 2° and 7° N. Finally, north of the

Tokelau or Union group, and not a great distance from the Kingsmill Islands, is situated the Phœnix cluster. Most of these we have named are of the usual type of lagoon island, are scantily populated, and produce little else besides guano or a few tons of copra.

Caroline Island was annexed in the year 1868. The few settlers raise stock and plant coco-nuts. Suwarrow, which is visited by the French, and has stores, a wharf, and a pearl fishery, is of importance as possessing a lagoon affording splendid anchorage. Manahiki or Humphrey Island has a population of 600 or more, who, as in many of these Pacific islands, are kept in a state of extreme submission by the native missionaries, aided by the Turi men or legislators. "If a Turi man suspects a man of having taken liquor," writes Mr. F. J. Moss, "he will stop him and order him to 'blow,' so that he may discover if his breath has lost its normal sweetness. The decision then come to is conclusive, adopted as a judgment by his fellow Turi men, and the culprit fined accordingly. A curfew drum is beaten at eight o'clock, and after that hour if any one is seen abroad the Turi men are down upon him with a heavy fine next day. . . . The people must extinguish all lights and go properly to bed. . . . Their lovely moonlight nights bring no enjoyment to these people. At Funafuti and other islands the Turi men go further. They march round the village during the night and quietly steal into the houses to see if all is right. It was found that the house-dogs barked and gave notice of their approach, so they forthwith decreed the destruction of all dogs on the island, and again became masters of the situation." In other islands the use of tobacco is strictly forbidden. Such a system, as Mr. Moss observes, must inevitably result in bringing out the worst points in the native character, and a reaction will doubtless set in which will leave the unhappy islanders in a worse state than before. Penrhyn or Tongarewa was at one time the seat of several different tribes living in a state of perpetual war with each other, but some years ago a Peruvian ship made a descent on the island, and kidnapped a large number of the natives, almost depopulating it. Since then the copra trade has made the people almost rich, and they are renowned as the best divers in the Pacific, pearl-shell being abundant in their lagoon.

Starbuck, about 5 miles in length and less than 2 in breadth, is a bare coral rock, without trees, lagoon, or proper landing-place—a worked-out guano island of little or no value. Malden, about 150 miles to the N.N.E., is populated, and in parts fertile. It produced a considerable quantity of guano, and still has on it the remains of some large *morais*—ancient sepulchral buildings to which reference has already been made. On the central ridge of the island are more than a hundred platforms of cruciform shape, built of coral slabs three feet high, and filled in with a compact mass of coral, shells, and stones. There are also a number of shelter-places or huts formed by three coral blocks, with a fourth on the top. More than thirty wells were also found cut in the coral rock from six to nine feet deep, and a number of shallow graves containing human bones much decayed, and shell ornaments.

Christmas, Fanning, Palmyra, and the few islets in their neighbourhood have been termed the America Islands, from being chiefly frequented by people of that nation for the guano they afford. The first-named is noteworthy as being perhaps the largest lagoon island in the Pacific. The Phœnix group was at one time the seat of operations of the "Phœnix Guano Company," but the islands have been exhausted, and the wharves and buildings abandoned, and the population probably now does not exceed 200 souls.

12. Easter Island.

Far out in mid-Pacific, 1400 miles beyond the lonely Pitcairn, over 2000 from the South American coast, and about 1900 from the island of Rapa or Oparo, whence its inhabitants are believed to have come, lies Easter Island, the farthest outpost of the vast series of Pacific Islands. Triangular in shape, with its major diameter 13 miles in length, it is entirely volcanic, with several large extinct craters, of which that at the N.E. point is the highest (1968 feet). Terano Kau, at the southern end, has a crater 700 feet deep and $2\frac{1}{2}$ miles in circumference, but is of lower altitude. The soil is composed entirely of decomposed lavas, and is very fertile. There is, however, no running water, although there are several springs near the shore, and deep pools in some of the craters. There are no trees, the tallest vegetation being bushes of *Hibiscus*, *Edwardsia*, and *Broussonetia*, 10 or 12 feet high. Decayed trunks of trees are nevertheless found, and the paddles and other wooden articles in possession of the natives show that formerly there must have been wood in some plenty.

The island was discovered on Easter Day, 1721, by Roggewein, and visited both by Cook and La Pérouse in their celebrated voyages, the latter giving a lengthy account of the curious monuments for which the island is celebrated. The population at that time was probably not less than about 3000, but in 1863 these numbers were greatly lessened by an atrocious outrage committed by some Peruvian vessels. Anchoring in the bay, these people rowed ashore and seized every person they could lay hands upon, taking them off to the guano diggings on the Chincha Islands, where the greater number of them perished. The following year a Jesuit missionary was sent from Tahiti with lay helpers, whose efforts in civilising the natives were completely successful. The task was rendered easy by the amiable disposition of the latter, who appear to have had few vices except immorality and a propensity for petty theft. Their numbers, however, were becoming so rapidly reduced that it was thought advisable to send some of them to Tahiti, and about 500 accordingly left in 1874. Four years later the missionaries left, taking with them 300 more, and establishing them on the Gambier group, the island having been purchased by Messrs. Salmon and Brander of Tahiti, to be converted into a stock farm. In 1891 there were only about 100 natives left. They are described as being a remarkably fine-looking people, and are all Christians. They are without a priest, but read prayer among themselves regularly in their small chapel. Sweet potato, taro, and sugar-cane are grown, but no species of grain. Bananas are cultivated in a most singular manner, great pits of 20 to 30 feet deep being dug and lined with masonry and the bananas planted within, so as to be sheltered from the wind. According to a recent writer there are on the island no less than 18,000 cattle, 20,000 sheep, and 70 horses, all belonging to the Tahitian firm above mentioned, but as the island only contains 45 square miles, these figures are most probably erroneous.

Easter Island is celebrated for its wonderful remains of some prehistoric people, consisting of stone houses, sculptured stones, and colossal stone images. Of these, various writers, from Cook and La Pérouse, have given accounts, but one of the fullest and most recent is that of Mr. Palmer in the *Journal of the Royal Geographical Society* for 1870. At the extreme south-west end of the island are a great number (80 or 100) stone houses built in regular lines, with doors facing the sea. The walls are 5 feet thick and 5½ feet high, built of layers of irregular flat stones, but lined inside with upright flat slabs. The inner dimensions are about 40 feet by 13 feet, and the roofing is formed by thin slabs overlapping like tiles till the centre opening is about 5 feet wide, which is then covered in by long thin slabs of stone. The upright slabs inside are painted in red, black, and white, with figures of birds, faces, mythic animals, and geometric figures. Great quantities of a univalve shell were found in many of the houses, and in one of them a statue, 8 feet high and weighing 4 tons, now in the British Museum. Near these houses, the rocks on the brink of the sea-cliffs are carved into strange shapes, resembling tortoises, or into odd faces. There are hundreds of these sculptures, often overgrown with bushes and grass.

Much more extraordinary are the platforms and images now to be described. On nearly every headland round the coast of the island are enormous platforms of stone, now more or less in ruins. Towards the sea they present a wall 20 or 30 feet high and from 200 to 300 feet long, built of large stones often 6 feet long, and accurately fitted together without cement. Being built on sloping ground, the back wall is lower, usually about a yard high, leaving a platform at the top 30 feet wide, with square ends. Landwards a wide terrace, more than 100 feet broad, has been levelled, terminated by another step formed of stone. On these platforms are large slabs serving as pedestals to the images which once stood upon them, but which have now been thrown down in all directions and more or less mutilated. One of the most

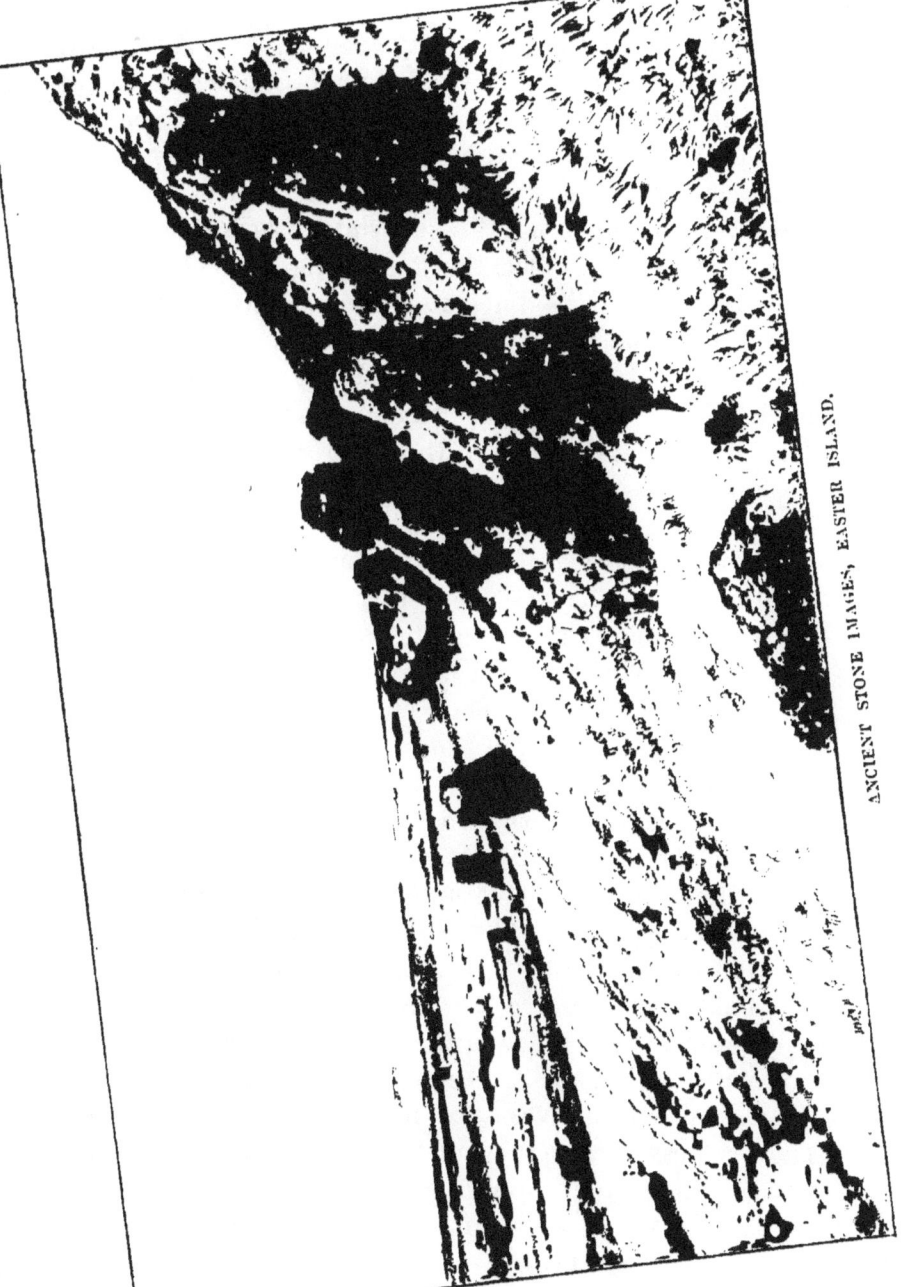

ANCIENT STONE IMAGES, EASTER ISLAND.

perfect of the platforms had fifteen images on it. These are trunks terminating at the hips, the arms close to the side, the hands sculptured in very low relief on the haunches. They are flatter than the natural body. The usual size of these statues was 15 or 18 feet high, but some were as much as 37 feet, while others are only 4 or 5. The head is flat, the top being cut off level to allow a crown to be put on. These crowns were made of red vesicular tuff found only at a small crater called Terano Hau, about three miles from the stone houses, and north of the large crater Terano Kau. At this place there still remain thirty of these crowns waiting for removal to the several platforms, some of them being $10\frac{1}{2}$ feet diameter. The images, on the other hand, are made of a gray, compact, trachytic lava found only at the crater of Otuiti, quite the east end of the island, and about 8 miles from the "Crown" quarry. Near the crater is a large platform, on which a number of gigantic images are still standing, the only ones erect on the island. The face and neck of one of these measures 20 feet to the collar-bone, and is in good preservation. The faces of these images are square, massive, and disdainful in expression, the aspect always slightly upwards. The lips are remarkably thin—the upper lip being short, and the lower lip thrust up. The eye-sockets are deep, and it is believed that eyeballs of obsidian were formerly inserted in them. The nose is broad, the nostrils expanded, the profile somewhat varied in the different images, and the ears with long pendent lobes.

The existing natives know nothing about these images. They possess, however, small figures carved in solid dark wood, with strongly aquiline profile differing from that of the images, the mouth grinning, and a small tuft on the chin. Wooden tablets, covered with strange hieroglyphics, have also been found, and it is evident that these wooden carvings, as well as those of stone, are the relics of a former age. The people have a tradition that many generations ago a migration took place from Oparo or Rapa-iti, one of the Austral group. Hence they call their present abode Rapa-nui, or Great Rapa, to distinguish it from Rapa-iti, or Little Rapa. An implement of stone, a mere long pebble with a chisel edge, is believed to have been the chief tool used in producing these wonderful statues; but it is almost incredible that with such imperfect appliances works so gigantic could have been executed, literally by hundreds, in an island of such insignificant dimensions, and so completely isolated from the rest of the world. At present Easter Island is the great mystery of the Pacific, and the more we know of its strange antiquities, the less we are able to understand them.

13. The Sandwich Islands or Hawaii.

Lying just within the northern tropic, over 2000 miles from San Francisco, and some 3000 from Fiji, is the isolated Hawaii or Sandwich Archipelago, forming a small and independent kingdom, though largely under the influence—both socially and politically—of the United States. It consists of eight inhabited islands, Niihau, Kauai, Oahu, Molokai, Lanai, Maui, Kahulaui, and Hawaii, of which the last is considerably the largest; and the three small rocky islets, Lehua, Kaula, and Molokini, together with a few shoals and small islands stretching to the N.W. They extend in a N.W. and S.E. direction over a distance of about 400 miles, and rise abruptly from great ocean depths of 16,000 to 18,000 feet. The land area is about 8500 square miles, and the population probably about 88,000. The islands are generally described as having been first discovered by Captain Cook, but there is no doubt that they were previously known to the Spaniards. They will always be connected with the name of the great navigator, however, as the place of his murder by the natives, on the 13th February 1779; the scene of the tragedy being Kealakeakua Bay on the west side of the island of Hawaii.

The Sandwich Islands are pre-eminently volcanic. Here, in Hawaii, rise three of the highest mountains in Polynesia—Mauna Kea, about 13,800 feet; Mauna Loa, hardly 200 feet less in elevation; and Mauna Hualalai, about 8000 feet, the two last active volcanoes. On the eastern slope of Mauna Loa is Kilauea, a remarkable volcano in constant activity, scarcely elsewhere surpassed in the awe-inspiring grandeur of its cauldron of seething lava, when contemplated on a moonless night. Its crater, of comparatively easy access, forms a vast irregular abyss, in which there is usually visible a glowing lake of lava, rising and falling independently of the action of other volcanoes. After a silence of eleven years, Mauna Loa was the scene of a terrific eruption on the 14th February, 1877. Fiery clouds of smoke and vapour were at first vomited with astounding velocity to a height of more than 15,000 feet, covering the heavens for a space of 100 square miles, and emitting such a strong glare that the whole island was lit up as vividly as by the mid-day sun, the light being clearly visible on the distant Maui. Ten days afterwards there occurred a fresh and most remarkable eruption, from a submarine volcano in the Bay of Kealakeakua. Countless red, blue, and green flames flickered over the surface of the waters, and huge glowing masses of lava emitting large volumes of steam, and diffusing dense sulphureous exhalations, were hurled into the air. This was accompanied by a loud rumbling noise, while the waters immediately over the crater were violently agitated and tossed about, as if rushing over high cliffs, or raised to the boiling-point by the subterraneous fires. Some vessels sailing near the spot were struck by the falling lava masses, without, however, suffering much damage. This eruption was preceded by a violent earthquake. Another great volcanic eruption took place in 1881. Craters large and small, thermal springs, and other evidences of volcanic activity are common throughout the islands. Among them the most striking is, perhaps, the great crater on Maui Island, Haleakala, which is stated to be 15 miles in circumference and about 2000 feet deep. Notwithstanding these potentialities, for disaster, the Hawaiian group may be regarded as one of the most pleasant places of abode in the Pacific, rejoicing in a most healthful climate, a rich vegetation, and a merry, light-hearted race of natives. The mean coast temperature is about 74° Fahr., and the rainfall at Honolulu below 40 inches. For these and other reasons the group has become a sanatorium for Americans, communication with San Francisco being now frequent and regular. The only severe endemic disorder is leprosy, which is said not to have existed in former years, though now rather common. The sufferers are segregated in the island of Molokai, and the memory of Father Damien's life and death among them will long remain as a conspicuous instance of heroic self-sacrifice.

Of all the islands of the Pacific, the Sandwich group are, so far as their fauna is concerned, the most interesting. In most cases, in Polynesia and Mikronesia, the birds and mammals are few in number, and apparently the descendants of stragglers from the west, which, in the course of centuries, have chanced upon these remote and lonely islets. In Hawaii, though the size of the islands is such as to forbid the existence of many mammals, we find a curiously rich and highly specialised avifauna, and a still more astonishing development of the land mollusca. The richness of the Passerine birds is most strongly marked in the *Drepanididæ*, of which there are no less than 32 representatives, most of them belonging to the genera *Himatione* and *Hemignathus*. The latter genus is

HEAD OF HEMIGNATHUS.

characterised by the extraordinary peculiarity of the prolongation of the upper mandible, so that in some cases it is twice the length of the lower, or even more, and the genus may be regarded as a midway form between the original immigrants and the more highly specialised *Drepanis*, with long, curved, and equal mandibles. Until recently these birds were regarded as Meliphagine, and therefore as having their nearest affinities in the Australian region, but Dr. Hans Gadow has recently proved conclusively that this is not the case, and that they are allied to the *Cœrebidæ*, a point of great interest, since the latter are American. The leading features of Hawaiian ornithology were first pointed out by Professor A. Newton in *Nature* (17th March, 1892), but are too technical to need more than mention here. It may be stated, however, that various finches found on the group may possibly own an Asiatic origin, and that *Acrulocercus* and *Chætoptila*, and the Rhipidura-like *Chasiempis*, point certainly to an Australian ancestry, although the three most numerous families of that region—parrots, kingfishers, and pigeons—are all wanting.

The land mollusca of the Sandwich Islands are described by Mr. A. H. Cooke as standing in marked contrast to those of the other Polynesian groups, in the possession of three entirely peculiar genera—*Achatinella*, *Carelia*, and *Auriculella*. More than 300 of the former genus have been described, every mountain valley on some of the islands containing its own peculiar species. *Partula*, so characteristic of all the other groups, is absent, while the small land operculates, with the sole exception of *Helicina*, are also wanting. The occurrence of one of the *Merope* group of *Helix*, otherwise known only from the Solomon Islands, is most remarkable. On the other hand, *Patula*, *Microcystis*, *Tornatellina*, and other small pan-Polynesian land pulmonata are well represented, and there is a rich development of *Succinea*. Among the marine littoral mollusca occur two *Purpura*, one of which is closely related to a tropical Mexican and the other to a temperate Californian species. On the whole, the molluscan fauna is unique in its peculiarities, both as regards its indigenous element and also as regards the apparently complicated relationships of the elements which are not indigenous.

It may thus be said that the Hawaiian Islands have received their fauna from the most varied and distant sources, and there is no doubt that a vast period of time has been necessary to bring about the differentiation of the species into such peculiar and interesting forms.

The Kanakas, as the natives are called, are amongst the finest and most intelligent peoples of the Pacific, and have become thoroughly Europeanised, or perhaps rather Americanised. The ladies model themselves quite after the American fashion, and speak English in preference to their mother tongue. All classes can read and write. But here, as elsewhere in the Pacific, we find that a decrease in the population has ensued since the advent of Europeans which is little short of appalling. At the time of Cook's visit the people were believed to number 300,000, while at the present time there are not more than 40,000. To what point this reduction will proceed cannot with certainty be predicated. Although extinction would appear at first sight to be the inevitable result, yet, judging from other instances, it need not be so, at all events not in the immediate future. European contact seems almost invariably to produce a sudden and rapid decline of this kind, but it appears also that a point may be reached beyond which this decline may not proceed, and that the balance may in due course establish itself; the race, if ultimately doomed, losing itself by absorption or fusion, rather than by the inability of the individual to resist disease or cope with the altered conditions of his environment.

What is the immediate cause of the depopulation of these and other islands of Polynesia, it is very difficult to say. Neither the diseases nor the ardent spirits introduced by Europeans are sufficient to account for it. By many writers who cannot be accused of bias, it is con-

sidered to be due in part to the missionaries, who, in their
zeal to rescue the uncivilised natives, have not always
gone to work with the necessary discretion. The repressive measures alluded to on a former page have
entirely altered the life and customs of the native, and
have been instrumental in depriving him of his former
light-heartedness and freedom, which, among an undeveloped, child-like race, is no small matter. The
Hawaiian Consul-General, Mr. Manley Hopkins, considers
that " the oppressive system of government, the dis-
continuance of ancient sports, and consequent change in
the habits of the people, have been powerful agents in
this work of depopulation; and the ill-judged enforcement
of cruel punishments and heavy penalties for breaches of
chastity have much aided it, by giving an additional
stimulus to the practice—always too common among
Polynesian females—of causing abortion, of which practice sterility is the natural result." And again: "The
missionaries have not attained the measure of success
which might have been expected from the long and
strenuous efforts they have made. They have not truly
Christianised or regenerated the nation. They have presented Christianity as a severe, legal, Jewish religion,
deprived of its dignity, beauty, tenderness, and amiability.
They have not made the people love religion. In their
rigorous Sabbatarian view of the Lord's day, in their desire
to enforce a Maine liquor law, and in some other matters,
they have attempted to infringe on the natural rights of
men, and have, in native eyes, reproduced the detested
tabu system—the nightmare from which the nation
escaped in 1820." The missionaries to whom these
remarks apply are those of the Congregational denomina-
tion of the United States, who, for nearly forty years,
from 1820 to 1860, had almost undisputed possession of

the field, and long exercised great influence over the government. That influence has now ceased, and a Church of England mission has been established; but it may be impossible to neutralise the evil effects of a system of repression and habits of hypocrisy which have been at work for nearly two generations.

In 1888, out of a population of less than 87,000, no less than 23,000 were Chinese; coolies of that race having been imported in large numbers for work on the plantations. There are now not more than 20,000, but the Japanese number nearly 8000. At the period just stated there were about 19,000 Europeans, of whom over 10,000 were Portuguese. These are almost without exception natives of Madeira and the Azores, who, unable from overpopulation to get land in their own country, though excellent and most industrious agriculturists, found in the land of their adoption a soil almost as good as that of their own, and an even better climate. With regard to the 40,000 or so of Kanakas still remaining, it is worthy of note that the men are greatly in excess of the women in number, a fact that perhaps more than any other augurs ill for the continuance of the race.

The main exports of the Hawaiian Islands are sugar and rice. American capital to the amount of five million sterling is invested in the sugar plantations, nearly five times that of any other nation: and the annual export, which rapidly increases, may be reckoned at about 120,000 tons. All is sent to the United States. From 5000 to 6000 tons of rice are exported, and the consumption of the island may be calculated as even exceeding this, when the large number of Japanese and Chinese labourers, who live upon little else, is taken into consideration. The banana trade with the United States has largely increased, and about £27,000 worth of the fruit was exported in 1889. Wool is another product of some importance, about half a million lbs. being annually shipped. The total value of the exports in 1889 scarcely fell short of three million sterling. The imports are chiefly manufactured goods, nearly four-fifths of which come from America. There is a small public debt of £200,000.

Hawaii was, up till quite recently, an independent monarchy, with two chambers, the upper composed of chiefs elected by the landholders, the lower chosen by universal suffrage. Political squabbles, however, have of late destroyed the peace of the islands, and retarded their progress. They culminated on July 4th, 1894, in a *coup d'état*, when a Republic was proclaimed. It is quite possible, however, that this form of government may not be of long duration. The capital, Honolulu, in the island of Oahu, has over 20,000 inhabitants, and is very progressive and European. Fine quays allow the largest steamers to lie alongside, the streets and shops are lit by electric light, and there are telephones everywhere. Cabs, tramways, schools, homes for aged natives, a racecourse, an opera-house, and excellent bands contribute to the comfort and amusement of the people. In the island of Hawaii, Hilo is the most important town, with 5000 inhabitants. There are two short railways in the group, and a good steamer service with San Francisco.

MIKRONESIA

CHAPTER XV

THE GILBERT, MARSHALL, CAROLINE, PELEW, AND LADRONE GROUPS

1. General.

NORTH of the Equator, between New Guinea and the south coast of Japan, the great ocean is studded with countless little islands, which, in consequence of their remarkably small size, are collectively called Mikronesia. The most easterly are the Gilbert and Marshall groups. Farther west are the Caroline Islands, and the Pelews, which by some writers are called the Western Carolines. North of them are the Ladrones or Mariannes, now peopled by the descendants of the Tagals and Bisayans of the Philippines. The inhabitants of the rest of Mikronesia are of very mixed race, the main elements being probably Indonesian (pre-Malay) and Polynesian. But in many parts there is strong evidence of Negrito and Papuan blood, while the junks of China and Japan, which are not infrequently wrecked upon Mikronesian reefs, have no doubt brought other elements into the ancestry of the present inhabitants. The Gilbert or Kingsmill group are British, and the Marshall Islands a German possession, while the Ladrone, Pelew, and Caroline Islands belong to Spain.

2. The Gilbert or Kingsmill Islands.

The Gilbert Archipelago, which was formally annexed by Great Britain in May, 1892, consists of sixteen islands, all coral reefs or atolls, and nowhere more than 20 feet above the sea. In some the land appears to be rising rather rapidly. The soil is only a few inches in depth, composed of coral sand and vegetable mould, in which hardly anything but coco-nuts and pandanus will grow spontaneously. There is no fern or grass, and not a single land bird with the exception of the migratory cuckoo *Urodynamis taitiensis*. A little taro (*Arum cordifolium*) is grown in trenches with great care. The food of the people is mainly procured from the sea, and ranges from the whale to the sea-slug. Great numbers of fish are taken in the lagoons, and turtle are abundant in the season. In such a barren group of islands the means of procuring the necessaries of life seem scanty enough, and it must require a constant expenditure of labour and skill to maintain life, yet nowhere in the most favoured portions of the Pacific is the population more dense or more healthy than in these sterile islets. Elsewhere in Mikronesia the sparseness of the population is painful, but here the overflowing swarms are a continual source of surprise. Some of the islands seem to form one great village. The very smallest of these atolls, only two miles across, has a population of from 1500 to 2000, while Taputenea has from 7000 to 8000. The population of the whole group is estimated at over 40,000, while the area of dry land is not more than 170 square miles, giving more than 230 persons per square mile, while in some of the islands it is said to reach 400 per square mile—a density of population certainly unequalled in the world in any area where the people depend for food solely on their own exertions.

The natives here are said to be darker and coarser than in the more western islands, so that there has probably been some intermixture of races, which, combined with the need for constant exertion in fishing, has created the energetic temperament which has rendered so large a population possible. They are tall and stout, 5 feet 8 inches or 5 feet 9 inches being the average height. They almost all go naked, except a conical hat of pandanus leaf. They make a kind of armour of plaited coco-nut fibres to protect themselves in war from their formidable swords armed with sharks' teeth. Their canoes are constructed entirely of coco-nut wood boards, sewn neatly together and fastened to well-modelled frames. The American Mission has stations in some of the northernmost islands of the group, and many of the children have been taught to read. The southern islands are under the London Missionary Society. The natives of the large island of Taputenea are said to differ from all the rest in their slender, well-proportioned bodies, fine black glossy hair, and projecting cheek-bones, and they are thought to have less of Polynesian blood than the inhabitants of the other islands. On the whole, this group offers one of the most remarkable social phenomena on the globe—a people in a state of almost complete barbarism, living under the most adverse physical conditions, and yet presenting a density of population not surpassed, if equalled, among the most civilised peoples in the most fertile countries of the world.

3. The Marshall Islands.

The Marshall Archipelago, running in a N.W. and S.E. direction for about 500 miles, is arranged in two parallel chains, that to the east being known as the Radack, and that to the west as the Ralick, group. Of the entire number of forty-six islands, the eight smallest only are flat coral islands encircled by reefs, all the rest being atolls. The entire land area has been estimated at 150 square miles, and the population at about 10,000. First seen by Saavedra in 1529, the group came into the possession of Germany in 1885. Their rule is not particularly successful, heavy taxes pressing hard upon the natives; but the large copra trade renders the islands valuable, and several trading firms, chiefly German, are established in the archipelago. Jaluit is the capital and seat of administration, if such a term can be used.

The vegetation of the Marshall group, though luxuriant as compared with that of the barren Gilbert Islands, is still inferior in exuberance and variety to that of the Carolines, and continually diminishes and becomes more stunted as we proceed northwards. From the coco-nut and pandanus the natives draw their chief supplies of food, and in some islands the bread-fruit is also found. From the root of *Tacca pinnatifida* a sort of flour is prepared. Yams, banana, and taro are also cultivated, and some species of *Hibiscus* yield a strong description of bast.

The natives, who are mostly pagans, are said to be decreasing rapidly in number, partly, no doubt, from the constant state of tribal war which prevails. Captain Cyprian Bridge describes the men as tall, and the women as singularly short, but often very good-looking, and extremely graceful. The former wear a short kilt of shreds of some vegetable fibre, but the women are clothed with *tapa* mats from the waist to the ankle. Tattooing is common, and the ear-lobes are distended to an enormous size by the insertion of a wooden hoop—the former custom showing evidence of Polynesian, the latter of Papuan influence. The natives are good sailors, making large canoes, in which they proceed on long voyages. "They actually make," Captain Bridge informs us, "curious charts of thin strips of wood tied together with fibres. Some of these indicate the position of the different islands with a surprising approach to accuracy. Others give the direction of the prevailing winds and currents." All the Marshall islanders speak dialects of one language, different from that of the Caroline Archipelago, though of similar grammatical structure.

4. The Caroline Islands.

The Carolines, thus called after Charles II. of Spain, lie between New Guinea to the south and the Ladrones to the north, and occupy a vast area. They form three main groups—the Eastern, Central, and Western—and the distance from Kusaie, on the east, to Babeltuap, the farthest western limit, is over 2000 miles. The Western group are better known as the Pelew Islands, and will be separately described under this name.

The majority of the islands are comprised in the Central group, and are of the usual character—low and coralline, and arranged round a central lagoon. Ponape and Kusaie are exceptions, being high and rugged; and Ruk consists of a lagoon reef 150 miles in circuit, within which are a number of little hilly islets. The fauna exhibits extreme poverty. The climate, tempered by cool breezes, is very healthy, and where sufficient soil is found most of the fruits of the Malay Islands flourish, not even excepting the durian. Such a condition is, however, not very generally existent, and the coco-nut, pandanus, and banana afford the chief support of the natives after the bread-fruit, which here supplies the place filled by taro in the eastern islands of the Pacific. The archipelago has a considerable trade in copra, and several German, American, and English traders are established.

The Carolines, like the Ladrones, belong to Spain, but were discovered by the Portuguese in the early part of the sixteenth century. At that period, with so much territory of value still unappropriated, they were not considered worthy of notice, but in 1696 and 1721, canoes from the islands having reached the Philippines and Ladrones, the Spanish sent an expedition to them. They were subsequently claimed as a Spanish possession, but no attempt at government was made until 1886, when, in consequence of Germany attempting to gain a footing by hoisting her flag on Yap, a Governor was appointed. The entire garrison were murdered in the following year, and a further massacre took place in 1890. Since then order is said to have been restored. Politically, the archipelago is divided into an Eastern and Western group, the capitals being at Ponape and Yap.

The natives of the Carolines are believed to number about 30,000, and the population is massed chiefly in the largest islands or groups—Ruk, Yap, Lukunor, and Ponape. They exhibit a considerable mixture of race and variation of colour, the latter passing from a very dark copper in the west almost to a light brown in the eastern islands. Many are of unusually tall stature and strongly built. In the east, Polynesian blood is more evident, and on the island of Nukuor, according to Mr. F.

J. Moss, the language spoken is pure but antiquated Maori. The Polynesian custom of tattooing is universal, but the pierced *septum nasi* and enlarged ear-lobes, together with the widespread existence of club-houses, point to a considerable Papuan influence. The people are singularly good navigators—a rude kind of navigation and astronomy being actually taught formally in schools instituted by them for this purpose; and charts are constructed much after the manner of those of the Marshall islanders. American missionaries have been established on the group for many years, but the progress hitherto made has not been great.

The Ruk Islands form the largest group of the Carolines, with an estimated population of about 15,000, and are the most densely peopled portion of the archipelago. Many different tribes inhabit them, and wars are thus of frequent occurrence. They are still regarded as dangerous by traders, whose vessels have not seldom been overpowered and plundered. Yap is much more in touch with civilisation, yet even here the natives are not entirely trustworthy. On this island, which is 17 miles long and of very irregular outline, are many German traders, by whom the commerce of the archipelago is principally carried on. The currency still appears to be shell money, and—more remarkable still, since they are not put to any use—large millstones or discs of arragonite, sometimes three tons in weight and eighteen feet round, which are quarried in the Pelew Islands, and are generally the property of the township, not the individual.

Kusaie or Ualan, a very picturesque island over 2000 feet in height, with a population not exceeding 300, is chiefly worthy of mention as the headquarters of the American Mission. Close to it is the little island of

Lele, remarkable for possessing ruins which appear to be very similar to those on Ponape, which we shall presently describe. Captain Cyprian Bridge speaks of them as forming a sort of fortress with cyclopean walls of large basaltic blocks, and there are also numerous canals and presumably artificial harbours.

Ponape, a rugged and mountainous island more or less circular in shape, and having a diameter of about 16 miles, is thickly wooded, and some of its trees attain a very large size. It has a population of 2500 living on the seaboard, but the interior is quite uninhabited. A coral reef extends round the island at about three miles from the shore, with nine openings, forming a number of excellent harbours. The climate is excessively equable, the extreme range of the thermometer during three years being only $19°$, the mean temperature being $80\frac{1}{4}°$. The trade winds blow for the greater part of the year; violent storms, as well as electrical disturbances, are rare; and rain falls more or less all the year round. The celebrated Malayan fruit, the durian, has been introduced here with success, and the vegetable-ivory nut flourishes. The soil is very fertile, but its surface in many parts is so covered with stones as to be unworkable. These consist almost entirely of regular basaltic prisms, and in their abundance and evident suitability for building purposes we have possibly two reasons to account for the extraordinary ruins on the eastern side of the island which have puzzled so many travellers.

The ruins of Metalanium are situated at the mouth of the port of that name, upon innumerable islets of the coral reef, distant about a mile or more from the mainland. They consist of one main building, which has a more or less central position in the midst of a vast number of other constructions whose *raison d'être* it is not easy to conjecture. The islets are here very numerous and closely approximated, and over a large area these have been built up in their entire circumference with high sea-walls composed of natural basaltic prisms of large size. The effect produced is that of a vast series of canals—" a Pacific Venice," as it has been termed by a traveller. These canals vary in width from 30 to 100 feet or more, and it is worthy of note that the walls, in many cases, have their bases submerged to some little depth—a fact which has led some observers to the not very certain conclusion that the land has sunk since their erection. On many of the islets raised platforms constructed of the same materials are to be seen.

The main building above mentioned demands separate consideration. It has been well described in his *Atolls and Islands* by Mr. F. J. Moss, who gives a ground-plan of it with measurements and a photograph of a portion of the wall. It may be roughly described as a massive quadrangle with sides about 200 feet in length, within which is another of smaller area, centrally placed, and enclosing in its turn a covered vault, behind which is erected a raised platform. The walls both of the outer and inner courts are provided with a western entrance 15 feet in width, and there are three other vaults placed between the outer and inner walls on the north, east, and south sides respectively. The walls of both the quadrangles are about 20 feet high, but while those of the inner have a uniform thickness of 10 feet, those of the outer are 18 feet thick at the base and only 8 feet in their upper part, so that a sort of terrace 10 feet wide is formed, which runs round the entire inner side at about 6 feet from the ground. The material of which these walls are composed is the same as that of those forming the canals, namely, natural basaltic prisms, without mortar, held together by their own weight. These stones are laid in alternate transverse rows, and are in many instances of great size, some being, according to Mr. C. F. Wood, as much as 25 feet in length and 8 feet in circumference.

The idea that these buildings could have been formed either by the present race of savages or by Spanish buccaneers, as some have thought, is preposterous, and they remain another mystery of the great Pacific, hardly inferior to that of Easter Island with its colossal images. There are other ruins in the island of a similar character, as well as mounds or platforms a quarter of a mile long and twelve feet high. The ruins on Lele Island, of which mention has already been made, closely resemble those of Ponape, but the latter are by far the most remarkable.

5. The Pelew Islands.

These are the most westerly group of Mikronesia, and less than 600 miles east of the Philippines. They consist of one large and a few small islands, several of which are high and mountainous, others being low and of coralline formation. Their entire area is about 200 square miles, and their population between 12,000 and 14,000. Babeltuap, the largest, is 30 miles long, with a mountain at the northern end. They are well covered with timber trees, from some of which the natives make good canoes capable of holding thirty persons. Yams and coco-nuts are the chief articles of food, but bananas are also grown. The inhabitants are quite distinct from the Caroline Islanders and Polynesians who prevail farther east, having a darker complexion and being of smaller stature. They are generally frizzly-haired, and paint their bodies in brilliant colours, especially yellow. Early voyagers were loud in praise of these people.

Captain Wilson of the *Antelope* packet, who was wrecked there in 1783, is said to have found the natives "delicate in their sentiments, friendly in their disposition, and, in short, a people that do honour to the human race"; and Captain Cheyne says that they are far more intelligent and polished in their manners than the Caroline islanders. Captain Wilson brought home with him Prince Lee Boo, son of the king, Abba Thulle, a young man who evinced so much aptitude for civilisation and such an excellent disposition, that his death from smallpox excited universal regret throughout England. Later travellers have given a less favourable account of the Pelew islanders; but, as in so many other cases, they have probably since had good reason to dislike their European visitors, and have had many injuries to revenge. Civilisation of a certain kind has reached the islands, and the customs are altering, but the wars still continue.

Dr. Carl Semper, who spent nearly a year upon the Pelews, has given a full account of the peculiar customs and political organisation of the natives. They have invented an order of knighthood which the king has the exclusive right to award, as well as to take back from those who may have fallen into disgrace. It is called "Klilt," and its insignia is the first cervical vertebra of the dugong or sea-calf (*Halicore*). The investiture and resumption of the order are alike a very formidable proceeding, the hand being violently thrust through the narrow ring of the fish-bone, whereby a finger is occasionally lost, and the skin in any case torn off. Yet the honour is purchased from the State for so much tripang by seafarers. Still more curious are the clubs and confraternities into which the people of various ranks are associated, with intricate rules and ceremonies which cannot here be given in detail. The women form similar associations, which, like the others, have their leaders, and enjoy the privileges of recognised corporations.

6. The Ladrone or Marianne Islands.

We have hitherto had to do almost entirely with groups of islands which have been arranged with their main axis in a direction roughly N.W. and S.E. The Ladrones form a marked exception to this rule. They lie in a single regular chain extending N. and S. for a distance of 500 miles; not in an absolutely straight line, but in a slight but even curve, with its concavity westward, thus forming as it were a segment of a vast circle. They are, for the most part, small and steep volcanic islets, some of which have active craters. The more southern islands are larger, extremely fertile, and well watered. The chain consists of seventeen islands, which lie between 13° and 21° N. latitude, and have a total area of 450 square miles. They are a possession of Spain, the Governor, who is dependent on the Captain-General of the Philippines, residing in Guam. The total population is a little over 10,000.

The Ladrones were discovered by Magellan in 1521, and were thus named by him from the thievish propensities of the inhabitants. In 1528 Saavedra took nominal possession of them, as did Legaspi later, in 1565, but no settlements were made. In 1668 the Jesuit, Luis de San Vitores, established his mission in Guam. The island became the port of call for the great Spanish galleons which went yearly between Manila and Acapulco, and it was in its neighbourhood that Anson waited in 1743 in the *Centurion* for his famous prize the *N. S. de Cavadonga*, which he eventually captured off Samar, her value being estimated at half a million sterling. The Spanish rule of the islands was characterised by harshness and oppression, and a desultory war of extermination was carried on for many years. When first known the islands had a population of at least 50,000. At the present day not one of the original race survives, and the islands are peopled chiefly by Tagals and Bisayans from the Philippines, with a few Caroline islanders, and numerous half-breeds, but also by the mixed descendants of natives of South American tribes.

The original Chamorros were in many ways a fine race. An ancient feudalism existed, the people being divided into nobles, priests, and plebeians. The religion was a sort of ancestor-worship. They have left behind them some memorials of a civilisation which was certainly higher than that existing among the natives at the present day. These structures, which are more numerous in Tinian than elsewhere, are very remarkable, and their service has never been satisfactorily explained. They consist of two ranges of massive stone columns, square in shape, 14 or more feet high, and about 6 feet in diameter. Enormous blocks of stone, in the shape of semi-globes, form the capitals. It has been suggested by Freycinet and others that they were the supports for the roofs of large buildings, and the theory is not unreasonable, but according to old Spanish accounts cinerary urns were discovered in the capitals of some of the columns. Whatever they may have been, they are undoubtedly of great antiquity, for the Spaniards regarded them as such on their first arrival three centuries and a half ago.

The Ladrones are favoured by a good and equable climate, but are occasionally visited by severe earthquakes and typhoons. The rainy season occurs in midsummer with the S.W. winds, but rain falls at intervals throughout the year, and droughts are rare. The thermometer varies between 70° and 80° Fahr. The country near Agaña in Guam is said to afford views which cannot be excelled for beauty, and the vegetation is exuberant. Maize, tobacco, and sugar are the chief crops, but cotton, coffee, rice, cocoa, and Manila hemp are also grown, and the coco-palm is abundant. There is, however, no exportation, for the islands lie far from ordinary trade routes and are rarely visited. Little is known either of the fauna or flora. Deer are numerous, especially on Saipan, and cattle, hogs, and fowls have run wild on Tinian for more than a century. No snakes are known, but rats, probably of late introduction, are numerous, and there is a peculiar species of *Pteropus*.

The chain begins in the north with Farallon de Pajaros, an active volcano about 1000 feet in height, and is succeeded by the three rocky islets known as the Urracas. Assumption, a very striking volcanic peak rising sharply from the water to the height of 2848 feet, is partially active. Agrigan, about 7 miles in length, and exceedingly rugged and mountainous, is the first inhabited island. Pagan is said to have no less than three active cones, but it is nevertheless peopled by a few natives, who have large coco-nut plantations. Five islands follow, Alamagan, Guguan, Sariguan, Anataxan, and Farallon de Medinilla, all of which are uninhabited. The islands farther south are larger and more fertile. Saipan is nearly 15 miles in length, and has a population of about 1000 persons. According to M. Marche, who explored it a few years ago, it has no sign of volcanic action. Tinian, the next island, was at one time the most populous of the group, and is said to have had 30,000 inhabitants; but when Anson visited it in 1742 to recuperate his scurvy-stricken crew, he found it utterly deserted. It is now inhabited by about 300 natives, and serves, like Molokai in the

Sandwich Islands, as a place of segregation for lepers. Aguijan Island is of no importance, and Rota, though considerably larger, has only 500 inhabitants.

Guam, the last island in the chain, is the most populous and important, and is the seat of the Spanish settlement. It is 32 miles in length, and is bordered by reefs in its southern portion. It has a population of 9000, two-thirds of whom are resident in the capital, Agaña, and almost all the rest upon the seaboard, the country inland being almost uninhabited. The Spanish residents are hardly more than 20 in number. A small force of 200 Manila soldiery are quartered here, and the militia comprises nearly all the native male population, and is commanded by native officers. Agaña is also a convict settlement, the prisoners usually numbering about a hundred. The town is beautifully clean, and possesses a hospital, good Government offices, a church, and schools. In 1888 there were 18 schools on the island. Many of the natives speak a little English, and it is said that 90 per cent can read and write. There is postal communication with the Ladrones only four times in the year, and they may be regarded as one of the most inaccessible and least-visited parts of the globe, but the occasional calling of the Spanish men-of-war brings them now somewhat more frequently in touch with the outside world than was formerly the case.

According to the soundings of the *Challenger* expedition, one of the deepest parts of the Pacific Ocean (4475 fathoms) occurs to the south-south-west of the Ladrones. East of this chain and that of the Bonin Islands the great depths are quickly reached, and a trough of this deep water, averaging over 3000 fathoms, continues hence nearly to Japan.

INDEX

ABACA, 41, 56, 80, 81
Abang volcano, 347
Abong-abong, Mount, 158
Abreu, Antonio d', 104, 316, 331, 338
Ache, 156, 157, 183, 211
Achenese language, 183
Admiralty Islands, 430
Adonara, 363, 364
Afzelia bijuga, 475
Agaña, 556
Agrigan Island, 555
Aguijan Island, 556
Agung volcano, 347
Agusan river, 85
Alamagan Island, 555
Alas, Mount, 370
Albay, 71, 72, 74
Albert Edward, Mount, 423
Albert mountains, 380
Albertis, Signor d', explores Fly river, 384, 421
Allor (*see* Ombay)
Amahai, 329
Amargura Island, 497
Amberno river, 381, 412
Amblyornis musgravianus, 394
  subalaris, 394
Amboina, 308, 316, 330
  wood, 333
Ambrym Island, 451
America Islands, 527
Amorphophallus titanum, 178
Ampanam, 352
Amuntai, 273
Anamba Islands, 273

Anataxan Island, 555
Andropogon austro-caledonicum, 462
  caricosum, 171
Aneitium Island, 449
Anglican Melanesian Mission, 409, 451
Anoa depressicornis, 283
Anson captures Manila galleon, 553
Ansus, 429
Antiaris toxicaria, 111
Antilocarpa sumatrana, 181
Antimony mines, 246, 457
Antique, province of, 79
Aoba Island, 453
Aparri, 72
Ape, Celebesian (*Cynopithecus*), 283, 286, 309, 325
Api Island, 451
Apia, 503, 504
Apo, Mount, 33, 85
Araucaria Cookii, 458
Arfak mountains, 379, 391
Argopura, 106
Arjuna, 106, 109
Arsenic in Sumbawa, 359
Aru Hassa, 354
Aru Islands, 425
Asahan mine, 246
Assumption Island, 555
Astrolabe Bay, 415
Atimano farm, 515
Aurora Island, 451
Austral Islands, 518
Australasia, 1
  extent of, 3

Australasia, geographical and physical features of, 4
  ocean depths, 5
  races of, 8
  zoological features of, 10
  geological relations of, 11
Australia, connection with New Guinea, 12
Awu volcano, 303

BABA Islands, 366
Babeltuap, 551
Babirusa, 283, 304, 309, 328
Babuyanes Islands, 72, 75
Bacalod, 80
Bacolor, 66
Bahu Solo river, 281
Bajaus, 90, 234, 240
Bala Island, 199
Balabac, 95
Balade copper mines, 457
Balagnini pirates, 240
"*Balai,*" 195
Balambangan Island, 253
Balbi, Mount, 442
Bali, 347
Baling, Mount, 223
Ballarod mines, 457
Bananas, 138
Banda, 316, 333
Bangka, 201
  straits, 202
Banguey Island, 253
Banjarmasin, 228, 270, 272
Banka or Banca (*see* Bangka)
Banks Islands, 451
Bantam, 145, 157
Barisan range, 158, 174
Barito river, 226
Bashi Islands, 72
Basilan, 90
Batam Island, 200
Batang-hari, 175
Batang Lupar, 226
Batanta Island, 427
Batavia, 145
  suburbs of, 148
  fort built at, 104
  rainfall of, 115
Batjan, 308, 309, 321, 325
Battak country and people, 186
Batu-angas, 321
Batu Islands, 199

Batu Kau volcano, 347
Batur volcano, 347
Bekasi, 149
Bencoolen (*see* Benkulen)
Benkulen, 157, 211
Benzoin, 180, 206
Beri-beri, 116, 177, 211, 230
Bernacci volcano, 74
Best, Captain Thomas, 184
Biak Island, 429
Bible burnt by the Dutch in Java, 129
Bickmore, Mr., on Celebesian burial, 291
Bicols, 50, 84
Bidi, 239, 246
Bilian wood, 243
Billiton (*see* Blitong)
Bima, 356
Bintang Island, 200
Birds' nests (edible), 92, 93, 244, 375
Birds-of-Paradise, 311, 322, 325, 429
  first brought to Europe, 381
  various genera of, 393
Birds of the Philippine Islands, 42
  of Java, 119
  of Sumatra, 182
  of Borneo, 232
  of Celebes, 285
  of Moluccas, 311
  of Timor Laut, 368
  of New Guinea, 392
  of Solomon Island, 444
  of New Caledonia, 458
  of Samoa, 505
  of Marquesas, 525
  of Sandwich Islands, 536
Bisayaus, 50, 79, 80, 81, 82, 83, 84, 87, 93, 554
Bislig, 88
Bismarck Archipelago, 413, 417, 430
  range, 380, 415
Bito lake, 83
Blanche Bay, 417, 434
Blitong, 204
Bohol, 83
Bonthain peak, 278
Borabora, 518
Borneo, 213
  history of, 214
  geology of, 217
  physical features of, 218, 221
  mountains of, 222

Borneo, plains and rivers of, 224
  lakes of, 228
  climate of, 228
  flora and fauna of, 230
  inhabitants of, 233
  agriculture and products of, 241
  British North Borneo, 248
  Labuan, 254
  Brunei, 256
  Sarawak, 259
  Dutch Borneo, 269
Boro-bodor temple, 132
Bos banteng, 231
Bosch, Gen. van den, 139
Bougainville Island, 442
Bounty, mutiny of the, 520
Bourail penitentiary, 464
Brambanam ruins, 131
Brantas river, 113
Bread-fruit, 333
Brine springs, 111
British North Borneo, 248
British occupation of Java, 104, 149
  of Benkulen, 157, 211
  mission to Ache, 184
  occupation of Bangka, 203
  settlement at Banjarmasin, 228, 272
  protectorate of North Borneo, 249
  occupation of Manila, 32
  of Balambangan, 253
  take Labuan, 254
  occupy Makassar, 277
  in the Moluccas, 317
  annexation of New Guinea, 418
  in Melanesia, 442, 467
  in Polynesia, 508, 509, 525
  in Mikronesia, 543
Brito, Antonio de, reaches Moluccas, 316, 322
Bromo volcano, 110
Brooke, Raja, 259, 261
Brown, Mount, 423
Brunei, 256
  visited by Pigafetta, 215, 238
  by Jorge de Meneses, 215
  river, 225
Buffalo in the Philippines, 59
  in Borneo, 241
Bugis language, 25
  race, 233, 273, 288, 293, 299, 339, 358, 361, 365, 375, 426
"Buitenbezittingen," 99, 100

Buitenzorg, 115, 149
Bulacan, 71
Buleleng, 350
Buluan lake, 86
Bulusan, 73
Buru, 308, 309, 314, 316, 327
Busuanga Islands, 93
Butak volcano, 106
Butung Island, 305
Butil, 301

CACAO in Philippines, 79, 80, 82, 87
Cagayan, 70
Cagud volcano, 75
Cajuput oil, 328
Calamianes Islands, 93
Calapan, 77
Calophyllum inophyllum, 475
Camarines, 71
Campbell, Lord George, on Tonga islanders, 488
Canloon volcano, 80
Cannibalism in Sumatra, 187, 188
  in New Guinea, 406, 433
  in Solomon Islands, 446
  in New Hebrides, 453
  in Fiji, 477
  in Marquesas, 524
Capiz province, 79
Caraballos mountains, 33, 35
Carestochelys, 395
Caroline Island, 526
  Islands, 546
Carteret, Philip, visits Admiralty Islands, 430; Solomon Islands, 443; Santa Cruz, 447
Cassia florida, 119
Cassowary, 311, 395, 436
Casuarius bennetti, 436
Catbalogan, 82
Cattle in Java, 138
Cave burial in the Philippines, 54, 93
Cavite, 65
Celebes, 275
  population of, 276
  history of, 276
  physical features of, 277
  rivers of, 280
  lakes of, 281
  climate of, 282
  fauna and flora of, 283
  inhabitants of, 288

Celebes, Dutch settled districts of, 292
  trade and products of, 300
  islands of, 301
Ceram, 308, 314, 328
Chalmers, Mr., 384
Chamorros of the Ladrone Islands, 554
Chandi Sewn ruins, 131
Charles Louis mountains, 379
Chepenche, 466
Cheribon, 145
Cherimai, 106
Cherry Island, 449
Chi Tarum, 113
  Manuk, 113
Chikurai, 106
Chilatjap, 144
Chinese in Australasia, 10
  in Philippines, 52, 92
  in Java, 125, 142
  in Bangka, 203
  in Borneo, 233, 237, 239, 247, 265
  in Ternate, 321
  in Sandwich Islands, 540
Chinrana river, 381
Christmas Island, 527
Cholera, 116, 177, 230
Chrome, 457, 458
Cigar factories in Manila, 66
Cinchona, 137
Civets, bred by the Achenese, 185
  in Moluccas, 309
Clarence, Mount, 423
Cloves, 309, 315, 317, 322, 324, 325, 330, 333
Coal in Philippines, 35, 79, 80, 81, 82, 87
  in Java, 105
  in Sumatra, 208
  in Borneo, 219, 245, 255
  in Celebes, 301, 304
  in Moluccas, 325, 326, 329
  in New Caledonia, 457
Cobalt, 457, 458
Cochlostyla, 43
Cock-fighting in the Philippines, 68, 69
Coffee in Philippines, 58, 79, 87, 92
  in Java, 136
  in Sumatra, 206
  in Celebes, 294, 295, 300
  in Moluccas, 325, 329

Coffee, in Bali, 349
  in Timor, 372
  in New Guinea, 418, 424
  in New Caledonia, 462
Communal system, in Java, 136
  in Sumatra, 185, 193
Conus millepunctatus, 402
Cook Archipelago, 509
Cook, Captain, 449, 456, 497
  on Tahiti, 513
  death of, 534
Cooke, Mr. A. H., on mollusca of Philippines, 44
  of New Guinea, 396
  of Hawaii, 537
Copal, 300
Copper in Philippines, 34, 79, 84
  in Sumatra, 208
  in Borneo, 246
  in Celebes, 301
  in Moluccas, 325
  in Timor, 370
  in New Hebrides, 453
  in New Caledonia, 457, 458
Copra, 274, 300, 303, 349, 418, 424, 450, 506, 516
Corvée in Java, 139
  in Minahasa, 297
Cota Batu, 88
Crocodiles, 233, 395
Crocodilus porosus, 395
Culion, 93
"Culture system," 139
  in Celebes, 297
Currents of the Lesser Sunda Group, 363
Cuscus, 283, 310
Cuyo, 93
Cuyos Islands, 93
Cyclops, Mount, 385
Cynopithecus nigrescens, 283, 286, 309, 325

Daendels, Marshal, 146, 149, 153
Dam, Van, defeats Portuguese off Makassar, 277
Damien, Father, 535
Damma Island, 365
Dammar gum, 180, 244, 300, 322
Dammara vitiensis, 475
Dampier visits New Guinea, 382, 431
Danau lake, 173
Davoa, 88

Dayman, Mount, 423
Dedica volcano, 76
Deep-sea soundings, 6, 556
Dempo volcano, 160
Demle mountain, 354
Dendrolagus, in Ké Islands, 344
D'Entrecasteaux Islands, 386, 437
"Dewarra," 435
Diahot river, 456
Diamonds in Borneo, 247
Didunculus strigirostris, 505
Dieng plateau, 134
Dili, tobacco district of, 207
Dilli, 371
Disraeli, Mount, 415
Dobbo, 426
"Dobbos," 403
Donda mountain, 278
Dorei. 411
Douglas, Mount, 423
Draper, Sir William, takes Manila, 32
Drawings, Rock, on Ké Islands, 343
Droughts of the Lesser Sundas, 18
Drums of New Hebrideans, 453
Duck-rearing establishment, 71
Duke of York Islands, 417
Dumaran Island and volcano, 94, 95
Dutch possessions in Australasia, 97
  their government, 98, 99
  their population, 99
Dyaks, 25, 234, 265
  in Paláwan, 95

EARTHQUAKES in the Philippines, 37, 66, 71
  in Java, 110
  in Nias Island, 198
  in Ternate, 321
  in Ceram, 329
  in Amboina, 331
  in Banda, 335
  in Timor, 370
  in New Guinea, 386
  in Fiji, 473
Easter Island, 528
  peopled from Rapa, 519
Eiau Island, 522
Elæis guineensis, 255
Elephant in Sulu, 91
  wanting in Java, 119
  in Sumatra, 181
  in Borneo, 231

Ellice Islands, 508
Ende Bay, 360, 362
Engaño Island, 200
Erromanga, 450, 452
Erskine, Captain, on the Tongan islanders, 488
  on the Samoans, 505
Espiritu Santo, 451
Eua Island, 497
Eucalyptus, 119
Euchirus longimanus, 313
Everill's, Captain, ascent of Strickland river, 385, 421

FANNING Island, 527
Farallon de Pajaros, 555
de Medinilla, 555
Fatuhiva, 522
Felis macroscelis, 181, 231
  marmoratus, 231
Ferguson Island, 386, 437
Fiji Islands, 467
  history of, 471
  geology and climate of, 472
  flora and fauna of, 475
  natives of, 476
  religion and education in, 480
  agriculture and trade of, 482
  government of, 484
  population of, 485
Finisterre mountains, 415
Finschhafen, 413
Flores, 359
Fly river, discovered, 383
  mouth of, 421
Forbes, Mr. H. O., on Dempo volcano, 160
  on Danau lake, 173
  on flora of Palembang river, 179
  on the *balai*, 195
  on natives of Buru, 327
  on Timor Laut, 367
  on Timor, 370
Forests of Malaysia, 17
Fort Defensie, 328
  Barneveld, 325
  de Kock, 210
  van der Capellen, 211
  Rotterdam, 293
  Oranje, 322
  Victoria, 332
  Nassau, 336
  Belgica, 336

French possessions in Australasia, 9, 510
Friendly Islands, 497
Fruits of Java, 119, 138 ; of Sumatra, 179

GALELA, 318
 sub-Papuan race at, 314
Gallus bankiva, 43, 121
 furcatus, 121
Galunggung, 106, 107
Gamakora volcano, 318
Gambier Islands, 520, 529
Gambir, 201, 243
"Gamilang," 124
Gas, Natural, at Tanjong Api, 280
Gaua Island, 451
Gaya, 252
Gazelle peninsula, 434
Gede volcano, 106
 its flora, 118
German Borneo Company, 92
German New Guinea, 412
German settlements in Australasia, 9, 412, 545
Gilbert Islands, 543
Gilolo (*see* Halmahera)
Gisser, 339
Gladstone, Mount, 415
Gloucester, C., volcanoes, 435
Goa, 289
Gold in Philippines, 34. 79, 81, 83, 84, 87
 in Rhio-Lingga Islands, 201
 in Bangka, 203
 in Sumatra, 208
 in Borneo, 247, 253
 in Celebes, 300, 301
 in Moluccas, 325
 in Sumbawa, 359
 in Timor, 370
 in New Guinea, 387, 437
 in New Caledonia, 457
Gongs, of Brunei, 248
Goodenough, Commodore, 447, 472
 Island, 437
Goram, 340
Gorontalo, 299
Goudberg, 158
Goura victoria, 429
Gressi, 144
 visited by Abreu, 104
Grobogan mud volcanoes, 111

Guadalcanar, 442
Guam, 555, 556
Guguan Island, 555
Guillemard, Dr., on Krakatau eruption, 170
 on Minahasan people, 298
 on Obi Major, 326
Guimaras, 78
Gnuong Api, 334, 335
Gunong-gunong Sewu, 112
Gunter, 106, 107
Guppy, Mr., on Solomon Islands, 443, 445
Gutta, 274

HALCON, Mount, 77
Haleakala, 535
Halmahera (or Gilolo), 308, 314, 318
Hare, Javanese, 119
 Sumatran, 182
Hat-making in Java, 151
Hatzfeldthafen, 416
Hawaii, 533
Head-hunting among Dyaks, 235
"Heerendienst," 98, 298
Hemignathus, 536
Hemileia vastatrix, 136
Hervey Islands, 509
Hickson, Dr., on "Culture system," 298
 on Sangir Islands, 301, 303
Hilo, 541
Himalayan genera found in Sumatra, 182
Hindu rule in Java, 103
 its traces, 101, 109, 130
 in Sumatra, 156, 196, 205
 in Borneo, 216, 273
 in Celebes, 277
Hinigaran, 80
Hiva-oa, 522
Honolulu, 541
Hopea dryobalanoides, 180
Hopkins, Consul, on Polynesian depopulation, 539
Houses, Dyak, 236
 Papuan, 403, 421, 425, 431, 433
 of Solomon Islanders, 446
 of New Hebrides, 453
 of New Caledonia, 459
 of Fiji, 478
 of Polynesians, 491
Houtman lands in Java, 104

INDEX 563

Huahine, 518
Humboldt Bay, 412
  Mount, 456
Humphrey Island, 526
Hymenophyllum tunbridgense, 391

IJEN, 106
Illanuns, 86. 240
Illimandiri, 360
Ilocanos, 50, 70
Iloilo, 79
Images, ancient, of Easter Island, 530
Indigo in the Philippines, 58
"Indios," 49
Indonesians, 8, 21, 25
Indragiri river, 176
Indrapura volcano, 159
"Infièles," 49
Iron in Philippines, 35, 79
  in Bangka, 203
  in Sumatra, 209
  in Borneo, 246
  in Celebes, 301
  in Timor, 370
Isabela, 90
Isarog, Mount, 74
Islamism in Java, 128
  in Sumatra, 156. 183, 205
  in Borneo, 234
  in Celebes, 277
Isle of Pines, 465

JACATRA (province) ceded, 104
  (town), 146
Jaluit, 545
Jambi river, 175
  tribes of, 189
Jambosa, 180
Jappen (*see* Jobi)
Jarnaram lake, 83
Java, 101
  islands of, 102
  history of, 103
  geology of, 104
  volcanoes of, 105
  rivers of, 113
  valleys of, 114
  climate of, 114
  diseases of, 116
  flora of, 116
  fauna of, 119
  inhabitants of, 121

Java, languages of, 126
  religion prevailing in, 128
  education in, 129
  antiquities of, 130
  agriculture in, 122, 135
  exports, 138
  "culture system" in, 139
  revenue of, 142
  population of, 142
  provinces and capitals of, 143
  towns of, 143, 145
Javanese nation, 121
Jembrana, 350
Jesuits, their work in Mindanao, 87
  in Guam, 553
Jobi Island, 429
Jokjokarta, 145
Jolo, sieges of, 32, 90
  province of, 89
Julia Hermina mine, 245
Jungle-fowl, 43, 121
Ju-ud, 341

KABA volcano, 160
Kabalaki, Mount, 370
Kadu valley, 114
Kaioa Islands, 322
Kaiserin Augusta river, 381, 385, 416
Kajeli Bay, 328
Kajuput-tree, 328
Kakian Society, 332
Kambing Island, 364
"Kambing utan," 181
Kamodo Island, 359
Kampar river, 176
Kanala mines, 457
Kanari tree, 336
Kandavu, 470, 472
Kao volcano, 497
Kapogo, Mount, 448
Kapuas river, 226, 272
Karang volcano, 106
Karbau peak, 366
Karons of New Guinea, 412
Katabelo, 360
Kauri pine, 470
Kawella, 364
Kawi language, 126, 349
  volcano, 106, 109
Kayan Dyaks, 273
"Kayu kuning," 362
Ké Islands, 341

Kealakeakua Bay, 534
Keane, Professor A. H., on the peoples of Australasia, 20
— on people of Nassau Islands, 199
— on the Polynesian languages, 496
Keizers Spits, 161
Kelut volcano, 109
Kema, 295
Kermadec, Huon, 456
Kettlewell's, Mr., exploration of New Guinea, 384
Kilauea volcano, 534
Kilkerran, Mount, 437
Kilwaru, 339
Kimanis river, 248
Kinabalu, 17, 221, 222, 229, 230
Kinabatangan, 227
Kingfishers, racquet-tailed, 395
Kissa Island, 366
Kiwai Island, 421
Klabat, Port, 203
— Mount, 278
Klings, 359
Knutsford, Mount, 423
Koen, General, founds Batavia, 146
Kolasi volcano, 74
Komodo strait, 363
Koningsplein, 148
Konstantinhafen, 415, 417
Korinchi tribe, 191
— volcano, 159
Korongo-eis tribe, 426
"Korowaar," 405
Kota Raja, 211
Koti (or Mahakkam) river, 227, 273
Krakatau, eruption of, 161, 335
Krama language, 127
Krätke range, 415
Krisses of Java, 124
— Menangkabo, 209
Kubu tribe, 183, 193
Kuching, 266
Kudat, 250
Kupang, 371
Kusaie Island, 546, 548
Kuta-baugan, ruins at, 205

Labot volcano, 74
Labour traffic in New Guinea, 418
— in New Hebrides, 451
Labua, Mount, 325
Labuan, 254
— coal mine, 246

Labuan-tring, 352
Ladrone Islands, 553
Lagerstroemia, 180
Laglaize, M. Leon, 384
Laguna de Bay, 71
— de Cagayan, 76
— de Canaren, 76
Laibobar Island, 367
Laipaka, 374
Lakahia, Mount, 379
Lakan, Mount, 370
Lalang grass, 171, 178
Lamararap volcano, 364
Lammas, Mount, 442
Lamongan, 106
Lampongs, people of the, 194
Lancaster, Sir James, visits Ache, 157
Landu Island, 370, 374
Langauan mud volcanoes, 280
Langen, Captain, on Ké islanders, 342
Languages of Malaysia, 24, 25
— of Polynesia, 496
Lante volcano, 354
La Pérouse visits Samoa, 500
— visits Easter Island, 528
— fate of, 447, 448
Larantuka, 360, 362
Larat, 367
Latimojong, Mount, 278
Latte, Mount, 497
Lauto, Mount, 503
Lavag, 72
Lawu, 106, 109, 134
Lead in Philippines, 34, 81
— in Borneo, 246
— in New Caledonia, 457, 458
Legaspi conquers the Philippines, 31, 54, 77
— takes Ladrone Islands, 553
— (town), 76
Lele, ruins at, 549
Leopard, 120
Lepers' Island, 453
Lepus netscheri, 182
Lesser Sunda Islands, 345
— droughts of, 18
Letti Islands, 366
Levuka, 468, 470, 486
Leyte, 82
Libocedrus papuana, 391
Lifu Island, 465, 466

INDEX 565

Liguasan lake, 86
Limbang river, 225
Limbotto lake, 280, 281
Linao lake, 86
Liugga Island, 200, 201
Liwong river, 146
Lobetobi volcano, 360
Lokon volcano, 278
Lombleu, 364
Lombok, 350
London Missionary Society, 409, 423, 504, 506, 511, 544
Loro-jongran ruins, 131
Louisiade Archipelago, 12
    Islands, 436
Low Archipelago, 519
Loyalty Islands, 465
Luar lake, 228
Lubu tribe, 189
Lusé, Mount, 158
Luzon, 70
    mountains of, 70, 73
    lakes of, 76
    population of, 76
Lycopodium clavatum, 391

Macacus cynomolgus, 41
Mace, 337, 339
Macgregor's, Sir W., exploration in New Guinea, 385, 421
"Maclay Coast," 384, 415
Macrodontism, 436
Madura, 99, 103, 143
    population of, 99, 143
Madurese nation, 121
Maer Island, 466
Magellan visits Sumatra, 156
    his ships in the Moluccas, 324
    in the Timor group, 364
    discovers Ladrones, 553
    death-place of, 30, 81
Magindano (*see* Mindanao)
Mahakkam (or Koti) river, 227, 273
Mahori, 20
    language, 495
Maimbun, 90, 92
Maitea Island, 518
Majaijay volcano, 74
Majapahit, 103, 130, 131
Makassar district, 292
Makassarese, 289
Makian, 321, 322, 323, 324
Maklai, Miklukho, 384

Malabar volcano, 106
Malabu, mines of, 208
Malacca, taking of, 104
Malaspina volcano, 80
Malay language, 19, 24
    race, 8, 19, 25
    characters of, 22
Malayo-Polynesians, 8, 21
Malaysia, geographical outline of, 13
    volcanoes of, 15
    forests of, 17
    ethnology of, 20
    languages of, 25
Malden Islands, 525, 527
Mallicolo, 451
Malu, Mount, 223
Malua, 504
Manahiki group, 525
    Island, 526
Mandar people, 289, 299
Mandayas, 86, 87
Mandeling, 171
Mangaia, 509
Mangerai strait, 359
Mango Island, 473
Manguianos, 77
Manila founded, 31
    taken by the English, 32, 53, 65
    rainfall of, 36
    description of, 65
    population of, 67
Manila hemp, 41, 56, 80, 81
Maninju lake, 173
Manis javanicus, 182
Manna Island, 502, 504
Manobos, 87
Manok Island, 366
Manowolko, 340
Maquiling volcano, 74
Maras, Mount, 202
Marchesa's exploration in New Guinea, 384
Marco Polo, 104, 155, 156
Maré, 322, 324
Mare Island, 465, 466
Marinda citrifolia, 344
Marionettes, 124
Marquesa Islands, 522
Marsden, Mr., on Rejang people, 192
Marshall Islands, 545
Marsupials of New Guinea, 392
Martapura, 272
Marud, Mount, 223

Masa Island, 199
Masbate, 84
Matabello Islands, 340
Mataram, 352
Matema Islands, 448
Maui Island, 535
Maumeri, 361, 362
Mauna Kea, 534
  Loa, 534
  Hualalai, 534
Mayon, Mount, 33, 70, 73
Meester Cornelis, 149
Megapodes, 311
Melaleuca viridiflora, 458
Mempakol, 252
Menado, 277, 293, 295
Menangkabo, 189, 238
  kingdom founded, 157
Mendaña discovers Solomon Islands, 443
  Santa Cruz Islands, 447
  Marquesas, 522
Meneses, Jorge de, visits Brunei, 215
  discovers New Guinea, 381
Mentawi islanders, 21
  Islands, 199
Merapi, Mount (Java), 106, 109
Merapi (Sumatra), 159
Merbabu, 106, 109
Metalanium, ruins at, 549
Meyer, Herr, in New Guinea, 384
Mikronesia, 542
Minahasa, 278, 293
  people of, 291
Mindanao, 84
  river, 86
  lake, 86
Mindoro, 76
Mioko, 417, 434
Misamis, 88
Misol island, 427
Mission work in Sarawak, 265
  in Minahasa, 294
  in Sangir, 302
  in New Guinea, 408, 431
  in Santa Cruz, 448
  in New Hebrides, 449
  in Loyalty Islands, 464
  in Fiji, 472, 480
  in Tonga, 499
Mitford, 253
Moa Island, 366

Modigliani, Dr., on Nias Island, 197
Mohammedanism in Java, 128
  in Sumatra, 156, 183
  in Borneo, 234
  in Celebes, 277
Molenvliet, 148
Mollusca of the Philippines, 43
  of Celebes, 286
  of the Moluccas, 311
  of New Guinea, 396
  of Sandwich Islands, 537
Molokai Island, 535
Moluccas, 306
  first visited by the Portuguese, 9
  geology and natural history of, 308, 315
  inhabitants of, 313
  "Residencies" of, 317
  "Lesser Moluccas," 322
Monotremes of New Guinea, 392
Monsoons in Java, 114
  in Sumatra, 176
  in Borneo, 228
  in Celebes, 282
  in Moluccas, 319, 342
  in Sumbawa, 356
  in New Guinea, 388
Montano's ascent of Mount Apo, 85
  journey across Mindanao, 86
Moörea Island, 518
Morais, 515, 518, 519, 527
Moresby, Captain, surveys S.E. New Guinea, 383, 436
"Moros," 49, 51, 86, 125
Morti, 308
Moss, Mr. F. J., on the Turi system, 526
  on Caroline Island ruins, 550
Motley, Mr., on geology of Borneo, 219
Mua peak, 502
Muara Takus, ruins at, 205
Mud volcanoes, 111, 364, 370
Muntok, 203
Muria volcano, 106
Murray Island, 466
Mus musschenbrocki, 232
Musa textilis, 41, 56
Music, Javanese, 124
Musi river, 175
Mutong, 301
Mydaus, 120

INDEX 567

Nacco Islands, 198
Nangamessi, 375
Nanjan lake, 78
Nanusa Islands, 302
Nassau Islands, 199
Natuna Islands, 273
Navigators' Islands, 500
Negara, 224, 273
Negrito race, 8, 21, 47, 54, 70, 80, 81, 82, 86, 95
Negros Island, 80
Nepenthes, 231
Neu Lauenburg (*see* Duke of York Islands)
Neu Mecklenburg (*see* New Ireland)
Neu Pommern (*see* New Britain)
New Britain, 431
New Caledonia, 12, 455
  mountains of, 456
  history of, 456
  geology of, 457
  climate of, 458
  flora and fauna of, 458
  natives of, 459
  trade of, 462
  administration of, 462
  penal establishment in, 463
New Caledonian Company, 451
New Guinea, 376
  title of Dutch to, 317
  physical features of, 378
  mountains of, 379
  history of, 381, 419
  annexation of S.E. by England, 384, 419
  geology of, 385
  climate of, 388
  flora and fauna of, 390
  the Papuans of, 397
  political divisions of, 410
  the Dutch territory, 410, 438, 440
  the German territory, 412, 440
  the British territory, 418, 439, 440
  islands of, 424
"New Guinea Company," 413, 417, 434
New Hanover, 432
New Hebrides, 449
New Ireland, 432
Newspapers of the Philippines, 56
Ngenges, Mount, 354

Ngoko language, 127
Nias Island, 197
Niauli-tree, 458
Nibong palm, 243
Nickel, 457, 458
Nila Island, 366
Nipa palm, 243
Niuē, 507
Niukalofa, 499
Noordwijk, 148
Normanby Island, 437
Noumea, 465
Nufur language, 430
  Papuans, 412, 430
Nuhu Roa, 342
Nui Island, 508
Nukahiva, 523, 524
Nukulailai Island, 509
Nukuor Island, 547
Nusa-Heli, Mount, 309, 329
Nusa-Tello, 341
Nutmeg, 300, 322, 334, 336, 339, 366

Obi Islands, 326
Obree, Mount, 385, 423
Ofu Island, 504
Oil-palm, 255
Olele, 211
Olosenga Island, 504
Ombay, 363, 364
  passage, 363, 369
Ombilin coal-fields, 208
Onin peninsula, 379, 411
Oparo, 519, 533
Ophir, Mount, 159
Opium-farming in Sarawak, 264
"Orang Sirani," 315, 329
Orang-utan, wanting in Java, 119
  found in Sumatra, 181
  in Borneo, 232
Order of the Sacred Heart, 410
Ornithoptera priamus, 313
Otaheite, 511
Otuiti, Mount, 532
Ovalau, 470
Ovulum ovum, 402, 445
Owen Stanley, Mount, ascended by Sir W. Macgregor, 385, 422, 423
  range, 380, 383, 422
  plants of, 391
Owhyhee, 533

PADANG, 177, 210
Padang-luwas, 171
"Padris" sect, 190
Pagan Island, 555
Pagi Islands, 199
Pagoat, 300
Pajagalon, 110
Paláwan (or Paragua), 93
Palembang, 174, 177, 209, 212
　river, 175, 212
　tribes of, 193
Palmyra Island, 527
Pam copper mines, 457
Pampanga, 71
Panay, 78
Pangium fruit, 179
Pango-pango, 504
Pantar, 364
Papandayang, 106
Papar, 252
Papawa, ruins at, 515
Papeete, 516
Papilio penelope, 396
　ulysses, 313
Papuan race, 8, 9, 21
Paragua (*see* Paláwan)
Parinarium laurinum, 444
Pasig river, 65, 71
Pasir, 273
Patani, 319
Pateros, 71
Patippi Bay, 412
Patteson, Bishop, 447
Patuwa volcano, 106
Paumotu Archipelago, 519
Pea-fowl, 120
　not found in Sumatra, 182
Pearls, 92, 245
Pearl-shell, 516
Pele Island, 453
Pelew Islands, 551
Peling Islands, 304
"Penakan," 125
Pengaron mine, 246
Penrhyn group, 525, 527
Penunggungan, 106
Pepper, 206, 243
"Pepper Coast," 191, 206
"Perkeniers," 338
Pertibi, plain of, 171
Petroleum in Java, 138
　in Sumatra, 209
　in Borneo, 246

Pheasant, Argus, 119, 182
　fire-back, 120, 182
Philippine Islands, 27
　area of, 28
　history of, 30
　conquest by Legaspi, 31
　geology of, 33
　climate of, 35
　typhoons in, 36
　earthquakes in, 37, 66, 71
　diseases prevalent in, 38
　fauna and flora of, 38
　past history of, 46
　natives of, 47, 53, 68
　population of, 53, 63, 64, 92
　religion and education in, 54
　agriculture, trade, and commerce, 56
　ports of, 60
　railways in, 60
　government and revenue of, 61
　army and navy of, 62
　budget of, 63
　volcanoes of, 73, 80, 85
Phœnix group, 526, 527
Phosphate of lime, 418
Pigafetta describes Borneo, 215,
　mentions Ombay, 364
Pigeon, Nutmeg, 338
　Crowned (*Goura*), 395, 429
　Marquesan, 525
Piña fabric, 59, 79, 80
"Pinag" 76
Pinag de Candava, 76
Pingi Island, 199
Pinus, genus, in the Philippines, 40
　in Sumatra, 179
Piracy, 88, 89, 92, 240, 254, 356, 412
Pitcairn Island, 520
Poggy Islands (*see* Pagi)
Pogoyama, 300
Poison shrub of Flores, 362
Pollok, 88
Polynesia, 487
Polynesian race, 9, 488
　languages, 493, 495
Ponape Island, 546, 549
Ponies, Javanese, 138
　Sumbawan, 359
　Timorese, 373
　Rotti, 374
　Sumban, 375

INDEX 569

Pontianak, 271
Population of Philippines, 63, 64
  of Dutch possessions, 99
  of Java, 141, 142
  of Sumatra, 209
  of Borneo, 214
  of Celebes, 276
  of Minahasa, 295
  of Bali, 350
  of Lombok, 353
  of Timor, 374
  of New Guinea, 424
  of New Caledonia, 461, 465
  of Fiji, 485
  of Sandwich Islands, 540
Port Moresby, 423
Royalist, 95
Portuguese first visit Moluccas, 9, 316
  possessions in Malaysia, 15
  visit Sumatra, 156, 157
  established in Moluccas, 316
  in Timor, 370
Posewitz, Dr., on Bornean geology, 217, 218
  on floods of Negara district, 224
  on Bornean diamonds, 247
Poso, Lake, 281
Powell, Mr. W., in New Britain, 384, 435
Prau, 106, 108, 134
Presbytes nasutus, 232
Primula imperialis, 118
Prince Frederick Henry Island, 425
Probubalus mindorensis, 41, 78
Proechidna, 392
Ptilopus roseicollis, 121
Pu, Mount, 223
Puerto Princesa, 95
Pulo Babi, 197
  Bras, 158
  Wai, 158
Puppet-plays, 124
Pura-pura, 366
Purdy Islands, 418

QUEEN CHARLOTTE Islands, 447
Quicksilver in Philippines, 79, 87
  in Borneo, 246
  in New Guinea, 388
  in New Caledonia, 457
Quiros discovers New Hebrides, 449, 451

Quiros discovers the Society Islands, 510
  the Low Archipelago, 519

RACES of Australasia, 8, 14, 19
Radack group, 545
Raffles, Sir Stamford, 104
  on Menangkabo, 189
Rafflesia, 178
Raiatea Island, 518
Railways in Philippine Islands, 60
  in Java, 145, 153
  in Sumatra, 211
  in New Caledonia, 464
  in Sandwich Islands, 541
Rainfall of Philippines, 36
  of Manila, 36
  of Java, 115
  of Sumatra, 177
  of Borneo, 229
  of Makassar and Menado, 283
  of Ternate, 319
  of Amboina, 333
  of Ké Islands, 342
  of New Guinea, 388
  of the Aru Islands, 425
  of New Caledonia, 458
  of Fiji, 473, 474
  of Honolulu, 535
Rakan river, 176
Ralick group, 545
Rana guppyi, 444
Rauken, Mr. W. L., on the "Mahoris," 20
Ranu lake, 281
Rapa Island, 519, 533
Rarotonga, 509
Rattan, 274, 300
Rattlesnake, H.M.S., survey of, 383
Raun volcano, 106
Rebello on Celebes, 276
Rejang river, 225
  tribes, 191
Reptiles of New Guinea, 395
Retes, Ynigo Ortiz de, 382
Rewa river, 468
Rhinoceros, 119, 120, 181, 231
Rhinoceros sumatranus, 181, 231
Rhio Island, 201
Rhio-Lingga Archipelago, 200
Rhododendrons, 231
Riamkina river, 272
Rijswijk, 148

Rindia Island, 359
Ringgold Islands, 472
Ringworm, Pacific, 389
Rinjani, Mount, 350
Rio Grande de Cagayan, 72
Ritabel, 367
Roggewein discovers Easter Island, 528
Rokka volcano, 360
Roma Island, 365
Romba mountain, 360
Rose-wood, 451
Rossel Island, 436
Rotti Island, 374
Rotuma Island, 472, 486
Ruang volcano, 303
Ruius in Java, 101, 109, 130
  in Sumatra, 155, 205
  in Borneo, 216,.238, 273
  in Celebes, 277
  on Espiritu Santo, 452
  in Tonga Islands, 500
  in Tahiti, 515
  in Austral Islands, 519
  on Pitcairn Island, 522
  on Malden Island, 527
  on Easter Island, 529
  in Caroline Islands, 549
  in Ladrones, 554
Ruk Island, 546, 548
Rumphius, 331
Rurukan, 295
Rusa Raja Island, 360, 361

SAAVEDRA, Alvaro de, 381, 545, 553
Sacripante, Mount, 83
Sadang river, 280
Sago, 243, 255, 264, 329
Saint Aignan, 437
  goldfields of, 387
Saint Panie, Mount, 456
Saipan Island, 555
Salaier Island, 305
Salak volcano, 106, 110, 116, 151
Salcedo, Juan de, 77
Salibabu, 302, 304
Salwatti Island, 427
Samar, 82
Samarai, 424
Samarang, 144
Samarinda, 227, 273
Sambas district, 247
Samoa Islands, 500

Samsum (or Samson) river, 379
Sanana Bay, 304
San Bernardino channel, 72
San Cristobal, 442
Sandakan, 250
Sandalwood, 375, 450, 458, 475
  Island (*see* Sumba)
Sandwich Island, 451, 452
  Islands, 533
Sangir Islands, 302
Santa Cruz Islands, 447
Sapan wood, 41, 58, 79, 362
Sapi strait, 359
Saputan mountain, 278
Sarawak, 259
  government of, 263
  army of, 264
  trade of, 264
  population of, 265
  capital of, 266
Sariguan Island, 555
Sarongs of Sumatra, 209
  of Borneo, 248
  of Makassar, 292
Sasak, Tana, 350
  race, 351
Sati, 349
Savage Island, 507
Savaii, 493, 502
Savo Island, 442
Savu Island, 374
Schouten Islands, 429
Scirpus cœspitosus, 391
Scratchley, Mount, 423
S. Cristobal volcano, 74
Seba, 374
Segaar Bay, 412
Segama river, 253
Selaparang, 350
Selaru, 367
Selawa-jantan, 158
Selwyn, Bishop, 448
Semao (or Semang) Island, 374
Semeru, 106, 109
Semioptera wallacei, 311, 312, 325
Sequeira, Diego Lopes de, 156
Seriang lake, 228
Sermata Island, 366
Serrao, Francisco, 331
Serresius galeatus, 525
Serua Island, 366
Serwatti Islands, 365
Shipbuilding among Ké islanders, 343

Siak river, 175
  tribes of, 189
Sialang tree, 179
Siamang, 181
Siamanga syndactyla, 181
Siau Island, 303, 338
Sibiru Island, 199
Sibutu passage, 92
Sidangoli, 319
Silam, 252
Silver in Philippines, 81
  in Borneo, 246
  in New Caledonia, 457, 458
Simalu Island, 197
Simpson, Mount, 423
Sindang Laja, 151
Singkara lake, 173
Singkel river, 176
Singkep Island, 200
Sipora Island, 199
Siquihor Island, 84
"Sirani, Orang," 315, 329, 332
S'lamat, 106
Slavery in Sulu, 92
  in Moluccas, 315, 322, 338
Socialism among the Papuans, 407
Société Calédonienne des Nouvelles Hébrides, 455
Society Islands, 510
Solomon Islands, 442
Solo river, 113, 114
Solor, 363
Soro Mandi mountain, 354
Sorsogon, 72, 73
Soundings in the Pacific, 6
  in Torres Straits, 12
  off North Borneo, 94
  on Celebes bank, 302
  in Ombay passage, 369
  near Ladrone Islands, 556
Spanish possessions, 15, 547, 553
  their conquest, 31, 32, 547
  settlements in Sulu group, 89
Spermonde Archipelago, 293
Spice Islands (*see* Moluccas)
Starbuck Island, 525, 527
Stirling range, 380
Straits of Sunda, 101, 154
  of Bali, 105
  of Surabaya, 114
  of Rhio, 201
  of Banka (Bangka), 202
  of the Timor group, 363

Strickland river, 385, 421
Styrax benzoin, 180, 206
Sual, 76
Submarine bank of S.E. Asia, 7
Suckling, Mount, 423
Sudara, Gunong, 278
Sudest Island, 436
  goldfields of, 387
Suk Island, 429
Sulla Islands, 304
Sulu, Spanish expeditions against, 32
  natives of, 52, 233, 238
  language of, 52
  population of, 63, 64, 92
  general description of, 89, 90
Sumatra, 154
  history of, 155
  geology, etc., of, 157
  lakes of, 159, 173
  volcanoes of, 159
  plains of, 160
  climate of, 171, 176
  rivers of, 174
  fauna and flora of, 177
  inhabitants of, 182
  languages of, 183
  islands of, 197
  religion and antiquities of, 204
  agriculture and trade of, 205
  population of, 209
  provinces of, 209
  chief towns of, 210
"Sumatras," 177
Sumba, 374
Sumbawa, 353
Sumbing, 106
Sunda straits, 101
Sundanese nation, 121
Sundara, 106, 108
Supiori Island, 429
Surabaya, 137, 143
Surakarta, 145
Surigao, 88
Suttee (*see* Sati)
Suva, 468, 470, 486
Suwarrow Island, 526
Swallow Islands, 448

Taal lake and volcano, 74
Tabu among the Papuans, 406
Tacloban, 83
Tafua peak, 503
Tafuti lake, 281

Tagals, 50, 71, 77, 554
Tagbiloran, 84
Tagbuanas, 50, 95
Tahiti, 511
Taiohai, 524
Tai-tai, 93, 95
Talang volcano, 159
Talaut Islands, 302
Talisse Island, 302
Tambilan Islands, 273
Tambora volcano, 354
　eruption of, 355, 358
Tambu river, 272
Tana Aropen, 412
Tangarung, 273
Tangerang, 149
Tangkamus mountain, 161
Tangkuban Prau, 106
Tanjong Priok, 149
Tanna, 450
Tapir absent from Java, 119
　in Sumatra, 181
　in Borneo, 231
Taprobana, 156
Taputeuea, 543, 544
Tarakan volcano, 318
Taraxacum officinale, 391
Tarsier (*Tarsius spectrum*), 283
Taruna, 303
Taschem crater-lake, 111
Tasman discovers Fiji, 471
　Tonga, 497
Taviuni Island, 470
Tawi-tawi, 90
Tayabas, population of, 76
Teak, 87, 90, 118, 138, 305
Tebang, Mount, 223
Tempe lake, 281
Temples of Java, 103, 109, 130
　of Sumatra, 155
　of Borneo, 216, 373
　of Fiji, 480
Tengar, 106, 109
Tenimber Islands (*see* Timor Laut)
Tepa, 367
Terano Hau, 532
　Kau, 528
Ternate, 313, 316, 319
Thakombau, King, 472
Tibi hot springs, 73
Tidor, 313, 316, 322
Tiger, 120, 124, 181
　unknown in Borneo, 231

Timor, 15, 345, 369
Timor Laut Islands, 367
Tin in Bangka, 202, 203
　in Blitong, 204
　in Sumatra, 208
Tinakula Island, 448
Tinian, 554, 555
Tionfoloka Islands, 341
Tior Island, 341, 344
Toba lake, 159, 173
Tobacco in the Philippines, 58, 79
　80, 84
　in Java, 137
　in Sumatra, 207
　in Borneo, 243, 253
　in Celebes, 300
　in Moluccas, 322
　in Bali, 349
Togian Islands, 304
Tokelau Islands, 508
Tolo volcano, 318
Tondano lake, 281
Tonga Islands, 497
Tongarewa Island, 527
Tongatabu, 497, 499
Tongkoko mountain, 278
Torres, Luis Vaz de, 382, 436
Torres Straits, soundings in, 12
Tortoiseshell, 92, 93, 245, 300, 333
Totoya Island, 473
Touata Island, 522
Trade returns of Philippines, 60
　of Netherlands India, 97
　of Java, 136
　of British North Borneo, 252
　of Dutch Borneo, 274
　of Celebes, 300
　of Moluccas, 322, 333, 339
　of Timor, 372
　of New Guinea, 424
　of New Caledonia, 462
　of Fiji, 483
　of Samoa, 506
　of Tahiti, 516
　of Sandwich Islands, 540
Tramways in Java, 153
Tridacna shell, 245
Trilithon in Tonga Islands, 500
Tripang, 92, 93, 245, 300, 424
Triton Bay, Dutch settlement at,
　382
Trobriand Islands, 438
Trusan river ceded to Sarawak, 263

Tual, 342
Tuamotu Archipelago, 519
Tubuai Islands, 518
Tucopia Island, 448, 449
Tufoa mountain, 497
Tugere tribe, 412, 421
Tukala, Mount, 278
Tulur Islands, 302
Tumahu, Mount, 327
Tunggul, 106
Tupinier Island, 435
Tutuila Island, 502, 504
Typhoons of the Philippines, 36

UAHUKA, 522, 523
Ualan Island, 548
Uapu Island, 522
Uea, 465, 466
Ulu tribe, 189
Union Islands, 508
Upas valley, 109, 110
   tree, 111
Upolu Island, 503
Urdañeta, Andrea de, 31
Urodynamis taitiensis, 543
Urracas Islands, 555
Urville, Dumont d', 471
Ussher, Mr., upon condition of Sarawak, 268
Uvaria aromatica, 58
Uvea, 465, 466

VALENTIJN, 331
Vanapa river, 423
Vanda Lowii, 231
Vanikoro, 448
Vanilla, 300, 516
Vanua Lava, 451
   Levu, 468
Varthema, Luigi, 104, 155, 214, 316, 338
Vate Island, 451, 452
Vatica eximia, 180
Vaux, Mr. W. S. W., on Polynesian languages, 20
Vavau Island, 497
Vele Island, 453
Victor Emmanuel range, 417
Victory, Mount, 385
Viti (*see* Fiji)
Viti Levu, 467, 468
Vitores, Luis de San, 553
Viverra tangalunga, 309

Volcano Island (Santa Cruz), 448
   (New Guinea), 435
Volcanoes of Malaysia, 15
   of the Philippines, 33
   of Luzon, 73
   of Paláwan Islands, 94
   of Java, 101, 105, 115
   of Sumatra, 159
   of Borneo, 221
   of Celebes, 278
   of Sangir, 303
   of the Moluccas, 308, 318, 319, 324, 331, 334
   of Lesser Sundas, 345, 347, 350, 354, 360, 364, 365, 366, 370
   of New Guinea, 385, 431, 434, 435
   of Melanesian Islands, 442, 452
   of Polynesia, 497, 504, 534, 555

WAHAI, 329
Waigiu, 427
Waikama hot springs, 470
Waikolo lake, 328
Waingapu, 375
"Wajang" (puppet-plays), 124
Waju tribe of Bugis, 288
Wallace, Mr., on Langauan mud volcanoes, 280
   on "culture system," 298
   on Batjan, 325
   his residence in New Guinea, 383
   on the characteristics of the Papuan, 400
"Wallace's line," 14, 347
Wa Sumsum river, 379
Waterfall, Tondano, 282
Weaving in Java, 124, 151
   in Sumatra, 209
Weltevreden, 148
Wesleyan missions, 409, 480, 499, 506
Wetta Island, 364
Wheat-growing in New Caledonia, 462
Whitehead, Mr., on weather experienced on Kinabalu, 229
   on Bornean birds, 232
Wilis volcano, 106, 109
Willem Schouten Islands, 429
Wilson's bird-of-paradise, 429
Winter Height, 423
Wokka, Mount, 364

Woodlark Island, 438
Wulur, 365

XULLA Islands, 304

YAMDENA, 367
Yamura, 158
Yap, 547, 548
Yasowa, Mount, 450
Ygarrotes, 51
Ylang-ylang, 58, 92
York, Duke of, Islands, 417
Ysabel Island, 442
Ysabela de Basilan, 90
Yule, Mount, 422

ZAMBOANGA, 87, 88
Zebu, 81
Zinc in Borneo, 246
Zonnegat, 335

Zoology of Australasia, 10
 of the Philippines, 41
 of Sulu group, 91
 of Paláwau, 94
 of Java, 119
 of Sumatra, 181
 of Bangka, 202
 of Borneo, 231
 of Celebes, 283
 of Xulla Islands, 304
 of Moluccas, 309
 of Timor Laut, 368
 of New Guinea, 391
 of New Britain, 435
 of Solomon Islands, 444
 of New Caledonia, 458
 of Fiji Islands, 476
 of Samoa, 504
 of Marquesas, 525
 of Sandwich Islands, 535

THE END

Printed by R. & R. CLARK, *Edinburgh.*